The Carter Presidency and Gay Rights

The Carter Presidency and Gay Rights

The Revolution That Dared Not Speak Its Name

Harris Dousemetzis

BLOOMSBURY ACADEMIC
LONDON • NEW YORK • OXFORD • NEW DELHI • SYDNEY

BLOOMSBURY ACADEMIC
Bloomsbury Publishing Plc
50 Bedford Square, London, WC1B 3DP, UK
1385 Broadway, New York, NY 10018, USA
29 Earlsfort Terrace, Dublin 2, Ireland

BLOOMSBURY, BLOOMSBURY ACADEMIC and the Diana logo are trademarks of Bloomsbury Publishing Plc

First published in Great Britain 2024

For legal purposes the Acknowledgements on p. xi constitute an extension of this copyright page.

Cover design by Adriana Brioso
Cover image © Bettmann/Getty Images

A catalog record for this book is available from the Library of Congress.

Library of Congress Cataloging-in-Publication Data

ISBN: HB: 978-1-3503-8109-4
PB: 978-1-3503-8108-7
ePDF: 978-1-3503-8111-7
eBook: 978-1-3503-8110-0

Typeset by Deanta Global Publishing Services, Chennai, India
Printed and bound in Great Britain

To find out more about our authors and books visit www.bloomsbury.com and sign up for our newsletters.

For Zak Kostopoulos, who was murdered in Athens, and to all LGBTQ+ people and activists who have been killed for seeking and promoting equal rights.

To my parents, for all they have taught me by word and by example.

And to my daughter Maya Allende, who I hope will one day become my teacher too.

Contents

Figures

Acknowledgements

This book would never have been completed without the goodwill and assistance of numerous people who gave unstintingly their time and knowledge to assist me. I am eternally grateful and indebted to the many people, both participants and academics (sometimes both), who agreed to be interviewed for this book. These people gave up their time to patiently share their memories and experiences with me. I've learnt from them much more than I had ever imagined, including many very interesting and amusing unpublished stories. I cannot refrain from mentioning one which does not appear elsewhere. Marilyn Haft told me how Abbie Hoffman, a friend and client of hers and a fugitive from justice at the time, joined her in disguise, and initially unbeknownst to her, in the parade at Carter's inauguration, shouting 'Free Abbie Hoffman!' He later even called her in the White House.

Professor Doreen Mattingly helped me in numerous ways in this project, and I am extremely grateful to her; she generously shared with me her experience and knowledge of Midge Costanza, she very graciously shared with me Costanza's personal papers from the Midge Costanza Institute and she very kindly read an early draft of the book and gave me very valuable feedback. Many thanks to Ambassador Stuart Eizenstat and Professor Lillian Faderman who honoured me by writing the book's foreword and afterword. My special thanks to everyone at the Jimmy Carter Presidential Library, especially to Keith Schuler, Billy R. Glasco, Jr and LaToya Devezin, for their enormous help throughout this project. Professor John Dumbrell, my primary PhD supervisor at Durham University, was also extremely helpful to me with his guidance and deep knowledge of presidential politics, I am very grateful to him. I also thank Eric Marcus, who not only shared his knowledge and experiences with me but kindly provided me with documents from his personal collection.

I would also like to extend my thanks to Mary J. Wallace at Walter P. Reuther Library, Jennifer Scott from the Bingham Centre of Duke University, Laura Smith and Graham Stinnett from the University of Connecticut Libraries and Mark Bowman of the LGBT Religious Archives Network, who very willingly and without charging me scanned numerous documents from the respective archival collections. Many thanks to Sharon Davidson and Michael Godfrey who proofread parts of this book, and to my daughter Maya Allende for helping me scan some of the books I used at Durham University's library.

I am also grateful to Nick Wolterman of Bloomsbury for introducing me to Atifa Jiwa, Bloomsbury's Senior Commissioning Editor, and to Atifa for her belief in this book and her tremendous assistance and patience during this whole process. Many thanks to Shoarko Patchiappan, Nadine Staes-Pole and Vishnu Prasad of Bloomsbury for their patience, collaboration and help. I have been very fortunate to have as friends Joe and Julie Horsfield, Sue Lipschitz, Gerry Loughran, Brian Stanners and

Majid Taghavi; these people have helped me in numerous ways throughout the years, for which I cannot adequately express my appreciation and gratitude. I owe a debt to the many historians whose work on President Carter, gay rights and the religious right inspired me and guided me in this project.

Above all, I owe a huge debt of gratitude to Dr Stephen Welch, initially my second supervisor at Durham, for his extraordinarily generous and consistent support, without which this book would be much the poorer. Not only did he offer wise suggestions from his knowledge of the era and of relevant academic literature, he invested countless further hours reading, re-reading and editing the manuscript, providing a necessary reworking of its architecture and considerably improving its language and readability. The book has benefited hugely from his efforts, and I am forever grateful to him.

As conventional as it is to say so, I remain acutely aware of my responsibility for any deficiencies that remain, and I beg forgiveness from anyone who helped me but despite my every effort I have omitted to mention.

Foreword

Stuart E. Eizenstat[1]

Harris Dousemetzis's book *The Carter Presidency and Gay Rights: The Revolution That Dared Not Speak Its Name* is important for several reasons. The first is particularly meaningful to me as President Jimmy Carter's Chief White House Domestic Policy Adviser, his policy adviser in the 1975–6 presidential campaign, and author of *President Carter: The White House Years (*2018, updated paperback 2020). It dramatizes an overlooked feature of the Carter presidency: the Carter administration's positive, courageous record in advancing gay rights at a time in the 1970s, when this was highly controversial, particularly for President Carter's conservative Southern base. I stressed in my book that he was one of the most underrated, under-appreciated, most consequential one-term presidents in modern American history. Several later books by major historians have come to similar conclusions. But none have stressed President Carter's record on gay rights.

President Carter was a champion of human rights abroad, making it a central feature of his foreign policy, and of civil rights for women and people of color at home. It is finally recognized that he appointed more women and minorities to federal judgeships and senior administration positions than all presidents before him put together. He supported affirmative action for Black and Hispanics in admissions to colleges and universities and implemented a novel minority set-aside programme for federal contractors. But it has taken Harris Dousemetzis through exhaustive, detailed review of administration records and dozens of interviews to finally illuminate President Carter's advancement of gay rights as an important civil right. Few civil rights issues have gained public acceptance faster than gay rights, and President Carter helped lay an important foundation for this result, improving the lives of millions of gay Americans.

Dr Dousemetzis describes how Jimmy Carter was the first presidential nominee to publicly seek the support of gay Americans through public advertising in gay media, sending his son Chip as a surrogate to gay rights events, and having gays on his campaign staff. As president he fulfilled his campaign promise to support gay rights by appointing openly homosexual men and women to numerous important federal posts. He opened the White House for the first time to gay rights advocates who had long been kept at arm's length, and sent administration representatives to gay community

1 Stuart E. Eizenstat has served as White House Domestic Affairs Advisor (1977–81), US Ambassador to the European Union (1993–6), Under Secretary of Commerce for International Trade (1996–7), Under Secretary of State for Economic, Business, and Agricultural Affairs (1997–9), Deputy Secretary of the Treasury (1999–2001) and as Special Advisor for Holocaust Issues for Presidents Obama, Trump and Biden.

meetings. And in the 1980 Democratic Convention Platform he supported the first-ever gay rights planks of a major political party. He proposed, passed and implemented the first piece of federal legislation to protect the rights of gay Americans: the landmark 1977 Civil Service Reform Act, which ended discrimination in federal employment in 95 per cent of the federal government's jobs. And his administration assured equal access to federal programmes, like the Peace Corps. President Carter also made gay organizations eligible for the first time to tax-exempt status from the IRS, making them eligible for the first time for federal funding and participation in federal programmes. And the administration re-interpreted existing law to allow gay tourists and legal migrants in the United States.

By upgrading the dishonourable discharges of gays in the military when they were disclosed, to honourable discharges, Mr Dousemetzis demonstrates that President Carter took the first step on the long, tortuous road, to granting gays equal status in the military, which went through President Clinton's later 'Don't Ask, Don't Tell', to final equal status in the Obama administration. In housing programmes under the Department of Housing and Urban Development gay families became eligible for the first time for housing benefits. And President Carter's White House Conference on Families, where my late wife Fran worked, gay families were included within the definition of a 'family'. Sadly and ironically, this book points out that for all of his championing of gay rights in so many different ways, much of the organized gay community supported the Democratic primary challenge of Senator Edward Kennedy, which split the party and weakened the president in his re-election campaign against Republican candidate Ronald Reagan.

A second reason *The Revolution That Dared Not Speak Its Name* is important is that it describes the rise of the rights movement in the United States and puts it in historical perspectives. As we continue to struggle with providing genuinely equal rights to people of color and women, a fight that goes back centuries, no other civil rights issue has gained broad acceptance in such a relatively short time as gay rights. This book helps explain this phenomenon.

Third, this remarkable book not only provides a deeper knowledge of the Carter presidency, which grows in importance with age, and documents the rise of the gay rights movement, but it illuminates the fierce political counter-reaction to gay rights by conservatives and Carter's own Southern Baptists, which persists to this day and has become a standard feature of Republican Party orthodoxy. The resulting 'culture wars' have bitterly divided the country, with too little middle ground found.

Harris Dousemetzis has done a great service with what I believe is a major piece of presidential and American history.

Introduction

Jimmy Carter was president at the climax of a time in which, as one understated book title has put it, 'something happened' in American political culture.[1] It marked the culmination of a long period in which a succession of what would nowadays be called 'culture wars' had erupted into American politics, beginning with the civil rights movement's brave steps to end the legal segregation and de facto political exclusion of Black people in the Southern states. A 'second wave' of feminism, succeeding that which had culminated in the granting of female suffrage across the nation, erupted in the 1960s with protests and writings that are well remembered today. Rights for 'homosexuals' (the terms 'gay' and 'lesbian' will primarily be used in this book, except when the legislative and regulatory context and its language is relevant, a context where indeed quite blatantly homophobic language is also to be found) began to be demanded on analogous grounds to these earlier movements for inclusion in the late 1960s. Demands grew in volume, but met little response from government until Carter's election. When it did begin to respond, gay people and their organizations enthusiastically pressed their demands, though ironically did not always recognize the progress that had been made – a function of their previous marginalization, the small circulation of the gay press, and the covert nature of many gay and lesbian lives. Even more ironically, the opponents of these developments, the cultural and increasingly the religious right, paid very close attention to every step of Carter's in this field, sensitized to it by the disappointment of the high expectations they had formed of a strongly religious candidate. Following Carter's defeat in 1980, and in part as a result of his successes in the field of gay rights, a field still not acknowledged as a legitimate area of government concern by many people, a long hiatus in the progress of gay rights began. In the wider context of political cultural change in the United States, then, the Carter presidency's response to the gay rights agenda occupies a crucial, and so far little appreciated, role.

Even among those interested in the history of gay rights, Carter's presidency is remembered as an era of intense activism by increasingly visible pressure groups which met a degree of frustration and disappointment, presaging if not provoking the rejuvenated conservatism of the 1980s, which in turn gave way to the more gay-friendly Clinton administration of the 1990s. In fact, President Carter contributed much more to the gay rights agenda in the United States than this narrative recognizes. He saw gay rights as a fundamental aspect of human rights, essential to his domestic civil rights policies. Carter, himself an evangelical Protestant, advanced its cause in the teeth of

[1] Edward D. Berkowitz, *Something Happened: A Political and Cultural Overview of the Seventies* (New York: Columbia University Press, 2007).

the growing forces of Christian evangelical conservatism, further strengthening them in the process. In addition to correcting the record, this book will also explain why it has been such an inaccurate one. Frank Kameny, one of the most important gay rights activists of the time, who dealt extensively with Carter's administration and witnessed first-hand its efforts and accomplishments on gay rights, wrote in October 1980 of 'a strange mythology' that had developed in the gay community that Carter had not done enough for gay rights.[2] This mythology continues to exist today, also extending to the community of scholars.

Today, Carter's presidency, and particularly his record on human rights, is a focus of renewed interest. However, his efforts and accomplishments in the area of gay rights have received very little attention,[3] and have often been completely ignored. This book reverses that neglect. The decisions Carter made and the policies he implemented contributed significantly to improving the lives of gay people, and at the same time he played an important role in changing public discourse about homosexuality in the United States.

By using previously unpublished archival material, along with personal interviews with prominent gay rights activists of the time and senior White House aides, the book documents the full range of government actions taken and policies implemented, and the numerous impediments they faced. The book's sources show that Carter did much more to advance gay rights than he has been credited with; when Carter could make a difference, he generally did, and when the impediments could not be overcome, his efforts still deserve acknowledgement. During Carter's presidency, gay people were for the first time drawn into government policy-making and accepted as part of the political community. At the White House, for the first time ever staffers were specifically assigned to monitor gay and lesbian concerns. Carter's policies and decisions contributed significantly to framing gay rights as a normal, legitimate concern, and activists in this area as legitimate political actors with the right to be listened to. Furthermore, the Carter administration's actions changed the public's sensitivity to gay rights and led to unprecedented political visibility for the gay community, certainly rousing opposition and hostility to it, but overall massively benefiting it in numerous ways.

In the mid-1970s, discrimination against gay people was almost a social norm; for most Americans, homosexuality was 'abnormal', and most of the public was not ready to accept such things as gay teachers in schools or gay soldiers in the Army. Ivy Bottini, one of the most prominent lesbian rights activists of the time, said 'Communists were the red herrings of the 50's, we're the gay herrings of the 70's'.[4] In 1977, 43 per cent of Americans believed that gay relationships between consenting adults should be illegal, with the same percentage disagreeing and the remaining 14 per cent undecided – a

2 Franklin E. Kameny, 'Gay Survival and Practical Politics: Support for Carter', *The Washington Blade*, 10 October 1980.

3 The only two other attempts to chronic Carter's efforts on gay rights are: William B. Turner, 'Mirror Images: Lesbian/Gay Civil Rights in the Carter and Reagan Administration', in John D'Emilio, et al. (eds), *Creating Change: Sexuality, Public Policy, and Civil Rights* (New York: St. Martin's Press, 2000), 3–28; and Claire Bond Potter, 'Paths to Political Citizenship: Gay Rights, Feminism, and the Carter Presidency', *The Journal of Policy History* 24, no. 1 (2012): 95–114.

4 'Coalition Politics: A Necessary Alliance', *LT*, September–October 1977.

recipe for burgeoning cultural conflict.[5] For most mainstream politicians, the issue of gay rights was ignored if not deliberately avoided.[6] At that point, the centre of gravity in Congress was moving to the right, in keeping with public opinion, which was becoming more conservative on both social and economic issues. In 1979, the *Washington Post* described 'Senate liberals' as 'an endangered species'.[7] As American liberalism was in decline, Carter was confronted by a Congress not only keen to assert its own will against his but unlikely to find majorities for legislation in furtherance of gay rights.

The institutions of the American state were indeed more generally resistant and hostile to gay concerns. Margot Canaday has argued that unlike other Western democracies where the state apparatus had origins in the distant past, prior to the 'discovery' of homosexuality by the medical profession in the nineteenth century, in the United States the engines of bureaucracy, which were then still being formed, incorporated contemporary attitudes towards homosexuality into the very structure of the state, making it a 'straight state'. Whatever the validity of this explanation, undoubtedly Canaday is correct to insist on the pervasiveness of homophobic assumptions and procedures in the US government apparatus, as will be thoroughly evidenced in later chapters. Throughout US history, she argues, when the government has got involved in the lives of gay people, it has usually been to exercise power over them: to police their private conduct, to bar them from accessing welfare benefits, to prevent them from even entering the country on the grounds that they were medically unfit, and to place them in constant fear of arrest or mistreatment.[8] Or as Louie Crew Clay, a member of the National Gay Task Force's Board of Directors, and founder of Integrity, a gay Episcopal organization said more simply to the author, before Carter ran for president, the only official body to show any interest in gay people was the police, and that was only in order to arrest them.[9]

The book therefore aims primarily to establish Carter's record in the area of gay rights and give the full amount of credit where it is due. Further, it will provide a broader description of the political cultural dynamics of US politics in the later 1970s with an emphasis on one of its more underexplored aspects – not the gay rights movement itself, which has been well documented, but its interactions with, and the response from, the government in this period. And discussing this relationship inevitably casts light on another one: between Carter and the emerging religious right. Carter's own religiosity, which is also explored below, gave special poignancy to this development, perhaps accelerating it. Finally, and also as a product of the book's aim to describe lobbying, interaction between administration and groups, and policy formation in detail, the book provides insight into the arduous dynamics of policy-making in the separated American system, attending to the complexities introduced by both the

5 'Does Support for Gay Civil Rights Spell Political Suicide?', GRNL, n.d. RMSF, G/L1, JCPL.

6 Randy Shilts, 'A Most Conventional Convention', *The Advocate*, 11 August 1976.

7 Jack Anderson, 'The Right Wing's Hit List', *WP*, 22 April 1979.

8 Margot Canaday, *The Straight State: Sexuality and Citizenship in the Twentieth-Century America* (Princeton, NJ: Princeton University Press, 2009), 1–15.

9 Louie Crew Clay, author interview. Henceforward, when interviews conducted by the author are paraphrased or quoted, and the identity of the source is clear from the context, such sources will not be referenced but rather indicated in the text with an asterisk.

multiplicity of agencies and departments that make up the executive branch and also the courts and Congress in impeding and sometimes facilitating progress on Carter's inclusive human rights agenda.

Aiming to achieve a close to comprehensive account of the administration's efforts and achievements means that, while the sheer volume of material to some extent speaks for itself, a challenge arises as to navigating the profusion of detail. To this end, the reader is assisted by two principal organizational devices. Aside from this Introduction and a concluding chapter, the early chapters and two at the end have a basically chronological pattern, dealing with Carter's accession to the presidency and his early actions, including appointments, and at the end with Carter's difficult route to his party's nomination in 1980, followed by his loss to Ronald Reagan. Individual sections within chapters also often follow a chronological structure, aiming as they do to trace the often complicated history of various initiatives. The central chapters are, however, thematic in their overall structure, addressing different policy areas, grouped into broad categories. A further aid to the reader, given the large number of names, acronyms and sources, is the frequent use of cross-referencing, and the provision of a set of glossaries. One distinctive feature of the book is its use of the recollections, and also the retrospective evaluations – sometimes different from their contemporaneous ones – of numerous participants. These words carry not only testimonial authority but often also emotional force, bringing the personal dimension of the administration's achievements into plain view.

1

Candidate Carter and gay rights

This chapter traces Jimmy Carter's emergence from national political obscurity to victorious presidential candidate. It describes the distinctive political and cultural conjuncture that made this possible, examines Carter's way of reconciling his religious faith and his philosophy of governing, and records the steps, many of them bold and pioneering, by which gay people and gay rights advocates were installed in Carter's primary and general election campaigns, as well as the initial signs of a conservative response.

The political conjuncture and the Democratic Party

Carter stood for election at a difficult time for the Democratic Party and for America in general. The country was still reeling after the disastrous Vietnam War and the Watergate scandal, and there was a general sense of dissatisfaction with political life and discontent at the cultural changes continuing from the previous decade. According to Byron Shafer, the Democratic Party was 'confused, divided, and disoriented' and 'a fractious, quarrelsome lot, characterized by incongruous elements, conflicting goals, and a notable lack of discipline'.[1] In embracing the civil rights movement, it had become less straightforwardly aligned with trade union and labour concerns. Becoming visible at the 1968 Democratic Convention, and put into formal and procedural effect by internal reforms leading to the 1972 McGovern candidacy, 'the rise of an alternative coalition', including minority civil rights, feminist and environmentalist forces, had weakened, if not pushed aside, the organized labour groups who had been very much at the heart of the party.[2] Among the new groups, the feminist movement emerged as particularly important. Led by influential women such as US Congresswoman Bella Abzug, feminists were actively pursuing greater representation for women at all levels.[3] The gay rights movement was also already looking to the Democrats for support, alongside other progressive and liberally oriented groups, although gay rights

1 Byron E. Shafer, *Quiet Revolution: The Struggle for the Democratic Party and the Shaping of Post-reform Politics* (New York: Russell Sage Foundation, 1983), 126.

2 Shafer, *Quiet Revolution*, 7–8, 157–9, 253; Michael Dukakis and Byron E. Shafer, author interviews.

3 Bella Abzug with Mim Kelber, *Gender Gap: Bella Abzug's Guide to Political Power for American Women* (Boston: Houghton Mifflin, 1984), 45–51; Shafer, *Quiet Revolution*, 466.

advocates were still seen as occupying 'niche' territory and had not been accepted into the mainstream.[4]

Internal party reforms responded to these pressures by democratizing the candidate selection process. After the McGovern-Fraser reforms following the 1968 nomination of Hubert Humphrey, which sought to reduce party officials' influence over candidate selection, more states selected delegates via primary elections, enabling 'outsider' candidates.[5] Prior to this reform process, Carter would have been a very unlikely choice. After it, and after Watergate, Carter's outsider status made him an ideal candidate – untainted by Washington, personally appealing, but also with few prior alignments other than what might be suggested by his religious faith, which also suggested personal qualities of integrity and trustworthiness.

Carter first announced his intention to seek the Democratic nomination for president in December 1974, a few weeks before his term as Georgia's governor ended. His nomination was resisted by the more liberal wing of the party, which was suspicious of his deep religious convictions and his close ties with conservatives.[6] A Gallup poll in October 1975 revealed that only 1 per cent of voters supported Carter for the nomination.[7] The 1970s were a key decade both for gay rights campaigners and evangelicals. The changes in political culture already alluded to were beginning to evoke a response, as yet largely unnoticed by the mass media, in the form of conservative Christian mobilization at the grass roots. In 1976, Carter benefited from this mobilization and from the greater openness to it of the Democratic Party. Unsurprisingly, as the Democratic candidate, he received the support of the organized left; but he also gained a following among progressive and conservative evangelicals who saw him as one of their own and mobilized to support him.[8] For some Democrats, Carter represented the opportunity to gain votes among the more conservative, while not alienating the Party's liberal base.[9] But not all took that view: newspapers featured a succession of off-the-record comments from prominent party figures calling for a 'Stop Carter' or an 'Anybody but Carter' campaign.[10] Nevertheless, although Carter failed to win significant support from party leaders and regulars,[11] this disadvantage was offset by the reformed selection procedures.[12]

4 Ginny Apuzzo's and Charlotte Bunch's author interviews.

5 Jeffrey S. Walz and John Comer, Jr., 'State Responses to National Democratic Party Reform', *Political Research Quarterly* 52, no. 1 (1999): 189–208.

6 Peter Bourne, author interview; Timothy Stanley, *Kennedy vs. Carter: The 1980 Battle for the Democratic Party's Soul* (Lawrence: University of Kansas Press, 2010), 22.

7 Leslie Wheeler, *Jimmy Who? An Examination of Presidential Candidate Jimmy Carter* (Woodbury, NY: Barron's Educational Series, 1976), v.

8 Randall Balmer and Mark J. Rozell, author interviews; David R. Swartz, *Moral Minority: The Evangelical Left in an Age of Conservatism* (Philadelphia: University of Pennsylvania Press, 2012), 213–17.

9 Dukakis, author interview.

10 Jody Powell, *The Other Side of the Story* (New York: Morrow, 1984), 183.

11 James I. Lengle and Byron E. Shafer, *Presidential Politics: Readings on Nominations and Election* (New York: St. Martin's Press, 1980), 21.

12 Michael Nelson, 'Resolved, Political Parties Should Nominate Candidates for the Presidency Through a National Primary', in Richard J. Ellis and Michael Nelson (eds), *Debating the Presidency: Conflicting Perspectives on the American Executive* (Washington, DC: CQ Press, 2006), 16.

Carter, a self-described 'born-again' Christian and a Southern Baptist, actively sought support from the gay community and evangelicals alike, causing both sides to believe that he accepted their views and intended to pursue their agenda. According to Clyde Wilcox, Carter 'publicly' asked evangelicals 'to abandon their historical distrust of politics',[13] and his 'campaign mobilized white evangelicals to vote in greater numbers than in past elections'.[14] Carter was honest when he told evangelicals that he considered homosexuality to be a sin, but he was equally honest in his belief that gay people should have the same rights as everyone else. These positions led later to a degree of disappointment all round, with evangelicals particularly unhappy. Unsurprisingly, Carter was accused of being vague in his policies,[15] and he admitted that the most frequent question he was asked during his campaign was whether he was a conservative or a liberal. His reply was that he was 'a fiscal conservative', but also 'quite liberal on such issues as civil rights, environmental quality, and helping people overcome handicaps to lead fruitful lives'. Often this answer was found evasive; Carter would then insist that it was 'the most accurate answer' he could have given in 'a few words'.[16] An unnamed Democratic Party insider said in 1976 that Carter was 'a liberal to liberals, a moderate to moderates, and a conservative to the conservatives'.[17]

During the 1976 Democratic primaries, in addition to Carter five presidential candidates publicly expressed their support for gay rights: Birch Bayh, Fred Harris, Milton Shapp, Sargent Shriver and Morris Udall. George Wallace declined to comment on the subject while Henry Jackson publicly opposed homosexuality.[18] Also among the candidates was the popular California Governor Jerry Brown, who would later come out as a strong supporter of gay rights and implement a series of gay-friendly policies as Governor. However, at the time, he considered the issue of gay rights to be politically 'threatening'.[19] Carter campaigned extensively, more than any other candidate, visiting thirty-seven states and travelling over 50,000 miles. Carter quickly moved into second place in polls, at 28 per cent, behind Hubert Humphrey (who was not campaigning in the primaries) at 30 per cent, with Bayh and Shapp dropping out of the race. By mid-May, having won the Iowa caucuses and the New Hampshire primary, Carter had not only overtaken Humphrey but was also ahead of President Ford. Helped by his status as a non-Washington politician, along with his apparent decency and honesty,

13 Clyde Wilcox, *Onward Christian Soldiers? The Religious Right in American Politics* (Boulder and London: Westview Press, 1996), 36.

14 Clyde Wilcox, *God's Warriors: The Christian Right in Twenty-First Century America* (Baltimore: Johns Hopkins University Press, 1992), 11.

15 Jack Knott and Aaron Wildavsky, 'Jimmy Carter's Theory of Governing', *The Wilson Quarterly* 1, no. 2 (1977): 49–50; Stephen Skowronek, *The Politics Presidents Make: Leadership from John Adams to Bill Clinton* (Cambridge, MA: The Belknap Press of Harvard University Press, 1997), 371–2.

16 Jimmy Carter, *Keeping Faith: Memoirs of a President* (Fayetteville: University of Arkansas Press, 1995), 78.

17 Wheeler, *Jimmy Who?*, xi.

18 Jonathan Bell, 'Beyond the Blue Denim: National Gay Rights Activism and the Democratic Party', in Jonathan Bell (ed.), *Beyond the Politics of the Closet: Gay Rights and the American State since the 1970s* (Philadelphia: University of Pennsylvania Press, 2020), 68 f227; Sasha Gregory-Lewis, 'What They're Saying: Bayh, Carter, Harris, Jackson, Shapp, Shriver and Udall', *The Advocate*, 28 January 1976.

19 Dudley Clendinen and Adam Nagourney, *Out for Good: The Struggle to Build a Gay Rights Movement in America* (New York: Simon & Schuster, 1999), 273.

Carter stayed in the lead throughout the nomination contest. In July, shortly before the Democratic convention, Carter chose Minnesota Senator Walter Mondale as his running mate. Carter was impressed with Mondale's credentials in the area of human rights, while he aimed to reconcile his Party's liberal wing and the uncomfortable Washington political establishment.[20] A month before the convention, and despite losing nine of the last fourteen primaries, Carter secured the nomination.[21]

Carter's religiosity and gay rights: A 'wall of separation'

The 1976 presidential election was very important for the gay community, which represented at least 5 per cent of the voting electorate ('at least', since the statistic referred only to those who acknowledged being gay in surveys).[22] Tom Bastow, a prominent gay rights activist and president of the Gertrude Stein Democratic Club (GSDC) from 1978 to 1979, claimed in 1980 that there were at the time at least eight million gay voters (with 84 per cent of them, about double the national average, being regular voters).[23]

In the presidential elections of 1972, gay rights activists had approached the Democratic Party and attempted to include a gay rights plank in its platform. Although the plank was not adopted, George McGovern, the Democratic nominee for president, had made statements in support of gay rights and had sought the gay vote.[24] Furthermore, Madeline Davis and Jim Foster, gay rights activists and themselves openly gay, were given by McGovern and the party the unprecedented opportunity to make televised speeches at the Convention.[25] However, McGovern failed to respond to a questionnaire sent to him by *The Advocate,* the biggest gay newspaper of the time and the only one with nationwide distribution, which sought his opinion on a number of gay rights concerns.[26] In August 1972, some thirty members of the Gay Activists Alliance (GAA) occupied McGovern's New York campaign headquarters demanding that he make a public statement regarding his stand on gay rights. Subsequently, McGovern's office issued a statement stating, 'Senator McGovern has repeatedly affirmed his commitment to civil rights and civil liberties for all Americans'.[27] McGovern's support for gay rights

20 Peter G. Bourne, *Jimmy Carter: A Comprehensive Biography from Plains to Postpresidency* (New York: Scribner, 1997), 250–7, 329–36; Charles Mohr, 'Choice of Mondale Helps to Reconcile the Liberals', *NYT*, 16 July 1976; Daniel K. Williams, *The Election of the Evangelical: Jimmy Carter, Gerald Ford, and the Presidential Contest of 1976* (Lawrence: University Press of Kansas, 2020), 229–30.

21 Lengle and Shafer, *Presidential Politics*, 41.

22 Jean O'Leary, 'From Agitator to Insider: Fighting for Inclusion in the Democratic Party', in D'Emilio, et al., *Creating Change*, 84.

23 Memorandum, Tom Bastow to Martin Franks, undated, but it is certainly late June or early July 1980. RMSF, G/L1, JCPL.

24 Lillian Faderman, *The Gay Revolution: The Story of the Struggle* (New York: Simon & Schuster, 2015), 250.

25 Clendinen and Nagourney, *Out*, 132–47.

26 Stacey Flores Chandler, 'Pride Month: The LGBTQ Rights Movement and the 1972 Presidential Campaign', The JFK Library Archives, https://jfk.blogs.archives.gov/2017/06/23/pridemonth-the-lgbtq-rights-movement-and-the-1972-presidential-campaign/.

27 'Gay Activists in Protest Occupy McGovern Office', *NYT*, 22 August 1972.

and other liberal issues caused controversy within his own party, alienating many Democrats and contributing to Nixon's landslide win.[28] Expectations of the Democrats within the gay community had nevertheless continued to grow.

During the 1976 presidential election race, incumbent and Republican nominee Gerald Ford, although generally moderate in his views, avoided making any substantive statement on gay rights.[29] Richard M. Scammon – director of the Census Bureau and elections analyst for NBC – said that for politicians 'In places like San Francisco, it might be OK for gay stuff, but anywhere else, it is a ticket to oblivion'.[30] In August 1976, David Nidiffer, a Bradley University student, asked President Ford to clarify his position 'on civil rights for gay people'. Ford replied, 'Civil rights for whom?' Nidiffer repeated, 'For gay people'. Ford then said,

> I recognize that this is a very new and serious problem. I've always tried to be an understanding person as far as people are concerned who are different than myself . . . that doesn't mean that I agree with or in what is done by them in their position in society. I think this is a problem we have to face up to, but I can't give you a pat answer tonight. It would be dishonest to say there is a pat answer.[31]

Carter certainly improved upon Ford's evasion by his readiness to engage with the issue of gay rights. He also went considerably further than McGovern had in embracing the gay rights cause. This, moreover, was a striking departure in particular for a candidate whose denominational religious commitments as a Southern Baptist, by no means the most progressive of churches, were strong and readily acknowledged. Carter negotiated this issue by relying on what could be called his own version of Thomas Jefferson's famous 'wall of separation' between church and state (a metaphor announced by Jefferson in a letter to the members of a Baptist church).[32] While the wall Jefferson took to be erected by the First Amendment of the Constitution has often been breached, it is nevertheless a venerable ideal of American politics, and subsisted sturdily inside Carter's own approach to politics and his philosophy of government. Carter repeatedly stated that he considered homosexuality to be a sin, but that gay people should not be harassed and should have equal rights with all other Americans. The implication was that his views on homosexuality had no bearing on matters of state. Throughout his campaign, Carter orally and in writing maintained his opposition to discrimination against gay people, stating that he would attempt to end it, for instance going on record as supporting the National Organization for Women's Pro-Gay platform.[33] Whenever

28 Dukakis, author interview; Rick Perlstein, *Nixonland: The Rise of a President and the Fracturing of America* (New York: Scribner, 2008), 693–724.

29 Larry Bush, 'The Carter Administration. More Done Than Said?', *The Advocate*, 12 June 1980; Roger Ricklefs, 'A New Constituency: Political Candidates Seek Out Gay Votes', *WSJ*, 20 October 1976; 'Does Support for Gay Civil Rights Spell Political Suicide?', *GRNL*, n.d. RMSF, G/L1, JCPL.

30 Randy Shilts, 'A Most Conventional Convention', *The Advocate*, 11 August 1976.

31 'Ford Has, "No Pat Answer"', *The Advocate*, 7 April 1976; NGTF Report, April 1976. RMSF, GR, B.7, JCPL.

32 Randal Balmer, 'Fundamentalism, the First Amendment, and the Rise of the Religious Right', *William and Mary Bill of Rights Journal* 18, no. 4 (2010): 889–91.

33 Carter Presidential Campaign Press Release, 'Jimmy Carter Speaks Out on Gay Rights', 23 May 1976. RMSF, GR, B.7, JCPL.

he was asked by the gay community, he responded that he opposed 'all forms of discrimination on the basis of sexual orientation'.[34] However, the gay community's scepticism, deriving from Carter's background, was not easily assuaged and had some concrete justification, such as Governor Carter's meeting in 1971 with three local gay rights activists, Beryl Boykin, Klaus Smith and Bill Smith, where he had refused to help them in their efforts to repeal anti-gay laws.[35]

During the election campaign, Carter received a large amount of correspondence from gay rights activists and gay organizations with questions regarding his opinion on the matter of gay rights. Carter was unequivocal in his replies, and equally importantly he actually *made* replies. For example, in March 1976, Carter responded to a letter from *Gay News*: 'I oppose all forms of discrimination on the basis of sexual orientation. As President, I assure you that all policies of the federal government would reflect this commitment'.[36] This letter made him the first presidential nominee from one of the two major parties to respond in writing to a request from the gay press.[37] It was one of many: 'Governor Carter is firmly opposed to discrimination in all forms including affectional preference. As President he will work to eliminate it';[38] to the Stonewall Democratic Club (SDC) in California Carter similarly declared that he 'opposed discrimination in all forms, including discrimination because of sexual preference'.[39] He consistently favoured 'the end of harassment or abuse or discrimination' against gay people and said that he did not have the right to 'cast the first stone' when it came to matters of sexual morality.[40] His statement on abuse, harassment and discrimination was widely circulated both in the gay community and by the Democratic Presidential Campaign Committee.[41]

On 12 March, while Carter was campaigning in Los Angeles, County Supervisor Ed Edelman arranged for him to meet with eight prominent local leaders over luncheon at the Hyatt Hotel. Four of them were openly gay and gay rights activists; among them were Dr Newton Deiter, founder of the Gay Media Task Force in Hollywood, and Rev. Troy Perry, founder of the Metropolitan Community Church (MCC), the first gay church in the United States. It was the first time a presidential candidate of one of the two major parties had agreed to meet with representatives of the gay community. Carter did not mention gay rights in his speech at the meeting, but offered

34 Carter Presidential Campaign Press Release, 'Jimmy Carter Speaks Out on Gay Rights', 23 May 1976. RMSF, GR, B.7, JCPL; Jean O'Leary-NGTF-Two Quotes, undated. SWSF, NGTF Correspondence, JCPL; 'Carter Aide Conferring with Gays on Rights', *NYP*, 26 March 1977.

35 OutHistory, 'Out in Atlanta: Atlanta's Gay and Lesbian Communities since Stonewall: A Chronology, 1969–2012', *OutHistory Org*, http://outhistory.org/exhibits/show/atlanta-since-stonewall/out_in_atlanta.

36 Carter Presidential Campaign Press Release, 'Jimmy Carter Speaks Out on Gay Rights', 23 May 1976. RMSF, GR, B.7, JCPL.

37 Clay and Ginny Vida, author interviews.

38 Letter, Charles Cabot to Christopher Larkin, 12 March 1976. MCSF, [GR: P], JCPL.

39 Letter, David Moran to Morris Knight, 4 March 1976. SDCR, B1, F20, ONE NLGA, USC.

40 For example: Carter Presidential Campaign Press Release, 'Jimmy Carter Speaks out on Gay Rights', 23 May 1976. RMSF, GR, B.7, JCPL; News Release, California Gay People for Carter-Mondale, undated. MCSF, GRJCV, JCPL; Jean O'Leary-NGTF-Two Quotes, undated. SWSF, NGTF Correspondence, JCPL.

41 Larry Bush, 'White House Claims Solid Record on Gay Issues', *The Sentinel*, 16 May 1980; Troy Perry, author interview.

afterwards to take questions. Perry asked whether a question from 'a member of the gay community' was acceptable, to which Carter replied 'of course'. To the question, 'If you become president of the United States, are you willing to sign an Executive Order to ban discrimination against gay people in the areas of military, housing, employment and immigration?' Carter replied: 'I could be supportive of all of those areas except one. The place I would have difficulty with is the area of employment where security clearances are involved, where there are employees who are not open about being gay'. Carter did not commit to signing an executive order, but pledged that he would work to end discrimination against gay people in the entire federal sector, apart from the security agencies which constituted about 5 per cent of it.[42] Perry was stunned and delighted by Carter's reply, commenting in retrospect 'that was brilliant, and light-years ahead of what other national politicians were saying in the campaign'. At the end of the meeting, Carter approached Perry and after he once again pledged his support for gay rights, handed Perry his business card and said, 'If you're interested, I need people to organize all over America'. Following the meeting, all four gay rights activists were thrilled with Carter's comments and unanimously endorsed him. They were impressed with Carter's openness and readiness to discuss the issue of gay rights, as well as his sincerity in admitting that he would maintain discrimination in the security sector, and with the fact that he practically asked them to join his campaign.[43]

After the meeting, Deiter suggested starting a Gays for Carter group in California, an idea supported by Carter's campaign team. Perry immediately joined the group, and they were soon joined by other local gay rights activists. Gays for Carter was endorsed by Carter himself and, to the activists' considerable surprise, he also agreed to send his wife Rosalynn to attend the group's opening gala and first fundraiser in Los Angeles. Wearing a coat lent to her by Perry after her luggage had been mislaid, Rosalynn pledged again that Carter would advance gay rights and end discrimination against gay people across the federal sector, apart from the security elements. Rosalynn's presence at the fundraiser was of major importance to the local gay community; it was the first time that the wife of a presidential nominee had met with the gay community and attended such an event.[44]

Carter's sincerity and commitment on the issue of gay rights was further proven to the gay community by the fact that he was happy to talk about the topic and express his support for gay rights on national television, and not only in Los Angeles and San Francisco, which had large and open gay communities. Carter's most explicit remarks on homosexuality were made in an interview on NBC's *The Tomorrow Show* on 19 March, where he said, 'I favor the end of harassment or abuse or discrimination against homosexuals', again making the security exception.[45] This was the first time that a presidential nominee had expressed his support for gay rights on national TV. As a

[42] News Release, California Gay people for Carter-Mondale, undated. MCSF, GRJCV, JCPL; Troy D. Perry with Thomas L. P. Swicegood, *Don't Be Afraid Anymore: The Story of Reverend Troy Perry and the Metropolitan Community Churches* (New York: St Martin's Press, 1992), 183–5; Perry, author interview.

[43] Perry, author interview.

[44] Ibid.

[45] Jimmy Carter on *The Tomorrow Show*, 19 March 1976. RMSF, GR, B.7, JCPL.

Gays for Carter leaflet put it, he was 'unafraid to go before the cameras for us'.[46] Jeanne Córdova, leading lesbian rights activist at the time and founder of *The Lesbian Tide* periodical, said of 'humble Democrat' Carter's public declaration of his opposition to discrimination against gay people, 'This was big! Perhaps it signaled a pivotal change. Maybe our gay and lesbian movement was entering a reformist swing into mainstream politics'.[47] Carter made comments along the same lines to the *Wall Street Journal*,[48] while in an interview with WHA-TV in Madison, Wisconsin, he was asked about a recent US Supreme Court decision to uphold the right of a state to declare same-sex relations between consulting adults to be illegal. He replied, 'I am not in favor of harassment of homosexuals', and that it was 'a hopeless case to enforce sex laws in the privacy of consenting adults'.[49]

On 21 May, Carter visited San Francisco and gave a news conference at the Hilton Hotel. He was asked by George Mendenhall, a gay rights activist and journalist, about his views on gay people and whether he considered them to be immoral or sinners. Carter replied that he considered them to be sinners since 'the Bible teaches against homosexuality', but he also invoked his version of the wall of separation by saying,

> the thing that I have meant in the past and that I still maintain is that I don't think that the government at the local, state or federal level should single out homosexuals for special abuse or special harassment, or special prosecution under existing laws . . . so, although I do look upon those and many other things as sinful, including lying, or a lack of showing respect to your own mother and father, abuse of the Lord's Day; no, I don't think it's right to single out homosexuals for abuse.[50]

In the same news conference, Carter was asked whether he would support Congresswoman Bella Abzug's bill to amend the 1964 Civil Rights Act to end discrimination against gay people in the federal government and replied in the affirmative. Asked how his religious faith could be reconciled with his support for gay rights, Carter replied,

> I don't consider myself one iota better than anyone else because I happen to be a Christian and I have never done anything other than keep strictly separated my political life from my religious life . . . the separation of Church and State is very vivid for me, is a very important factor for me . . . there would be no conflict in my life as President, having my own personal, deeply felt religious beliefs. I don't consider myself any better than anyone else.[51]

46 Gays for Carter leaflet, undated. RMSF, GR, B.7, JCPL.
47 Jeanne Córdova, *When We Were Outlaws* (Midway, FL: Spinsters Ink, 2011, Kindle edition), location 6700.
48 Quoted in 'Carter Election Will Aid Gay Rights, Voeller Claims', *Centre Daily Times*, 9 November 1976.
49 Charles Fulkerson, 'Carter Would Use Tough Tactics in Another Arab Oil Embargo', *Wisconsin State Journal*, 31 March 1976.
50 'Jimmy Carter Takes a Stand on Gay Rights, But What Does It Mean?', *The Advocate*, 16 June 1976.
51 Ibid.

Carter's comments pleased the gay community, which saw them as further signs of his commitment to their cause.[52] Larry Little John, a member of Carter's Advisory Committee on Gay People (see later in this chapter), said,

> Carter could have easily ducked supporting the Abzug bill because of the numerous pieces of legislation before Congress. Carter could have claimed to be uninformed about the topic. Carter is right down the line on gay rights when we cannot find one Senator in one hundred to sponsor the Abzug bill.[53]

On 23 May, Carter's Campaign team in California issued a press release entitled, 'Jimmy Carter Speaks Out on Gay Rights'. It outlined Carter's position and included several of his public statements on the subject, for example his support for Abzug's bill and his response on *The Tomorrow Show*.[54] Subsequently, Mendenhall expressed his opinion of Carter in the *Bay Area Reporter*. After listing Carter's statements in support of gay rights, as well as his religious beliefs and his blackmail theory about gay employees in the security sector, Mendenhall wrote,

> Carter is consistently being upfront on gay rights. He makes no hesitation in speaking out on the subject at all times – not just in closeted meetings with a few gay leaders. . . . We may not buy all of Jimmy Carter, but at this point, he is a person gay activists should be seriously considering.[55]

Carter's strong and public statements of opposition to discrimination against gay people were quoted repeatedly in communications from gay rights activists. For example, in a letter written by Robert Osborn to Thomas Hastings, the New York Chief of Police, on 24 August, calling for police officers to receive training and instruction on how to deal with the gay community and for an end to police harassment of gay people and transvestites. Osborn's letter used wording almost identical to Carter's.[56]

Further consolidation of the gay community's support for Carter followed his response to events in his home state of Georgia. When Mayor Maynard Jackson of Atlanta proclaimed 26 June to be a Gay Pride Day, he received hundreds of letters of protest and was sued by seven local businessmen. A local Southern Baptist minister gathered about sixteen thousand signatures demanding the event's cancellation or Jackson's resignation, and a number of Southern Baptists formed a group called Citizens for a Decent Atlanta and made an abortive attempt to persuade a court to annul the announcement. The same month, the Southern Baptist Convention, to which Carter belonged, passed its first resolution against homosexuality.[57] Carter was asked his opinion and publicly expressed his support for Jackson's proclamation. In

52 Apuzzo, Charlotte Bunch, Clay, Adam DeBaugh and Perry, author interviews.

53 Phil Cappetta, 'Gays for Carter', *Gotham Ledger*, 9 July 1976. RMSF, GR, B.7, JCPL.

54 Carter Presidential Campaign Press Release, 'Jimmy Carter Speaks out on Gay Rights', 23 May 1976. RMSF, GR, B.7, JCPL.

55 George Mendenhall, 'Carter for President', *BAR*, 27 May 1976.

56 Letter, Robert Osborn to Thomas Hastings, 24 August 1976. MCSF, [GR: MECOCL], JCPL.

57 OutHistory, 'Out in Atlanta: Atlanta's Gay and Lesbian Communities Since Stonewall'; Roger Ricklefs, 'A New Constituency: Political Candidates Seek Out Gay Votes', *WSJ*, 20 October 1976'.

the end, Jackson stood his ground and the event took place as planned.[58] Gay people, especially in Georgia, were 'enthusiastic' about Carter publicly declaring his support for the mayor's decision and for the Gay Pride Day. During the parade, some of the participants held placards with Carter's picture or name, and below them his remarks regarding his support for gay rights. Other placards simply stated, 'Carter for President' or 'Vote Carter'. Clay said to the author,

> We all knew that Carter didn't really approve of homosexuality, but at least he recognized that we had equal rights like everyone else. For us, this was the most important thing. In those days, anti-gay rhetoric and feelings were so widespread, that a public figure who recognized us as equal members of society was an ally by definition.*

The inclusive campaign

Carter publicly sought the gay vote and publicly opposed discrimination against gay people.[59] According to Peter Bourne, Carter's Deputy Campaign Director at the time, it was Carter's own idea to seek the gay vote: 'There is no doubt that Carter, very early on, apart from his personal inclinations, did see the gay community as a constituency to be recruited to support him'.* After their meeting at the Hyatt Hotel, Perry had declared, 'I am strongly supporting Jimmy Carter because of his commitment to civil rights for all people and because of his opposition to non-job related employment discrimination'. Carter's campaign team included this quote in its press releases, showing his intention to reach out directly to the gay community.[60] The press releases also contained statements of Carter's endorsement by other prominent gay and lesbian activists such as Earl Stokes of the San Francisco Board of Permit Appeals, Del Martin, Chairperson of the San Francisco Commission on the Status of Women, and Phyllis Lyon of the San Francisco Human Rights Commission. Lyon and Martin made a strong statement in support of Carter, saying, 'As lesbians and as women, we support Jimmy Carter for President because of his strong stand on the ERA [Equal Rights Amendment], because he is committed to appointing women to key positions in his administration and because he supports gay civil rights. President Ford has failed women and gay people'.[61]

58 Clay, author interview; Roger Ricklefs, 'A New Constituency: Political Candidates Seek Out Gay Votes', *WSJ*, 20 October 1976.

59 Phil Cappetta, 'Gays for Carter', *Gotham Ledger*, 9 July 1976; Clay and Perry, author interviews; Rick Valelly, 'How Gay Rights Activists Remade the Federal Government', *WP*, 1 October 2018.

60 News Release, California Gay people for Carter-Mondale, undated. MCSF, GRJCV, JCPL; Perry with Swicegood, *Don't Be Afraid Anymore*, 184–5.

61 News Release, California Gay people for Carter-Mondale, undated. MCSF, GRJCV, JCPL. The ERA in its most recent form had been passed by Congress in 1972 and with bipartisan support had been on course for ratification by three quarters of the states. By the start of Carter's presidency Phyllis Schlafly's 'Stop ERA' campaign had begun to reverse its progress and the Amendment was becoming a bellwether of emerging cultural divisions. Jane J. Mansbridge, *Why We Lost the ERA* (Chicago: University of Chicago Press, 1986), 8–110; Joan Williams, *Unbending Gender: Why Family and Work Conflict and What to Do About It* (Oxford and New York: Oxford University Press, 1999), 147. Eventually, the ERA was defeated and remains to this day not ratified. Randall Balmer

In a highly significant move for the gay community, Carter appointed Margaret 'Midge' Costanza as co-chair of his campaign team in New York State. Costanza was an ardent feminist and avid supporter of gay rights, also known by those close to her, including Carter, to be lesbian. Carter was also very well aware of Costanza's ideology and her support for women and gay rights; her commitment to human rights was the main reason he chose her for his campaign.[62] Costanza played a crucial role in the campaign, making speeches, recruiting people to the campaign staff and accompanying Carter on his tours all over the country.[63] In appointing Costanza, who was a very vocal supporter of gay rights, Carter was also signalling to the wider public that such a position was no barrier to participation at the highest levels of politics.

Costanza was not the only gay rights activist with an active and visible role in Carter's election campaign. Bella Abzug joined Carter's campaign at his request.[64] Costanza and Abzug were tasked with 'introducing' Carter to New York State and both women actively campaigned there with him as well as alone on his behalf.[65] In addition to Abzug, several other prominent feminists supported Carter and campaigned for him, such as Betty Friedan, co-founder and first president of the National Organization for Women (NOW), and Mary E. King, founder and president of the National Association of Women Business Owners.[66] Shortly before the Democratic Convention, King, who had been appointed as Carter's chief adviser on women, suggested he create a women's committee dedicated to increasing women's voices in his campaign. Carter found the idea 'excellent' and on 13 June, he announced the formation of the Committee, appointing King as its director.[67] It was named the 51.3% Committee, referring to the female percentage of the American population, and its three basic purposes as outlined by Carter were to advise him on his 'campaign for President and how women can best and most fully be involved in it'; to advise him 'on the issues – not only such traditional "women's issues" as health and education, but on all issues – war, and peace, the budget and the economy, and other matters of importance to the American people'; and 'To assist him in seeking out well-qualified women to serve' in his administration.[68]

Carter's campaign team went on to appoint a number of openly gay people to various visible and important positions all over the country.[69] Carter had instructed his campaign team to appoint as many people from minorities as possible. Although he had not given specific instructions about gay people, he had insisted that there should

told the author that Carter confided to him in later life that 'one of the deep disappointments of his presidency was his failure to shepherd the Equal Rights Amendment to ratification'.*

62 Bourne, Stuart Eizenstat and Sarah Weddington, author interviews.

63 Midge Costanza interview to Ashley Boyd, 2010. MCI; Doreen Mattingly, *A Feminist in the White House: Midge Costanza, the Carter Years, and America's Culture Wars* (New York: Oxford University Press, 2016), 67–76.

64 Abguz with Kelber, *Gender Gap*, 50–1; Roger Ricklefs, 'A New Constituency: Political Candidates Seek Out Gay Votes', *WSJ*, 20 October 1976.

65 'Just Like Old Times, Mrs. Abzug Is on Stump Again but for Carter', *NYT*, 20 October 1976.

66 Judith Adler Hennessee, *Betty Friedan: Her Life* (New York: Random House, 1999), 224; Mim Kelber, 'Carter and Women: The Record', *The Nation*, 24 May 1980; Mattingly, *A Feminist*, 78.

67 Statement by Jimmy Carter on Women's Rights before the Committee of 51.3 Percent, 13 June 1976. NSSF, Carter's Briefings and Statements, B.69, JCPL; Kandy Stroud, 'Mary King: A Key Carter Brain Truster from the Beginning', *NYT*, 8 July 1976.

68 Ibid.

69 Clay and Perry, author interviews; Gays for Carter! A Message to the Gay Community, undated. RMSF, GR, B.7, JCPL; Randy Shilts, 'A Most Conventional Convention', *The Advocate*, 11 August 1976.

be no discrimination against anyone. Several people in a number of posts who were appointed at the time, or people who had continued working with him since his days as governor, were openly gay and Carter was aware of this, having even appointed some of them himself. According to Peter Bourne and Stuart Eizenstat the appointment of openly gay people to visible posts in Carter's campaign team was a deliberate public statement on Carter's part.*

Three of the openly gay people who were appointed by Carter's campaign team were hired to important staff jobs in California.[70] When asked why they were hired, the state's campaign co-chairman stated, 'We hired them because they are pros, that's why',[71] sending a clear message that Carter did not discriminate in words or in actions. Two such appointments were those of John Roberts,[72] as scheduler, and Charles Graham, a professional fundraiser who was hired as press aide and fundraising coordinator in California. Graham pointed to the appointment of openly gay people as confirming Carter's sincerity about gay rights.[73]

Carter also placed four openly gay people on his delegate slate in California.[74] One of them was Clayton Wells, who was also Carter's delegate and SDC's secretary, and who went on to play an active and important role throughout the election campaign – 'hard evidence of a commitment to gay people', according to *The Advocate*.[75] A number of gay rights activists were also appointed by Carter for his campaign in New York State. Among them was Jean O'Leary, co-executive director of the National Gay Task Force (NGTF) and former chairwoman of Lesbian Feminist Liberation, who at Costanza's urging, and with Carter's approval, joined the campaign team and campaigned among the gay community in New York. O'Leary's high profile as a gay rights activist made this appointment a particularly notable one for the gay community. O'Leary obtained many votes for Carter among the gay community by reporting that he was open to dialogue and addressing their concerns.[76] Clay said about O'Leary's appointment that it

> was very important for us. Having an open lesbian and one of the NGTF's directors appointed by the Presidential nominee was of major significance for us. We felt that we could make our voices heard. Most importantly, it was obvious to us and to everyone that Carter was against discrimination.*

Furthermore, Carter advertised in gay publications, an unprecedented step for a presidential candidate. One such advertisement was in *The Advocate*; it contained a picture of Rosalynn Carter 'discussing community issues' with Deiter and Perry during the Gays for Carter fundraiser in Los Angeles. The ad also contained a list of names of prominent

70 Gays for Carter leaflet, undated, and Gays for Carter! A Message to the Gay Community, undated, both in RMSF, GR, B.7, JCPL.

71 Gays for Carter leaflet, undated. RMSF, GR, B.7, JCPL.

72 George Mendenhall, 'Carter for President', *BAR*, 27 May 1976.

73 Randy Shilts, 'A Most Conventional Convention', *The Advocate*, 11 August 1976.

74 Gays for Carter! A Message to the Gay Community, undated, and Gays for Carter! 'Mondale Affirms Carter Anti-Discrimination Stand', 12 September 1976, both in RMSF, GR, B.7, JCPL.

75 Randy Shilts, 'A Most Conventional Convention', *The Advocate*, 11 August 1976.

76 Apuzzo and Bunch, author interviews; Midge Costanza interviews to Dudley Clendinen, 1994–1995. MCI.

openly gay people who had endorsed Carter, and Perry's quote about his support for Carter.[77] In this way, Carter was the first presidential nominee to reach out so explicitly to the gay community, assuring them that he would not discriminate against them, and that he valued them as voters and as citizens. It was a daring thing to do in the face of rising opposition to the gay rights cause and a powerful message to the gay community as a whole. It was also an important act of validation in which Carter showed that one did not personally have to accept gay sexual behaviour in order to accept gay people, and to recognize their concerns as valid matter government concerns. According to Charles Graham the ads were 'very well received' by the gay community and 'counteracted the "homosexuality is a sin" statement'.[78] These ads contributed to Carter's endorsement by a number of gay rights activist leaders (Figure 1).

Eddie Sandifer, a gay veteran who in 1973 had founded the Mississippi Gay Alliance, summarized the impact as follows:

> Seeing Carter's ads in the gay press was really quite unexpected, quite a shock even. This was something that was never done before, as far as I can tell. Politicians were not advertising themselves in such publications, not even those who were gay. It was certainly very important. We were all very surprised to see the US President nominee placing advertisements in the gay press, but it was a pleasant surprise. It must have taken Carter a lot of courage to do it, considering the volatile atmosphere at the time, but it certainly sent out a big message.*

Carter continued his outreach to the gay community by sending his 26-year-old son Chip to California to campaign in the community there. Chip toured gay areas in San Francisco and attended events organized by gay rights activists. He repeatedly highlighted his father's support for gay rights and for an end to discrimination. He even accepted the invitation of the Harry S. Truman Democratic Club to attend the annual Great Tricycle Race in San Francisco, a fundraiser for guide dogs organized by the Mint Tavern, a local gay bar. Sharing a tricycle with gay rights activist Mike Delaney, Chip rode throughout the race, which made a circuit of all the gay areas of the city, including the gay bars, asking the gay community to support his father.[79] On one occasion he acknowledged that his father 'doesn't think homosexuality is right, but he doesn't want to inflict his morals on other people'. Chip also stated that he was there to 'show support for gay peoples' political situation'[80] and rode the tricycle 'to designate the acceptance of that lifestyle'.[81] A picture of Chip riding the tricycle and his comments regarding his father's support for gay rights appeared in newspapers all over the country, much to the delight of the gay community.[82] Local gay rights activists compared Chip's campaign in California's gay community to Eleanor Roosevelt's 1930's campaigning in Harlem, where

[77] 'Advertisement: Jimmy Carter', *The Advocate*, 2 June 1976.

[78] Charlie Graham quoted in one of Carter's ads that appeared in gay publications, n.d. RMSF, GR, B.7, JCPL.

[79] Harry Britt, author interview; 'The Great Tricycle Race', *BAR*, 10 June 1976; Bob Kiggins, 'Outrageous', *The Advocate*, 30 June 1976.

[80] Clendinen and Negourney, *Out*, 276.

[81] Costanza interview to Boyd. MCI; Bob Kiggins, 'Outrageous', *The Advocate*, 30 June 1976.

[82] Britt, Clay, DeBaugh, David McReynolds, author interviews; Clendinen and Negourney, *Out*, 275.

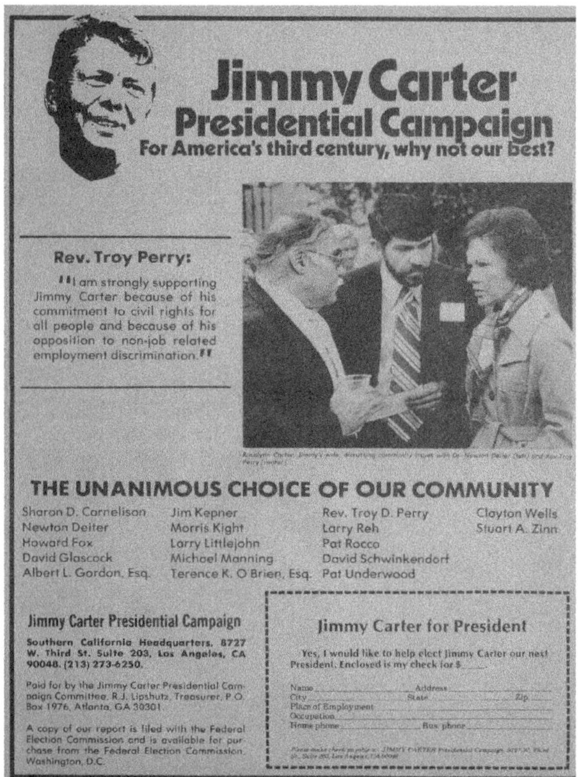

Figure 1 One of the several Carter ads that appeared in six gay publications. According to Charles Graham, an openly gay professional fundraiser who had been appointed as fundraising coordinator for Carter's campaign in California, the ads were 'very well received' by the gay community and 'counteracted the "homosexuality is a sin" statement which was widely noted'. RMSF. GR, B.7. JCPL.

she asked the Black population to vote for her husband.[83] Costanza recalled telling the gay community about Chip's presence in San Francisco: 'I'm here to tell you Chip Carter does not go to a Gay Rights celebration without the approval of the president and this campaign. He didn't just happen to show up or accidentally run into it, he wants your support'.[84] Jeffrey Montgomery, founding executive director of *Triangle Foundation*, a gay and civil rights organization in Michigan, commented:

> It was a difficult period for us. A lot of people in the US were talking about us in demonic ways, and were seeing us as abnormal and even dangerous. Having the son of the Presidential candidate attending our meetings and talking to us probably made a lot of these people reconsider their opinion about us.*

83 Phil Cappetta, 'Gays for Carter', *Gotham Ledger*, 9 July 1976.
84 Midge Costanza interview with Dudley Clendinen, 24 February 1994. MCI.

Another act of the Carter campaign which appealed to the gay community was the commissioning of Andy Warhol, one of the most famous living artists as well as one of the most famous openly gay people in the world, to print a hundred copies of a Carter portrait he had made for the *New York Times Magazine*. These were to be sold for fundraising, priced at one thousand dollars each. Warhol's silkscreens, entitled *Portrait of Jimmy Carter*,[85] raised about $50,000 for the campaign, and were later described by Carter as 'the turning point in the financing of my campaign'.[86]

As a result of Carter's outreach to gay voters, his public statements in support of gay rights, and the appointment of openly gay people to visible posts in his campaign team, the gay community mobilized to support him. A large number of openly gay people joined his election campaign in various positions, while some began forming local volunteer groups in support of Carter in order to mobilize the gay vote. Such groups were formed in cities with large gay communities, such as Atlanta, Houston, Miami, New York, Seattle and Washington, D.C.[87] Carter's support for the Gay Pride Day in Atlanta, as well as his public statements in support of gay rights, led the vast majority of gay people in Georgia to declare their support for their former governor in the election race. To show their appreciation, several openly gay people turned up at Carter's Campaign Committee offices in Atlanta, volunteering to join the election campaign team in the state. As a result, more than twenty gay people joined the campaign team in various positions and went on to campaign for him all over the state; one of them was Ray Kluka, a prominent gay rights activist who later became the director of the Atlanta Gay Center.[88]

In California, the Harry S. Truman Democratic Club and the Alice B. Toklas Memorial Democratic Club (ABTMDC) endorsed Carter and promoted his candidacy.[89] Perry and the state's Gays for Carter were soon joined by a number of other prominent local gay rights activists like Sheldon Andelson, Harry Britt, Donald Knutson, Bill Kraus, Rev. Ray Broshears and Morris Kight who all actively campaigned for Carter.[90] Volunteers were numerous: Charles Graham said that 'gay people were calling me up and asking how they could help Carter'. As a result of this, Graham and other gay people in Carter's campaign team formed an Advisory Committee on Gay People as part of Carter's national election organization, in order to advise him on gay rights issues. The team consisted of more than seventeen prominent gay people and feminists, including Perry.[91] It was the first time that a presidential nominee had had such a committee, and that a nominee had received advice on gay rights issues.[92]

85 Victor Bockris, *The Life and Death of Andy Warhol* (New York: Bantam Books, 1989), 298–9.

86 Jo Ann Lewis, 'An Artful Thank-You from President Carter', *WP*, 15 June 1977.

87 Larry Bush, Clay, ABilly S. Jones-Hennin, Norman Elliot Kent and David McReynolds, author interviews.

88 Clay, author interview.

89 'Chit Chat from "Alice B"', *BAR*, 28 October 1976; 'Election Endorsements', *BAR*, 27 May 1976.

90 Britt and Perry, author interviews.

91 Gays for Carter! A Message to the Gay Community, undated, and Gays for Carter! 'Mondale Affirms Carter Anti-Discrimination Stand', 12 September 1976, both in RMSF, GR, B.7, JCPL; Phil Cappetta, 'Gays for Carter', *Gotham Ledger*, 9 July 1976.

92 Gays for Carter! A Message to the Gay Community, undated, and Gays for Carter! 'Mondale Affirms Carter Anti-Discrimination Stand', 12 September 1976, both in RMSF, GR, B.7, JCPL; Perry, author interview.

In late May and early June, prior to the California primary on 8 June, the Gays for Carter in the state, with the approval of Carter's Presidential Campaign Committee, took out ads in several gay publications. The ads highlighted Carter's public comments and commitments in support of gay rights and an end to discrimination, the fact that he had appointed openly gay people to prominent posts within his campaign team, that he had an Advisory Committee on Gay People, that he supported Abzug's bill, and that he was 'unafraid to go before the cameras' and express support for gay rights. Furthermore, the ads assured gay readers that, despite Carter's deep religious convictions, he did not 'believe in legislating morals' and he 'opposed all forms of discrimination on the basis of sexual orientation'.[93]

Conventional hurdles

In 1975, the Stonewall Democratic Club had submitted a gay rights plank, promising to provide equal protection under civil rights law, to the California Democratic Council, but the Party's Platform Committee had not so far adopted it.[94] A few weeks before the 1976 Democratic Convention, the committee met. There were only four openly gay delegates: O'Leary, who had earlier been elected on Birch Bayh's delegate slate; Josephine (Jo) Daly, of the San Francisco Human Rights Commission and former co-chairwoman of the ABTMDC, and Jim Foster, co-founder of the ABTMDC and Clayton Wells. The gay delegates aimed to convince the party to adopt the gay rights plank.[95]

As the Convention approached, with Carter having secured the nomination after seventeen primary election victories out of thirty-one, some gay rights activists perceived a cooling of his attitude towards gay rights.[96] One of the reasons for this perception seems to have been a statement Carter made to *The Advocate*; 'I have never told anyone that I favor total equality. I have not made up my mind on it [regarding a gay rights bill]. I do not feel that people should be abused because of their sexual preference, but I don't know how we could deal with the issue of blackmail in federal security jobs. But with that possible exemption, I would probably support this legislation'.[97] While this statement only reiterated his earlier view, *The Advocate* nevertheless wrote, 'In good conscience we cannot recommend that gay people vote for him'.[98]

Meanwhile, O'Leary and Ginny Apuzzo, co-chair of the Gay Rights National Lobby (GRNL) and a member of the NGTF at the time (becoming its executive director in the 1980s), had been trying to mobilize the gay community to lobby the party for a gay rights

93 For example, see: 'Jimmy Carter advertisement', *BAR*, 27 May 1976, and Advertisement for Carter's 1976 campaign, *BAR*, undated. RMSF, GR, B.7, JCPL.

94 SDC, 'Gay Rights Plank', undated. SDCR, B1, F20, ONE NLGA, USC.

95 Clendinen and Nagourney, *Out*, 276–9; Press advisory, undated. NGTFR, B.6, F.2, CU; Randy Shilts, 'A Most Conventional Convention', *The Advocate*, 11 August 1976.

96 Clendinen and Nagourney, *Out*, 276; Wheeler, *Jimmy Who?*, viii.

97 Randy Shilts, *Conduct Unbecoming: Gays & Lesbians in the U.S. Military, Vietnam to the Persian Gulf* (New York: St. Martin's Press, 1993), 275.

98 Clendinen and Negourney, *Out*, 286.

plank. Throughout the year, Apuzzo had been travelling around the country attending hearings of the Democratic Platform Committee, trying without much success to raise the issue of gay rights.[99] Simultaneously, O'Leary had been lobbying Democrats who were sympathetic to gay rights and had written to Costanza asking her to help push for a gay rights plank in the platform. O'Leary and Costanza, who had happily agreed to help, attempted to introduce sexual orientation language to three different platform committees, but failed.[100] Subsequently, thousands of gay rights activists in New York marched from Greenwich Village to Central Park to protest against the two major parties for not paying significant attention to the issue of gay rights.[101]

On 14 June, Costanza and Mary Ann Krupsak, New York Lieutenant Governor and member of the National Women's Political Caucus, which supported gay rights, met with Carter in person and told him about the proposed plank. Carter told them that he was in favour of gay rights and of the plank and that he would ask Stuart Eizenstat to push for inclusion of sexual preference in the civil rights section. Eizenstat, a senior member of Carter's campaign team and one of his top political advisors, was in charge of the platform.[102] Furthermore, Carter pledged to appoint to his administration and the federal government people who were sensitive to the concerns and rights of the gay community.[103] News of this pledge delighted the gay community.[104] However, Eizenstat and other leading members of the campaign feared the reaction of conservative voters and objected to the inclusion of the plank. Costanza said that Eizenstat had decided to 'overrule' Carter 'on this one'.[105] Eizenstat told *The Advocate* on 15 June,

> I took it upon myself, because I thought it would be undesirable for this to be in the document, to make this an important vote, to keep it out. I told him [Carter] that if he didn't mind me using my judgment, I had the feeling that it ought not be in the document. We weren't backing away on his personal stand on it, but it was not advisable to have it in the platform document.[106]

O'Leary protested to Costanza, who took the protest to Eizenstat. Eizenstat's response illuminates the sensitivity of the issue of gay rights, which was still far from the mainstream:

> In our country we should not discriminate against anyone, but if we endorse these issues, we're going to lose. . . . Let's do what we have to for the gay rights movement,

99 Ginny Apuzzo, author interview.

100 O'Leary, 'From Agitator to Insider', 88–9.

101 J. Brooks Flippen, *Jimmy Carter, The Politics of Family, and the Rise of the Religious Right* (Athens: The University of Georgia Press, 2011), 82–3.

102 David Aiken, 'Carter Henchmen vs. Human Rights: Democratic Platform Purged of Gay Plank', *The Advocate*, 14 July 1976.

103 Jeanne Córdova, 'Carter Aide Wants Nation to "Hear What I Heard"', *LT*, May–June 1977; 'NGTF-Federal Agency Meetings Set Second White House Conference in September', News from NGTF, 31 March 1977. NGTFR, B.145, F.47, CU.

104 Apuzzo and Clay, author interviews.

105 David Aiken, 'Carter Henchmen vs. Human Rights: Democratic Platform Purged of Gay Plank', *The Advocate*, 14 July 1976.

106 Ibid.

> but let's do it after we get to the White House. For God's sake, don't let us carry this albatross going into the election. We have to win this election.[107]

Costanza commented in 1994 that Eizenstat

> tried desperately to keep that issue out of the platform. But not because he didn't support gay rights, but I think mostly because how would it affect the election . . . he wanted to serve the needs of the Gay Rights Movement, but at the same time, he didn't want us coming off looking like – in other words – we didn't want – we wanted to take the middle of the road.[108]

Despite the setback, gay rights activists were not yet willing to give up. Costanza, at O'Leary's urging, took the issue of the plank to the Party's Platform Committee.[109] Senior Carter aides, like Eizenstat, asked Daly and O'Leary to stop their effort, claiming that the plank would divide the party and cost it the election. They promised that Carter would support gay rights if elected.[110] Nevertheless, the effort continued, meeting further rebuff when Apuzzo was told by a Carter aide that she and the other activists 'were an embarrassment to Candidate Carter', and by Joseph Duffey, Eizenstat's deputy, 'your issue is not a priority' when he excluded her from an open meeting.[111] In any case, these incidents and behaviours were not really representative of Carter's or most of his associates' opinions and attitudes. Graham defended Carter's actions and pointed out the fact that Carter had appointed several openly gay people to his campaign team. He added, rather provocatively,

> Most gay political people simply are not clever enough to recognize the difference between an enemy and a friend. Yes, we have been fucked over by a number of politicians. But Jimmy has spoken on the gay issues. He supports gay rights. Once elected, he'll act upon it. What more do they want?[112]

In the end, the Platform Committee voted against the gay rights plank by 57–27. Two other attempts to add 'sexual preference' or 'sexual orientation' were also defeated.[113] The California Committee for Equal Rights commented, 'Considering the pitch Carter made for gay votes, the dumping of the gay plank is an outrage'.[114] The NGTF had also unsuccessfully attempted to include gay rights in the Republican Party platform.[115] Despite the failure to pass the plank, gay rights activists were half-satisfied due to

107 Clendinen and Nagourney, *Out*, 277; Costanza interviews with Clendinen. MCI.

108 Costanza interview with Clendinen, 24 February 1994. MCI.

109 David Aiken, 'Carter Henchmen vs. Human Rights: Democratic Platform Purged of Gay Plank', *The Advocate*, 14 July 1976; Clendinen and Nagourney, *Out*, 277.

110 Tracy Baim (ed.), *Gay Press, Gay Power: The Growth of LGBT Community Newspapers in America* (Chicago: Prairie Avenue Productions and Windy City Media Group, 2012), 348; Eizenstat, author interview.

111 Apuzzo, author interview.

112 Randy Shilts, 'A Most Conventional Convention', *The Advocate*, 11 August 1976.

113 David Aiken, 'Carter Henchmen vs. Human Rights: Democratic Platform Purged of Gay Plank', *The Advocate*, 14 July 1976; Clendinen and Nagourney, *Out*, 277.

114 Paul D. Hardman, 'Carter Dumps Gay Plank', *BAR*, 8 July 1976.

115 'NGTF Lobbies Democrats for Gay Rights Plank', News from NGTF, 8 June 1976. NGTFR, B.36, F.1, CU.

Carter's pledge to support gay rights and open the doors of the White House to them once he was elected. For most activists, this was far more important than the failure to adopt the plank.[116]

By the time of the Democratic Convention in Madison Square Garden in New York City on 12–15 July, Carter had largely won over the Democratic Party, and his nomination saw arguably the greatest party unity in decades. Whereas the Convention had often been the culmination of candidate selection, making it politically fraught, Carter had been chosen several weeks before.[117] In addition to the four openly gay delegates, several openly gay people had been appointed to work for Carter's campaign team at the Convention.[118] Paul Kuntzler, co-founder of the GSDC and of the GAA, put forward the idea of nominating a gay person for president in order to give some visibility to gay rights, as the nomination speech would have given the speaker fifteen minutes of coverage on primetime television. The proposal was endorsed by the GSDC, but dismissed by other activists who claimed it was 'unworkable', a 'waste of time and energy', and too controversial for party officials. Furthermore, acknowledging the progress that had been made with Carter's appointments and public support, activists did not want to jeopardize their relationship with him.[119] Nevertheless, some gay rights activists held a march on the Sunday of the convention, displaying gay power, anti-Carter and anti-Democratic placards, criticizing the party for not accepting a gay rights plank and comparing its silence on gay issues to that of the Germans on the genocide of gay people by the Nazis. One demonstrator said, 'Gay people have been shut out of this convention. They've just ignored us, but we won't go away'. However, there were also some gay demonstrators supporting Carter, from New York's Gays for Carter group, who were holding a 'Gays for Carter' sign.[120]

At the Convention, O'Leary faced repeated blockage of her attempt to book a room for a 100-person caucus meeting. She was informed that she needed to provide a hundred signatures in advance, despite the fact that this requirement was not enforced on other groups.[121] Ultimately, the openly gay delegates formed a Gay Rights Support Caucus and presented their proposal to Robert Strauss, Carter's close confidant and chairman of his election campaign, and also chairman of the Democratic National Committee. Strauss accepted the Caucus and it was given the Cinema Room, an official caucus room. This was the first time that one of the two major parties had accepted a gay rights caucus at its convention. Daly said in the Caucus's opening statement, 'We are delighted that Chairman Strauss has officially recognized the First Gay Rights Caucus to be held before the Democratic National Convention of 1976'. O'Leary

116 Apuzzo, Bunch and Perry author interviews; Paul D. Hardman, 'Carter Dumps Gay Plank', *BAR*, 8 July 1976.

117 Bourne, *Carter*, 336.

118 Randy Shilts, 'A Most Conventional Convention', *The Advocate*, 11 August 1976.

119 Apuzzo, author interview; Lou Romano, 'Gay to Be Nominated at Dem. Convention', *The Blade*, July 1976.

120 'National Gay Task Force Deplores Defeat of Gay Rights Plank by Democratic Party Platform Committee', NGTF Press Release, 15 June 1976. NGTFR, B.36, F.1, CU; Randy Shilts, 'A Most Conventional Convention', *The Advocate*, 11 August 1976.

121 Jo Freeman, 'Something Did Happen at the Democratic National Convention', *Jo Freeman.com*, http://www.jofreeman.com/conventions/DemCon1976.htm; Randy Shilts, 'A Most Conventional Convention', *The Advocate*, 11 August 1976.

commented, 'They weren't going to recognize us, but they were forced to. We were given the credibility of a viable caucus'.[122] The gay delegates recognized the importance of this act of acceptance and thanked Strauss repeatedly. However, to the intense disappointment of the activists, none of this was mentioned in the television coverage of the Convention.[123]

The gay rights caucus was not the activists' only accomplishment during the Convention. More than 650 delegates signed petitions supporting decriminalization of consensual sex and the enactment of gay civil rights guarantees, both the Women's and the Youth caucuses publicly expressed their support for equal rights for gay people, and important contacts were made with politicians and others who were willing to support the cause. Furthermore, Carter expressed his support for gay rights and declared that Mondale would be in charge of the issue of 'gay liberation'.[124] Mondale then stated in his acceptance speech that he was opposed to all forms of irrational discrimination.[125] The activists, despite their disappointment at the exclusion of the gay rights plank, were pleased with Carter and Mondale's public statements.[126] A sign of things to come for gay rights as well as of Carter's esteem for Costanza was the fact that he chose her, along with Andrew Young, to give his two seconding speeches.[127]

Gay rights in the presidential campaign: 'Strange territory'

After the Convention and during his presidential campaign, Carter continued seeking the gay vote. Carter's aides campaigned relentlessly in all the major gay communities in the country, while he continued advertising in gay publications. Despite the exclusion of the gay rights plank, Carter continued to receive the overwhelming support of the gay community because of all his other actions. In August, Robert Rygor, a gay rights activist from New York, started a Gays for Carter group that, unlike the group in California, aimed to be a national coalition. On 21 August, Gays for Carter kicked off their national campaign with a press conference in New York where speeches were delivered by Costanza and O'Leary. The group proudly advertised the presence of the two women at the conference, stating their positions in Carter's campaign and highlighting the fact that O'Leary was the co-executive director of the NGTF. The group argued that Gays for Carter would be 'recorded as a milestone in the history of the Gay Civil Rights movement'.[128] It was indeed, as it was the first time that a gay group had been formed to support a presidential nominee in a national campaign. The group

122 Randy Shilts, 'A Most Conventional Convention', *The Advocate*, 11 August 1976.
123 NGTF press release, 30 July 1976. NGTFR, B.152, F.46, CU.
124 Apuzzo, author interview; NGTF press release, 30 July 1976. NGTFR, B.152, F.46, CU; Shilts, 'A Randy Shilts, 'A Most Conventional Convention', *The Advocate*, 11 August 1976.
125 Press Release, *Northwest Gay Review*, undated. NGTFR, B.152, F.46, CU.
126 Apuzzo, Bunch, Clay and Perry, author interviews.
127 Bourne, *Carter*, 334; Mattingly, *A Feminist*, 67–76.
128 Gays for Carter! Announcement of Press Conference and Kickoff Benefit, undated. RMSF, GR, B.7, JCPL.

quickly expanded with branches in several other cities and states, for example Atlanta, Florida, Seattle and Washington, D.C.[129]

The SDC publicly endorsed Carter, although Mondale was unable to commit to attending one of the Club's events.[130] Another group, California Gay People for Carter-Mondale, led by Martin and Lyon, also campaigned for Carter. Meanwhile, Perry and the MCC repeatedly expressed their support for Carter and urged their followers to vote for him. Furthermore, the MCC's pastors and members all over the country campaigned for Carter, especially among the gay community.[131] A number of prominent gay rights activists also organized fundraisers for Carter's campaign. Such fundraisers took place at least in the District of Columbia, Florida, Georgia and New York State; the majority of them took place in California.[132] One of those who generously donated to Carter's campaign was Jack Campbell, president of the Dade County Coalition for the Humanistic Rights of Gays. He later received from Carter a silver peanut for this contribution.[133] One of Carter's most passionate supporters in Florida was Bob Basker, executive director of the Coalition for the Humanistic Rights of Gays and co-founder of one of the first gay rights organizations in America, the Mattachine Midwest. Basker organized a number of fundraisers among the gay community in South Florida.[134] Finally, the vast majority of the gay press endorsed Carter, highlighting his active and continuous seeking of the gay vote, his pledge to support gay rights legislation and his hiring of several openly gay people to his campaign team.

On 18 August, the NGTF wrote to Carter asking him to pledge that if he were elected President, he would:

- support the passage of H.R.13928 'which would guarantee gay women and men the same rights to employment, housing and public accommodations as all other citizens'
- 'issue an executive order forbidding discrimination in any branch of federal service, including the military; revoking all less-than-honourable discharges of those dismissed from the armed service for homosexuality; and restoring all such persons to full veterans' rights and benefits'
- order the Immigration and Naturalization Service to stop prohibiting gay migrants and tourists from entering the United States
- 'repeal archaic laws [sodomy statutes] which still exist in two-thirds of our states'
- appoint 'qualified openly gay Americans to positions on your personal staff and all levels of the federal government'.[135]

129 Clay and McReynolds, author interviews; Gays for Carter! Announcement of Press Conference and Kickoff Benefit, undated. RMSF, GR, B.7, JCPL; Gays for Carter Official Statement, 15 July 1976. RMSF, GR, B.7, JCPL; Randy Shilts, 'A Most Conventional Convention', *The Advocate*, 11 August 1976.

130 Letter, Eliot Cutler to Clayton Wells, 1 September 1976. SDCR, B.1, F.21, ONE NLGA, USC.

131 DeBaugh and Perry, author interviews.

132 Britt, Kent, McReynolds and Perry, author interviews.

133 Faderman, *The Gay Revolution*, 341.

134 Kent, author interview; James T. Sears, 'Bob Basker (1918–2001): Selling the Movement', in Vern L. Bullough (ed.), *Before Stonewall: Activists for Gay and Lesbian Rights in Historical Context* (New York: Harrington Park Press, 2002), 193–202.

135 Letter, Jean O'Leary and Bruce Voeller to Governor Carter, 18 August 1976. NGTFR, B.152, F.46, CU.

It seems that Carter did not respond to the letter.[136] However, in late September or early October, O'Leary met and talked with Robert Havely, head of Carter's National Issues and Policy, and asked him to send to her in writing Carter's position on gay rights. Havely wrote to O'Leary on 4 October, stating that Carter had 'repeatedly expressed his opposition to all forms of discrimination, including discrimination based on sexual preference. He supports the principles of H.R.5452 [another version of Abzug's Civil Rights Amendments bill] and will sign the bill if it reaches his desk'. Havely also mentioned that although 'Governor Carter is not entirely comfortable with homosexuality for personal reasons', he nonetheless 'has strongly expressed his feeling that homosexuals should not be singled out for special harassment, abuse or discrimination'.[137]

On 2 September, Harvey Milk, one of the most prominent gay rights activists at the time and co-founder of the San Francisco Gay Democratic Club, clearly expressed his support for Carter in the *Bay Area Reporter*. Although Milk acknowledged that Carter considered homosexuality to be a sin, he argued that more important were his public statements in support of gay rights and his willingness to support a bill like Abzug's. Milk wrote, 'Can you "live with" a president that regards you as a sinner but feels that the government has no business interfering with your personal life and will sign into law that point?'[138]

In October, Carter somewhat countered the suspicion that he had cooled towards gay rights by appointing three openly lesbian women to the council of his 51.3% Committee: Jo Daly; Elaine Noble, the first openly gay member of the Massachusetts House of Representatives; and despite the fact that she had previously served as a Bayh Convention delegate, Jean O'Leary.[139] The gay community commended the appointments,[140] which meant that the three women were advising Carter and had the power to appoint staff.[141] In her first meeting with Carter, O'Leary asked him directly why he had not pressed for the gay rights plank. Carter was taken aback by this directness, and to her pleasant surprise, he was 'very apologetic'. Carter apologized for not pushing hard for it, taking the blame himself and not shifting it to Eizenstat, though citing the same reasons. Carter pledged to O'Leary to open the doors of the White House and the federal agencies to gay rights activists and to advance gay rights if elected, a response that pleased O'Leary and delighted her colleagues at the NGTF.[142]

While Carter's campaign enthusiastically publicized the appointments, pointing out that it was 'the first time that known gay people have been appointed to an important

[136] This is the assumption since no such letter was found at CU or at the JCPL.

[137] Letter, Robert Havely to Jean O'Leary, 4 October 1976. MCSF, [GR: MECOCL], JCPL; Letter, Robert Havely to Clayton Wells, 31 October 1976. SDCR, B.1, F.21, ONE NLGA, USC.

[138] Harvey Milk, 'Milk Forum: "Uncertainty" of Carter or the "Certainty" of Ford', *BAR*, 2 September 1976.

[139] 'Dykes Out Front for Carter', *LT*, November–December 1976; 'Lesbians Appointed to Carter/Mondale 51.3% Committee', News from NGTF, 15 October 1976. NGTFR, B.152, F.46, CU.

[140] Apuzzo and Bunch, author interviews; Letter, Jean O'Leary and Bruce Voeller to President Carter, 26 December 1978. NGTFR, B.152, F.46, CU.

[141] Carter/Mondale News Release, 14 October 1976. MCSF, MCSF, GRJCV, JCPL; 51.3%. Who Are We? Undated. 1976 Presidential Campaign, TCFODF, Women-51.3% Committee, JCPL.

[142] O'Leary's report to the NGTF, as recalled by Clay and Nancy Higgins, author interviews.

national advisory committee',[143] the announcement was not covered at all in the vast majority of newspapers and went unnoticed by most Americans.[144] Gay people, however, did notice. Daly, Noble and O'Leary were the first, but not the only openly gay people to join Carter's campaign team. Numerous 51.3% Committee staffers appointed to branches all over the country were openly lesbian; they went on to actively campaign for Carter in their states, including in the local gay communities. For example, in California, Daly appointed dozens of open lesbians; one of them was Nancy Higgins, who was appointed as the Committee's District Assistant Coordinator.[145] The 51.3% Committee also worked very closely with the National Women's Political Caucus, which in August voted in favour of two gay rights resolutions.[146]

Meanwhile, members of the Carter campaign team, including Abzug, Costanza, Daly, Noble and O'Leary, members of the 51.3% Committee, and several other openly gay people campaigned on Carter's behalf in the gay community all over the country, highlighting his support for gay rights.[147] This marked the first time that openly gay members of a presidential nominee's staff had campaigned on his behalf, and also the first time that members of the nominee's team had campaigned in gay communities. However, what was more important for the gay community at the time was the presence and high visibility of many openly gay people in Carter's team. Higgins told the author that to see many open lesbians campaigning for a presidential nominee was 'really wonderful and quite unique. It never happened before and it was truly elevating. I think we all felt that the times were changing. Of course, Carter deserves the credit for it'.* On the appointments of the many openly gay people in Carter's campaign team and on their contributions in campaigning for Carter, Montgomery said:

> Carter proved by appointing them that he did not care about the people's sexual preferences and that all were equal to his eyes. I think it was also a symbolic move; if the president has appointed a gay then it is OK for us to do so to and that kind of thing.*

On 28 October, just a few days before the election, Milk made another appeal to the gay community to vote for Carter via his regular article in the *Bay Area Reporter*.[148] Nevertheless, the newspaper avoided endorsing a candidate.[149] Around the same time, Lillian Carter, Carter's mother, revealed to journalists in Philadelphia that her son's hairdresser was gay. She went on, 'now, don't you print any of that or I'll kill you. His mother doesn't even know'.[150]

Although some members of the gay community were suspicious of Carter because of his background, many realized, having observed his public pledge to support gay

143 Carter/Mondale News Release, 14 October 1976. MCSF, MCSF, GRJCV, JCPL.
144 Mattingly, *A Feminist*, 81.
145 Higgins, author interview.
146 David Brill, 'Women's Political Caucus Endorses Gay Rights', *The Advocate*, 13 August 1975; Higgins, author interview.
147 Apuzzo and Higgins, author interviews.
148 Harvey Milk, 'Milk Forum: A Heartbeat Away and Others', *BAR*, 28 October 1976.
149 'Editorial', *BAR*, 28 October 1976.
150 'Mizz Lillian Learns a New Word', *The Advocate*, 29 December 1976.

rights and his very significant step in appointing supporters of gay rights activism, as well as openly gay individuals, to his campaign, that Carter was the candidate most likely to help their cause, thus deserving their vote.[151] A converse trajectory for conservative voters was of course a risk. During his campaign, Carter received the support of most religious voters, including evangelicals and conservative Christians who traditionally supported the Republican Party.[152] However, his appeal to them was shaken by an interview he gave to Robert Scheer for *Playboy* magazine. In the interview, which was distributed to the press in late September (the actual *Playboy* issue came out in November), Carter defended his religious beliefs while also making clear that they were not going to affect his political decisions and that he did not wish to impose them on anyone else. Carter was also asked about homosexuality and admitted that he considered it to be a sin, just like stealing, lying and 'sexual intercourse outside marriage', but also admitted that he was sinful too, making the famous admission, 'I've looked on a lot of women with lust. I've committed adultery in my heart many times'. His Christian faith therefore required him to maintain a non-judgemental attitude towards other people, and he did not consider himself to be better than anyone else because he was Christian. Carter also stated that 'on human rights, civil rights, environmental quality, I consider myself to be very liberal'. Scheer asked Carter about his comment on homosexuality and 'what does that mean in political terms?'

> *Carter:* The issue of homosexuality always makes me nervous. It's obviously one of the major issues in San Francisco. I don't have any, you know, personal knowledge about homosexuality and I guess being a Baptist, that would contribute to a sense of being uneasy.
>
> *Scheer:* Does it make you uneasy to discuss it simply as a political question?
>
> *Carter:* No, it's more complicated than that. It's political, it's moral and it's strange territory for me. At home in Plains, we've had homosexuals in our community, our church. There's never been any sort of discrimination – some embarrassment but no animosity, no harassment. But to inject it into a public discussion on politics and how it conflicts with morality is a new experience for me. I've thought about it a lot, but I don't see how to handle it differently from the way I look on other sexual acts outside marriage.[153]

Carter was severely criticized for the interview by conservatives, though it was his remark about 'adultery in his heart' that attracted the most attention, and in the view of Bourne and Eizenstat the interview almost cost him the election.* At the same time, the *Playboy* article was significant for reaffirming Carter's 'wall of separation' between his religious faith and his philosophy of government; that is, his view of homosexuality as equivalent to heterosexual sex before marriage – sinful in the eyes of God, but not a matter for government, and not something that should automatically prevent gay people from full and active participation in American society and politics. In this way,

[151] Bunch, DeBaugh, Kent and McReynolds, author interviews.

[152] Bourne and Dukakis, author interviews; Robert L. Maddox, *Preacher at the White House* (Nashville, TN: Broadman Press, 1984), 166.

[153] 'Jimmy Carter Interview', *Playboy*, November 1976.

Carter was engaging in one of many actions of his that helped to frame homosexuality as an ordinary aspect of life. The interview also hints at the large scope of Carter's own view of 'sin', which he understood as an inevitable consequence of human fallibility. This view, attributable to his appreciation of theologian Reinhold Niebuhr, had led Carter to remark in 1974 that 'the sad duty of the political system is to establish justice in a sinful world'.[154]

Despite this setback, and in a very close race, Carter won the election with 50.1 per cent of the vote against Ford's 48.0 per cent. About 80 per cent of Carter's votes came from the South and the Northeast.[155] Evangelicals helped him win not only in the South but also in key northern states like Pennsylvania and Ohio with large rural populations that usually voted Republican.[156] An NGTF poll of gay voters showed that 67 per cent of those surveyed voted for Carter, a rather low figure considering that Carter was the only candidate who had taken a clear pro-gay stance and the mobilization of the gay community in his support.[157] Nevertheless, the community was pleased with Carter's win. Bruce Voeller, the co-executive director of the NGTF, stated that Carter's election was a major step forward for the gay rights movement.[158]

☙

The 1976 elections represented a pivotal moment for the gay rights movement. During his campaign, Carter recognized and engaged with the gay rights community as a legitimate part of the citizen body, with legitimate representative organizations. Carter's asking gay voters for their support, his advertising in gay publications, his public support for gay rights, and the presence of openly gay people and prominent gay rights activists in his campaign team, all clearly played important roles in making visible both the gay rights movement and homosexuality itself to many Americans. While gay rights activists had been campaigning for their rights for years, this was the first time that a presidential candidate had broached the issue with such openness, and the first time that gay rights activists could think with justification that the highest officer in the United States was ready to do business with them. These engagements with the cause, even before any actions of the Carter administration, were a watershed moment for the movement as it began to shift from the fringes of society closer to centre stage. In this way, Carter was engaging in one of many actions that helped to frame homosexuality as an ordinary aspect of life, making the topic part of the national conversation, 'speaking the name' of gay people for the first time at this level. That his

154 On Carter's debt to Niebuhr see Kevin Mattson, *'What the Heck Are You up to, Mr President?' Jimmy Carter, America's 'Malaise', and the Speech That Should Have Changed the Country* (New York: Bloomsbury, 2009), 59–60, quotation at 60.

155 J. Dumbrell, *The Carter Presidency: A Re-evaluation* (Manchester and New York: Manchester University Press, 1995), 4.

156 A. James Reichley, 'The Evangelical and Fundamentalist Revolt', in Richard John Neuhaus and Michael Cromartie (eds), *Piety and Politics: Evangelicals and Fundamentalists Confront the World* (Washington: Ethics and Public Policy Center, 1987), 78.

157 Lou Chibbaro, Jr., 'Carter's Efforts Not Enough Activists Warn', *The Blade*, 10 July 1980.

158 'Carter Election Will Aid Gay Rights, Voeller Claims', *Centre Daily Times*, 9 November 1976.

advisers were well aware of the potential electoral risks strongly confirms the sincerity of Carter's interest in the gay rights issue.

Carter's repeated assertion of the 'sinful' character of homosexuality requires, given its seemingly homophobic character, some contextualization, which this chapter has provided. There is first of all the pragmatic judgement of Milk, representative of many gay rights activists, including those interviewed by the author, that the promise of movement on longstanding exclusionary policy was of far greater importance. For Carter himself, an insistence on the separation of such concerns from his political values, bolstered by a firm belief that politics should not proceed from a position of claimed moral infallibility, offset the apparent discriminatory implications of the category of 'sin'. So broad was Carter's conception of sin, extending even to his own lustful thoughts, that even pastors among gay rights advocates found it lacking in critical force.[159]

Increased visibility for gay rights was of course a double-edged sword. The 1976 election was important for the religious right as well as for the gay rights movement. It too received a form of validation from Carter's candidacy and election, given his religious background, which was a novelty in a presidential candidate (there had also been no Southern president, other than Eisenhower and Lyndon Johnson from Texas, since Andrew Johnson just after the Civil War). While this chapter has traced the steps taken by Carter that legitimated and reduced the marginality of gay people and gay rights, the election of a president from the South and fully committed to the Southern Baptist tradition gave religion, including evangelical religion, greater prominence and legitimacy too, in stark contrast to its relative absence in preceding decades of presidential politics. Both forces thus gained legitimacy from Carter's successful candidacy. In addition, however, the activation of hopes and the boosting of confidence of both sides created increased tensions between them. The mutual exclusivity of their interests, and Carter's symbolic representation of both, would be one of the major tensions that he would face as president.

[159] Bob Arthur, Clay, DeBaugh, Bush, Kent, McReynolds and Perry.

2

Carter's people

This chapter explores Carter's implementation, with regard to its last element, of his declared 'policy of appointing qualified individuals without discrimination based on race, color, sex, religion, national origin or sexual orientation', to which he remained committed until the end of his presidency.[1] Presidential appointment power extends from his immediate advisory and senior managerial staff through a series of widening circles of White House and Executive Office functions and ad hoc positions in presidential commissions and committees, into the broader executive branch, consisting of Cabinet appointments and other appointments to senior positions in government departments and agencies. Among the most consequential of presidential appointments – though like many in the executive branch they are subject to Senate confirmation – are those to the federal judiciary. Naturally these require different degrees of presidential attention, and the president must often rely on the advice of the initially selected senior advisers and officials. From the perspective of the gay community and gay rights advocates, two aspects are important: that gay people be included as candidates for such appointments, and that the appointees, gay or not, should adopt inclusive policies, and seek to remove discriminatory ones, in their area of responsibility. While the two considerations obviously overlap, this chapter considers them separately, but it begins where Carter himself had to begin, with the creation of his transition team.

On the threshold

In December 1976, just a few weeks after Carter's election, the NGTF, through its *Action Report,* urged 'gay groups and individuals' to 'write letters to Carter' asking him, among other things, to 'fulfil the pledge to bring those who have been discriminated against into government by appointing qualified openly gay Americans to positions on the Presidential staff and at all levels of the Federal government'.[2] Carter appointed Jack Watson, a lawyer from Atlanta who had also worked in his election campaign, as director of his transition team. Watson was a supporter of gay rights and was well-liked and well-known among the gay community in Atlanta; his appointment pleased gay

1 Letter, Robert Strauss to Charles Brydon and Lucia Valeska, 3 March 1980. RMSF, GH1, JCPL.
2 'Write Letters to Carter', NGTF Action Report, December 1976. SWSF, NGTF F+P, JCPL.

rights activists.[3] Soon afterwards, Carter announced that some members of the 51.3% Committee would join his transition team and work with it in recommending qualified women for appointed jobs in the new administration. Carter was quick to prove that his commitment to gay rights was sincere and re-appointed Daly, O'Leary and Noble to the 51.3% Committee to work with his transition team. It was the first time that a president's transition team had included open gay people. Gay rights activists applauded Carter for this and O'Leary publicly stated that 'the appointments of three open lesbians to a committee for the next President of the United States is a history-making event'.[4]

The 51.3% Committee remained active throughout Carter's presidency. Although it had a secondary role in recommending appointments, it cooperated with various Democratic women's clubs around the country, holding a number of events over issues of concern for women, including lesbian rights. Some of the original Committee members retained their positions, including Daly and O'Leary, while several open lesbians were appointed or re-appointed to a number of positions in the Committee's apparatus; one of them was Higgins, who was appointed on Daly's recommendation as the Committee's Assistant Congressional District Coordinator in San Francisco.[5]

Gay rights advocates in the White House

The White House appointees who played the most crucial roles in the progressing of gay rights issues are discussed individually in the following sections, arranged alphabetically.

Midge Costanza

After his election, Carter began working on structuring the White House's Office of Public Liaison (OPL) so that it could provide access 'to all groups which have complaints or ideas to share with their government'.[6] This was Carter's way of meeting the pledge he had made as a candidate to open up the White House to citizens, and for his government to keep in touch with and respond to public opinion. Phil Strickland, an official, and from 1980 executive director, of the Baptist General Convention of Texas' Christian Life Commission, suggested that the new director of the OPL should not only deal with interested groups, but also establish a formal relationship with the religious community, and suggested that the ideal person for the post should be someone 'religious enough to understand religious mind-sets and political enough

3 Clay, author interview.

4 'Briefs: O'Leary on Carter Committee', *It's Time*, December 1976. SWSF, NGTF F+P, JCPL; 'Lesbians Join Carter Committee', *The Blade*, January 1977.

5 Letter, Gretta Dewald to the 51.3% Committee Coordinators, 3 April 1978, and Gretta Dewald's Excerpt from 15 February 1978 Proposal, both in NGTFR, B.152, F.46, CU; Higgins, author interview.

6 Margaret Costanza draft letter, undated. MCSF [H-GRPH], JCPL.

to understand issues'.[7] To the disappointment of Strickland and even more of conservatives,[8] Carter instead chose to appoint Midge Costanza as director of OPL and as his Assistant. She became the first woman to hold the title of Assistant to the President.[9] Carter hoped that the OPL would show that the White House was open to everyone, and that his government would be both honest and responsive to the public; he wanted Costanza 'to be the window to the nation'.[10]

The NGTF hailed Costanza's appointment as 'very gratifying and reassuring to us'.[11] Professor Charlotte Bunch, who was a good friend of Costanza at the time, told the author that Costanza's appointment was '*very* important. Every time that we [the gay and lesbian community] wanted something, we could talk to her'. Bunch also said about Carter's relationship with Costanza, 'I knew that he liked her. That was very clear. And that, on some level, he was proud of what she was doing. I'm sure'.* Clay told the author that the NGTF and the gay community were 'enthusiastic' about Costanza's appointment, which was 'a strong indication' of Carter's intention to attend to gay rights.*

Costanza made her support for gay rights publicly known almost the moment Carter hired her. In the press conference for her presentation after her appointment, and with Carter present, the first question she was asked was about her support for gay rights. Costanza explicitly stated her strong support for gay rights and that her aim, as well as Carter's, was to eliminate discrimination against gay people. It was the first time that a president's top aide had been asked about gay rights. Costanza's public support for gay rights, in the presence of Carter, delighted the gay community, who viewed it as a positive sign of things to come. Shortly afterwards, she again expressed her strong support for gay rights in an interview with the Associated Press.[12] Not public, but also significant, was the fact that Costanza had shortly before her appointment begun an intimate relationship with Jean O'Leary, but had kept it a secret. Costanza was in the closet when she began working in the White House.[13] However, the relationship very quickly became known to Carter and Costanza's associates and colleagues. No one, including Carter, had an issue with it.[14] Carter both liked and trusted Costanza and publicly characterized her as a 'member' of his 'family'.[15] He was in the forefront at a

[7] Memorandum, Phil Strickland to Jimmy Carter, 3 December 1976, and Letter, Jimmy Carter to Phil Strickland, 17 December 1976, both in LBSF, B.91, [CLC], JCPL.

[8] Letter, Phil Strickland to Landon Butler, 16 February 1977. LBSF, B.91, [CLC], JCPL.

[9] Edward Walsh, 'Carter Names 12 Key Staff Aides', *WP*, 15 January 1977.

[10] Mattingly, *A Feminist*, 89.

[11] Letter, NGTF to Midge Costanza, 1 February 1977. MCSF, [GR: C], JCPL.

[12] DeBaugh, 'A White House Ally', *The Blade*, February 1977; 'Carter Names Pro-Gay Woman as Top Aide', *LT*, March–April 1977; DeBaugh, Perry and Vida, author interviews.

[13] Costanza's reticence later abated. In mid-August 1979, she received the MCC's first Human Rights Award at its conference in Los Angeles, in recognition of her efforts for gay rights. In her speech, Costanza joked, 'I was the woman Jimmy was lusting after. But I wouldn't fool around – not with someone who thought the place to lust was in the heart'. She then added to big applause that she had 'learned what it's all about' from Jean O'Leary, who was also present, 'in the ladies room of the White House!' Turning to Perry, she said, 'You may be a preacher, but she's one hell of a teacher!' (Steve Warren, '9th MCC Meet: Taking Stock', *The Advocate*, 4 October 1979).

[14] Bourne, Eizenstat, Haft, Malson and Weddington, author interviews.

[15] OWHPS, Remarks of the President at a Reception for IWY, 22 March 1978. MMSF, IWY, JCPL.

surprise birthday party for her in the White House and showed his appreciation by inviting her to Camp David for Thanksgiving.[16]

Once in the OPL, Costanza went on to appoint to her staff a number of dedicated supporters of gay rights, such as lawyers Marilyn Haft and Seymour Wishman. Feminism and support for gay rights were both essential conditions for Costanza to appoint someone in her office. Bunch told the author that 'there was a very strong staff that Costanza had that were supportive of gay rights', and this was 'absolutely vital'.* Carter hoped that Costanza would mastermind changes in difficult areas, such as securing progress on gay rights, without upsetting evangelicals, while at the same time deflecting attention from his own role. Carter positively encouraged her to consult with outside interest groups.[17]

During her time in the White House, Costanza was the person gay rights activists called to have their issues of concern addressed. She became the biggest ally of gay rights activists in the White House and the driving force for the advancement of gay rights during the first twenty months or so of Carter's administration. In addition to opening up the White House to the gay community, Costanza provided gay rights activists with constant access to federal agencies by facilitating, and normally attending, numerous meetings between the two sides, a key role that will be discussed at the relevant points in later chapters. On 21 February 1978, the NGTF recognized this role in a unanimous commendation for her efforts, writing that her 'support and leadership' had 'strengthened' the gay rights movement and they were 'deeply grateful' for her efforts.[18] The organization later that year honoured her for 'outstanding contributions to the human rights of gay people'.[19] The plaque she received read, 'For opening the White House to all Americans including lesbians and gay men'.[20]

This was perhaps an exaggeration. Costanza's outspokenness, public stances and political actions over controversial issues such as abortion and gay rights upset conservatives.[21] Although Carter never objected to Costanza over her efforts on gay rights – on the contrary, he admired her dedication to the subject, according to Bunch, Eizenstat and Haft* – he was concerned about all the negative publicity and criticism she received. Carter, as well as some White House aides like Eizenstat, also believed that she was dedicating most of her time to issues like gay rights and abortion and was neglecting other important issues such as poverty, unemployment and other human rights. Costanza had closed her office's door to people and groups whose ideas she did not agree with, such as conservative Christians, thus failing to make the White House open to all Americans as Carter had promised.[22] As Officer for Public Liaison, communicating with religious bodies was part of Costanza's remit, and religious leaders felt somewhat alienated by her.[23] Conservative Christians expressed their frustration

16 Hays Gorey, 'That Woman in the West Wing', *NYT*, 22 January 1978.
17 Bunch and Haft, author interviews.
18 Letter, C. F. Brydon to Midge Costanza, 21 February 1978. MCI.
19 Letter, Jean O'Leary to Chip Carter, 27 January 1978. NGTFR, B.152, F.46, CU.
20 Picture with caption from *Sappho*, 6, 10, 1978. NGTFR, B.145, F.47, CU.
21 Mattingly, *A Feminist*, 89–182.
22 Eizenstat and Weddington, author interviews.
23 Memorandum, Phil Strickland to Midge Costanza and Chip Carter, 21 March 1977. LBSF, B.91, [CLC], JCPL.

at failing to meet with Carter and Costanza for the first time in October 1977 when they demonstrated outside the White House against child abuse, sex textbooks in schools and pornography. They 'demanded' to see Carter on the grounds that they were 'the President's people'. They said they had been trying to meet with Costanza for six months and felt she was giving them 'the run-around'. The demonstrators told two White House aides, 'The gays can get into the White House, but we can't. What kind of administration is this?'[24]

That Carter nevertheless valued Costanza's efforts, and did not himself have an altogether ecumenical attitude towards outside pressure groups, was demonstrated privately in November 1977. After Costanza had met three times with gay rights activists in the White House and facilitated several meetings between gay rights activists and federal agencies, she found herself in the spotlight as a target for conservative and homophobic forces. Carter 'reconfirmed' his 'confidence in her' and 'asked her to stay closer' to him. He wrote in his diary that day, 'I've been concerned about her involvement in the abortion and gay rights business, but she takes a tremendous burden off me from nut groups that would insist on seeing me if they couldn't see her'.[25] On another occasion, after Costanza had received a barrage of attacks in the media, Carter called her into his office, expressing his admiration for her work and reminded her that he got far more bad press than she did.[26]

Carter's stance on abortion was an issue of conflict between the two; he was against the banning of abortions, but he also opposed the use of federal funds for them. Carter had made known his opinion on the matter during the 1976 election campaign, and it remained the same throughout his presidency.[27] Even so, Costanza retained Carter's support and trust at least until mid-1978. In April 1978, Carter appointed Anne Wexler as his special assistant and her arrival reduced Costanza's responsibilities, although Carter made Costanza head of his Interdepartmental Task Force on Women, which was tasked to monitor the status of women in the administration. Costanza was left in charge of the attempt to get the ERA ratified, and of putting into effect the International Women's Year Plan of Action (see Chapter 5), as well as advising on the impact of domestic policies on women.[28] She also continued working very closely with the NGTF on a number of gay rights issues.[29] Despite her diminishing role, Costanza remained, as she put it, 'fiercely loyal' to Carter'.[30]

In mid-1978, Haft left the OPL to become Mondale's Deputy Counsel, depriving Costanza of her most trusted ally in the administration. Meanwhile, Costanza's relationship with the administration was quickly unravelling. The dissatisfaction of some White House aides with Costanza grew as they were unhappy at her insistence on appointing only people who were supportive of all the issues on her agenda and

24 Memorandum, Ed Smith to Midge Costanza, 19 October 1977. MCI.

25 Jimmy Carter, *White House Diary* (New York: Farrar, Straus and Giroux, 2010), 127.

26 Hays Gorey, 'That Woman in the West Wing', *NYT*, 22 January 1978.

27 Dumbrell, *The Carter Presidency*, 71–4; Mattingly, *A Feminist*, 118–36.

28 Mattingly, *A Feminist*, 174–96.

29 Bunch and Clay, author interviews; George Mendenhall, 'Midge Costanza: Have We Lost the White House Key', *BAR*, 8 June 1978.

30 Karen De Witt, 'Miss Costanza Resigns as Assistant to Carter, Citing Problems of Style', *NYT*, 2 August 1978.

her refusal to meet with interest groups who represented views that she opposed. White House aides, like Hamilton Jordan and Beth Abramowitz, had complained to Carter about both these issues, but he had taken no action.[31] Finally, on 1 August 1978, dismayed by her weakened role, Costanza resigned, citing her differences in style and in approach with that of Carter and his administration. Carter asked Costanza to reconsider her resignation, and when she insisted, he accepted it with 'much regret', and asked her to remain for another month to ensure a smooth transition and to help with the selection of her replacement. Costanza agreed and helped Carter to choose Sarah Weddington as her replacement.[32]

After she left the White House, on some rare occasions Costanza publicly criticized Carter and of his overall performance as president,[33] and she harboured some private resentment: according to Doreen Mattingly (her close friend and biographer), Costanza 'felt like she got sacrificed by the Carter administration, and they used her as a token, rather than advancing the issues'.* However, she often spoke enthusiastically about Carter's efforts on gay rights and of how 'proud' she was to have worked for him in the White House. She emphasized that they were 'still friends', that they had stayed in touch and that he had even been advising her on her next career move.[34] Costanza pointed out that Carter was constantly under pressure from the evangelical right and especially from his own church over her appointment and her involvement with gay rights, the ERA and abortion and commended him for the fact that he had not capitulated to the demands of conservatives and anti-gay rights forces.[35] In 2015, Carter told Mattingly that he was 'in harmony' on the gay rights issue with Costanza.[36] Mattingly told the author that Costanza would not have disagreed with this observation.*

Despite Carter's record-breaking number of appointments of women officials, including many feminists and open lesbians, Costanza's resignation cost him considerable support from feminist and lesbian voters.[37] The NGTF promptly wrote a letter to Carter expressing its 'deep regret' over Costanza's resignation and stating their view that she had been an exceptional public servant, their hope that her successor would continue her great work in the area of gay rights, and their sorrow at having lost her as a friend in the White House, concluding:

31 For example, see Memorandums of Hamilton Jordan to President Carter, undated. MCI, and Beth Abramowitz to Stu Eizenstat, 10 August 1978. WHCOF, SFE, FG300, JCPL.

32 Jean Córdova, 'White House Link Resigns. Costanza Cites "Approach Differences"', *LT*, September/ October 1978; Karen De Witt, 'Miss Costanza Resigns as Assistant to Carter, Citing Problems of Style', *NYT*, 2 August 1978.

33 Stanley, *Kennedy vs. Carter*, 70; Don L. Volk, 'Community Interview: Midge Costanza', *L.A. Edge*, 15–29 June 1983.

34 Numerous Costanza interviews; for example see M. A. Karr, 'Midge Costanza Speaks Out on Gay Rights and the ERA', *The Advocate*, 27 December 1978; Karen West, 'Costanza Feels She Did Some Good', *Seattle Post*, 21 November 1978, and Dwight Gaut, 'Costanza Addresses Dorian Group', *Seattle Gay News*, 24 November 1978; Jean Córdova, 'White House Link Resigns. Costanza Cites "Approach Differences"', *LT*, September/ October 1978; 'Miss Costanza Ponders a Carey Job Offer', *NYT*, 17 November 1978.

35 Costanza interviews to Clendinen, 1994–1995. MCI; Jim Marko, 'Midge Costanza: Gay Rights Proponent at the White House', *GCN*, 9 July 1977.

36 Mattingly, *A Feminist*, 112.

37 Bunch, author interview; Susan M. Hartmann, 'Feminism, Public Policy, and the Carter Administration', in Gary M. Fink and Hugh David Graham (eds), *The Carter Presidency: Policy Choices in the Post-New Deal Era* (Lawrence, Kansas: University Press of Kansas, 1998), 225–30.

> Millions of lesbians and gay men have been heartened by Ms. Costanza's sensitivity to the concerns of all Americans, including the gay community. We believe that her departure from her present White House position represents a great loss to our community, to your administration and to the people of this nation.[38]

However, the NGTF anticipated further progress with its agenda, mostly due to the 'many contacts Ms. Costanza has helped us to make within the Federal government'.[39] Voeller also remained confident that Costanza's loss was not 'fatal' and told *Gay News* that the NGTF did not 'see this in any way debilitating or hurting our efforts. Although it is quite a disappointment, the groundwork for future advances on the federal level has been laid very solidly'.[40]

Voeller turned out to be correct in his assessment. Other White House staff who were assigned to the issue of gay rights were also very effective, and the White House's commitment to it had a broad base. During Costanza's twenty months in the OPL, gay rights activists met with her and Marilyn Haft five times, but after both women were gone, in the next twenty-eight months the activists met with other members of the Carter administration at least fifteen times. Carter also continued appointing to his administration, to presidential commissions and to governmental agencies people who were friendly to gay rights, or were openly gay themselves. Costanza's departure was not the blow for gay rights that it might have initially appeared to be.

Stuart Eizenstat

As Chief Domestic Policy Adviser and Executive Director of Carter's Domestic Policy Council, Eizenstat was one of the most powerful people in the Carter administration. He was initially not very popular with gay rights activists due to his blocking of the gay rights plank at the Convention, and his highly pragmatic approach to politics, but he was true to his commitment to Costanza at the Democratic Convention and went on to play a very important role in the advancement of gay rights. Larry Bush, journalist and gay rights activist, who interviewed Eizenstat in 1980 and dealt with him during the last two years of the Carter administration, said that Eizenstat was supportive of gay rights but was also aware of the political consequences of this support and always carefully calculated the political risks of each decision regarding it.*

In any case, throughout Carter's tenure in the White House, Eizenstat's Domestic Policy Office was heavily involved with gay rights: it initiated or supported a number of policies and decisions that massively contributed to the advancement of gay rights, to be discussed in later chapters. Eizenstat assigned Bob Malson[41] to be his office's liaison

38 Letter, Jean O'Leary and Bruce Voeller to President Carter, 18 August 1978. NGTFR, B.152, F.49, CU.

39 'NGTF Leaders Express Regret over Costanza Resignation', *AGN*, 11 August 1978.

40 'Costanza Loss Not Fatal to Federal Dealings', *GN*, October 1978.

41 Malson is an attorney and graduate of Harvard Law School. He served as Counsel to the US Senate Judiciary Committee from 1974–1977 before moving to head one of Carter's Transition Teams and then, following the Inauguration, onto Eizenstat's Domestic Policy Staff as Associate Director for Justice and Civil Rights. While in the Senate, he had worked on the Omnibus Judgeship Act for Sen. Tunney. Malson, author interview.

with the gay community, and Malson told the author that Eizenstat was fully aware and 'very supportive' of his efforts on gay rights.* Eizenstat told the author that he and his deputies, Bert Carp and David Rubenstein, gave Malson their 'blessing and support' for these efforts because of their and Carter's 'strong belief in non-discrimination based on any basis including sexual preference'.* Eizenstat told Bush in May 1980 that his duties included 'making non-discrimination a reality in government policy' and 'a substantive contribution to the gay community. . . . We are now looking into areas where there is discrimination against homosexuals overtly'.[42] A few months later, Eizenstat successfully lobbied Democratic delegates to include a gay rights plank in the party platform at the 1980 National Convention (see Chapter 13).

Marilyn Haft

Immediately after Costanza was appointed by Carter, O'Leary and Voeller of the NGTF asked her to appoint Marilyn Haft as her assistant in the OPL. Haft, a lawyer and a prominent gay rights activist, was a good friend of O'Leary and especially of Voeller. She was very left-wing, worked with the American Civil Liberties Union (ACLU) and was also well known to the gay community as she was the only non-gay member of the Board of Directors of the NGTF and of the GRNL. A few years earlier, she had co-written the ACLU's book *The Rights of Gay People.* Haft had also participated in a number of notable gay rights cases; one of the most notable was the case of Leonard Matlovich, an Air Force sergeant who had been dishonourably discharged from the military in 1975 because he was gay, despite having an exemplary service record (Matlovich had made a public announcement of his sexuality in order to create a test case; he became widely known for the case and appeared on the cover of *Time* magazine). Haft had also, along with Seymour Wishman, acted pro bono as Voeller's lawyer in his trial against his former wife, who had taken him to court in an attempt to restrict his visitation rights to his children after he had come out as gay.[43] O'Leary and Voeller believed that Haft would be ideal in advancing their issues through the White House since she was very experienced in working for gay rights. Her White House appointment meant that Haft had to resign from the board of the GRNL and the NGTF as these positions constituted a conflict of interest with her new role.[44] Florence Isbell wrote in July 1977 in the *Civil Liberties Review* that 'No other president has appointed so many avowed civil libertarians to high office'. Among the appointments, Isbell paid specific attention to Haft's, which she characterized as 'particularly striking' because 'her entire career has been as a civil liberties activist'.[45]

The NGTF welcomed Haft's appointment; it knew she would be another important ally in the White House and that she would also be able to assist Costanza in her

[42] Larry Bush, 'White House Claims Solid Record on Gay Issues', *The Sentinel*, 16 May 1980.

[43] The judge eventually ruled in favour of Voeller's ex-wife due to his openness about homosexuality and his visitation rights were significantly restricted (Carlos A. Bell, *The Rights to Be Parents: LGBT Families and the Transformation of Parenthood* [New York and London: New York University Press, 2012], 65).

[44] Haft, author interview.

[45] Florence Isbell, 'Carter's Civil Libertarians', *The Civil Liberties Review*, 4 July–August 1977: 55–6.

efforts for gay rights. Haft did not disappoint the activists and did much more than they had hoped for.[46] In mid-1978, Haft was appointed White House Deputy Counsel to Vice President Mondale; although her engagement with gay rights efforts reduced significantly due to her new responsibilities, she did continue her advocacy and remained in touch with and assisted gay rights activists.[47]

Robert (Bob) Malson and Allison Thomas

Shortly after Costanza's departure, and responding to a request from the NGTF, Malson, Assistant Director of the White House Domestic Policy Staff, and Allison Thomas, Anne Wexler's assistant in the Office of Public Liaison, were specifically assigned by the White House to monitor gay and lesbian concerns; it was the first time that an administration had appointed White House staff members to deal specifically with gay issues.[48] Like Costanza, Malson and Thomas were committed to the cause. Bush told the author that in Carter's administration, 'there were some wonderful people who really went the full distance' with regard to gay rights and that 'Allison Thomas and Bob Malson in particular were helpful'.*

Although Costanza and her office were the main driving force for gay rights while she was in the White House, Eizenstat had assigned Malson to monitor developments and assist Costanza's efforts. Malson accompanied Costanza and Haft to most of their meetings with gay rights activists, including meetings they facilitated with federal agencies. Malson also participated as a White House representative in several meetings between gay rights activists and federal agencies. After Costanza's departure, Malson and Thomas considerably expanded their contact with gay rights activists, and both went on to play major roles in the advancement of gay rights. Malson arranged most of the White House meetings with gay rights activists and was present at most of them, and he and Thomas became the first White House aides ever to meet activists in gay communities (see Chapter 4). Malson enjoyed a very close relationship with gay rights activists, especially with Charles Brydon, Larry Bush, and Lucia Valeska, meeting, corresponding and talking on the phone regularly with them. The NGTF, as it had with Wexler, addressed Malson and Thomas in its correspondence by their first names and without any formalities.

Indeed their interactions included friendly meetings during unrelated business. For example, on a visit to New York in April 1979, Malson had lunch with NGTF's Co-Executive Directors Brydon and Valeska,[49] and in January 1980, when Donald Knutson of the Gay Rights Advocates and attorney and activist William Dillingham flew from San Francisco to Washington on a business trip, Malson took them for dinner and on a tour of the White House. Both men wrote to him thanking him for his hospitality, with Knutson also offering, 'when you next come to the West Coast,

46 Bunch and Clay, author interviews.

47 Haft, author interview.

48 Robert Malson memorandum for Stu Eizenstat, 19 April 1980. SESF, Gays [CF], JCPL; WH memorandum: Talking points on gay issues, 5 August 1980. RMSF, G/L2, JCPL.

49 Letter, C. F. Brydon and Lucia Valeska to Bob Malson, 13 July 1979. RMSF, GR, B.7, JCPL.

I hope that you will let me buy you lunch'.[50] Thus the White House staffers who were dealing with gay rights issues did more than address their concerns: they formed friendly relationships with them. As Malson told the author about this interaction, 'I just remember that it was warm, and it lasted, fundamentally, throughout the four years we were there. And Midge had a great deal to do with the initiation of it. And Allison and I, as support staff, were fortunate to be involved in such an important manner'.*

Bush reported that Malson 'was a person of real integrity who played an important role in the Carter administration in seeing that obstacles were removed so that progress could be made. He had a good heart'.* Clay found Malson to be 'a real gentleman', someone who displayed 'a genuine interest in our concerns' and who was 'willing to go the extra mile for us'.* Key Whitlock, co-chair of the NGTF, wrote similarly of Malson's genuine interest in *The Advocate*.[51] Malson contributed importantly to the advancement of gay rights during his time in the White House, not only by acting on the activists' requests but also by taking several significant initiatives, which will be examined in due course. For his part, Malson said that working on gay rights issues and with gay rights activists was 'an honour and a privilege' and that he 'was honoured to be able to be of assistance'.*

Thomas was an important ally of gay rights activists in the White House, enjoying very good and close relationships with several of them, for example Frank Kameny and Adam DeBaugh, and she played a significant role in the advancement of gay rights during Carter's presidency. Kameny characterized her as a 'willing ally' of the gay rights cause,[52] Randy Shilts, one of *The Advocate*'s most celebrated journalists, described her as someone 'who had always been comfortable around gay people',[53] and Bush spoke of her to the author as 'a very key person throughout this whole process'.* Thomas was the person the NGTF contacted to facilitate meetings with federal agencies. She also became the first White House aide to invite to the White House a gay rights organization, the National Committee for Sexual Civil Liberties, in order to receive advice on how to legally deal with a number of gay rights issues (see Chapter 13).

Furthermore, Thomas and Anne Wexler had a particularly good and close relationship with Ginny Apuzzo, then the Director of the Fund for Human Dignity, whom Thomas characterized in a White House memorandum as 'a friend of ours'.[54] Apuzzo for her part argued that Thomas was 'always very responsive' to gay rights issues and that generally Wexler's staff 'were wonderful, they were always helpful, and I believe that's Anne's influence'.* Like Malson, Thomas was on first-name terms with the gay rights activists, she often called them on the phone while they also called her at the White House, she had informal dinners with them, and even sent them her greetings

50 Letters to Robert Malson by Donald Knutson, 6 February 1980, and William Dillingham, 7 February 1980; both in RMSF, GTFN1, JCPL.

51 '"Serious" Consideration of Gay Rights, White House Says After Talks', *The Advocate*, 21 February 1980.

52 Letter, Franklin Kameny to Allison Thomas, 29 May 1980. ATSF, B.265, GR, JCPL.

53 Shilts, *Conduct Unbecoming*, 332.

54 Memorandum, Allison Thomas for Bob Berenson, 21 October 1980. ATSF, B.265, GR, JCPL.

when they met with one of her White House colleagues.[55] Adam DeBaugh, a prominent gay rights activist and MCC member, singled out Thomas's assistance among others who gave 'significant support', saying that she was 'very helpful. Allison was always very supportive – on behalf of Anne Wexler and President Carter, of course'; he had had several formal and informal meetings and telephone conversations with Thomas, and they worked closely on a number of gay rights issues, for example the resettlement of gay Cuban refugees. After Carter's loss to Reagan, DeBaugh received a letter from Thomas in which she thanked him for 'being in touch and working together' and wished him well for his struggle to achieve gay rights;[56] Thomas and Malson indeed wrote such letters to all the gay rights activists with whom they had worked closely, for example Brydon and Valeska.[57]

Jane Wales

Shortly after his inauguration, Carter appointed Jane Wales, who had worked as a volunteer in his election campaign, as Coordinator of Public Liaison; she was among the few appointments in the OPL that were made by him and not by Costanza. Wales remained in the OPL, working with both Costanza and Wexler, before moving to the State Department as Deputy Assistant Secretary of State in October 1979.* Wales was very progressive and a supporter of gay rights. She worked on several gay rights issues and met on a number of occasions with gay rights activists in the White House and outside it; she was also invited to and attended a number of functions organized by gay rights organizations. Wales also developed very good relationships with the gay rights activists she encountered, such as Kameny and Voeller, often talking and meeting with them, even outside the White House; for example, she had dinner with Voeller in January 1979.[58]

Anne Wexler

On 19 April 1978, Carter appointed Anne Wexler as his special assistant, and she took over some of Costanza's duties, including dealing with most of the interest groups.[59] Wexler, former Associate Publisher of *Rolling Stone*, had worked in a number of capacities in Carter's 1976 election campaign, and in January 1977, Carter had appointed her as Deputy Under Secretary of Commerce.[60] Wexler went on to become Carter's most important female advisor. Her status as a political insider gave her strategic depth, filling a gap in the collective skill set of Carter's leading advisers and offering a legislative strategy that featured the use of interest groups in support of the

[55] Several documents in RMSF and ATSF, in JCPL; e.g. Memorandum, Allison Thomas for Mike Chanin, 27 November 1979, and Letter, C. F. Brydon to Allison Thomas, 12 August 1980.

[56] DeBaugh, author interview.

[57] Malson, author interview.

[58] Note, Jane Wales to Joe Norton, 8 January 1978 [sic; the correct year is 1979]. JWSF, GR, JCPL.

[59] Announcement of Anne Wexler Appointment, 19 April 1978. GRSF, B.64, Anne Wexler Folder, JCPL; 'Carter Picks Replacement for Costanza', *WP*, 30 August 1978.

[60] Biographical Information: Anne Wexler. Records of Anne Wexler. JCPL.

administration's proposals. An unnamed senior Carter adviser said, 'in the first year we didn't have Anne Wexler – she came in later – who was able to mobilize the public interest groups in support of proposals'.[61] Douglas Martin of *The New York Times* wrote that 'some said Ms. Wexler gave the administration a measure of political skill it had been lacking'.[62] Furthermore, White House officials considered her to be, as the *New York Times* put it, 'more politically sophisticated than the controversial Costanza'.[63]

Although Wexler did not share Costanza's passion for gay rights issues, she was as willing as her predecessor to meet gay rights activists, and to assist with their agenda.[64] Furthermore, and very importantly, she designated her assistant Thomas as the White House's Public Liaison with the gay community.[65] Thanks to her political experience and know-how, as well as her less controversial profile compared to Costanza, Wexler turned out to be no less willing and perhaps even more effective in addressing gay rights issues, as will be described in later chapters. She also accepted invitations to attend a number of gay rights events organized by the NGTF. Wexler enjoyed a very good and close relationship with the NGTF and the gay community. Ginny Apuzzo argued that Wexler was 'incredibly helpful' to her and to other gay rights activists: 'I was Anne Wexler's contact in the gay community, and she was very responsive, I could call her any time, she would take my call, I would tell her what we needed, she would help'.* Apuzzo and Larry Bush also said that Wexler's door in the White House 'was always open' to the gay community and gay rights issues.*

Seymour Wishman

On Haft's recommendation and at Voeller's urging, Costanza appointed Seymour Wishman, a civil rights and criminal lawyer who supported gay rights, as Deputy Assistant to the President for Public Liaison. Wishman turned out to be a very important ally for gay rights activists and made significant contributions to a number of cases they brought to the White House's attention. Indicative of the relationships between Costanza, Haft and Wishman at the White House and O'Leary and Voeller of the NGTF is the fact that on 22 May 1979, the three attended a benefit dinner in New York City organized by the Fund for Human Dignity and the NGTF to honour O'Leary and Voeller, who were retiring from their posts as Co-Executive Directors of the organization.[66] Wishman left his post after Costanza's departure, after which the issue of gay rights became a more collective effort from the White House, with the OPL cooperating with the White House's Domestic Policy Council to address the issue.

61 Quoted in Mark A. Peterson, 'The Presidency and Organized Interests: White House Patterns of Interest Group Liaison', *American Political Science Review* 86, no. 3 (1992): 612.

62 Douglas Martin, 'Anne Wexler, An Influential Political Operative and Lobbyist, is Dead at 79', *NYT*, 8 August 2009.

63 Karen De Witt, 'Miss Costanza Resigns as Assistant to Carter, Citing Problems of Style', *NYT*, 2 August 1978.

64 Apuzzo, author interview.

65 Robert Malson memorandum for Stu Eizenstat, 19 April 1980. SESF, Gays [CF], JCPL.

66 Apuzzo and Haft, author interviews.

Beyond the White House

Until 1977, only three women had ever served as US Cabinet secretaries. Carter's Cabinet included three women who believed strongly in gay rights: Juanita Kreps, Secretary of Commerce, Judge Shirley Hufstedler, the first cabinet-level Secretary of Education, and Patricia Roberts Harris, Secretary of Housing and Urban Development (HUD) and later Secretary of Health, Education, and Welfare (HEW). Carter also appointed a number of civil rights activists who were supportive of gay rights to various posts across his administration, the executive branch and in presidential commissions; several are briefly described below.

Bella Abzug, a lawyer, feminist and gay rights advocate, and since 1970 a member of the House of Representatives (where she introduced the first federal gay rights bill in 1974), was held in high esteem by Carter and was seriously considered for a prominent post in the administration.[67] The two met in the White House in February 1977, and discussed 'many things of mutual concern', as she put it.[68] Carter offered her the position of Director of the Equal Employment Opportunity Commission, which would have made her the first woman to hold this role, but she turned it down as she had already agreed to back Eleanor Holmes Norton for the job. She declined several other positions, as she was only interested in becoming Secretary of the Department of Transportation or chair of the Federal Trade Commission.[69] She was, however, appointed at Costanza's recommendation to two of Carter's presidential commissions, with significant implications for gay rights, as was noticed by conservative critics, including some Democrats. Despite this, Carter went on to appoint Abzug in 1978 as co-chair of his newly established National Advisory Committee for Women, though he would dismiss her in January 1979 (see Chapter 5).

Daniel J. Bradley, a lawyer from Georgia, was a closeted gay man, although his homosexuality was known to his immediate circle and to the gay community where he lived. He declined an administration post in 1977 but was appointed in 1979 president of the Legal Services Corporation, a source of funding for legal representation for those unable to afford it. In 1982, Bradley came out and then became a board member of the GRNL and the Lambda Legal Defense Fund.[70] **Margaret McKenna**, a civil rights attorney, at the time Deputy White House Counsel, was suggested by the NGTF in August 1979, on account of her 'interest' in their 'concerns' as their liaison at the White House; Carter, however, appointed her as Undersecretary of the Department of Education, and Malson was instead assigned to this role.[71] **Monroe H. Freedman**, a Harvard law professor, had in the early 1960s been a volunteer General Counsel of the Mattachine Society, one of the earliest gay rights organizations in the country. Described by Kameny as 'an outstanding advocate of civil liberties in general, and gay

[67] 'Bella Abzug Sees Carter', *NYT*, 15 February 1977; Martin Tolchin, 'Post for Mrs. Abzug with Carter Urged', *NYT*, 30 November 1976.

[68] Edward C. Burks, 'Mrs. Abzug Confirms Talks with Carter on F.T.C. Job', *NYT*, 19 February 1977.

[69] Abguz with Kelber, *Gender Gap*, 55–6.

[70] 'Dan J. Bradley, 47, Dies of AIDS; Ex-head of Legal Services Agency', *NYT*, 9 January 1988.

[71] Letter, C. F. Brydon to Evan Dobelle, 1 August 1979. NGTFR, B.6, F.3, CU.

rights in particular', he was made executive director of the US Holocaust Memorial Council.[72]

Aware that the Equal Employment Opportunity Commission was extremely important for gay and women's rights, Costanza recommended that Carter appoint as its director **Eleanor Holmes Norton**, former ACLU Assistant Legal Director, who had served for six years as chair of the equivalent commission in New York City and was a strong supporter of gay rights.[73] **Patricia Wald**, previously a Litigation Director of the ACLU-sponsored Mental Health Law Project, was appointed as Assistant Attorney General for Legislative Affairs at the Justice Department, and was described by O'Leary as being 'good on the issues. . . . She's like Midge [Costanza], she was very helpful in getting us in to see people.'[74] Georgia Democratic Congressman **Andrew Young** became Ambassador to the United Nations. Young had often publicly spoken against anti-gay discrimination.[75] Bush commented about him, 'I think, of *all* the politicians I ever interviewed, Young was the most well versed, most sympathetic . . . most concerned about fairness and equality'.*

The FBI's new director **William Webster** had been a judge at the US Court of Appeals for the Eighth Circuit in St Louis. In a landmark case, he had ruled in favour of a Missouri gay student group's request for legal recognition; Kameny said that Webster's record as a judge 'is generally considered very progressive and his concern for due process has been clearly demonstrated by his decisions'.[76] Other appointees who had publicly expressed their support for gay rights included Patricia M. Derian as Coordinator for Human Rights and Humanitarian Affairs and then as Assistant Secretary of State for Human Rights and Humanitarian Affairs; Barbara Babcock as head of the Civil Division of the Justice Department; Carol Tucker Foreman, as Assistant Secretary of Agriculture. Liz Carpenter as Assistant Secretary of Education for Public Affairs and to his IWY Commission (see Chapter 5); John J. Gilligan as Administrator of the Agency for International Development; F. Ray Marshall as Secretary of Labor; and James B. King, as White House Personnel Director and then as Chairman of the National Transportation Safety Board.[77]

The case of **Reubin Askew** is distinctive as an example of a government appointment which the growing influence of the gay community nearly prevented. In September 1979, Carter nominated the former Governor of Florida to be the US Trade Representative, a cabinet-level position at the head of an office based in the Executive Office of the President. While having a strong liberal record as governor (an office to which he was elected at the same time as Carter became governor of Georgia), for instance on desegregation and on the ERA, he had joined the campaign against a non-discrimination ordinance in Florida (see Chapter 11), saying, 'I do not

72 'Holocaust Staff Calls for Input', *The Blade*, 6 March 1980.

73 Memorandum, Midge Costanza to the President, 29 January 1977. MCSF, [Norton, Eleanor Holmes: Costanza Recommendation to President], JCPL.

74 Larry Bush, 'Bible Thumpers Attack Court Nominee', *The Blade*, 5 July 1979.

75 Bush and Clay, author interviews.

76 Lou Chibbaro, Jr., 'Kameny Charges FBI Coverup', *The Blade*, 7 June 1979.

77 Larry Bush, 'The Carter Administration. More Done Than Said?', *The Advocate*, 12 June 1980; Bush and Higgins, author interviews; Marilyn Fleener, 'Carter's People, Some Good News', *The Advocate*, 23 February 1977.

want a homosexual teaching my child',[78] and told his Senate confirmation hearing that he would not appoint known gay people to work in the Office of the US Trade Representative. Vigorous protest and lobbying from gay rights groups ensued. After some hesitation by Carter, who presumably had a degree of political fellow-feeling with Askew, gay rights activists pressed their objections, which by then had the support of anti-discrimination employment legislation, at the confirmation hearing. The confirmation was suspended at the instigation of Senator Robert Packwood (R-OR). Askew then reversed his position; in a written statement to Packwood and the Senate, he pledged not to discriminate against any employee on the basis of sexual preference in both government- and non-government-protected positions. This was accepted by the activists and his appointment was confirmed.[79]

Openly gay people in the White House and beyond

In addition to appointing people who were 'sensitive' to the gay community's concerns, Carter fulfilled his promise to appoint openly gay people to governmental and other public posts, even though gay rights organizations, unlike other minority groups, had not nominated any candidates.[80] Carter had made it clear to all his staff not to discriminate against anyone and had encouraged them to have diversity in their appointments.[81] Margaret McKenna told the author about this,

> He was clear that he was [in support of gay rights], and I think people were surprised about how strong he was about women and gay rights. And I think people [of his administration] stepped in line, because that's what he wanted. I think that there was general agreement that this is what the administration wanted and this was what we were going to do.*

Inclusiveness was, moreover, not only a matter of numbers but also of the atmosphere encountered by people who were just emerging from exclusion. According to several of the gay rights activists who spoke to the author, Carter's White House was a comfortable and welcoming workplace for openly gay employees.[82] Illustrative is the report to the author by Eric Marcus, a journalist, broadcaster and author specializing in gay rights issues, of a tour of the White House which his openly gay romantic partner at the time, Jim Mayer (appointed by Eizenstat to the Domestic Policy Staff) arranged; he said, 'I don't know if Carter knew he was gay, but my boyfriend found it a very comfortable place to work'.* Higgins made a similar comment to the author about her lesbian

78 Faderman, *The Gay Revolution*, 339.

79 Tom Bastow, author interview; Lou Chibbaro, Jr., 'Askew Recants Anti-gay Remarks', *The Blade*, 27 September 1979.

80 Larry Bush, 'The Carter Administration. More Done Than Said?', *The Advocate*, 12 June 1980.

81 Bourne, Eizenstat, Margaret McKenna and Weddington, author interviews.

82 Apuzzo, Bastow, Bush, DeBaugh, Haft, Higgins, Kent, McReynolds and Eric Marcus, author interviews.

partner: 'She said there were several gays and lesbians in the White House and most people were comfortable with it; Carter certainly was'.*

Carter's willingness to appoint openly gay people to important and visible public posts was demonstrated only a few months after his inauguration, when his administration offered positions to Jo Daly and Elaine Noble, two of the most prominent open lesbians and lesbian rights activists of the time, as well as members of Carter's 51.3% Committee. However, these appointments did not materialize. Daly was offered a senior position in the Women's Bureau, but not the Directorship that she wished for, so she declined the offer.[83] Sam Brown, the Director of ACTION, a US government agency (see Chapter 6), offered Noble three different 'top jobs'. She eventually decided against them as she believed that she would be able to serve the gay community better as State Representative than in any of the posts she was offered.[84] Nevertheless, Carter went on to appoint several openly gay people to his administration and other public posts. For example, Ruth Abram, executive director of the Women's Action Alliance and member of the NGTF's Board of Directors, and openly lesbian, to his IWY Commission.[85] Other important examples are profiled below.

Virginia 'Ginny' Apuzzo

Apuzzo was one of the most prominent lesbian rights activists of the period as she was Co-Chairperson of the GRNL and Director of the Fund for Human Dignity; in the early 1980s she became Executive Director of the NGTF. In June 1980, about five months before the presidential election, Carter, on Wexler's recommendation, approved Apuzzo's appointment to the Democratic Party's Platform Committee, where she was instrumental in the party's adoption of a gay rights plank (see Chapter 13). Apuzzo worked very closely with the administration and developed a very good relationship with many White House aides, especially Wexler. One of the happiest moments of Apuzzo's life, she told the author, and one that also indicates how personal her relationship with Carter and his administration became over time, happened in 1980, when she received an invitation from Carter to attend the White House function for the honourees who had been given that year's Kennedy Centre Honors (Figure 2). The function would take place a few weeks before Carter left the White House, and this was to be his last big party there. A few weeks before the function and the 1980 presidential election, Wexler called Apuzzo and said: 'Ginny, the president wants you to know to bring your partner to this'. Thus, Apuzzo and her partner attended the function, making them the first openly lesbian couple to be personally invited by the president of the United States to an official event.*

83 Higgins, author interview.

84 'Noble Refuses Federal Post', *GN*, June 1977; Randy Shilts, 'Noble Nixes Appointment', *The Advocate*, 15 June 1977; Randy Shilts, 'Administration Mulls Noble Appointment', *The Advocate*, 1 June 1977.

85 'Jean O'Leary Named to IWY Commission', News from NGTF, 30 March 1977. NGTFR, B.36, F.29, CU.

Figure 2 President Carter welcomes Ginny Apuzzo to the White House in 1980 (Courtesy of Ginny Apuzzo).

Aaron Henry

Dr Henry was a Black closeted gay, or at least bisexual, man. He was one of the most renowned civil rights activists of the 1960s. Henry often denied that he was gay, and did not publicly express support for gay rights. However, his sexuality was widely known in Mississippi, in political circles and among those who knew him, as he had been arrested by the police at least four times in 'moral arrests' and had been charged with 'homosexual sodomy' and with 'disorderly conduct' for soliciting men in order to engage 'in an unnatural sex act'. Henry publicly attributed the arrests to white racists' efforts to slander him, pointing out that he was married.[86] However, members of the gay community in Mississippi were aware of Henry's homosexuality and he was forthcoming with them about the subject.[87]

Henry had campaigned for Carter in Mississippi in 1976 and had a very good relationship with him; Carter was of course aware of his friend's arrests and almost certainly of his sexual preference too. Henry's history attracted renewed interest and controversy during Carter's presidency due to his friendship with the president and his nomination by Carter to public posts. In early 1979, Carter cooperated with Henry and the National Caucus on the Black Aged to organize a luncheon in the White House to honour with the Living Legacy Award seventeen elderly Black Americans who had made

[86] Aaron Henry with Constance Curry, *Aaron Henry: The Fire Ever Burning* (Jackson: University Press of Mississippi, 2000), 126–8; John Howard, *Men Like That: A Southern Queer History* (Chicago: The University of Chicago Press, 2001), xv–xvi, 158–66, 171–3; 'Miss. NAACP Leader Arrested on Drug and Moral Charges', *Philadelphia Tribune*, 11 November 1972.

[87] Sandifer, author interview.

significant contributions to the nation in various fields such as art, education, medicine and sports.[88] Soon afterwards, Henry ran for the Mississippi House of Representatives, and it became known that Carter was considering appointing him to the Federal Commission for Aging. This news prompted white supremacists, conservatives and political foes of Henry to point out his arrests and his homosexuality. Some men who had had sexual relationships with Henry came forward and other evidence of gay relationships, 'moral arrests' and 'homosexual sodomy' became publicly known, with his political enemies attempting to derail his run for the state House and keep him from being appointed to the Commission.[89]

Nevertheless, Carter stood by Henry and invited him to the White House in February 1979, publicly endorsing his nomination and praising his character. Carter's endorsement and public comments about Henry, as well as their picture in the White House together, which was widely circulated in the local press in Mississippi, boosted his candidacy. Later that year he was elected to the Mississippi House of Representatives, in which he served until 1996.[90] Furthermore, in December 1979, despite the protests, Carter appointed him to the Federal Commission for Aging. During the official appointment ceremony, Carter described Henry as 'my good friend'.[91] Carter remained a good and loyal friend of Henry despite the controversies and later appointed him to the President's Council.[92]

Although we are not in a position to know for certain whether Carter knew that Henry was gay or bisexual, this is of secondary importance. More important is his reaction to what was publicly known about Henry, which was to ignore it, to continue his friendly relations with Henry and to appoint him to public posts on his merits.

Jean O'Leary

Costanza was aware that the appointment of an openly gay person to Carter's administration, to a presidential commission or a government post, would be of great symbolic importance. Thus, she suggested to O'Leary, presumably with Carter's approval, that she should apply for a top post in the Women's Bureau, an agency within the Department of Labor. O'Leary had already been appointed by Carter three times, twice to his 51.3% Committee and also to his election campaign team. However, she was only willing to consider leaving her post in the NGTF for the position of Director of the Women's Bureau – a post for which Carter had already lined up Alexis Herman.[93] Costanza then suggested that Carter appoint O'Leary to his National Commission on

[88] Memorandum, Gretchen Poston to the President and Mrs. Carter with attached list of the honorees, 22 February 1979, and The White House: Luncheon Honoring Elderly Blacks, 22 February 1979, both in OSS, Presidential Files, B.108, F.2/23/79 Afro-Americans, JCPL.

[89] Jared E. Leighton, 'Freedom Indivisible: Gays and Lesbians in the African American Civil Rights Movement' (Ph.D. Thesis, University of Nebraska-Lincoln, 2013), 234–5; Sandifer, author interview.

[90] Sandifer, author interview.

[91] Memorandum, Gordon Stewart and Richard Conn to President Carter, 7 December 1979, and White House Announcement of Appointment Affecting Senior Citizens, 10 December 1979, both in OSS, Presidential Files, B.141, F.12/10/79[4], Presidential Appointments, JCPL.

[92] Henry with Curry, Aaron Henry, picture section and back cover.

[93] Higgins and Robin Tyler, author interviews.

the Observance of International Women's Year (The IWY Commission; see Chapter 5). Carter told Costanza, 'Well, all right, but does she have to use her title [Co-Executive Director of the NGTF]?' She replied, 'Do you have to use yours, sir?'[94] Carter accepted Costanza's recommendation and in March 1977 appointed O'Leary to the IWY Commission, making her the first openly gay person to be appointed to a presidential commission. O'Leary served on the commission until it was disbanded in March 1978.[95] The NGTF was delighted with her appointment and made sure to mention in its reports and press releases that O'Leary was appointed to the post by President Carter himself,[96] maximizing the legitimation benefit.

O'Leary's appointment caused considerable outrage and dissatisfaction among conservatives, and Carter received a lot of criticism for it; she was characterized by *The National Enquirer* as 'a militant pro-lesbian who advocates lesbian sex education in America's public schools', and the newspaper expressed its surprise that Carter had appointed such a person 'to a position of prominence and high visibility which she could use as a public platform to promote her pro-lesbian views'.[97] Costanza and Carter also received homophobic letters from conservative Christians.[98]

In June 1978, despite the criticism he had received from conservatives for O'Leary's appointment, Carter, again on Costanza's recommendation, appointed her to the National Advisory Committee for Women (NACW), the successor to the IWY Commission. O'Leary expressed her pleasure at being given the chance to represent the concerns of lesbians and all American women. These appointments made O'Leary the first openly gay person ever to be appointed to a presidential commission, and she was appointed by the president himself,[99] obviously a clear statement by Carter of his anti-discrimination position. In December 1978, in a letter to Carter, the NGTF praised and emphasized the importance of O'Leary's various appointments: 'You honored our organization and gave recognition to the gay-rights issues when you appointed one of us to the International Women's Year Commission and to your 51.3% Committee on Women'.[100]

Bayard Rustin

Rustin was one of the most prominent civil rights activists and had been a close associate of Martin Luther King Jr. Rustin was also openly gay and in 1953 had been arrested and jailed for two months after being found with two men in the back seat of a car. Although King had embraced gay people involved in the civil rights movement

94 O'Leary, 'From Agitator to Insider', 91.
95 Ibid.
96 Several NGTF's press releases and newsletters, e.g., 'IWY', NGTF Action Report, April–May 1977. JWSF, NGTFJW, JCPL.
97 Arline Brecher, 'Carter Appointed Lesbian Rights Leader to National Post', *The National Enquirer*, the date is not visible. MCI.
98 See several letters at MCI.
99 Costanza interview to Boyd. MCI; 'O'Leary Appointed by President Carter to National Advisory Committee for Women', News from NGTF, 30 June 1978, NGTFR, B.36, F.85, CU.
100 Letter, Jean O'Leary and Bruce Voeller to President Carter, 26 December 1978. NGTFR, B.152, F.46, CU.

of the 1950s and 1960s, such as Rustin, Rustin remained largely in the background in comparison to other civil rights leaders.[101] Carter, who was of course aware that Rustin was gay, held him in high esteem and the two developed a good relationship during his presidency.[102]

In November 1978, Carter appointed Rustin to his Commission on the Holocaust, and two years later, he appointed him again to the Holocaust Memorial Council (see Chapter 10).[103] Furthermore, in 1979, Carter invited Rustin to be part of the official US delegation that travelled to Israel for Golda Meir's funeral; this would have made Rustin the first openly gay American delegate on a foreign mission, had he not been prevented from attending by being on a human rights mission to Southeast Asia.[104] In 1980, Rustin campaigned for Carter's re-election and organized a committee called Black Americans to Re-elect the President.[105]

Jill Schropp

Carter did not appoint open lesbians only on the basis of recommendations by Costanza. In July 1979, he appointed Jill Schropp, campaign manager of Citizens to Retain Fair Employment, to his newly reorganized President's Advisory Committee on Women, which replaced the NACW (itself a successor of the IWY Commission; see Chapter 5).[106] The NGTF wrote to Carter approvingly, 'We consider it a positive sign that you have *again* appointed a member of America's gay community . . . to your Advisory Committee on Women . . . Our congratulations'.[107] The organization characterized Schropp as 'an outstanding representative of the concerns of lesbians and all American women'.[108] Carter appointed Schropp again in 1980 as press secretary of his re-election campaign in Washington state.[109]

A long reach: 'You have to love these Carter judges'

As in other cases discussed in this chapter, it would be implausible to say that Carter's choices in the judicial branch rested solely, or even primarily, on the nominees' positions on gay rights. Carter had pledged during his election campaign to appoint

101 John D'Emilio, *Lost Prophet: The Life and Times of Bayard Rustin* (New York: Free Press, 2003), 191–3; Eric Marcus, 'Bayard Rustin', Making Gay History, https://makinggayhistory.com/podcast/bayard-rustin/; ABilly S. Jones-Hennin, author interview.
102 Walter Naegle, author interview.
103 Phil McCombs, 'The Politics of Creating the Holocaust Memorial', *WP*, 13 April 1983; Ellie Wiesel, President's Commission on the Holocaust, 'Report to the President', 27 September 1979; Naegle, author interview.
104 Jervis Anderson, *Bayard Rustin: Troubles I've Seen* (New York: HarperCollins Publishers, 1997), 341.
105 Naegle, author interview.
106 'Carter Appoints Lesbian', *LT*, July/August 1979.
107 Letter, Jean O'Leary and C. F. Brydon to President Carter, 18 May 1979. SWSF, PACW-Correspondence from Members, JCPL.
108 Scott P. Anderson, 'Carter Taps Lesbian for Women's Commission', *The Advocate*, 14 June 1979.
109 White House News on Women, II, VIII, December 1980.

judges 'whose judgment and integrity were sound' and not because they shared the same beliefs or religion,[110] a quite conventional position for a presidential candidate to take, though perhaps a more necessary one from a candidate with Carter's background. More substantively, he had also said that all his appointments would reflect his opposition to all forms of discrimination, including on the basis of sexual preference.[111] He appointed to the federal bench record-breaking numbers of women and members of minorities, with many of them being civil rights activists, and like his other appointments, his judicial picks were centrists or leaned to the left.[112] The effects of these appointments have been felt well into the twenty-first century. This section describes some of the Carter appointees' (highlighted in **bold** when introduced) most important and pioneering contributions to the advancement of gay rights.

Some expository clarification is first needed. Aside from some specialized areas of law, the federal judiciary consists of three levels: district courts serving between one and four districts per state (and the District of Columbia), which are the initial trial courts; appeal courts organized into multi-state regions known as numbered 'circuits' (with in addition a D.C. Circuit which mainly deals with government-related cases, from whose bench Supreme Court nominees are disproportionately drawn); and the Supreme Court, which unlike the circuit courts is not obliged to hear appeals referred to it. Circuit courts are thus responsible for establishing many important precedents within their regions, and non-bindingly in others. Typically a panel of three judges decides appeal cases, but the full set of judges of the circuit is sometimes convened (termed 'en banc'). District court decisions have a greater risk of being overturned and do not set formal precedent, but their advances in argument can be influential, as we will see.

The best known of Carter's judicial appointments, thanks to their later elevation to the Supreme Court (as nominees of President Bill Clinton), were **Stephen Breyer** to the Court of Appeals for the First Circuit and **Ruth Bader Ginsburg** to the Court of Appeals for the District of Columbia Circuit. In 2013, Ginsburg, who as General Counsel of the ACLU had initiated programmes for gay rights, became the first US Supreme Court justice to officiate at a same-sex wedding.[113] The Court of Appeals for the District of Columbia Circuit was the most important court in the country for gay rights cases. In addition to Ginsburg, Carter's other three appointees to this court, Harry T. Edwards, Abner Mikva and Patricia Wald, also strongly supported gay rights.[114] The nominations of Mikva and Wald came under severe attack by evangelicals and conservatives on this account. During her time at the Justice Department, to which

110 'Jimmy Carter Interview', *Playboy*, November 1976.

111 Eizenstat, McKenna and Weddington, author interviews; 'NGTF-Federal Agency Meetings Set Second White House Conference in September', News from NGTF, 31 March 1977. NGTFR, B.145, F.47, CU.

112 M. Glenn Abernathy, 'The Carter Administration and Domestic Civil Rights', in M. Glenn Abernathy et al. (eds), *The Carter Years: The President and Policy Making* (London: Frances Pinter, 1984), 106–8; W. Gary Fowler, 'A Comparison of Initial Recommendation Procedures: Judicial Selection under Reagan and Carter', *Yale Law & Policy Review* 1, no. 2 (1983): 299–320.

113 Raffy Ermac, 'Ruth Bader Ginsburg Highlights Constitution at D.C. Same-Sex Wedding', *The Advocate*, 18 May 2015; Paul Richter, 'Clinton Picks Moderate Judge Breyer for Supreme Court Spot', *LAT*, 14 May 1994.

114 Larry Bush, 'The Carter Administration. More Done Than Said?', *The Advocate*, 12 June 1980.

she had been appointed by Carter, Wald had worked with the NGTF and had assisted the organization in various ways. In June 1979, Senator Gordon Humphrey (R-N.H.) attacked Wald during her confirmation hearing by the Senate Judiciary Committee, denouncing her as an 'instrument of the devil' and likely to ruin the American family by ruling in favour of gay people. Nevertheless, Wald's nomination was approved.[115] Mikva, a Democratic Illinois Congressman, had a strong liberal voting record, having been a co-sponsor of the national gay rights bill in the previous two Congresses, and in past elections he had been endorsed by *Gay-Life*, a gay newspaper in Chicago, while in 1961 he had been instrumental in the removal of the anti-sodomy law from the criminal code of the state of Illinois. Mikva's nomination was attacked by the religious right, but in the end his appointment was confirmed.[116] Many key gay rights cases were also heard in the Court of Appeals for the Ninth Circuit, which is the largest circuit by population, containing California and eight other states. Carter appointed six judges to this court, who during their tenure ruled a number of times against discrimination on the grounds of sexual preference.[117]

In the case of *Ben-Shalom v. Secretary of the Army* in a Wisconsin district court (May 1980),[118] Judge **Terence Evans** made the first major gay rights ruling against the US Army. He ruled that Miriam Ben-Shalom, who had been honourably discharged on account of her 'homosexual tendencies', should be reinstated, holding that the Constitution (through the First, Fifth and Ninth Amendments) protected people from being punished for their private sexual preferences, furthermore rejecting for lack of evidence the Army's contention that gay people lacked fitness for military duty and noting the 'readily available tool for intimidation and harassment' provided by the discharge provision. He argued that its breadth would, if allowed to stand, make soldiers afraid to read 'anything that might be construed as a homosexually-oriented book or magazine', or 'to make any statements that might be interpreted as supporting homosexuality'.[119] Evans's ruling was hailed by the gay community at the time as a landmark. Larry Bush titled his article about it in *The Sentinel*, 'Federal Court Strikes at Homophobia in Army'.[120]

Carter appointees played significant roles in another case involving separation from the military, *Watkins v. U.S. Army*.[121] Perry Watkins had acknowledged he was gay when he was drafted in 1967, but was nevertheless allowed to remain in the Army, and had, while remaining open about his homosexuality, successfully re-enlisted on two further occasions. He remained in the military throughout the 1970s; investigations

[115] Larry Bush, 'Bible Thumpers Attack Court Nominee', *The Blade*, 5 July 1979; Larry Bush, 'Wald Wins Approval', *The Blade*, 19 April 1979.

[116] Larry Bush, '2nd Court Nominee to Be Opposed', *The Blade*, 5 July 1979; Larry Bush, 'Wald Wins Approval', *The Blade*, 19 April 1979.

[117] 'Betty Binns Fletcher Dies at 89', *LAT*, 25 October 2012; Sheldon Goldman, 'Carter's Judicial Appointments: A Lasting Legacy', *Judicature* 64, no. 8 (1981): 347.

[118] *Ben-Shalom v. Secretary of Army*, 489 F. Supp. 964 (E.D. Wis. 1980).

[119] Larry Bush, 'Federal Court Strikes at Homophobia in Army', *The Sentinel*, 30 May 1980; 'Lesbian Sergeant Ordered Reinstated', *The Blade*, 29 May 1980; The United States Law Week, 'New Court Decisions: Armed Forces', *The Bureau of National Affairs, Inc.*, Washington, DC 48, 47, no. 3 (1980): 1–2.

[120] Larry Bush, 'Federal Court Strikes at Homophobia in Army', *The Sentinel*, 30 May 1980.

[121] 875 F.2d 699 (9th Cir. 1989).

into his sexuality were conducted and the Army did consider discharging him but did not do so. On one occasion, it decided that his own admissions were not enough in the absence of any other evidence that he was gay. In 1979, he re-enlisted a third time intending to achieve twenty years of service so that he could retire with a pension. His re-enlistment was not challenged at the time; however, when his security clearance came up for review, the Army decided to revoke it, denying him a promotion. In 1981, Watkins appealed against this decision and the Army immediately moved to discharge him.[122]

The complex history of Watkins's relationship with the Army was echoed in the litigation that ensued, consisting of several district court decisions followed by a series of decisions by the appeals court. The final outcome, in 1989, was a victory for Watkins, but on narrow grounds. En route to this conclusion, however, Carter-appointed judges made significant arguments advancing the cause of gay rights on constitutional grounds. In the trial court in Washington State, Judge **Barbara Jacobs Rothstein** considered the Army's history of acquiescence in Watkins's admission of his sexuality to be a key factor (invoking thereby the legal doctrine of 'estoppel'), and found in his favour. Later appeals to the Ninth Circuit Court produced, amid much additional argument, a notable decision in Watkins's favour authored by **William A. Norris**, who with **William Cameron Canby Jr** formed the majority in a three-judge panel. Norris's opinion, written against the backdrop of the Supreme Court's recent decision in the notorious case *Bowers v. Hardwick* (see below) that a constitutional right of privacy did not extend to homosexual acts, developed instead an argument that homosexual *orientation* (which was what the Army regulation in fact prohibited) should be considered a 'suspect category', inviting, like the category of race, 'strict scrutiny' by the courts in terms of the equal protection provision if the government discriminated with respect to it.[123] Norris's opinion had far-reaching consequences and went on to influence the decisions of many state and lower federal courts that struck down bans on gay marriage in the early twenty-first century.[124] Raymond Fisher, a Ninth Circuit Judge, said that Norris 'was a big hero in the gay community for that opinion and for advancing the constitutional theory ahead of its time. It sent a signal to the gay community that there was support in the federal courts. There was hope'.[125]

The Army requested an en banc hearing and the case was heard in 1989 in San Francisco.[126] The court ruled again, 7 to 4, in favour of Watkins, ordering the Army

[122] Shilts, *Conduct Unbecoming*, 79–83, 155–62, 218–42, 309–10.

[123] *Watkins v. U.S. Army*, 837 F.2d 1428, 1452 (9th Cir. 1988). Stephen Reinhardt dissented, though 'with great reluctance'. He considered that *Hardwick* was indeed binding in this case, remarking ruefully 'I am sometimes compelled to reach a result I believe to be contrary to the proper interpretation of constitutional principles'. Nicholas Bamforth, *Sexuality, Morals and Justice: A Theory of Lesbian and Gay Rights Law* (London and Washington: Cassell, 1997), 38–42; Leonard, *Sexuality and the Law*, 507–19; Joyce Murdoch and Deb Price, *Courting Justice: Gay Men and Lesbians v. The Supreme Court* (New York: Basic Books, 2001), 394–8.

[124] Sam Roberts, 'William A. Norris, 89, Federal Judge Whose Opinion Presaged Gay Marriage', *NYT*, 30 January 2017.

[125] Maura Dolan, 'Judge William A. Norris, Author of Early Ruling That Boosted Gay Rights, Dies at 89', *LAT*, 27 January 2017.

[126] *Watkins v. U.S. Army*, 875 F.2d 699 (9th Cir. 1989).

to allow him to re-enlist and holding that the Army could be sued for treating gay people and other soldiers unfairly, a ruling that potentially held the military accountable to the courts for a broad spectrum of military decisions that had historically been immune from judicial review. However, the ruling stopped short of the constitutional issues of equal protection invoked by Norris and Canby, relying instead on the 'estoppel' grounds used in the district court. Norris was moved to repeat his constitutional argument, more-or-less word for word, in a concurring opinion, again supported by Canby. Judge **Harry Pregerson**[127] wrote for the majority, 'This is a case where equity cries out and demands that the Army be estopped from refusing to re-enlist Watkins on the basis of his homosexuality'. Gay rights groups throughout the country hailed the new decision, while expressing regret that it did not go as far as the court's earlier ruling. 'This opinion is a victory, not only for Watkins, but for all gay Americans', said Nan D. Hunter, director of ACLU's Lesbian and Gay Rights Project.[128]

An 'equal protection' defence of gay rights had in fact already been advanced at the district court level, by Judge **Thelton Henderson** in the California case *High Tech Gays v. Defense Industrial Security Clearance Office*.[129] Henderson determined that the Department of Defense's policy of conducting a time-consuming 'expanded investigation' of gay applicants for security clearances, possibly resulting in refusal if they had participated in homosexual activity in the preceding fifteen years, was illegal, and he issued a nationwide injunction accordingly. His argument was based primarily on the equal protection clause, and he cited the prevalence of 'unfounded, degrading stereotypes' in support of a 'strict scrutiny' analysis of equal protection, as well as the implausibility of even the weaker 'rational basis' for unequal treatment resting on the supposed vulnerability of gay people to blackmail. Gay rights activists applauded the judge's verdict, with the plaintiffs' counsel Richard Gayer saying, 'Three cheers for Judge Henderson. This is a courageous act on his part to end discrimination'.[130] The case was appealed to the Ninth Circuit, a three-judge panel of which reversed the district court,[131] prompting a further defence of the equal protection argument in its 'strict scrutiny' form by Canby, who concluded resoundingly:

[127] Pregerson also contributed to an appeal court victory for hotel worker Medina Rene, who had faced a hostile work environment due to anti-gay prejudice: co-workers and a male supervisor had subjected him to a daily round of name-calling, rude jokes and unwanted touching. The case, *Rene v. MGM Grand Hotel*, 305 F.3d 1061 (9th Cir. 2002), was complicated by the fact that sexual orientation was not listed among the grounds of discrimination prohibited by Title VII of the 1964 Civil Rights Act. More indirect analysis was needed to bring the offending behaviour under the scope of Title VII, and Pregerson in a concurring opinion contributed one such analysis, based on the illegality of discrimination based on sexual stereotyping. A different analysis, highlighting the sexualized nature of the assaults, was however the argument of the plurality opinion.

[128] Kim Murphy, 'Court Tells Army to Reinstate Gay; Skips Wider Issue', *LAT*, 4 May 1989.

[129] 668 F. Supp. 1361 (N.D. Cal. 1987).

[130] 'Homosexuals Win Case on Security', *NYT*, 22 August 1987; Arthur S. Leonard, 'Chronicling a Movement: 20 Years of Lesbian/Gay Law Notes', *New York Law School Journal of Human Rights* 17 (2000): 440–1.

[131] 895 F.2d 563 (9th Cir. 1990).

> Homosexuals are hated, quite irrationally, for what they are, what they did not choose to be, and what they cannot easily change. Mainstream society has mistreated them for centuries. If the equal protection clause means anything, it should mean that the government cannot, on the slightest of justifications, join in the discrimination.[132]

As inadequate as he found it, Canby made use of the appeal court's decision in *High Tech Gays* in another case, in which an appeal from Dusty Pruitt, a woman discharged from the Army for her lesbian orientation (revealed in a newspaper interview) was remanded back to the district court with a requirement that the Army substantiate, rather than merely assert, factual grounds for its discrimination against her: 'we will not spare the Army the task . . . of offering a rational basis for its regulation'.[133] Another member of the three-judge panel was **Betty Binns Fletcher**. Gay rights activists were pleased to see the courts standing up to the military by demanding that it provide reasons for its actions, and rejecting appeals to prejudice. Paula Ettelbrick of the Lambda Legal Defense and Educational Fund said at the time that the ruling is 'yet another nail in the coffin for this policy. I don't know what argument they will have left to justify this policy'.[134]

A further nail was rather loudly hammered home by district court judge **Terry J. Hatter** in California, in a similar case of military discharge, this time from the Navy, following a public revelation of homosexuality. Hatter ordered Keith Meinhold's reinstatement, and also issued a nationwide injunction banning similar discharges, announcing:

> Gays and lesbians have served, and continue to serve, the United States military with honor, pride, dignity and loyalty. The Department of Defense's justifications for its policy banning gay people from military service are based on cultural myths and false stereotypes. These justifications are baseless and very similar to the reasons offered to keep the military racially segregated in the 1940's.[135]

The Pentagon appealed Hatter's ruling, and in 1994, a three-judge panel of the Ninth Circuit heard the case; one of the judges was **Otto R. Skopil Jr**. The judges unanimously backed Hatter's decision regarding Meinhold but reversed its extension to other cases.[136]

In 1993, **Louis Oberdorfer**, district court judge for the District of Columbia, blocked the Navy from discharging Lieutenant Richard Selland after he had admitted to his commander that he was gay. Oberdorfer, noting that distress Selland had suffered from escalating taunts from his shipmates had motivated his disclosure, and that this in turn had prompted not the sympathetic intervention he had hoped for but rather his expulsion from the ship, described Selland as resembling 'a sparrow caught in a badminton game' and added that the Navy had strayed 'perilously close to being in

[132] 909 F.2d 375, 382 (9th Cir. 1990).
[133] *Pruitt v. Cheney*, 963 F.2d 1160, 1166 (9th Cir. 1991).
[134] 'Court Reinstates Lesbian's Lawsuit against Army', *NYT*, 20 August 1991.
[135] *Meinhold v. U.S. Department of Defense*, 808 F. Supp. 1455, 1458 (C.D. Cal. 1993).
[136] 34 F.3d 1469.

contempt' of Judge Hatter's injunction in the *Meinhold* case.[137] District court judge **Milton L. Schwarz** ruled similarly, in the same year, in the California case of Mel Dahl, whom he ordered be reinstated by the Navy. Schwartz, invoking the 'rational basis' test as developed in *High Tech Gays* and *Pruitt*, said in his ruling that the exclusion of gay people from the Navy lacked any rational basis; indeed, even '[the Navy's] evidence *supports* if not confirms the conclusion that the policy both effectuates and is solely motivated by prejudice against homosexuals'.[138]

This set of cases concerning gay rights in the military demonstrates, as well as the complex interconnections within a rapidly emerging body of anti-discrimination case law, the key role in that process made by Carter-appointed judges. While they sometimes made decisions ahead of what the judicial apparatus as a whole would countenance, a direction of travel was nevertheless clearly set. In 1993, Arthur Leonard, Professor of Law at New York Law School, commented about these cases to *The Advocate*, 'You have to love these Carter judges'.[139] But more severe headwinds for judicial enforcement of gay rights were evident in cases concerning homosexual behaviour and same-sex marriage, where Carter-appointed judges could make decisive change only after they had ascended to the Supreme Court.

A notable but failed push against this growing headwind was made by Texas district court judge **Jerry Buchmeyer**, who adjudicated a test case brought by Donald F. Baker, a former teacher (in fact dismissed on grounds of his sexuality) and the president of the Dallas Gay Alliance, against the provision of the Texas criminal code which outlawed 'deviate sexual intercourse with another individual of the same sex' and defined the former as 'any contact between any part of the genitals of one person and the mouth or anus of another person'.[140] Sodomy, under various definitions (including oral sex, anal sex, and sex with an animal) had been prohibited in Texas since 1860, but only in 1974 had the offense been limited to homosexuals (though with a much reduced penalty). Buchmeyer found the Texas statute unconstitutional on the grounds of its violation of a right to privacy which numerous Supreme Court cases, beginning with *Griswold v. Connecticut* (overturning a ban on the sale of contraceptives), had derived from the Constitution and had progressively expanded; a right which encompassed private consensual sexual relations between adults and could not be withheld from homosexuals on the basis of any plausible state interest in banning homosexual sodomy.[141] Accordingly, the statute also violated the equal protection clause. However, the Fifth Circuit Court of Appeals overturned the decision in 1985.

The legal headwinds strengthened considerably with the outcome of the case *Bowers v. Hardwick*,[142] which addressed Georgia's sodomy law. As with *Baker v. Wade*, it was a test case. Michael Hardwick, a gay man in Atlanta, had been arrested in his house when a police officer who had arrived with a warrant against him for

137 *Selland v. Aspin*, 832 F. Supp. 12, 13, 16 (D.D.C. 1993).
138 *Dahl v. Secretary of U.S. Navy*, 830 F. Supp. 1319, 1332 (E.D. Cal. 1993).
139 John Gallagher, 'Don't Know, Can't Tell', *The Advocate*, 2 November 1993.
140 *Baker v. Wade*, 553 F. Supp. 1121, 1124 (N.D. Tex. 1982), rev'd 769 F.2nd 289 (5th Cir. 1985) (en banc).
141 553 F.Supp 1121, 1125–6, 1134–5, 1142.
142 *Hardwick v. Bowers*, 760 F.2d 1202 (11th Cir. 1985); *Bowers v. Hardwick*, 478 U.S. 186 (1986).

not turning up in court found him having consensual oral sex with another man, but the local District Attorney had declined to prosecute. Hardwick sued Michael Bowers, the state's Attorney General, in federal court, seeking, as Baker had, to have the law found unconstitutional.[143] The district court dismissed the case for lack of a legal claim, noting the Supreme Court's summary affirmance in 1976 of a Virginia case, *Doe v. Commonwealth's Attorney*.[144] In that case, the appeal court, and hence the Supreme Court when it affirmed, found the expanding privacy right to be irrelevant, 'since [homosexuality] is obviously no portion of marriage, home or family life'.[145] The Eleventh Circuit, to which Hardwick now appealed, found 2 to 1 in a three-judge panel that the Supreme Court precedent had limited weight, with two Carter appointments **Frank Johnson** and **Phyllis Kravitch**, on either side of this debate, Kravitch agreeing that there was no legal claim. The Supreme Court, which the case now reached, unsurprisingly stuck to its earlier position, and indeed expanded it as a full opinion, deciding in *Bowers v. Hardwick* that the right of privacy elaborated in previous cases 'bears [no] resemblance to the claimed constitutional right of homosexuals to engage in acts of sodomy', and that, furthermore, no such constitutional right existed.[146] A considerable block was therefore placed on further progress regarding the criminal status of homosexual intimacy, and regarding same sex marriage. Carter appointees, as noted, played opposing roles in this outcome, but the Supreme Court was the main player. Shortly afterwards the Court declined to hear an appeal of *Baker*.

Kravitch nevertheless made contributions sympathetic to gay rights when the precedents were less confining. In *Shahar v. Bowers*, another case involving the Attorney General of Georgia, in which Robin Shahar sued him after he rescinded an offer of employment upon learning of her plans to get married to her female partner, Kravitch participated in the Eleventh Circuit cases when Shahar appealed her district court loss. Kravitch, in first a panel decision (finding for Shahar) and then a full court hearing (finding for Bowers), argued in support of Shahar's 'intimate associative interest', to which she argued the en banc majority gave 'short shrift'.[147] She was also among the three appeal court judges who unanimously found in favour of Vandy Beth Glenn, a transgender person who worked at the Georgia General Assembly, but was sacked after she informed her employer that she intended to have a sex change operation to transition from male to female, and sued him for sex discrimination in violation of the equal protection clause.[148]

A significant change of direction in the Supreme Court began to be apparent in the mid-1990s, by which time **Breyer** and **Ginsburg** had joined the court. They contributed to the 6–3 majority in the case of *Romer v. Evans*,[149] the first major ruling

143 William N. Eskridge, Jr., *Gaylaw: Challenging the Apartheid of the Closet* (Cambridge, MA: Harvard University Press, 1999), 149–52; Arthur S. Leonard, *Sexuality and the Law: An Encyclopaedia of Major Legal Cases* (New York and London: Garland Publishing, 1993), 153–64; Murdoch and Price, *Courting Justice*, 25, 84–7, 272–337.

144 *Doe v. Commonwealth's Attorney for City of Richmond*, 403 F. Supp. 1199 (E.D. Va. 1975).

145 403 F. Supp. 1199, 1202.

146 *Bowers v. Hardwick*, 478 U.S. 186, 190–1 (1986).

147 *Shahar v. Bowers*, 70 F.3d 1218 (11th Cir. 1995), 114 F.3d 1097 (11th Cir. 1997).

148 *Glenn v. Brumby*, 724 F. Supp. 2d 1284 (N.D. Ga. 2010), aff'd, 663 F.3d 1312 (11th Cir. 2011).

149 517 U.S. 620 (1996).

by the Supreme Court in favour of gay rights. This decision annulled an amendment to the constitution of Colorado which barred municipalities from introducing laws recognizing people of 'homosexual, lesbian or bisexual orientation, conduct, practices or relationships' as a protected class. The amendment had been introduced via a statewide referendum in response to a series of municipal enactments which had expressly banned such discrimination. The Supreme Court found that the amendment, by allowing such discrimination to continue, violated the Federal Constitution's equal protection clause.[150]

Breyer and Ginsburg joined another 6–3 majority in the landmark case of *Lawrence v. Texas*,[151] which the court took with the express intention of inquiring whether Bowers should be overruled. The circumstances with which the cases began are quite similar: arriving on unrelated business, the police discovered John Geddes Lawrence engaged in anal sex with another man and arrested them both. But in *Lawrence*, unlike *Bowers*, the court undertook a detailed examination of the history of anti-sodomy laws, in part to undermine the reliance of *Bowers* on a 'longstanding criminal prohibition of homosexual sodomy'. It also pointed to a more recent trend of abandonment by states either of such laws themselves, or of their enforcement. Drawing both on *Romer* and on the abortion case *Planned Parenthood v. Casey*, the Court found a substantive guarantee of liberty in the due process clause of the Constitution, which protected private consensual sexual conduct, whatever might be the moral claims of a state's governing majority.[152]

In 2013, Breyer and Ginsburg were among the US Supreme Court Judges who heard two key cases, both decided on 5–4 votes, that opened the path for the legalization of same-sex marriage. The first, *United States v. Windsor*,[153] concerned the constitutionality of a key part of a federal law passed during the Clinton administration, the 1996 Defense of Marriage Act (DOMA), which denied benefits to same-sex married couples. The second, *Hollingsworth v. Perry*,[154] involved Proposition 8, a voter-approved California state law enacted in 2008 that banned gay marriage. In *United States v. Windsor*, the Court struck down Section 3 of DOMA, which limited the definition of marriage to a bond between a man and a woman for the purposes of federal benefits, as a violation of the Constitution's guarantee of equal protection under the law. This meant that gay married couples would be entitled to receive support and that the government was now obliged to recognize same-sex marriages that had been legally conducted in states which allowed them. After lower courts had ruled that Proposition 8 failed the equal protection test, in *Hollingsworth v. Perry* the Supreme Court affirmed that finding. The Court did not, however, rule on the issue of whether all state bans on gay marriage contravened the Constitution; therefore, this ruling had no impact in the majority of US states, which at this point still did not recognize gay marriage. That issue was finally

150 Arthur S. Leonard, 'From *Bowers v. Hardwick* to *Romer v. Evans*', in D'Emilio, et al., *Creating Change*, 66–77.

151 539 U.S. 558 (2003).

152 539 U.S. 567–71; Dale Carpenter, *Flagrant Conduct – The Story of Lawrence v. Texas* (New York: W.W. Norton & Company, 2013), 61–74, 209–78.

153 570 U.S. 744 (2013).

154 570 U.S. 693 (2013).

Figure 3 President Carter with Ruth Bader Ginsburg at the Reception for Women Federal Judges, 3 October 1980. WHSPC, nlc19532.14, JCPL.

decided in 2015, when Breyer and Ginsburg were in the 5–4 majority in the case of *Obergefell v. Hodges*[155] which granted same-sex couples the right to get married in all fifty US states (Figure 3).[156]

According to Ginsburg, Carter intended that judges 'be drawn from all of the people, not just some of them', and hence saw it as his mission to help previously underrepresented groups to gain more equal standing in the judiciary. She commented, 'After Carter, things never went back to old ways. The first time I ever thought of being a judge was when Jimmy Carter announced to the world that he wanted to change the complexion of the U.S. judiciary, which he did'.[157]

It would be an overstatement to claim that sensitivity to gay rights was the first criterion for the nominations that he did make; Ginsburg probably has the better analysis of his motivation. Nevertheless, this section has shown that Carter's appointments did make important contributions to gay rights at various levels of the federal court system, many of them in the early phase in relation to military service, and had a reach long enough to help secure in the twenty-first century both an end to discriminatory prosecutions for gay sex and the legal establishment of same-sex marriage across the United States. In 2001, Deb Price, former editor at the *Wall Street Journal* and the *Washington Post,* and Joyce Murdoch, managing editor for politics at the *National Journal,* acknowledged that Carter's judicial appointments had 'been responsible for many of the gay civil rights movement's legal victories'. They lamented

155 576 U.S. 644 (2015).

156 Ruth Bader Ginsburg with Mary Hartnett and Wendy W. Williams, *My Own Words* (New York: Simon & Schuster, 2018), xxi, 139–49, 154–72, 174–5; Amisha Padnani and Celina Fang, 'Same-Sex Marriage: Landmark Decisions and Precedents', *NYT*, 26 June 2015.

157 Mark Joseph Stern, 'Carter's Quiet Revolution', *Slate*, 14 July 2019.

the lost progress that would have happened if Carter 'had gotten the chance to appoint progressive civil rights advocates to the Supreme Court'.[158]

ꕥ

In January 1977, before Carter had even been inaugurated, O'Leary and Voeller of the NGTF wrote in its newsletter, 'We are hopeful that a new administration will produce some liberal appointments'.[159] From the instances described in this chapter, it can be seen that the hope was hardly disappointed, even though, in this period of rapid cultural change, in part promoted by Carter's appointments themselves, expectations also developed rapidly. These instances, moreover, are far from exhausting the account that could be given of the inclusiveness towards gay advocacy and gay people across the full reach of presidential appointment power during the Carter years.

Carter's administration saw a dramatic increase in the number of minorities and members of progressive organizations elevated to important government roles. As many as 20 per cent of the top executive positions were filled by women or minorities; unremarkable by today's standards, but creating an unprecedented level of diversity in the executive branch of government.[160] But the presence of openly gay people and gay rights advocates among this new cohort is even more striking, given that the baseline inherited from previous presidencies was not just small, but practically non-existent. Not only the number of cases but the number of *firsts* is notable. Indeed it could have been greater still if some of the offers made by Carter (several at Costanza's urging) had not been rejected by candidates with higher aspirations. Moreover, Carter's ability to appoint even more openly gay people to his administration was limited by a lack of obvious candidates, despite the pool of connections opened up by appointments he did make. Gay rights organizations did not recommend or nominate anyone to the White House as they lacked the resources to monitor vacancies and therefore propose candidates, or indeed any experience in the task. That the potential opportunities for appointments outpaced the capacity of advocacy groups to suggest candidates, starkly contrasting with the situation today, is itself an indication of the rapidity with which inclusiveness expanded.

There were, of course, limits to the changes. Not all of Carter's appointees gave gay rights the highest priority. Hamilton Jordan, like Eizenstat, was fully aware of the threat that attention to gay rights posed to the president's relationship with the evangelical right and generally with conservatives. It was not a case of ideologically opposing and objecting to gay rights, but more of a calculated political reticence as they believed that open support for such issues was politically harmful for the administration. But Carter had instructed all his staff and appointees to not discriminate against anyone when

[158] Murdoch and Price, *Courting Justice*, 337.
[159] Jean O'Leary and Bruce Voeller, '1976: A Year of Growth', *It's Time*, January 1977. SWSF, [NGTF-Need for Federal Legislation], JCPL.
[160] James D. King and James W. Riddlesperger Jr., 'Diversity and Presidential Cabinet Appointments', *Social Science Quarterly* 96, no. 1 (2015): 96.

making appointments on their own, and strongly encouraged them to pursue diversity in their appointments, their departments and their offices.[161]

The presence of Costanza, along with other openly gay people or supporters of gay rights aides in the White House, contributed substantially to the legitimacy of the gay rights movement in the eyes of a growing number of Americans, helping to establish them as a mainstream part of the progressive movement in general. They also facilitated access to other parts of government by the activists, with whom they had a warm relationship, contrasting in both respects with the usual failure to get even a response from previous administrations. The practical impact of Carter's appointments described in this chapter will become obvious in the following chapters.

[161] Bourne, Eizenstat, McKenna and Sarah Weddington, author interviews.

3

Opening the White House to the gay community I

Setting the agenda

Gay rights activists had been trying to secure a White House hearing since 1962, when a letter with such a request was sent to President Kennedy. Over the next few years, several attempts were made to obtain a meeting, but they were all unsuccessful. In most, if not all, cases the White House had not even bothered to respond.[1] Carter's arrival as president marked a radical change. This chapter describes the transformation in recognition and access that the gay community experienced, practically from the very first day of the new presidency. A crucial meeting with gay rights advocates, of which Costanza was the prime mover, took place in the White House, a signal moment for the community, even though the president, who had of course authorized it, was not in attendance. Much of the later agenda of the Carter administration in the area of gay rights was established at this meeting, as were vital channels of communication, though the symbolic effects were just as important. Chapter 4 continues the story after the departure of Costanza.

The first steps

Important indications of Carter's seriousness about gay rights had already been given by the appointments to his transition team, as discussed in the preceding chapter. The inauguration, on 20 January 1977, reinforced the message. To this first official event of the new presidency, Carter invited some of those who had worked in his election campaign, including Jack Campbell, Daly and O'Leary. This marked the first time that openly gay people had been invited to attend the inauguration ceremony and also the first time that they had been invited to an official government event by any president.[2] Carter had asked five of the most prominent American artists of the time to help him fund the cultural events held during his inauguration. Two of the five were openly

1 Randy Shilts, 'White House Meeting. Concrete Results Soon?' *The Advocate*, 20 April 1977; Clay and McReynolds, author interviews.

2 Clay, Higgins and Kent, author interviews.

gay – Robert Rauschenberg and Andy Warhol. The artists were commissioned to create their own portfolios that could be sold in order to raise funds for the events. Later, on 14 June, Carter invited the five artists to the White House to honour them and to thank them for their contribution to his inauguration.[3]

In his religiously inflected inaugural speech, Carter introduced the theme of human rights as a pathway to redemption, saying that promoting human rights offered an opportunity for America to renew itself – essentially to be 'born again', as he had been through his faith. While Carter did not directly reference homosexuality, it was already clear from his campaign statements, actions and appointments that his conception of human rights embraced gay rights.[4]

Carter was no sooner in the White House than he came under pressure from gay rights activists to act for their causes. Carter had put Vice President Mondale in charge of it, later jokingly saying that he did this not only because he thought so highly of him, but also because it was one of the hot issues, along with abortion laws, the Concorde and Northern Ireland, that nobody wanted to touch. Carter and Costanza began receiving huge amounts of correspondence from gay people seeking reassurance that the president would act on his campaign promises.[5] Almost immediately after she had been appointed to the OPL, Costanza had been asked by O'Leary to set up a meeting in the White House between the administration and gay rights activists. Costanza, although very willing in principle, was initially a bit hesitant.[6] Haft said that Costanza was 'nervous' and 'frightened by all of this' because she was still 'in the closet' and she thought that her relationship with O'Leary would become known. However, O'Leary according to Haft 'wanted it very badly', and Haft insisted too. O'Leary asked Haft to be more the face of the meeting and organize it so that it would take some of the pressure off Costanza.[7]

Finally, O'Leary and Haft convinced Costanza to proceed with the meeting as soon as possible. On 1 February 1977, just over ten days after Carter's inauguration, at Costanza's suggestion, the NGTF wrote to the OPL and officially requested a White House meeting in order to examine how they could 'work together to end discrimination against gay people'.[8] Subsequently, Costanza told Carter about the request and of her intention to meet with gay rights activists in the White House in the near future. When Carter did not object, Costanza abandoned her fear and hesitation.[9] Costanza and Haft then began planning the meeting and invited Voeller and O'Leary of the NGTF to informal and preliminary discussion at the White House. This preliminary meeting took place on 8 February 1977, the first time that gay rights activists had entered the White House for talks. The meeting lasted two hours and its main topic was discriminatory policy against gay people on the part of various federal

3 Bockris, *Andy Warhol*, 305; Jo Ann Lewis, 'An Artful Thank-You from President Carter', *WP*, 15 June 1977.

4 William Steding, *Presidential Faith and Foreign Policy: Jimmy Carter the Disciple and Ronald Reagan the Alchemist* (New York: Palgrave MacMillan, 2014), 48.

5 Various letters addressed to Costanza and Carter. MCI.

6 Faderman, *The Gay Revolution*, 299–300; Haft, author interview; Mattingly, *A Feminist*, 109.

7 Haft, author interview.

8 Letter, NGTF to Margaret Costanza, 1 February 1977. MCSF, [GR: C], JCPL.

9 Haft, author interview.

departments and agencies.[10] O'Leary and Voeller were asked by Costanza to make 'a full, formal presentation of the needs of gays in the federal area to her and her staff' at a meeting scheduled for March.[11]

After the February meeting, on the same day, Costanza wrote to O'Leary and Voeller, 'I have been impressed with the presentation you have made and wish to explore more fully the role my office and I can play; specifically in facilitating meetings with those persons who will be most helpful to you in the areas we have reviewed', while she assigned Haft to work with the NGTF 'in setting-up the specific development of the agenda'.[12] The NGTF characterized the meeting in a letter to its members as 'very successful and promising', while it described the forthcoming official meeting as 'the biggest opportunity in our movement's history', which would address discrimination in areas including housing, the military, federal prisons and employment.[13] The NGTF also distributed to the press copies of Costanza's letter to the organization along with a press release that read, 'For the first time in the history of the United States, a top-level official at the White House has met with representatives of this nation's second-largest minority, the estimated 20 million lesbians and gay men'.[14]

As a result of the announcement of the forthcoming meeting, the NGTF received mail from all around the country offering congratulations, encouragement and suggestions. The NGTF said that everyone in the organization felt 'very excited' about the meeting, which it considered to be 'the first major step in a series of meetings that will bring about some real changes for the gay community'.[15] Costanza, Haft and the NGTF began making their respective preparations for the meeting, which was clearly going to attract huge attention from the media. For her efforts, Costanza was hailed by the NGTF as a 'friend in the White House'.[16] The meeting garnered enthusiastic support from gay organizations across the country.[17] For example, the Alice B. Toklas Memorial Club, the first registered lesbian, gay, bisexual and transgender club for Democrats in the United States, wrote to Carter praising him for taking a stand on the issue of gay rights and for his 'willingness to take action in this heretofore neglected area of human rights', something, they said, that 'no other world leader had done'.[18]

Many conservative Christians were displeased with the news, although not all religious organizations objected.[19] While American Catholics were broadly opposed to homosexuality, they generally adopted a more compassionate stance than the evangelical right. For example, the bishop of Michigan, H. Coleman McGehee Jr, wrote to Carter to indicate his approval of the meeting and the administration's move towards amending policies that currently discriminated against gay people. He felt, he

10 Letter, Midge Costanza to Ms. O'Leary and Mr. Voeller, 8 February 1977. SWSF, NGTF Correspondence, JCPL; 'NGTF Meets with White House Aide', *GN*, March 1977.
11 Letter, Jean O'Leary and Bruce Voeller to 'Dear friends', 9 February 1977. NGTFR, B.2, F.60, CU.
12 Letter, Midge Costanza to Ms. O'Leary and Mr. Voeller, 8 February 1977. SWSF, NGTF Correspondence, JCPL.
13 Letter, Jean O'Leary and Bruce Voeller to 'Dear friends', 9 February 1977. NGTFR, B.2, F.60, CU.
14 'Carter Aide to Meet with Gay Activists', *Miami News*, 15 February 1977.
15 Letter, NGTF to the participants of White House meeting, 15 March 1977. SWSF, [Gay] CR, JCPL.
16 'A Friend in the White House', *The Advocate*, 23 March 1977.
17 See letters of support at MCSF [GR: P], JCPL
18 Letter, D. K. Hughes-Oldenburg to President Carter, 3 March 1977. MCSF, [GR: P], JCPL.
19 See letters in MCSF [GR: P] and in RLMSF, GI, both in JCPL.

wrote, that the administration was moving 'in a valuable direction', and he was 'proud' of Carter's leadership 'in this and many other ways'.[20] Carter also received several letters from Congressmen such as John L. Burton, Donald M. Fraser, Edward I. Koch and Henry A. Waxman supporting his efforts.[21] Paul N. McCloskey Jr, a Republican member of the House of Representatives, was the most enthusiastic, expressing to Carter his 'delight' that he would entertain a meeting with the gay community in the White House and characterized this as a 'courageous political initiative'.[22]

However, the forthcoming White House meeting also created some tension within the gay community as to who would participate in it, a decision that was in the hands of the NGTF. Numerous activists, from all over the country, asked to be included. For example, Clayton Wells, the Secretary of the SDC, asked O'Leary to include Morris Kight, the Club's co-founder and one of the most prominent gay rights activists of the time;[23] he was not included on account of his outspokenness and some of his beliefs, which the NGTF considered to be too extreme for the White House.[24] This decision added fuel to the emerging tension between the New York-based NGTF and gay rights activists on the West Coast. Charles Brydon, who succeeded Voeller as Co-Executive Director of the NGTF in 1979, later diagnosed this rivalry as follows:

> There was this antagonism here between East and West. Generally the people in California had this attitude that they were far more successful. They didn't need NGTF. And of course we're dealing with the people in New York City who needed NGTF and then resented it at the same time.[25]

David Goodstein, *The Advocate*'s publisher, also based in California, was another who wanted to participate; he got in touch with Costanza and asked to be included in the activists' delegation. Unlike the other activists, Goodstein had not written to the NGTF as he was involved in an ongoing feud with Voeller and the organization generally.[26] O'Leary told Costanza that there was 'no way' that Goodstein should be included, and he was not.[27] Goodstein did not take kindly to this and for about the next two years *The Advocate* downplayed or did not mention the efforts and achievements in gay rights of both the NGTF and Carter's administration, in contrast to its effusive praise since the election. The newspaper later changed course, after Goodstein was invited

20 Letter, Reverend H. Coleman McGehee Jr. to President Carter, 7 March 1977. MCSF, [GR: P], JCPL.

21 These letters can be found in MCSF [GR: P], JCPL.

22 Letter, Paul N. McCloskey, Jr. to President Carter, 8 March 1977. MCSF [GR: P], JCPL.

23 Letter, Clayton Wells to Jean O'Leary, 18 February 1977. SDCR, B.1, F.21, ONE NLGA, USC.

24 Clay, author interview.

25 Charles Brydon interview to Eric Marcus, 19 November 1989. Eric Marcus's Personal Collection.

26 Several interviewees, such as Bush, Bunch, Clay and Ginny Vida mentioned this feud (as have some published sources, such as William B. Turner, 'Mirror Images: Lesbian/Gay Civil Rights in the Carter and Reagan Administration', in John D'Emilio et al. (eds), *Creating Change: Sexuality, Public Policy, and Civil Rights*, New York: St. Martin's Press, 2000), which seems to have had a personalistic aspect involving Goodstein and Voeller, but none were able to provide more substantive details. Whatever its origin, the issue of power and priority among gay rights groups and their leading personalities was enough to keep it going (Bunch, Bush, Clay and Vida, author interviews).

27 Clendinen and Negourney, *Out*, 286.

to Carter's White House,[28] and Larry Bush, who wrote for *The Advocate*, became the first openly gay reporter accredited to the White House in late 1978 (see Chapter 10).[29] Eventually a larger-than-planned fourteen-member delegation was formed, consisting of Pokey Anderson, Charles Brydon, Charlotte Bunch, Ray Hartman, Frank Kameny, William B. Kelley, Elaine Noble, Reverend Troy Perry, Achebe Betty Powell, George Raya, Myra Riddell, Charlotte Spitzer, and Voeller and O'Leary.[30]

Before the meeting, another meeting of note took place in the White House. On 10 March, Carter and Mondale met with the Ad Hoc Coalition for Women, a coalition consisting of representatives of fifty women's groups. Among those invited was O'Leary as a representative of the NGTF, and thus of lesbian women. It was the first time that an openly gay person, a person representing lesbian women, and indeed a representative of any gay rights organization, had been invited to, and attended at, the White House for official and direct talks with the president. Topics discussed at the meeting included the appointment of women to federal posts, the Equal Rights Amendment, and the creation of a women's advocacy cabinet post. O'Leary commented that the meeting had been a productive one and that she had been impressed with the responses from Carter and Mondale. She said: 'Both Carter and Mondale expressed a sincere interest and commitment to the issues discussed, especially the ERA and to strengthening enforcement procedures for existing sex discrimination legislation'.[31]

The March Meeting: 'What just happened?'

The much-anticipated and highly consequential meeting (which will be mentioned in numerous places below, and will henceforward be referred to as the 'March 1977 Meeting') took place on Saturday 26 March in the White House's Roosevelt Room, and lasted almost three hours instead of the planned ninety minutes. Costanza had chosen a Saturday for the meeting to make it easier to attend, as most of the activists had full-time jobs and some had to travel some distance, and because she wanted to use the Roosevelt Room, the room where all the important meetings in the White House took place, which was available for the required length of time on a Saturday. Carter was at Camp David.[32] Costanza later affirmed that his absence was coincidental and that 'under no circumstances did I keep it from him'.[33] Carter had given Costanza the freedom to meet in the White House with anyone she pleased at any time, and had, as she remarked in a speech in November 1978, 'accepted her efforts to hold a meeting of the NGTF in the White House'.[34]

28 Fred Fejes, *Gay Rights and Moral Panic: The Origins of America's Debate on Homosexuality* (New York: Palgrave MacMillan, 2008), 106.
29 Bush, author interview.
30 'Fourteen Gays Attend White House Meeting', *It's Time*, Apr–May 1977. JWSF, NGTFJW, JCPL.
31 'O'Leary on IWY Commission', *It's Time*, Apr–May 1977. JWSF, NGTFJW, JCPL.
32 Costanza interviews to Clendinen. MCI.
33 'Leaders Recount Historic White House Meeting 30 Years Later', National LGBTQ Task Force, May 2007. MCI.
34 Mayumi Tsutakawa, 'Midge Costanza. Dynamo Lauds Gay Win', *Seattle Post*, 22 November 1978.

Figure 4 The participants of the ground-breaking March 1977 White House; (clockwise from centre) Midge Costanza (back to the camera), Robert Malson, Jean O'Leary, William B. Kelley, Achebe Betty Powell, Charles Brydon, Charlotte Spitzer, Myra Riddell, Cooki Lutkefedder, Ray Hartman, Pokey Anderson, George Raya, Frank Kameny, Troy Perry, Charlotte Bunch, Elaine Noble, Bruce Voeller and Marilyn Haft. WHSPC, nlc00800.8. JCPL.

Two other White House officials attended, Haft and Malson, while Cooki Lutkefedder, a civil rights specialist with the Office of Domestic Affairs of the Democratic National Committee, also attended as an observer.[35] Walking into the White House, Brydon thought, 'Incredible! We're Here! The heartbeat of the country'. Perry thought, 'I am a homosexual, and I am walking through the front door of the White House, where I've been invited for coffee and a chat'.[36] The meeting opened with Costanza's welcoming words: 'It is a pleasure to meet you. I'm sorry that it has taken so long for you to come into a house that belongs to you as much as it does to anyone in this country'[37] and continued, 'The President believes that human rights will be the new weapon. He knows that he cannot support human rights overseas unless he supports it here'.[38] Costanza assured her guests of Carter's approval of the meeting (Figure 4).[39]

The activists then made a series of representations and requests. Their main focus was on government agencies and departments that they felt had discriminatory policy, a long list consisting of the Civil Service Commission, the Commission on Civil

[35] 'NGTF-Federal Agency Meetings Set Second White House Conference in September', News from NGTF, 31 March 1977. NGTFR, B.145, F.47, CU.

[36] Faderman, *The Gay Revolution*, 298–9.

[37] 'Costanza Praises Gay Leaders: "Sorry It Took So Long"', *NewsWest*, 14–28 April 1977.

[38] NGTF-White House meeting-3/26/77, Notes by Bob Malson. MCI.

[39] 'Homosexuals Confer with Carter Aide', *San Francisco Examiner*, 27 March 1977.

Rights, the Department of Defense, the Department of Health, Education and Welfare (HEW), the Department of Housing and Urban Development (HUD), the Federal Bureau of Prisons, the Federal Communications Commission (FCC), the Immigration and Naturalization Service (INS), the Internal Revenue Service (IRS) and the State Department.[40] The NGTF requested the White House's assistance in arranging a series of meetings with all these bodies,[41] and the delegation made the following specific requests:

- A change of policy in the armed forces so that gay people could be allowed to serve and the upgrading of all the dishonourable discharges for gay veterans (the NGTF was aware that Carter was about to launch his Special Discharge Review Program; see Chapter 9), and wished the programme to include those discharged on account of their sexual preferences);
- Reversal of the IRS policy of denying tax exempt status to non-profit gay organizations;
- Provision of HEW funding for gay counselling and health problems, including research on hepatitis;
- Amendment of HUD regulations to include a requirement that all federal housing grants include a policy forbidding discrimination against gay people, and generally ensuring that HUD provided equal access to housing opportunities for gay citizens;
- Reversal of the INS policy which did not allow gay people into the country, to take up permanent residency and to become naturalized citizens;
- Improvement of the conditions of gay prisoners;
- Expansion of the Commission on Civil Rights' jurisdiction to include discrimination on the basis of sexual orientation, as well as an expansion of the Civil Rights Act in order to eliminate discrimination on the basis of sexual orientation;
- Ending the State Department's policy of denying security clearances to gay employees;
- Investigating and ending Civil Service Commission discrimination against gay people in hiring;
- Support for research in the area of homosexuality, training of mental health professionals in the area of human sexuality, and educational programmes in sex education;
- Assistance to the gay community 'in its effort to obtain full recognition by the FCC as a group whose right to access to the broadcast media is firmly established';[42]

40 Memorandum, Margaret Costanza to President Carter, 8 April 1977. SWSF, [Gay] CR, JCPL.

41 Memorandum, Marilyn Haft to Margaret Costanza, 11 April 1977. SWSF, [Gay] CR, JCPLI.

42 Memorandums, Marilyn Haft to Margaret Costanza, 11 April 1977 and Margaret Costanza to President Carter, 8 April 1977, both in SWSF, [Gay] CR, JCPL; George Raya's presentation on Health, Education and Welfare, 26 March 1977. SWSF, NGTF–Health 3/77 [O/A 4496], JCPL; NGTF, 'Needs of the Gay Community with Respect to FCC and Community Ascertainment', 26 March 1977. SWSF, [NGTF: FCC1], JCPL; NGTF presentation on fair housing policy, 26 March

The activists also made presentations on vandalism against gay churches and on the psychological oppression suffered by gays and their parents because of exclusionary social perceptions, and they presented Costanza with a dossier of evidentiary materials on the issues discussed.[43]

Malson responded that the delegation had made a 'brilliant and very moving' presentation. Lutkefedder, who had attended many such White House sessions, judged this one to be 'the most professional job I've seen'.[44] Costanza, Haft and Malson assured their guests that they were going to take immediate action on all the matters they brought up, and committed to setting up meetings between the NGTF and all the federal agencies in question.[45] Costanza, who was well prepared, also informed the activists that she had already set up a meeting between the NGTF and Attorney General Griffin Bell and Assistant Attorney General Patricia Wald, and that she had assigned Malson and Haft as liaisons between the Bureau of Prisons and the activists. She also handed the activists a paper with the contact details of the relevant people in the federal agencies and elsewhere.[46] Costanza also stated that Carter had pledged that 'sensitivity to the rights of gay people will be very seriously considered in considering nominees for vacancies' in the federal departments, commissions and agencies.[47] The parties exchanged telephone numbers and arranged to meet again in the White House in September 1977 to assess the progress of their agenda and to stay in touch and hold additional meetings if necessary.[48] Leaving the White House, the gay rights activists were still astonished that they had been there. Voeller asked O'Leary and Perry, 'Can you believe what just happened?' Moreover, they had been there before conservatives and homophobic activists like Anita Bryant, who had just begun her crusade against gay rights. Thirty years later, Perry remembered 'how incredibly gracious Midge Costanza and the White House staff were to us'.[49]

Immediately after the meeting, Costanza spoke movingly to journalists about the testimony she had heard about discrimination, and affirmed that the administration viewed the situation facing gay people as an important human rights issue.[50] When asked if she thought that the meeting would be criticized for affording the prestige of the White House to the gay community, she replied,

> I just wish that the citizens of this nation could have joined me in that room to listen to the examples of oppression I heard today. Perhaps the issue of homosexuality

1977. SWSF, [NGTF–Fair Housing] 3/77 [O/A 4496], JCPL; Lou Romano, 'Gays Meet with Carter Aides', *The Blade*, April 1977.

43 Memorandum, Margaret Costanza to President Carter, 8 April 1977. SWSF, [Gay] CR, JCPL.

44 'NGTF-Federal Agency Meetings Set Second White House Conference in September', News from NGTF, 31 March 1977. NGTFR, B.145, F.47, CU.

45 Bunch, Haft and Perry, author interviews.

46 Details of contacts in Federal Agencies, undated. MCI; 'NGTF-Federal Agency Meetings Set Second White House Conference in September', News from NGTF, 31 March 1977. NGTFR, B.145, F.47, CU; Lou Romano, 'Gays Meet with Carter Aides', *The Blade*, April 1977.

47 'NGTF-Federal Agency Meetings Set Second White House Conference in September', News from NGTF, 31 March 1977. NGTFR, B.145, F.47, CU.

48 Haft and Perry, author interviews; Lou Romano, 'Gays Meet with Carter Aides', *The Blade*, April 1977.

49 'Leaders Recount Historic White House Meeting 30 Years Later', National LGBTQ Task Force, May 2007.

50 Austin Scott, 'Carter Aide Meets with Gay Activists', *WP*, 27 March 1977.

> would be better understood and perhaps more widely accepted in this country if they could have heard what I did.[51]

Costanza told the *Washington Post* that Spitzer's presentation (on parents of gay children and the discrimination they had faced) was 'the most moving' and that 'there weren't too many dry eyes in the room after she spoke'.[52] When she was asked whether she had Carter's permission for this meeting and what the president thought of gay people, she replied, 'I am not in the position where I need permission to do anything . . . the point is homosexuals are being discriminated against; the point is not their sexual views'.[53] At an NGTF press conference only a few hours after the meeting, O'Leary stated that this was

> The first time in the history of this country that a President has seen fit to acknowledge the rights and needs of some 28 million Americans. This meeting was a happy milestone on the road to full equality under law for gay women and men, and we are highly optimistic that it will soon lead to complete fulfilment of President Carter's pledge to end all forms of Federal discrimination on the basis of sexual orientation.[54]

The meeting brought the issue of gay rights to the forefront of American politics, making it a national issue. O'Leary and Shilts characterized it as 'historic' and Voeller said that it demonstrated Carter's 'courageous commitment' to human rights, comparing it to 'the type of change' initiated by President Lincoln in freeing the slaves and President Truman in desegregating the military. Kameny said, 'it looks as if we will be having activist assistance from the topmost levels of government. I am very, very optimistic about the outcome'. Kameny also highlighted that this meeting marked the first time that anyone in the White House had responded to a request for a meeting with gay rights activists in all the years of repeated requests, starting with President Kennedy.[55] The day after the meeting, Noble said that she was 'quite amazed' and 'surprised that the Carter administration made as many commitments as it did, to open doors for us', also comparing the situation favourably to that during the Kennedy administration, when all of their requests for a meeting had been ignored, adding, 'we have no illusions that anything is going to happen overnight, [but] a lot of us have picketed on the outside. Now we see ourselves inside the fence'.[56]

An NGTF press release that followed sounded a triumphant note, announcing the follow-up meeting that would be held in September 1977, that Costanza would recommend a meeting with Carter himself, that various crucial issues had been discussed, and that future meetings between the NGTF and a range of government

51 'Costanza Praises Gay Leaders: "Sorry It Took So Long"', *NewsWest*, 14–28 April 1977.
52 Lou Romano, 'Gays Meet with Carter Aides', *The Blade*, April 1977.
53 Faderman, *The Gay Revolution*, 304.
54 'Gays Optimistic after Historic White House Session', News from NGTF, 26 March 1977. NGTFR, B.36, F.24, CU.
55 Lou Romano, 'Gays Meet with Carter Aides', *The Blade*, April 1977; Randy Shilts, 'White House Meeting. Concrete Results Soon?' *The Advocate*, 20 April 1977.
56 Austin Scott, 'Carter Aide Meets with Gay Activists', *WP*, 27 March 1977; Lou Romano, 'Gays Meet with Carter Aides', *The Blade*, April 1977.

officials would be held. The press release further stated: 'Ms. Costanza also promised to relay several special requests to the President, who was asked to "champion the cause" of human rights for gay Americans the way he has done for oppressed minorities around the world'.[57] The NGTF had many reasons to feel optimistic and was grateful to Carter for his efforts. In its *Action Report* of April/May 1977, it stated that 'it never hurts to show appreciation', urging the gay community to 'send letters of thanks and encouragement to President Carter' for opening the White House and the federal agencies to them.[58]

Over the two weeks following the meeting, Costanza sent Carter two detailed memorandums on the meeting and what was discussed in it, including the activists' requests. She also informed him that she had agreed to help the NGTF with its requests, including by facilitating meetings between the organization and federal departments, and that they were going to meet again with her in the White House to report on their progress.[59] Carter agreed with Costanza's plans, and she and Haft began working to arrange these meetings.[60] According to Costanza, Carter did not respond in any kind of explicit way to the March meeting. She said that there was 'no special reaction . . . he didn't say gee, that was awful, why did you do it. Or gee, that was great, I'm glad you did it'.[61] According to Haft and Mattingly, Carter never complained to Costanza about the meeting or about her efforts on gay rights.* Furthermore, Costanza 'vehemently rejected' the notion that the meeting was a result of her relationship with O'Leary and insisted that her motives for organizing it 'stemmed from an overall commitment to social justice'.[62] In an interview with Jim Marko of the *Gay Community News* two months after the meeting, Costanza reflected on its direct impact on the gay community in America and its relationship with the White House:

> At the outset you have to admit that simply the symbolic gesture of holding the meeting has brought about a great deal of activity. There has been a rising of consciousness and new organization in the gay community. Gays had not been welcome or invited ever before to the White House. Concretely? There are meetings being held with the Justice Department, the Immigration and Naturalization Service, the Department of Housing and Urban Development and other agencies. Gays are getting this and that's concrete. There is a commitment from me and from these agencies to continue the dialogue with the gay community.[63]

57 'NGTF-Federal Agency Meetings Set Second White House Conference in September', News from NGTF, 31 March 1977. NGTFR, B.145, F.47, CU.

58 'White House Follow-Up', NGTF Action Report, April–May 1977. JWSF, NGTFJW, JCPL.

59 Memorandums, Margaret Costanza to President Carter, 28 March and 8 April 1977; both in MCI.

60 Haft, author interview.

61 Costanza interviews to Clendinen. MCI.

62 Doreen J. Mattingly and Ashley Boyd, 'Bringing Gay and Lesbian Activism to the White House: Midge Costanza and the National Gay Task Force Meeting', *Journal of Lesbian Studies* 17 (2013): 366.

63 Jim Marko, 'Midge Costanza: Gay Rights Proponent at the White House', *GCN*, 9 July 1977.

Uplift, backlash and division

The meeting received extensive coverage in the mainstream press and was reported on all major television and radio networks. Ron Gold, co-founder of the NGTF, said the meeting would 'have an important psychological effect. It was on television and people saw all these pariahs entering the temple'.[64] At a time when the gay rights movement was still struggling for visibility and legitimacy, the meeting was a turning point, as it offered both. Two days after the meeting, the *New York Post* confirmed this in an article entitled 'From Closet to Street to Respect'.[65] Voeller also highlighted the vast symbolic importance of the meeting, 'even if specific actions turn out to be slow in coming, the symbolic act of meeting directly across the hall from the Oval Office, in a room regularly used for meetings of the National Security Council, gave gay leaders a lift'.[66] The gay community also finally had access to the highest officials in government, while in Costanza, Haft, Malson and Wishman it had found friends who could help it achieve its goals. As Larry Bush accurately observed, this 'was the first time gays had talked to their government outside the courtroom'.[67]

However, the rapid enhancement of the visibility and legitimacy of the cause also produced 'backlash' effects, as it rallied homophobic activists, and even ordinary, not especially politicized Americans, to express their horror that the gay community had been in the White House. Conservative voices railed against homosexuality and its supposed pernicious impact on society. Evangelicals were particularly unhappy; several prominent leaders denounced Carter and wrote to him expressing their clear disappointment with him for allowing such a meeting to take place.[68] Catholic Americans had already expressed their horror before the meeting. The headline on the front page of the *National Catholic Register* proclaimed that 'Carter Aide Meets Gays', and the article began by stating, 'One of President Carter's top assistants will meet with ten members of a sexual deviate organization' and quoted Gary Potter, executive director of Catholics for Christian Political Action, who stated his opposition to any actions that would confer 'respectability or social acceptance on the practice of homosexuality'. Potter also urged 'Catholics and other Christians, especially family people', to 'write letters to the President and send copies to their senators and representatives expressing their strong belief that as taxpayers they are opposed to the public employment of anyone who acknowledges himself or herself as a practicing homosexual'.[69]

Costanza and Carter received numerous homophobic letters of 'criticism and abuse', as Costanza put it,[70] from irate citizens complaining about the meeting.[71] Costanza responded to all of the letters she received, defending the meeting and repeating that it had taken place 'in keeping with the President's commitment that access be given to

64 Robert Lipsyte, 'From Closet to Street to Respect', *NYP*, 28 March 1977.
65 Ibid.
66 Randy Shilts, 'White House Meeting. Concrete Results Soon?' *The Advocate*, 20 April 1977.
67 Larry Bush, 'White House Claims Solid Record on Gay Issues', *The Sentinel*, 16 May 1980.
68 See numerous letters in MCI and in JCPL, e.g. JWSF, GI-HC and MCSF, [H-GRPH].
69 'Carter Aide Meets Gays', *National Catholic Register*, 27 March 1977.
70 Letter, Midge Costanza to James Woodward, undated. MCI.
71 See numerous letters in MCI and in JCPL, e.g. JWSF, GI-HC, JCPL.

all groups'.[72] On 27 March, just a day after the meeting, Jody Powell, the White House Press Secretary, appeared on CBS's news programme *Face The Nation* and was asked about it. Powell defended the meeting, being 'extremely positive' about it.[73] Haft, and Powell again, publicly defended the meeting and the right of gay people to equal rights and to be heard.[74]

A further effect of the meeting was to exacerbate some divisions within the gay community's organizations, as the NGTF had been the principal interlocutor with the administration, although it was not the only one. *The Advocate* and its publisher Goodstein, excluded from the delegation, could not ignore the meeting altogether but attempted to downplay its significance by relegating a report on it to page 35. Nevertheless, the report was substantial: under the title 'White House Meeting: Concrete Results Soon?' O'Leary was quoted as saying:

> In the next two or three years we will see federal agencies one by one reverse their policies, once they see that it is not just us, but 20 million people supporting us. [Gay people can expect] a couple of victories and a lot of attitude change because of the publicity.[75]

Shortly afterwards, however, Goodstein banned the NGTF's advertisements from *The Advocate*. This led to a complete breakdown of the relationship between the NGTF and the magazine and the feud continued almost throughout Carter's presidency (see also Chapter 13).[76] As for O'Leary's statement, it would turn out to be a bit off the mark: as we will see, thanks to the combined efforts of the NGTF and Carter's administration, as well as Carter's appointments to the federal agencies, it would take just a few months to see the first reversals of discriminatory policies.

In May 1978, after a series of major accomplishments for gay rights by the NGTF, Randy Shilts attacked the organization with a long article in *The Advocate*, entitled 'Political Lion or Paper Tiger?' Shilts attempted to downplay the NGTF's success so far. Although over a year had passed since the March 1977 Meeting, he wrote that some members of the gay community were still unhappy with the selection process; most because they were excluded from it, others because they felt that those who had been selected were not 'experts' in the areas they had covered in their presentations, and as a consequence they had lost an opportunity to adequately present issues of concern for the gay community. Among the targets for criticism were Raya, who had presented the issue of gay health needs, and Bunch, who had presented the issue of discriminatory immigration and naturalization policies. The critics argued that both knew little or nothing about the subjects they had talked about and that Bunch was selected to attend the meeting simply because she was on the NGTF's board and Raya because of his close

72 Letter, Margaret Costanza to Joanna Clark, 19 May 1977. MCSF, [H-GRPH], JCPL.

73 Memorandum, Richard Reiman to Margaret Costanza, 28 March 1977. MCI.

74 'Costanza Praises Gay Leaders: "Sorry It Took So Long"', *NewsWest*, 14–28 April 1977; 'Homosexual Leaders Meet at White House with Presidential Aide to Discuss Discrimination in Federal Law', *NYT*, 27 March 1977; George Mendenhall, 'White House Opens Doors', *BAR*, 31 March 1977.

75 Randy Shilts, 'White House Meeting. Concrete Results Soon?' *The Advocate*, 20 April 1977.

76 Bush, author interview; Clendinen and Negourney, *Out*, 286–7; Turner, 'Mirror Images', 14.

ties with the organization. Anthony Sullivan, a gay immigrant from Australia who had been fighting for naturalization for several years, was reported to be very critical of the selection of Bunch, arguing that with this the NGTF had 'sold gay aliens down the river' and 'was more concerned with getting its own name in the paper than helping us out'.[77]

Beyond *The Advocate*'s feud, other members of the gay community were unhappy with the NGTF as they felt that it was not representative of the entire community, that it was not as forceful as it should have been, and that its members cared more for their own power and visibility than for securing concrete results for gay people. Some thought they had a privileged relationship with the White House, mostly because of what they alleged to be the 'preferential treatment' given to Voeller and O'Leary.[78] An example is an angry letter to Haft by Gary Van Ooteghem, co-chairperson of the GRNL. He wrote:

> It is becoming extremely obvious that both Bruce Voeller and Jean O'Leary have pretty much 'locked out' anyone but themselves from ever reaching into The White House – due, it appears, to both you and Costanza and your combined effective screening process. Call it what you like, but in aiding them in becoming the sole representative and contacts of the gay community you are, in fact, inadvertently doing our movement a great disservice. We do not need more power-hungry czars, but less. . . . You and Costanza, both should also realize that many of us out here are witnessing the erosion of our own access to the president . . . it is absolutely mad to believe that only those two can and will represent all of us.[79]

Bunch, Clay, Ron Gold and Ginny Vida, prominent members of the NGTF at the time, argued that the criticism of the organization stemmed mostly from 'jealousy' rather than mistakes on its part.[80] Gold said in 1977, 'They're really worried that we have too much power. But if we have power, it's because we work. If they worked, they'd had power, too'.[81] The criticism of the NGTF was in any case somewhat inaccurate as other gay rights organizations, including the GRNL and the MCC, and individuals who had no connection with the NGTF, had participated in the meeting, as they would in several others. With regard to the selection process for the meeting, Bunch and Clay pointed out that the aim of the fourteen activists was to simply raise the issues of concern of the gay community and they did not really need to be 'experts' on the subjects.* But Bunch acknowledged to the author,

> What Randy Shilts said has a *grain* of truth. Whenever a group like the NGTF gets an inroad into the White House and then that evolves into something larger, of course, there are ways in which that shuts out some other people. I don't think the

77 Randy Shilts, 'Political Lion or Paper Tiger?', *The Advocate*, 31 May 1978.
78 Apuzzo, Bastow, Bunch, Bush, Jones-Hennin and McReynolds, author interviews.
79 Letter, Gary Van Ooteghem to Marilyn Haft, 31 August 1977. JWSF, GR-FG, JCPL.
80 Bunch, Clay and Vida, author interviews; Randy Shilts, 'Political Lion or Paper Tiger?', *The Advocate*, 31 May 1978.
81 Randy Shilts, 'Political Lion or Paper Tiger?', *The Advocate*, 31 May 1978.

> NGTF was *intentionally* shutting out other people, but it's true. In a way, Randy Shilts is *right* to some extent.*

In other words, the fact that the March 1977 Meeting portended such dramatic change inevitably created tensions and resentments. In practical politics, the emergence of the gay community from its 'pariah' status could not be a process of uniform advance across all fronts and on the part of all organizational actors equally; the leading front would tend to acquire advantage, and others would perceive disadvantage. As unfortunate and petty as they might seem, these differences were themselves a sign of the absorption of the gay community into ordinary politics; a sign, in other words, of the success of the meeting in achieving a significant degree of political incorporation.

☙

Positive evaluations of the March 1977 Meeting nevertheless abounded, and these, as later chapters will document, would prove to be fully justified. The administration moved quickly to address all the requests made by the activists at the meeting; O'Leary and Voeller correctly later argued that it 'served as a prelude to considerable progress in ending anti-Gay discrimination at Federal level'.[82] But symbolic effects were even more immediate. As Costanza later recalled, 'Never before had gay rights been an issue discussed within the walls of the White House as a national issue. For most gay men and women in this nation – and the world – it provided a level of pride that had never been felt before'.[83] In O'Leary's words,

> this meeting meant a lot to the whole community. It meant that we had been recognized by the highest institutional establishment in our country. And for gay people who were looking for signs, for symbols, for recognition, for anything along those lines that would make their lives valid, it was a wonderful breakthrough.[84]

[82] 'NGTF Leaders Express Regret over Costanza Resignation', *AGN*, 11 August 1978.

[83] Don L. Volk, 'Community Interview: Midge Costanza', *L.A. Edge*, 15–29 June 1983.

[84] Eric Marcus, *Making History: The Struggle for Gay and Lesbian Equal Rights: An Oral History* (New York: HarperPerennial, 1993), 270.

4

Opening the White House to the gay community II

Broadening the agenda

This chapter continues chronologically from Chapter 3 and shows that despite the departure of Costanza, and a short period of relative inactivity, the radically new openness of the White House continued to develop, indeed to intensify. Administration officials began to recognize different components of the gay community and the gay rights movement, whose appearance marked the continuing political development of the movement itself. The White House started to reach out more proactively, to the extent of visiting gay groups where they lived, and asking them for input rather than responding to requests and demands.

After Costanza: 'A kind of quiet period'?

By September 1978, Costanza and Haft had left the OPL. In October 1978, Carter appointed Sarah Weddington, General Counsel at the Department of Agriculture and a widely known supporter of feminist causes, as his new special assistant. Weddington enjoyed a high profile on account of her role as legal counsel to Jane Roe (Norma McCorvey) in the *Roe v. Wade* case, where her argument had achieved a radical liberalization of abortion law. Her main task was to promote the ratification of the ERA, but she also took on the part of Costanza's portfolio that was focused on interest groups, including the NGTF. Weddington became a key staff member on women's issues in Carter's administration.[1]

Shortly after her appointment, Weddington invited the NGTF and NOW to the White House for an introductory meeting. It took place on 27 October 1978, with O'Leary and Voeller representing the NGTF, and Eleanor Smeal and Arlie Scott, its President and Vice President, NOW. Weddington assured the gay rights activists that although her top priority was the ERA and economic issues of interest to women, she would continue working with them on gay rights issues, including facilitating meetings

1 Weddington, author interview.

between the activists and federal agencies and departments, and on the aims that were set out at the March 1977 Meeting.[2]

After the introductory meeting, Weddington, and Wexler who had now also been tasked by Carter to deal with gay rights issues, made no new attempt to reach out to the gay community, while the departures of Voeller and then of O'Leary as Co-Executive Directors of the NGTF in early 1979 led to a temporary breakdown in communication between the organization and the White House.[3] Weddington did not share Costanza's passion about gay rights and later suggested that she was going to channel any requests to 'the proper agencies', and would focus on women's issues and the ERA.[4] Gradually, Wexler took over the issue of gay rights, while Bob Malson and Allison Thomas became the White House's liaisons with the gay community. Nevertheless, although Weddington went on to play a largely secondary role with regard to gay rights, she turned out to be attentive to gay rights issues that were brought to her, and established a close relationship with Lucia Valeska, who had replaced O'Leary as Co-Executive Director of the NGTF. In late June or early July 1979, Weddington accepted an invitation to visit the organization's office in New York.[5]

The hiatus in communication between the NGTF and the White House was thus short-lived. The relationship that existed prior to Costanza's departure was quickly restored, with Carter's administration maintaining its open-door policy for gay rights activists and meetings between the two sides continuing to take place regularly in the White House until the end of Carter's presidency. The turning point came in mid-1979 when Charles Brydon and Valeska took over as Co-Executive Directors of the NGTF, and they both immediately resumed contact with the White House.[6] In June 1980, Brydon and Valeska stated that they still had 'friends at the White House' and were still working with them 'on a variety of issues'.[7] In May 1980, Wexler told *The Sentinel*, one of the biggest gay newspapers at the time:

> There may have been a kind of quiet period there. We weren't being approached, nor were we reaching out . . . When Charlie and Lucia came to us again and said we need to discuss some of these things that have sort of been sitting here, we found out two things. One, that a number of things had been done, without any fanfare but in a very substantive way. Second, that there certainly was no problem in responding to other issues that were raised in a very prompt way, which we did.[8]

2 'Midge's Gay Rights Work Continues', *AGN*, undated. NGTFR, B.152, F.49, CU; 'Weddington Continues Efforts of Costanza', *The Advocate*, 27 December 1978; 'Weddington Tells NGTF She'll Continue Work on Gay Concerns', News from NGTF, n.d. NGTFR, B.36, F.107, CU.

3 Voeller, co-founder of the NGTF, announced his resignation in November 1978, with effect in January 1979 (Scott P. Anderson, 'Voeller Quits NGTF', *The Advocate*, 15 November 1978). O'Leary, citing personal reasons, announced in December 1978 that she would leave her position in June 1979 ('O'Leary to Resign as Co-Executive Director of NGTF in June', News from NGTF, 12 December 1978, NGTFR, B.36, F.110, CU).

4 Larry Bush, 'White House Claims Solid Record on Gay Issues', *The Sentinel*, 16 May 1980.

5 Letter, Sarah Weddington to Jean O'Leary and Charles Brydon, 16 May 1979. NGTFR, B.144, F.57, CU; Weddington, author interview.

6 Larry Bush, 'White House Claims Solid Record on Gay Issues', *The Sentinel*, 16 May 1980.

7 Charles F. Brydon and Lucia Valeska, 'Notes from the Co-Execs', *It's Time*, May–June 1980, and 'White House Meetings', *It's Time*, May–June 1980, both in RMSF, G/L1, JCPL.

8 Larry Bush, 'White House Claims Solid Record on Gay Issues', *The Sentinel*, 16 May 1980.

In fact, the NGTF and the gay community's relationship became even stronger than it had been during Costanza's tenure, with the White House providing constant and unlimited access to several gay rights activists and organizations. At least fifteen meetings between the administration and gay rights activists took place after Costanza departed, in comparison to the five that had occurred during her time in the White House. Malson, Thomas, Jane Wales and Wexler provided the activists with constant telephone access, while the White House's facilitation of meetings between gay rights activists and federal agencies continued as before.[9] Very importantly, during Wexler's time in the White House and after Costanza's departure, Carter's administration made overtures to other parts of the gay community and other gay organizations, vitiating suggestions that the administration was displaying preferential treatment to the NGTF and had excluded other gay rights activists (see Chapter 3). Furthermore, in December 1979, Wexler, who, like Costanza, was aware of the importance of the White House's Roosevelt Room, welcomed there fifteen gay rights activists who presented the administration with a petition for gay rights (see Chapter 6).[10]

In February 1979, six months after Costanza's departure, Brydon confirmed the continuation of the relationship with the White House as he explained to fellow NGTF members in a memorandum that 'the White House project' remained 'the most important NGTF undertaking in terms of practical results benefiting lesbians and gay men'.[11] The NGTF on the first page of its May–June 1980 newsletter stated that 'these meetings continued on a variety of questions',[12] while in August 1980, the White House stated that 'the dialogue continues and will continue, and it has produced significant results'.[13] The same year, the NGTF highlighted the fact that Carter not only opened the White House doors to the gay community but also kept them open 'even after he got flack' from conservatives.[14]

On 10 December 1979, Brydon, Valeska and Larry Bush met at the White House with Carter's aides Mike Chanin, Malson, Diana Rock and Thomas. Among their demands was that Carter should himself meet with gay leaders.[15] Carter never personally met with a delegation of gay rights activists for official talks in the White House.[16] However, Carter met and had unofficial talks with them individually on several occasions. As already noted, an early conversation was with O'Leary on 10 March 1977, while a few months later he personally welcomed to the White House Rev. Bob Arthur, an openly gay preacher from the MCC who was there to meet with Costanza to discuss a number

9 See several documents at RMSF; for example, Tom Bastow note to Bob Malson, 27 November 1979. RMSF, GTFN1, JCPL.

10 OWHPS, 'NGTF Presents Petition to the White House', 20 December 1979. SESF, NGTF Presents Petition to White House – 12/20/79, JCPL; 'White House Meeting', *The Advocate*, 21 February 1980; 'White House Receives Gay Rights Petition', News from NGTF, 21 December 1979. ATSF, B.271, NGTF, JCPL.

11 Charles Brydon Memo, 6 February 1979. NGTFR, B.144, F.57, CU.

12 'White House Meetings', *It's Time*, May–June 1980: 1. RMSF, G/L1, JCPL.

13 WH memorandum: Talking points on gay issues, 5 August 1980. RMSF, G/L2, JCPL.

14 NGTF, 'What Has Jimmy Carter Ever Done for Gays?', 1980. NGTFR, B.6, F.3, CU.

15 Letter, Charles Brydon and Lucia Valeska to Bob Malson, 7 January 1980, and NGTF's Requests to the White House, 10 December 1979, both in RMSF, GH1, JCPL.

16 It was President Clinton, over fifteen years later, who became the first president to personally meet with a delegation of gay rights activists in the White House. Apuzzo, author interview.

of gay rights issues; Carter expressed to him his support for gay rights (see p. 191).* Carter had several further informal discussions in the White House about progress on gay rights with O'Leary, whom he had appointed to two presidential commissions. Carter was probably deliberately attempting to avoid further controversy on the matter by not meeting publicly with the leaders, while his administration was nevertheless doing much to advance gay rights. As Bourne said, 'politics is a balancing game and you have to try to accommodate everybody and not antagonize everybody'.*

Opening to racial minorities within the gay community

Although the NGTF was meant to represent the entire American gay community, gay people who belonged to racial minorities formed several other organizations as they felt they were not adequately represented by it. The biggest one was the National Coalition of Black Gays (NCBG), the first national organization for gay Black Americans. It was formed in 1978 by Rev. Delores P. Berry, Darlene Garner, John Gee, Gil Gerald, Louis Hughes, ABilly S. Jones-Hennin and Rev. Renee McCoy. Encouraged by the recently found success of the NGTF, the NCBG aimed to give Black gay people who thought their lives or attitudes were ignored by existing gay groups a voice of their own at the national level. The organization's motto was 'we are as proud of our blackness as we are of our gayness'.[17] Jones-Hennin said at the time, 'we are not yet comfortable with NGTF or GRNL acting as spokespersons for third world gays. Their structures – which are geared toward the one-issue perspective of sexism against the Gay community – do not reflect adequate concerns for third world Gays'.[18] Perry Watkins, a gay rights activist, said in 1993 about Black gays:

> Racism within the gay community is a big problem. The primary reason is that we are a direct reflection of the society from which we come, which is controlled by white males. When the gay community was formed and became political, the leaders were white men, and they brought their prejudices with them.[19]

Seeing the access that other gay organizations had to the White House and the success and visibility they had achieved as a result of this, the NCBG decided to seek a meeting, and on 26 January 1979 Berry and Jones-Hennin wrote to Jane Wales requesting 'an opportunity to discuss our concerns, organization, goals, philosophy and projects with you'.[20] Given that the organization had been formed only the year before and was not widely known – even within the Black gay community – the activists were not optimistic about their request. Wales's affirmative response took everyone by surprise.

17 Gil Gerald and Jones-Hennin, author interviews; Eric Darnell Pritchard, '"As Proud of Our Gayness, as We Are of Our Blackness": Race-ing Sexual Rhetorics in the National Coalition of Black Lesbians and Gays', in Jonathan Alexander and Jacqueline Rhodes (eds), *Sexual Rhetorics: Methods, Identities, Publics* (New York and London: Routledge, 2016), 161–2.

18 Don Michaels, 'White House Invites Third World Gays', *The Blade*, 12 April 1979.

19 Lena Williams, 'Blacks Rejecting Gay Rights as a Battle Equal to Theirs', *NYT*, 28 June 1993.

20 Don Michaels, 'White House Invites Third World Gays', *The Blade*, 12 April 1979.

The meeting was set for 5 June, and Berry and Jones-Hennin also invited, in addition to members of the NCBG, representatives of other minority gay communities, Latin, Asian and Native American, with a minimum of two representatives from each community. The other participants were Ernie Acosta, Sidney Brinkley, Rev. Darlene Garner, Jon Gee, Gil Gerald, Louis Hughes, Rev. Renee McCoy, Siu Ming Ng, Carolyn Pickett and Stephanie Wilson.[21]

On 5 June 1979, shortly before her meeting with the activists, three clergymen attempted to meet with Wales to protest about and stop the meeting. Wales ignored them and the meeting took place as planned. Wales, accompanied by Abigail Havens of the Department of Labor and Special Projects Coordinator of Carter's Interdepartmental Task Force on Women, met with the activists. It was the first time that activists representing minorities of the gay community had entered the White House for talks with the administration. The issues discussed included support for legislation that would end discrimination against foreign aliens who wished to enter the country, support for the ERA, intervention with the INS to stop its anti-gay and anti-Hispanic practices, budget cuts in social programmes, continued provision of CETA funds (see Chapter 7) for job training of poor and gay people in urban areas, a request that the NCBG would be invited in the future to any human rights conferences organized by the White House and a request that Carter's administration publicly endorse the forthcoming Conference of Third World Gays.[22] Gerald told the author that they wanted to show to Wales that 'they may be concerns on the same issues [as the NGTF], but from a different community perspective'.* The activists also gave Wales a copy of Jonathan Katz's book *Gay American History* and asked her to forward it to Carter.[23]

Wales assured the activists that Carter 'strongly support affirmative action, gay rights and the Equal Rights Amendment' and that the administration had already been working on a number of the issues they had raised. She informed them about its achievements to date. The activists had been for the most part unaware of these administration efforts and accomplishments. Very importantly, Wales informed them about federal programmes that could provide their organizations and their communities with federal funding and offered to assist them with their applications. She pledged that the administration would continue providing funding for poor and gay people, and although she avoided making any promises, she assured them the administration would continue working on some of the issues they had raised, while she would discuss with her White House colleagues the issues that had been brought to her attention for the first time. She also made an interesting response to the request that Carter endorse the Conference of Third World Gays: that 'public statements can often be counter-productive. In some instances it is far better to act than to make public statements'. Finally, Wales told the activists that she would convey their concerns to

21 Gerald and Jones-Hennin, author interviews.

22 Ernie Acosta, '3rd World Gays Take Issues to White House', *The Blade*, 7 June 1979; Gerald and Jones-Hennin, author interviews.

23 Ernie Acosta, '3rd World Gays Take Issues to White House', *The Blade*, 7 June 1979.

Carter and pass on Katz's book, and assured them that the White House's door was always open for them.[24]

The activists were absolutely 'thrilled' and 'delighted' with the meeting and considered it to have been 'very successful'. They were also all very impressed with Wales's positive attitude towards them and her sincerity, and they detected a genuine interest on her part in the issues they raised. According to Gill, the meeting was 'a landmark' for Black LGBT visibility, while Jones-Hennin characterized it as 'a highlight' in the history of the NCBG. They both argued that it had multiple benefits not only for their organization, but for the Third World gay movement. The meeting's two biggest contributions were that it helped to legitimate the NCBG and the Third World gay movement in the eyes of the public, and it increased the movement's and the organization's visibility, especially among gay minority communities.[25] According to Gerald, the NCBG's 'visibility exploded' as a result of the meeting and this led to considerable expansion, as well as a great growth in Black gay rights activism:

> The meeting helped this fire. On a level of building our credibility as an organisation, it was an early stage of Black LGBT visibility and involvement in the political and policy sphere, so we were pioneers in that. And the very fact that we had a meeting with the White House was important to us in establishing our own visibility and credibility as an organization.*

The NCBG held a press conference immediately after the meeting, but despite the fact that the organization had informed the press, including the gay press, about it, only one journalist turned up; from the *Manchester Union-Leader*, an ultra-conservative newspaper from New Hampshire. Eventually, the meeting made it into the gay press thanks to Ernie Acosta, who wrote about it in *The Blade,* one of the biggest gay newspapers of the time.[26] Despite the lack of media coverage, news of the meeting nevertheless reached the ears of conservatives, who fiercely criticized Carter for allowing it. Among those who reacted to the meeting were a group of clergymen from New York, who accused Carter of ignoring the Bible's teachings and of 'lending respectability to the breakdown of moral values', as this meeting was 'one of the several actions of Carter's administration that encourages homosexuality'. The anti-gay clergymen demanded from Carter a comparable White House meeting for themselves. Wales said that the anti-gay clergy group 'would be given the same opportunity' as the gay groups.[27] However, such a meeting never materialized.[28]

Wales's observation that public statements can 'often be counter-productive' is worthy of emphasis, accurately capturing the backlash phenomenon that the administration's efforts, and the ensuing visibility and legitimation of gay rights, were evoking. In the following chapters it will be seen that the more publicity the issue of

24 Ernie Acosta, '3rd World Gays Take Issues to White House', *The Blade*, 7 June 1979; Gerald and Jones-Hennin, author interviews.

25 Gerald and Jones-Hennin, author interviews.

26 Ernie Acosta, '3rd World Gays Take Issues to White House', *The Blade*, 7 June 1979'; Gerald, author interview.

27 Scott P. Anderson, 'Fundamentalists Blast Carter for Gay Support', *The Advocate*; 26 July 1979; Andy Soltis, 'Carter under Fire over White House Gay Meet', *NYP*, 5 June 1979.

28 Jane Wales, author interview.

gay rights gained, the more resistance it stirred up, not only from conservatives but also from Congress. Thus, although the administration supported gay rights through *policy*, it acknowledged that equal support in *politics* could be counter-productive and ineffective. By way of illustration, no succeeding administration accepted a request from the NCBG for a meeting. On 19 December 1979, Jones-Hennin visited the White House again, this time as a representative of the NCBG in a delegation of gay rights activists who presented Carter's administration with a petition (see Chapter 6). These two visits within the space of six months were the only times in its history that the NCBG was admitted to the White House.[29]

Reaching out to the gay religious community

In 1968, Rev. Troy Perry, after being excommunicated from the Pentecostal Church because of his homosexuality, founded a church in Los Angeles in which people could be both gay and Christian, citing a need for a church that welcomed gay people rather than condemning them. The Metropolitan Community Church (MCC) was by 1980 the biggest national gay organization with a membership of about 20,000 and 113 parishes all over the country.[30] The MCC's staff, however, were often harassed, and the church's buildings frequently vandalized, burgled and set on fire. For example, in 1976, a church's building in Riverside, California, was destroyed by arson.[31] The success and visibility of the MCC led to the creation of other similar gay congregations such as Integrity, founded in 1974 by Louie Crew Clay and bishops of the Episcopal Church, and Dignity, founded in 1969 by Dr Patrick Nidorf, a Roman Catholic priest, a church for gay Catholics. Meanwhile, several congregations and denominations such as the Union of America Hebrew Congregations, the Unitarian Universalists and the United Church of Christ began accepting gay members and ministers.[32]

In mid-1977, the Cleveland chapter of Dignity sent a letter to Rosalynn Carter introducing the organization and requesting her to send them a food recipe to include in a book they were going to publish. Rosalynn sent both a recipe, for flank steak, and her best wishes 'for a successful project' to the organization.[33] A year later, Clay invited Lillian Carter, the president's mother, to attend an Integrity fundraiser in Atlanta, Georgia, and asked whether her son could donate one of his books to be sold at the event. Lillian accepted the invitation and President Carter donated a copy of *The Adventures of Tom Sawyer* that contained notes he had written as a child, along with a newly written signed dedication to the organization. The activists were much impressed by the gift. In her speech at the event, Lillian clearly expressed her son's, as well as her own, support for gay rights. Carter's gesture with his book and his mother's

29 Jones-Hennin, author interview.
30 Perry, author interview; 'Rights Groups to Aid Homosexual Cuban Refugees', *NYT*, 8 July 1980.
31 Perry, author interview.
32 Fejes, *Gay Rights*, 72.
33 'Rosalyn Contributes to Dignity', *The Blade*, September 1977.

appearance at the event delighted the gay community in Georgia and were catalysts in the expansion of Integrity and the legitimacy it gained in the eyes of the public.[34]

Meanwhile, the MCC, despite its success in expanding, still lacked respectability and recognition. In October 1977, after an arson attack on the church's building in Phoenix, Arizona, Perry received a phone call from Malson who expressed the administration's sympathy over the incident and support for the church's activities; a move that was highly appreciated by Perry.[35] On 10 December 1979, Malson and Thomas, along with two other White House aides, Mike Chanin and Diana Rock, met in the White House with Brydon, Bush and Valeska. The activists made a series of requests to the administration (discussed further in Chapter 13); one of them was for Carter or his family to attend a service of the MCC, to boost the profile and legitimacy of the Church.[36] Carter did not attend such a service but sent his mother Lillian to attend an MCC service in Atlanta in 1980, which essentially fulfilled the activists' request and again delighted the local gay community and the Church.[37]

Furthermore, the administration attempted direct outreach to the gay religious community. In 1979, Carter appointed Rev. Dr Robert Maddox as his special assistant for Religious Liaison. Maddox, a minister of the evangelical Southern Baptist Church and Carter's close friend, was liberal and supportive of gay rights. Larry Bush, who met Maddox, reported that he 'was *very* sympathetic and open to lesbian and gay people, and he was opposed to discrimination'.* After his appointment, Wexler informed Maddox that the gay community had religious organizations led by gay people. She expressed her and Carter's concern about the violence and harassment these organizations suffered and asked Maddox to set up a meeting in the White House with gay religious leaders to meet them and to find ways to help them. Maddox immediately agreed and invited to the White House forty-one representatives of gay churches and gay religious caucuses in American churches.[38] It was the first time that the White House had sent personal invitations to representatives of the gay community without such a meeting having been requested. The gay religious community was surprised and thrilled with the unexpected invitation; they had never even thought of asking for such meeting.[39]

The meeting took place on 28 April 1980, lasted two hours and included, apart from gay religious leaders, also a few heterosexual pastors who were supportive of gay rights, while Maddox was accompanied by Allison Thomas. The delegation was the biggest delegation of gay rights advocates to have been invited to the White House up to that point; it included pastors and members of the United Church of Christ, the Episcopal, Presbyterian, Quaker, Brethren, Mennonite, American Baptist and Seventh Day Adventist denominations, the Bet Mishpochech congregation, while an independent

34 Clay, author interview.
35 Perry, author interview.
36 Letter, Charles Brydon and Lucia Valeska to Bob Malson, 7 January 1980, and NGTF's requests, 10 December 1979, both in RMSF, GH1, JCPL; Perry, author interview.
37 Clay and Perry, author interviews.
38 Maddox, author interview.
39 DeBaugh, Perry and Wilson, author interviews.

gay synagogue in Washington was also represented. Among those attending was Dr Nancy Wilson, an openly lesbian MCC minister.[40]

Each participant offered a presentation on their church or group, advanced issues of concern for them around employment, housing, discrimination and continuing the process of decriminalization, and discussed ways of eliminating the perception among most Americans that Christianity condemned and was incompatible with homosexuality.[41] One of the questions put to Maddox was about a remark that Bob Jones III, the conservative and anti-gay President of Bob Jones University, had alleged that he had made. Jones had claimed that Maddox had told him that Carter 'was not going to do anything to hasten homosexuals' acceptance into society'. Maddox denied making the remark, saying that President Carter 'fully endorses, encourages the civil rights of homosexuals'.[42] At the end of the presentations, Maddox asked his guests how the administration could help the gay churches and generally the gay religious community. One of them, weeping, replied that just by inviting them to the White House, Carter had already done more good for them than it could do in any other way.[43]

At the end of the meeting, Maddox expressed Carter's 'wholehearted' support for gay rights, pledging that this administration would continue working to advance gay rights. However, he did not promise anything specific and told his guests that he would personally communicate to Carter what he had learnt that day. He thanked his guests and said, 'You've blown a number of stereotypes for me today. The kind of careful preparation you have done will carry the day for you eventually', but suggested caution about expectations for quick results on gay issues in church and government. He also told them, 'I feel at home and very comfortable with you folks today – more so', he said, than he had felt with the delegation of Christian fundamentalist ministers who had visited him in the White House with an anti-gay rights petition signed by 74,000 people about a month before (see Chapter 6).[44] Everyone in the religious leaders' delegation was impressed with Maddox's attitude and frankness. They were happy to have been assured that Carter supported gay rights, but also that Maddox had been frank and had avoided making specific promises. Wilson recalled that Maddox 'was very gracious, I have to say, and welcoming to us. I remember him being particularly, I would say, moved or overwhelmed by what he did not know before this meeting – how invisible LGBT people, and especially people of faith, were. He was very moved'.*

After the meeting, Allison Thomas told reporters who were there to cover the event, 'This is an open Administration. The President stands firmly for civil and human

40 'Gay Religious Leaders Visit White House', *BAR*, 22 May 1980; Maddox and Wilson, author interviews.

41 Wilson, author interview.

42 'Gay Religious Leaders Visit White House', *BAR*, 22 May 1980.

43 Maddox and Wilson, author interviews.

44 Family Protection Report, 'Carter's Adviser "More Comfortable" with Homosexuals than with Fundamentalists', July 1980. RLMSF, GI, JCPL; 'Gay Religious Leaders Visit White House', *BAR*, 22 May 1980; Maddox and Wilson, author interviews.

rights for all Americans, and I'm proud to say that includes homosexuals'.[45] As for the meeting's impact, Wilson said,

> Very few people get that opportunity, at the highest level, to simply present your case or your beliefs and your ideas. So I think, for us, it was just amazing that in about . . . I guess it was twelve years' time from our birth, from our origins, that we had this great opportunity to be able to say something – and of course, to touch Robert Maddox, and maybe, to some degree President Carter who has continued to evolve on the issues. He's a remarkable example of someone who has come a long, long, long way in his views, and he was always gracious and open-hearted in many ways.*

The meeting received a lot of attention and criticism from conservatives and the conservative press, who once again accused Carter of endorsing and encouraging homosexuality. Maddox received more than sixty letters of protest and condemnation from conservatives, including a very critical one from Phyllis Schlafly's Eagle Forum, all demanding to know whether he had really made the comment about the fundamentalist preachers. Maddox responded to all of them and attempted to calm things down. He claimed that he and Carter did not encourage homosexuality as a 'viable alternate life-style', but that he and Carter believed that '[gay people] must not be discriminated against before the laws of the land . . . [President Carter] does not want any American citizen deprived of their civil rights because of his or her private sexual orientation'.[46]

Meeting California's gay community at home

In addition to the meetings held in the White House, on some occasions, gay rights activists asked Carter's aides to meet them in other locations in order to listen to their concerns. Costanza, Haft, Malson, Thomas and Wales accepted several invitations to such meetings, some of them informal, mostly with Washington-based gay organizations such as the GSDC and the GAA. They met with them in their offices or in other venues.

However, the most important and ground-breaking of these meetings took place in May 1980 in California. In early 1980, Sheldon Andelson, the first openly gay person to be appointed to the Board of Regents of the University of California, conceived of inviting White House staff to California to meet the local gay community. Andelson's aim was to get Carter's administration to meet the gay community itself, to see how it lived, and to listen to *it* rather than to its leaders and organizations. Andelson and other activists in California did not feel adequately represented by gay rights organizations, especially the NGTF, for which they had little regard, and wanted their own voices

[45] Family Protection Report, 'Carter's Adviser "More Comfortable" with Homosexuals than with Fundamentalists', July 1980, and Letter, George Schroeder to Everett Sneed, 6 September 1980, both in RLMSF, GI, JCPL.

[46] Several letters in RLMSF, GI, JCPL.

to be heard by Carter. To achieve this, the meetings were to take place in local gay establishments, like gay community centres. Andelson and other prominent local gay rights activists agreed to invite Malson and Thomas to Los Angeles and San Francisco for direct talks with the local gay community. The activists were not particularly optimistic about their proposal, believing that it was a step too far to ask the White House to allow two top aides to be involved in public talks with the gay community, especially in public gay places, and so close to the 1980 Presidential elections.[47] Malson and Thomas discussed the invitation with (respectively) Eizenstat and Wexler, receiving support for the visit. Eizenstat told the author that he did not have to ask for Carter's permission to authorize such meetings because he 'knew what his general policy was, which was against any form of discrimination including sexual preference', and that the administration had 'made that very clear'.* Thus, in the first week of May, Malson and Thomas travelled to California to meet with the two local gay communities and listen to their concerns.[48]

The planned visit created great anticipation among the gay communities, who began to prepare for it. Professor Eric Schockman, a gay rights activist, participated in several of the meetings between the gay community and Malson and Thomas in San Francisco. He told the author of the feelings of the local gay community about Malson and Thomas's visit: 'So we were just, "The White House is coming," we were all excited because it's what a blessing does, it gave us the energy and vitality to continue working'.* The meetings took place in San Francisco and Los Angeles between 1 and 4 May, and all but one (to be mentioned shortly) were held in local gay establishments such as community centres and coffee shops. Several hundred people from both local gay communities attended these meetings and expressed their concerns to Carter's aides. Malson and Thomas attended a fundraiser at the Los Angeles Gay Community Services Center and another one in San Francisco, with the visitors providing drawing cards for these events. Andelson, who was on the founding board of the Los Angeles Gay Community Services Center, and Jim Kepner, the curator of the recently opened National Gay Archives in Los Angeles, invited Malson and Thomas to the Archives in order to promote them; they accepted the invitation. The only meeting not to take place at a gay establishment, a party to thank Malson and Thomas for their visit, took place at Andelson's house in Los Angeles on 2 May. About three hundred members of the local gay community were present; it lasted for four or five hours and ended well past midnight.[49]

In the meetings, Malson and Thomas listened to the activists' concerns, but also talked about the administration's efforts and accomplishments so far. Among the requests they heard were that Carter would issue an executive order to eliminate discrimination in the 5 per cent of the federal sector that was not covered by his Civil Service Reform Act (to be discussed in Chapter 6), that he would end the INS's

47 Paula Fiscal, Higgins, Eric Schockman and Carol Ruth Silver, author interviews.

48 Letters, Allison Thomas and Robert Malson to Carol Ruth Silver, Art Agnos, Sheldon Andelson and others. All dated 9 May 1980 and in RMSF, GTFN2, JCPL.

49 Britt, Fiscal, Higgins and Schockman author interviews; Letters, Allison Thomas and Robert Malson to Carol Ruth Silver, Art Agnos, Sheldon Andelson and others. All dated 9 May 1980 and in RMSF, GTFN2, JCPL; Memorandum, Bob Malson to Stu Eizenstat, 8 May 1980. RMSF, GH1, JCPL.

discriminatory policy against gay aliens, that he would support a gay rights plank at the 1980 Democratic Convention, that he would support any gay rights bill, that he would end the discrimination against gay people in the military, and that he would appoint open gay people to public posts. Malson and Thomas were surprised to discover that a number of the administration's accomplishments on gay rights were unknown to their interlocutors; for example military discharge upgrades and new federal funding (discussed below), and Carter's appointments of openly gay people like Abram, O'Leary, Rustin and Schropp to various presidential commissions. In addition, the activists learnt that the White House was already working on a number of their requests.[50]

Malson and Thomas's presence in California was very important for the local gay community, who rushed to meet and talk with them. The meetings were so popular that at most of them a large number of people had to remain outside the rooms where the discussions were taking place, while almost all of them lasted much longer than the arranged time. Indeed the trip itself was extended by one day to allow Malson and Thomas to meet members of San Francisco's Black gay community.[51] The activists could not believe that two aides were meeting with them in their houses and in gay establishments. It was the first time that an administration had accepted such an invitation and the first time that the White House had engaged in direct dialogue with the gay community rather than gay leaders and gay rights organizations. The locations of the meetings, in local establishments and not government offices, were also found significant by the participants.[52] Even those who were not entirely happy with Carter's efforts on gay rights, like Harry Britt, were impressed with Malson and Thomas and praised their professionalism, courtesy and attention to their concerns.* Schockman said to the author:

> I think the White House visit was a hypodermic, a shot in the arm. . . . It sort of recognized we weren't just a little island on the West Coast, we weren't just the lefties, but that this could be a mainstream issue that a Democratic president eventually could embrace. . . . That visit alone was a milestone in a large degree. It's a blessing that we started something that was unparalleled at the time.*

Upon their return to the White House, Malson and Thomas followed up with 'thank you' letters to their hosts.[53] To Andelson, addressing him as 'dear Shelley', and thanking him for inviting them to his house and for arranging the meeting there, they wrote: 'Your house was lovely and the company thought-provoking. We are both busy following up on the many concerns raised. We both look forward to continuing discussions either in California or here in Washington'.[54] They also wrote memorandums for Eizenstat and Wexler. Malson wrote that some of the gay community's proposals and requests,

[50] Ibid.

[51] Britt and Higgins, author interviews.

[52] Britt, Fiscal, Higgins, Silver and Schockman, author interviews.

[53] Letters, Allison Thomas and Robert Malson to Carol Ruth Silver, Art Agnos, Sheldon Andelson and others. All dated 9 May 1980 and in RMSF, GTFN2, JCPL.

[54] Letter, Allison Thomas and Robert Malson to Sheldon Andelson, 9 May 1980. RMSF, GTFN2, JCPL.

especially regarding gay people in the military, 'would be very difficult to implement, but we can gain important support in the gay community by moving on some of them'.[55] Malson displayed again his genuine concern about the issues raised by suggesting politically feasible ways of addressing them; for instance he suggested that the request for public acknowledgement by Carter or Mondale through their attending a gay-oriented event such as Gay Pride, or visiting a gay community centre in California, could be met 'in the context of similar visits to other distinctive communities' such as a 'Hispanic daycare center'.[56] Thomas suggested that Mondale could attend the ACLU National Gay Rights Project dinner at the Beverly Wilshire Hotel in Los Angeles on 15 May.[57] Wexler agreed with Thomas's idea and calculated that the political benefits of Mondale's appearance at the event would 'far outweigh the possible liabilities',[58] though as far as can be established, Mondale did not attend the dinner, most likely due to the short notice. Eizenstat commented on Malson's memorandum, 'Glad you made a trip, I think you did well'.[59]

Despite their ground-breaking character, these meetings did not receive any attention in the press, including the gay press; thus they did not become widely known beyond the gay community in California. David Goodstein was not invited to participate in the organization of these meetings by the local gay community; in consequence the meetings were not reported in *The Advocate*. The NGTF, although it usually publicized in its newsletters all the important news regarding gay rights, also made no mention of the meetings, probably because of the ongoing feud that existed between gay rights activists on the West Coast and the organization on the East Coast; probably for the same reason the meetings were also ignored by the East Coast-based gay press.

☙

By meeting with gay rights activists in the White House, as well as outside it, Carter's administration provided the gay community with unprecedented visibility and legitimation. The breakthrough meeting and the meetings that followed were as much a milestone in the modern gay rights movement as the Stonewall Riots and played a major role in the expansion of the movement. The riots had galvanized gay rights activists by providing a focus for their anger, but the White House meetings had multiple effects. Many more people joined the gay rights movement as a result of seeing that, collectively, they could make a difference – they would be heard, and their efforts would result in tangible outcomes. The NGTF modelled to gay rights activists all over the country the sort of behaviours and approaches that had the capacity to grant them access to leaders with the power to make dramatic changes in the area of gay rights.

55 Memorandum, Bob Malson to Stu Eizenstat, 8 May 1980. RMSF, GH1, JCPL; clarification in author interview with Malson.
56 Ibid.
57 Memorandum, Allison Thomas to Anne Wexler, 8 May 1980. RMSF, GTFN2, JCPL.
58 Memorandum, Anne Wexler for Dick Moe, undated. AWSF, B34, NGTF, JCPL.
59 Stu Eizenstat's notes on Bob Malson's 8 May 1980 memorandum. RMSF, GH1, JCPL.

The practical effects of the meetings were equally important: they facilitated access to other parts of the executive branch where, often with White House assistance, important gains could be, and were, made. These effects are documented in several succeeding chapters. Throughout Carter's tenure as president, gay rights activists enjoyed an unprecedented level of access to the White House, a level of access that would not be repeated until Obama's presidency, almost thirty years later.

5

The National Women's Conference

The lesbian dimension

The United Nations initiative to promote the cause of women's equality through an International Women's Year, to which the Ford administration had already made a commitment, brought an intensified effort by President Carter. The timing of his accession to the presidency increased the hopes of lesbians to gain a presence and achieve both policy and legitimation goals at the anticipated conference. However, opposition to the feminist agenda was already mounting strongly after the *Roe v. Wade* decision on abortion rights, and conservative forces were of course further provoked by the more vocal promotion of the political agenda of lesbians. The conference represents a vivid display of the emerging political complexities of Carter's embrace of gay rights within the framework of human rights.

A conference for the year of women

In 1973, the United Nations announced that 1975 would be International Women's Year (IWY). In January 1975, President Ford created the National Commission on the Observance of International Women's Year (IWY Commission), whose members were mostly part of the centrist feminist establishment. The Commission aimed to identify the 'remaining barriers to women's full and equal participation in American society', to recommend measures the government could take to remove them, and to suggest ways to 'promote equality between men and women'. In the summer of 1975, the UN Conference on Women in Mexico City adopted a World Plan of Action to improve the lives of women worldwide. In June 1976, Ford's IWY Commission produced a report, *To Form a More Perfect Union . . . Justice for American Women*, which contained 115 recommendations for the improvement of women's lives through government action. Despite the efforts of Charlotte Bunch, Jean O'Leary and other lesbian rights activists, it made no reference to lesbian rights. Congress directed the IWY Commission to convene a National Women's Conference (NWC), preceded by state and regional meetings, and preparatory work began. One of the IWY Commission's tasks was to appoint coordinating committees for the state and regional meetings (sometimes called conferences) in each of the fifty states and six specified territories. The Commission sent state coordinating bodies a list of sixteen topics to consider while preparing recommendations for a final plan of action and again lesbian rights were not included. The Ford administration had already introduced a procedure whereby women who were not federal officials could take part in drawing up action plans via government-funded IWY conferences at the state and national level. This legislation had been drafted by Bella Abzug; Abzug had requested $10 million to fund the conferences, but Congress approved only half of it. Ford insisted that the national conference take place after the 1976 election.[1]

The IWY Conference was seen by lesbian rights activists as an excellent opportunity to raise their profile, legitimize their cause and make their voices heard.[2] Phyllis Schlafly, founder of the conservative, pro-family, anti-gay and anti-feminist Eagle Forum and leader of the Stop-ERA campaign, attempted to stop the IWY programme by petitioning Congress and the courts. When this failed, she called on her supporters to prepare for war against the feminists, telling them that they could 'make the "libbers" sorry they ever held the IWY conference'.[3] Arriving in office in 1977, Carter inherited the already controversial project and asked Costanza and Alexis Herman to recommend members for a reconstituted IWY Commission.[4]

Conference preparation: 'Holy battlegrounds'

The NWC was arranged to take place in Houston on 18–20 November 1977. Preparations for the Houston Conference were massive, involving fifty-six preliminary conferences, one in each state and territory, with women voting not only for delegates to the NWC itself but also on a number of issues proposed by the IWY Commission. If an issue was approved by twelve or more State or Territorial conferences, it would be included, along with the IWY Commission's recommendations, in a proposed National Plan of Action to be debated and voted on in Houston. The final National Plan of Action was going to be submitted to Congress and President Carter for their consideration and help in adopting it.[5]

Costanza clearly realized that the NWC would provide an excellent opportunity to promote many of her favoured causes, such as the ERA, access to abortion and gay rights. She was one of the most influential actors in the organization of the Conference. Ford's IWY Commission consisted of thirty-five members, and although they were all feminists, the vast majority of them were against lesbian rights and not particularly progressive. Many prominent feminists at the time believed that the

1 Bunch, author interview; IWY Commission, 'Background on the National Women's Conference and the IWY Commission', August 1977. MMSF, IWY, JCPL; Alice S. Rossi, *Feminists in Politics: A Panel Analysis of the First National Women's Conference* (New York: Academic Press, 1982), 24–6.

2 Bunch, Higgins and Tyler, author interviews.

3 Marjorie J. Spruill, *Divided We Stand: The Battle Over Women's Rights and Family Values That Polarized American Politics* (New York: Bloomsbury Publishing, 2017), 133–4.

4 McKenna, author interview.

5 IWY Commission, *The Spirit of Houston*, 11; IWY Commission, 'Background on the National Women's Conference and the IWY Commission', August 1977. MMSF, IWY, JCPL.

association of lesbian rights with feminism would hurt the women's movement and the ratification of the ERA.[6] Costanza's aim was to make Carter's Commission more diverse and progressive than the one Ford had set up. Thus, she suggested that Carter expand the Commission to forty members, replace twenty-two of Ford's appointments, keeping only thirteen, and appoint Bella Abzug as chair.[7] Carter quickly accepted the last recommendation, shortly afterwards also appointing Abzug, again on Costanza's recommendation, as chair of the Conference itself. Abzug was someone who understood the tensions within the women's movement over homophobia, racism and classism, a time when the women's movement was somewhat riven by these factors.[8]

Objection to the reconstitution was not the sole prerogative of conservatives, but also had a pragmatic basis, as in the case of Betty Friedan. Friedan, founder and former president of NOW, one of the founders of the National Women's Political Caucus, and among the most prominent feminists, had herself admitted she was known for being 'violently opposed to the lesbian issue'.[9] She believed that lesbian rights were of lesser importance in comparison with other women's movement issues such as abortion, childcare, discrimination and most importantly the ERA; 'anti-ERA protagonists', she later said, sought to 'enflame [*sic*] the lesbian issue to undermine support for the constitutional amendment'.[10] Friedan, a Democrat, had campaigned for Carter in the 1976 elections and was widely expected to be appointed to Carter's IWY Commission. However, Bunch and O'Leary, worried that she might block a lesbian rights resolution, convinced Costanza to exclude her from the Commission despite strong protests from Abzug, many leading feminists, and prominent women of the Carter administration. Bunch said, 'Friedan was considered, at that point, *very* anti-lesbian, and anything we could do to block her, we would do'.* In the event, however, Abzug later appointed Friedan as delegate-at-large, enabling her to attend the Conference.[11]

Carter eventually increased the number of Commissioners to 42 and made all of the appointments recommended by Costanza and other feminist members of the administration, particularly Alexis Herman. Carter's IWY Commission thus contained numerous supporters of lesbian rights such as Maya Angelou, Coretta Scott King and Gloria Steinem. As Costanza had recommended, Carter also re-appointed the more progressive feminist members of Ford's Commission.[12] The most important appointment of all for lesbian rights was that of O'Leary. Her appointment as Commissioner meant that she was the first openly gay person to be appointed to a government post, and more importantly, she was appointed by the president himself. O'Leary was in fact not the only open lesbian to be appointed by Carter as Commissioner, as he also

6 Betty J. Blair, 'Support for Lesbian Rights Splits Feminist Ranks', *The Detroit News*, 20 December 1977; Bunch, author interview.

7 Memorandum, Margaret Costanza to President Carter, 16 March 1977. MMSF, IWY, JCPL.

8 Bunch, author interview.

9 IWY Commission, *The Spirit of Houston* (Washington, DC: National Commission on the Observance of International Women's Year, 1978), 166.

10 Betty Friedan, *Life So Far: A Memoir* (New York: Simon & Schuster, 2001), 248–9, 294–5.

11 McKenna, author interview.

12 Midge Costanza's IWY Commission Nominees, undated, and Members of the IWY Commission, 1977, undated, both in MMSF, IWY, JCPL; McKenna, author interview.

appointed Ruth Abram, co-executive director of the Women's Action Alliance and a board member of the NGTF.[13]

Bunch wrote in her essay *A Brief History of Lesbian Organizing for IWY*, 'The first IWY national commission appointed by President Ford offered us little hope. While a few individuals were responsive to our concerns, the commission clearly did not intend to include lesbianism in its deliberations'.[14] But prospects for lesbian rights massively improved after Carter's changes to the Commission. *Off Our Backs*, a feminist periodical, wrote, 'When Carter took office, the Ford-appointed commission was dumped in favor of a more zippy crew headed by Bella Abzug'.[15] But Carter's appointments, especially of Abzug as chairwoman and of O'Leary, caused outrage among conservatives who bombarded the White House with angry letters. Schlafly attacked Carter for appointing O'Leary and 'many of the most militant women's libbers in the country'.[16] Pat Robertson denounced Carter after Abzug's appointment saying, 'I wouldn't let Bella Abzug scrub the floors of any organization I was head of. But Carter put her in charge of all the women of America'.[17]

When the newly appointed IWY Commission held its first meetings on 11 and 12 April, O'Leary suggested that lesbian rights should be on the agenda for workshops at the state conferences.[18] However, only Smeal supported O'Leary's proposal; all the other members, even Abzug and others who supported lesbian rights, were against it, believing the word 'lesbian' in the title of a resolution was too controversial. The Commission's rejection was a disappointment to O'Leary, who felt betrayed by Abzug.[19] However, it agreed to include a resolution entitled 'Sexual and Affectional Preference', which, as O'Leary later said, provided an 'organizing tool' as 'lesbians could go to state committees and say that they wanted this issue discussed in pre-convention workshops'.[20]

The passage of the 'Sexual and Affectional Preference' resolution was followed by a flurry of mailings from the NGTF urging lesbians and non-lesbian feminists to turn up in full strength at the state conferences since lesbian rights was now a 'legitimate' women's issue. However, there was still work that needed to be done for a pro-gay resolution to be added to the National Plan of Action. O'Leary argued that 'in order to get any pro-gay resolutions passed at the National Conference, we need a groundswell of support coming out of the earlier (state) meetings'.[21] The organization urged the gay community to talk to state coordinators as soon as possible to set up workshops on these issues, and to ensure that the maximum number of the state conferences passed

13 Higgins, author interview; 'Sexual Preference Added to List of International Women's Year Issues', News from NGTF, 15 April 1977. NGTFR, B.36, F.32, CU.

14 Charlotte Bunch, 'A Brief History of Lesbian Organizing for IWY', 1977. MCI.

15 AH and JK, 'National Women's Conference', *OOB*, January 1978.

16 Spruill, *Divided We Stand*, 133–4.

17 William Martin, *With God on Our Side: The Rise of the Religious Right in America* (New York: Broadway Books, 1996), 166.

18 'Sexual Preference Added to List of International Women's Year Issues', News from NGTF, 15 April 1977. NGTFR, B.36, F.32, CU.

19 Bunch, author interview; O'Leary, 'From Agitator to Insider', 91–2.

20 Doreen J. Mattingly and Jessica L. Nare, 'A Rainbow of Women and Unity at the 1977 U.S. International Women's Year Conference', *Journal of Women's History* 26, no. 2 (2014): 98–9.

21 Bunch, 'A Brief History of Lesbian Organizing for IWY'.

resolutions in support of four key aims: 'Passage of laws prohibiting discrimination on the basis of sexual preference in employment, housing, etc; Repeal of laws governing private sexual behavior between consenting adults; Passage of laws making sexual preference irrelevant in determining child custody and visitation rights; and Inclusion of more and better lesbian visibility in the media'.[22]

Furthermore, thanks to extensive lobbying by Costanza and O'Leary, the IWY Commission affirmed via a public statement that lesbian rights was a feminist issue and that the organizers of state conferences should not discriminate against lesbians and should allow them to participate and hold workshops on lesbian concerns. Finally, thanks again to Costanza and O'Leary's efforts, the IWY Commission appointed several open and closeted lesbians as members of each state and territory coordinating committee, ensuring that lesbian rights would be considered in all the state meetings.[23]

The Commission set out its aims for the main conference in a report entitled *Plan for Action*; the ERA was the lodestar, but a sexual preference plank was also included. The planks in the report were intended to be discussed at the state-level conferences and were then open to debate on the floor at the main conference in Houston.[24] The passage of the 'sexual and affectional preference' resolution was followed by a flurry of mailings from the NGTF urging lesbians and non-lesbian feminists to turn up in full strength at the state conferences since lesbian rights was now a 'legitimate' women's issue.[25] The organization also suggested that activists talk to state coordinators as soon as possible to set up workshops on these issues, and to ensure that the maximum number of the state conferences passed resolutions in support of two key aims: 'Passage of laws prohibiting discrimination on the basis of sexual preference in employment, housing etc. [and] Repeal of laws governing private sexual behavior between consenting adults'.[26]

The NGTF launched a campaign 'to promote lesbian participation' and to improve lesbian visibility in the media. It urged all lesbians to 'get involved immediately on their state level', as 'an active lesbian presence in these state conferences is crucial . . . because resolutions emerging from them will have a great influence on shaping the legislative goals of the women's movement'.[27] Particularly relevant to the preparations were O'Leary's activities within the NGTF where she developed a Women's Caucus, described as 'a formally constituted body of lesbians and lesbian-feminists', whose aim was to facilitate 'a lesbian presence in all women's issues, projects, and organizations throughout the country' and to 'reflect our commitment to feminist principles and to the integration of the battles against both sexism and heterosexism'.[28]

22 Ibid.

23 Bunch and Higgins, author interviews; Harry Langhorne, 'Lesbians Plan Women's Year Conference', *GN*, June 1977.

24 IWY Commission, 'Women's Conference: National Plan of Action', 1977. MCI.

25 Bunch, 'A Brief History of Lesbian Organizing for IWY'.

26 'Sexual Preference Added to List of International Women's Year Issues', News from NGTF, 15 April 1977. NGTFR, B.36, F.32, CU.

27 'National Gay Task Force Urges Lesbians to Participate in International Women's Year Conference', NGTF Press release, June 1977. NGTFR, B.35, F.15, CU; 'Urge Lesbian Role in Int'l Women's Year Series', *It's Time*, March 1977. SWSF, NGTF F+P, JCPL.

28 'Women's Caucus Formed at NGTF', 1 NGTF Press Release, August 1977. NGTFR, B.9, F.40. CU.

In O'Leary's view, full lesbian participation at the NWC would upgrade lesbian rights from 'a minority concern' to a 'core' and 'vital issue'.[29] O'Leary expressed fears that 'without a strong lesbian-feminist presence . . . our issues and our needs will consciously or unconsciously be overlooked', and asked lesbians to 'spread the word and encourage lesbians to join the fight for full participation in the goals of International Women's Year'.[30] O'Leary also got in touch with the lesbian and pro-lesbian members of Carter's 51.3% Committee and with NOW's Lesbian Rights Task Force and asked them to collaborate with the NGTF's Women's Caucus on the planning and organization of lesbian participation in the state conferences; the cooperation of these three organizations was crucial for the mobilization of lesbians.[31]

At the same time, several women's groups, including lesbian groups like the NGTF's Women's Caucus, received federal funding to organize for the forthcoming NWC, including organizing workshops in the state conferences on lesbianism and lesbian rights. It was the first time in American history that lesbian organizations had received federal funding, and also the first time that workshops on lesbianism and lesbian rights had been funded by the government; lesbian rights groups had requested funding from Ford's IWY Commission but had been turned down.[32] Bunch recalled that the federal funding the lesbian organizations received was 'very important for the lesbian movement', for both practical and symbolic reasons.*

However, with the exception of Smeal, who remained strongly in favour of lesbian rights, and to an extent Steinem – as well as Abram who, however, had little influence over the other Commissioners – the IWY Commission was not as supportive of lesbian rights as Costanza and O'Leary wished. Fear of harmful controversy persisted. A cause of friction had been the Commission's reluctance to use the word 'lesbian' in its official documents and communications.[33] For example, the Commission was going to publish guides that were designed to assist in setting up workshops on nineteen topics regarding women's rights; among them was a guide for Sexual Preference. Experts on each of these nineteen subjects were hired by the Commission to write these guides, while the NGTF was asked to write the one about Sexual Preference.[34] The NGTF, with federal funding, produced a 61-page guide, the fifth-longest of the nineteen guides,[35] but it was not distributed. O'Leary said about it, 'For other issues they contracted the work out, but for this NGTF had to do it all, and then the Commission staff second-guessed and challenged us on almost every word. It went back and forth and it became later and later, until it was just too late'.[36] Nevertheless, in almost all state conferences, workshops on lesbianism took place, with many, if not all, of them being funded by

29 Bill Sievert, 'Lesbians Plan for IWY Battle', *The Advocate*, 21 September 1977.
30 'Lesbian Voices Needed: I.W.Y. State Conference', *The Lesbian Feminist*, June 1977.
31 Bunch and Higgins, author interviews.
32 Jeffery St. John, 'Now Taxpayers Are Financing Homosexual Causes' (the newspaper title is unfortunately not visible in the archive record), MCSF, [H-GRPH], JCPL; Bunch and Higgins, author interviews.
33 Bunch, author interview.
34 Mattingly and Nare, 'A Rainbow of Women', 100.
35 US Department of State Archive, 'The President's Interagency Council on Women', US Department of State, https://1997-2001.state.gov/picw/archives/npa.html.
36 Mattingly and Nare, 'A Rainbow of Women', 100.

the government, while the Commission allowed workshops with the word 'lesbian' in their title to take place. The workshops were the core of the conferences, as they were to make recommendations for a platform of women's issues to be adopted by the NWC proper. For example, in New Jersey's IWY Conference (24–26 June) there were two workshops on lesbianism, 'Loving Women – The Lesbian Lifestyle' and 'Finding Our Sexual Center-Views', while in Delaware (17–18 June) there was a workshop on 'Sexual Lifestyles' which included lesbianism.[37]

Conservatives had already been angered by the mere provision of federal funding to the IWY programme, but the revelation that lesbian groups had received a portion of this taxpayers' money to advance their causes further infuriated them. For example, Jeffery St. John, a two-time Emmy Award-winning journalist who contributed commentary among others to the *New York Times*, wrote an article entitled 'Now Taxpayers are Financing Homosexual Causes'. North Carolina Republican Senator Jesse Helms held informal hearings on the IWY, calling for a Congressional investigation and an audit by the General Accounting Office into the $5 million appropriated for it.[38]

O'Leary's energetic and well-planned campaign had met with great success. However, so too did that of her leading opponent, Schlafly. Homophobic and anti-feminist backers of Schlafly saw the women's movement as socially radical and destructive of the traditional family and expressed their opinions in angry and uninhibited rhetoric.[39] Schlafly warned that the state conferences would be full of 'Libs and Lesbians, Frauds and Follies',[40] and characterized the IWY Commission as 'a front for radicals and lesbians'.[41] She believed, correctly as a matter of fact, that it was 'entirely pro-ERA' and that it aimed to prevent her and other pro-family activists from taking part in the Conference.[42] She predicted that 'Houston will finish off the women's movement' and the ERA due to their association with abortion and lesbianism,[43] and did everything in her power to fulfil her prediction. Schlafly was not the only one who felt excluded by the Conference, as this was the general feeling among conservatives and pro-family forces. Alarmed by the feminists and lesbians' mobilization and by their early successes in the state conferences, conservatives all over the country willingly joined Schlafly's call to arms. Several groups of Catholics, Mormons and Baptists, and groups such as Stop ERA, Right to Life, the Conservative Caucus, the John Birch Society and the Ku Klux Klan, formed an informal coalition with Schlafly and her Eagle Forum at the forefront that aimed to stop the advancing feminists and lesbians.[44]

Lesbian activists realized what sort of opposition they would face in Houston when anti-feminists mobilized their forces at several of the state conferences. As a result, the local conferences turned out to be a sour affair with feminists and conservative

37 Bunch and Higgins, author interviews; Harry Langhorne, 'Lesbians Plan Women's Year Conference', *GN*, June 1977.

38 Jeffery St. John, 'Now Taxpayers Are Financing Homosexual Causes' (the newspaper title is unfortunately not visible in the archive record), MCSF, [H-GRPH], JCPL.

39 'Home from Houston', *WP*, 27 November 1977.

40 Ellen Goodman, 'At Stake in Houston: Perception of Power', *WP*, 17 November 1977.

41 Robert O. Self, *All in the Family: The Realignment of American Democracy since the 1960s* (New York: Hill and Wang, 2012), 313.

42 Nadine Brozan, 'White House Conference on the Family: A Schism Develops', *NYT*, 7 January 1980.

43 IWY Commission, *The Spirit of Houston*, 119.

44 Vera Glaser, 'Women's Year Peril on the Right', *The Philadelphia Inquirer*, 23 August 1977; IWY Commission, *The Spirit of Houston*, 109–19; Mattingly, *A Feminist*, 150–3.

and anti-feminist activists fighting bitterly to gain delegates. The three major issues of conflict were the ERA, abortion and lesbian rights. On several occasions anti-feminists attempted, sometimes successfully, to break up workshops on these topics.[45] The massive mobilization of conservative forces brought quick results. In the Utah state conference in Salt Lake City in July 1977 nearly 12,000 of the 14,000 women participants were Mormons who had answered their church's call to support the 'correct principles' and stop the feminists. As a result, the resolutions put forward by the IWY Commission for the ERA, abortion and lesbian rights were easily voted down, while twelve of the fourteen delegates who were selected by the state were members of the conservative Mormon Church.[46] In addition to Utah, the states of Alabama, Indiana, Florida, Nebraska, Montana, Missouri, Oklahoma, South Carolina, Ohio, Kansas and Mississippi were won by the conservatives who voted down the IWY Commission's proposals for the three conflicted issues and elected conservative delegates.[47]

Bunch characterized the state conferences as a conflict of lesbians and feminists against conservatives and recalled that conservatives and anti-feminists far outnumbered the lesbian community. To counter this, Bunch and O'Leary sent emergency calls to their rank and file to get to the conferences and neutralize the numerical advantage enjoyed by their opponents, resulting in a massive grassroots organizing and mobilizing of open and closeted lesbians all over the country.[48] The mobilization bore fruit and the feminist and lesbian forces scored their biggest win in the state of New York on 8 and 9 July. Costanza had played an active role in the preparations for this state conference as she had helped the coordinating committee plan it.[49] Another big win came in California, the state where most workshops on lesbianism took place, on 16–19 June. Thirteen lesbian delegates, the most in any state delegation, were elected, while 99 of the other 101 delegates were feminists. Particularly important for this success was the mobilization of the local lesbian community and local gay men and the efforts of Carter's 51.3% Committee.[50]

These closely matched mobilizations meant that Costanza and O'Leary still had work to do to ensure that feminists and pro-lesbians would be in a majority at the NWC. They took a drastic measure to achieve this. The IWY Commission, taking advantage of a regulation stating that the Conference had to reflect the demographic makeup of women nationally while including delegates from groups that 'work to advance the rights of women', went on to appoint 370 extra delegates-at-large; the vast majority, if not all of them, being not just feminists but sympathetic to lesbian rights.[51] The NGTF had asked lesbians who wished to be selected as delegates to send in their names, along with a statement stating whether they were 'out front lesbians' and why

45 Bunch, author interview; IWY Commission, *The Spirit of Houston*, 103–11.
46 John M. Crewdson, 'Mormon Turnout Overwhelms Women's Conference in Utah', *NYT*, 25 July 1977.
47 Vera Glaser, 'Women's Year Peril on the Right', *The Philadelphia Inquirer*, 23 August 1977.
48 Bunch, author interview.
49 Mattingly, *A Feminist*, 154.
50 Kathleen Hendrix, '"Inherent Tension" in Women's Meeting', *LAT, 21* June 1977; Higgins, author interview; Terry Wolverton, 'Lesbian Activists Confer on IWY Meet Strategy', *Out!* 29 July 1977.
51 Bunch, author interview; IWY Commission, *The Spirit of Houston*, 119.

they wished to be delegates.[52] Among the 370 selected delegates were several lesbians whom O'Leary and Bunch had found and asked to be put down as candidates and whose names were submitted to Costanza and to the IWY Commission.[53] Thanks to the Commission's appointment of the delegates-at-large, and despite the conservative mobilization and their wins in at least ten states, only a quarter of the delegates who were elected to participate in the NWC were anti-feminists.[54] The appointment of the extra 370 delegates was seen by conservatives as confirmation that the administration planned to pack the Conference with lesbians. The White House received hundreds of angry protest letters from outraged conservatives, as well as threatening phone calls.[55]

Observing the controversy that the state conferences attracted, Beth Abramowitz, Eizenstat's adviser on women's issues and Assistant Director in the Domestic Policy Staff, began to argue that it might be best for the administration to distance itself from them. She told Eizenstat that the state conferences had been turned into 'holy battlegrounds. Over abortion, over homosexual rights. Real tacky stuff', and that 'it was best not even to try to deal with that'.[56] However, the administration remained active and played a visible role during the state conferences. For example, Costanza, in addition to her participation at the state conference in New York, was the keynote speaker at the state conference in Massachusetts in late July 1977.[57] Carter's 51.3% Committee also had a visible role in the state conferences and helped in their planning and organization, while Betty Blanton, one of its most prominent members, was a spokesperson at the state conference in Tennessee. All over the country, the local branches of the 51.3% Committee, which included several open lesbians like Daly and Higgins, assisted feminist and lesbian women at the state conferences, contributing significantly to the mobilization and visibility of lesbians. They also distributed to the participants a questionnaire regarding women's rights and concerns that included questions regarding lesbian rights.[58] Furthermore, members of the IWY Commission participated in a number of state conferences; for example, Jean Stapleton was a spokesperson at the conference in the state of New York.[59] The Commission also proposed a series of lectures, entitled *Briefings from the Top: Distinguished Women in Government Lecture Series*, to be delivered in Houston by the forty most senior woman aides in Carter's administration, including of course Costanza. The women, who were chosen by Costanza and Herman, were asked to give one-hour lectures on subjects related to their professional role or generally about women.[60]

52 Jeanne Córdova, 'IWY: Most States Back Lesbian Rights', *LT*, September–October 1977.
53 Bunch, author interview; NGTF Women's Caucus Minutes, Part I, IWY Plans, 14 August 1977. MCI.
54 Jeanne Córdova, 'IWY: Most States Back Lesbian Rights', *LT*, September–October 1977; IWY Commission, *The Spirit of Houston*, 11.
55 McKenna and Wales, author interviews; see also letters in MCI.
56 Mattingly, *A Feminist*, 153–4.
57 Ibid.
58 Letter, Gretta Dewald to the 51.3% Committee Coordinators, 3 April 1978. NGTFR, B.152, F.46, CU; Higgins, author interview.
59 University of Massachusetts Amherst, 'New York State Women's Meeting and the First National Women's Conference', http://exhibits.library.umass.edu/scua/s/diana-mara-henry/page/fnwc.
60 Memorandum, Jane Wales to Midge Costanza, 22 November 1977. MCI; McKenna, author interview.

A couple of months before the Conference, O'Leary suggested to Costanza, and then to the IWY Commission, that it hire Barbara Price, an openly lesbian stage producer, lawyer and the national chair of the lesbian caucus of the National Women's Political Caucus, as the producer of the Conference's cultural programme. The proposal was accepted, O'Leary and Price submitted a list of about forty women artists they proposed hiring to perform at the Conference, the vast majority of whom were open or closeted lesbians. O'Leary believed that the presence of lesbian artists and a lesbian-themed cultural programme would increase lesbian visibility and transform lesbian rights into a 'core issue'. She was also aware that the Conference would be televised all over the country and that it would be the first time that openly lesbian artists would perform on national TV. Among the performers selected by Price and O'Leary were Maxine Feldman and Robin Tyler, two of the most prominent openly lesbian artists at the time. Feldman was a singer-songwriter and stand-up comedian whose song *Angry Atthis*, the first openly distributed *lesbian*-themed song, had become an anthem of the lesbian movement. Tyler was the first openly lesbian stand-up comic, and along with Patty Harrison, she had formed Harrison and Tyler, the first openly lesbian comedy duo.[61] Costanza and the Commission accepted all of O'Leary and Price's recommendations, thus providing an additional lesbian theme to the Conference. However, the booking of lesbian performers, as well as the appointment of several lesbians as delegates-at-large, were steps too far for Catherine East, one of NOW's founders, who resigned as the IWY Commission's Deputy Coordinator. She later cited the lesbian issue as being the main reason for her resignation.[62]

An NGTF survey showed that at least fifty-seven 'up-front lesbians' had been elected to participate in the NWC in addition to 'many more "closeted" lesbian delegates'. Despite strong opposition from organized conservative groups, a wide variety of pro-gay resolutions were adopted by at least thirty[63] out of the fifty states, with six more including those resolutions in minority reports; anti-gay resolutions were passed in only four states.[64] This meant that a pro-gay plank had to be, and was, included in the National Plan of Action.[65] The NGTF acknowledged Carter's contribution by stating:

> Thanks in considerable measure to President Carter's appointment of Jean as one of the select group of commissioners of IWY, the high point of the past months was undoubtedly the major role played by NGTF in so successfully mobilizing lesbian visibility and passage of the 'lesbian' resolution at the International Women's Year convocation at Houston.[66]

61 Tyler, author interview.
62 Mattingly and Nare, 'A Rainbow of Women', 100.
63 Some sources, such as the NGTF Action Report, 'October 1977'. MCSF [H-GRPH], JCPL, give the number of states adopting such resolutions as twenty-nine, while O'Leary later wrote that it was 'more than' thirty-five. O'Leary, 'From Agitator to Insider', 91.
64 Bunch, 'A Brief History of Lesbian Organizing for IWY'.
65 'Lesbian Rights Proposal Controversial Issue at Houston's National Women's Conference', News from NGTF, 18 November 1977. NGTFR, B.36, F.61, CU.
66 NGTF, 'Minutes from the Executive Committee's meeting', 13 August 1977. NGTFR, B.2, F.60, CU.

The IWY Commission considered that Carter's presence at the Conference was a necessity. On 25 April, Stapleton wrote to Carter and his wife inviting them both to attend.[67] On 12 May, Abzug wrote to Carter to the same effect, arguing that his appearance there 'will signify to the people of America' that his administration intended to 'respond to the problems of women as a high-priority human-rights issue'.[68] Carter had not responded to these requests and as the NWC approached, he was undecided whether to attend. On 27 July, Lee Novick, one of the IWY staff, wrote to Costanza that 'the question we are being asked most frequently by the press is, "What time will the President speak?"'[69] It had become clear to the White House that the Houston Conference was certain to be contentious, and some of Carter's aides, like Eizenstat and Jordan, thought that it would be best to put some distance between it and the White House, including limiting the number of presidential aides who would attend. Eizenstat warned Carter that his close association with the Conference could open a 'can of worms' and urged him not to participate in person. On the other side, Costanza insisted to Carter that women 'do need that much representation' from the administration in the Conference. Meanwhile, the Commission asked Rosalynn Carter to attend, pointing out that two other First Ladies were going to be present, Betty Ford and Lady Bird Johnson.[70] In early August, Costanza informed the Commission that Carter was planning not to attend. On 12 August, Abzug wrote to Carter urging that the campaign against the NWC was precisely why he had to attend. If he did not, she argued, this would not only show that he was not interested in women's issues; it would also 'give heart to the ultra-right forces that have sought to disrupt the state meetings and to stop the national conference altogether, and to prevent further progress in the area of women's rights'.[71]

Carter seriously contemplated attending the NWC, but he eventually accepted his advisers' suggestion to not do so. However, he strongly insisted that his administration should have a large and vocal presence as a statement of its support for the ERA and for women's rights. Thus, it was agreed that his wife Rosalynn, and Judy Carter, his twenty-seven-year-old daughter-in-law, whom he had appointed to be his unofficial and unsalaried personal spokesperson on the ERA, would attend and speak at the Conference on his behalf. Despite some of his advisers' strong opposition, Carter also approved the Commission's request for the series of lectures by the forty most prominent women of his administration; there would thus be a large administration presence.[72]

Bunch, Costanza and O'Leary's efforts had ensured prominence for lesbians and lesbian rights at Houston. Although Carter had accepted all of Costanza's recommended appointments, the reconstituted Commission had turned out to be not as supportive of lesbian rights as O'Leary and Costanza had intended. Even so, the Commission's contribution to the lesbian issue was indisputable. Ford's Commission

[67] Letter, Jean Stapleton to President and Mrs. Carter, 25 April 1977. MCI.

[68] Letter, Bella Abzug to President Carter, 12 May 1977. MCI.

[69] Mattingly, *A Feminist*, 154.

[70] Flippen, *Jimmy Carter*, 140–1.

[71] Mattingly, *A Feminist*, 154–5.

[72] Eizenstat and McKenna, author interviews; Memorandum, Jane Wales to Midge Costanza, 22 November 1977. MCI.

had completely ignored lesbian rights and lesbian participation. Eleven months later, Carter's Commission, which included two open lesbians, had appointed 370 lesbians or pro-lesbian feminists as delegates-at-large, had seen pro-gay resolutions adopted by numerous states, and had included a resolution on sexual preference among the twenty-six planks of the National Plan of Action that would be debated and voted on Houston. Furthermore, lesbian rights organizations had received government funding, while numerous workshops on lesbian rights, also funded by the government, had taken place all over the country. Finally, the hiring of over thirty lesbian artists to perform at the Conference had ensured additional visibility. This tremendous turnaround should clearly be credited to Costanza, who was the driving force behind the organization of the Conference but also to Carter, who accepted all her recommendations and provided her and the Commission with the necessary authority to achieve it. In addition to recommending appointees to the IWY Commission and helping with the preparations for the Conference, Costanza had also worked hard throughout this period to help keep Rosalynn Carter, women in the administration who were involved in the planning of the Conference, and colleagues who were scheduled to give lectures aware, informed and positive about the lesbian dimension at the upcoming event.[73] Bunch, who had been critical of Ford's Commission for ignoring lesbian rights and lesbian participation, wrote shortly before the NWC,

> In January of 1977, lesbian issues were not mentioned in ANY of the literature for IWY and there were no open lesbians involved in the planning of the conference on a national or state level. Eleven months later as we move into Houston for the national conference, the Plan of Action includes a major agenda item on sexual preference, based on resolutions that were passed in 30 states, and there are at least 60 open lesbian delegates and scores more closeted lesbians and supporters of gay rights in the state delegations.[74]

On 17 November, one day before the opening of the Conference, the *Washington Post* carried an editorial declaring, 'What is at stake in Houston is the perception of political power. Everyone agrees that the conference will be a symbol, a message, a test of clout'.[75]

The conference takes place: 'We are everywhere'

The National Women's Conference opened in Houston on Friday 18 November 1977, led by Chairwoman Abzug, who was described by the *Washington Post* as 'the mother of this convention'.[76] In total, there were about 20,000 people present, including 2,006 delegates, plus 2,000 official observers and invited guests, along with 1,500 journalists

[73] Bunch and McKenna, author interviews.
[74] Bunch, 'A Brief History of Lesbian Organizing for IWY'.
[75] Ellen Goodman, 'At Stake in Houston: Perception of Power', *WP*, 17 November 1977.
[76] Sally Quinn, 'The Pedestal Has Crashed: Pride and Paranoia in Houston', *WP*, 23 November 1977.

and 3,000 volunteers.[77] At least 120 of the delegates were lesbians, with 60 of them being open and wearing orange armbands to show it, while at least 320 were conservatives. The three organized lesbian groups were the Lesberadas, a Houston lesbian collective, the California IWY Support Coalition, and the NGTF. The three main issues were abortion, ratification of the ERA and gay rights.[78] The Carter administration had a very strong presence, as in addition to Rosalyn and Judy Carter, and Costanza and the other thirty-nine senior administration women aides who would be giving lectures, several other lower-ranking female staff from the administration were in the audience. Furthermore, Carter's 51.3% Committee, which included several open lesbians, had an active role, distributing among the Conference participants a questionnaire about issues of concern to women, which included lesbian rights.[79] Fearing that the Sexual Preference plank might not be put to the vote before the end of the Conference – the voting would take place in alphabetical order, and it was twenty-third out of the twenty-six planks on the list – O'Leary and the NGTF's Women's Caucus convinced several delegates to wear buttons reading 'Keep the agenda moving – Let every issue be heard',[80] while they distributed a pamphlet entitled 'Lesbian Rights' and other educational fliers on lesbianism. Conservatives were outraged at the distribution of these publications; what added salt to their wounds was the fact that they had been produced with federal funding.[81]

That the women's movement was now a mainstream feature of American life was demonstrated by the massive media coverage the Conference received. Hundreds of television cameramen and newspaper reporters gave minute-by-minute accounts of the proceedings, highlighting the prestigious presence not only of First Lady Rosalynn Carter but also of Betty Ford and Lady Bird Johnson.[82] Rosalyn said in her speech,

> Jimmy is sorry that he could not be here today. His concern about the outcome of your agenda is deep. He cares about what is going on here this weekend. And I trust you don't think he's sent a woman to do a man's job. . . . Jimmy asked me to be his personal emissary today and to talk to you briefly about his concerns and his goals . . . of course I am here for myself too.

She lauded the goals of the Conference and listed some of her husband's achievements to date with regard to women's issues.[83] Judy Carter also gave a speech and urged the delegates to support the ERA and all the other women's issues on the agenda. Costanza

77 IWY Commission, *The Spirit of Houston,* 11, 119–24.

78 Vicki Gabriner, 'International Women's Year: "Mommy, When I Grow Up, Can I Be a Lesbian?"' *Atalanta* 12 (1977): 12; 'Lesbian Rights Proposal Controversial Issue at Houston's National Women's Conference', NGTF Press Release, 18 November 1977, NGTFR, B.36, F.31, CU.

79 Letter, Gretta Dewald to the 51.3% Committee Coordinators, 3 April 1978. NGTFR, B.152, F.46, CU; Higgins, author interview.

80 O'Leary, 'From Agitator to Insider', 91.

81 Maria Braden, 'Lesbian Pictures A Weapon in Ky. ERA Battle', *WS*, 12 February 1978; Bunch, author interview; Jean O'Leary, 'IWY: Strategy for Action', *It's Time*, November 1977. NGTFR, B.147, F.2, CU.

82 Bill Curry and Megan Rosenfeld, 'Crucial Test for Women's Conference: Momentum in the Mainstream', *WP*, 19 November 1977.

83 IWY Commission, *The Spirit of Houston,* 138, 219–20.

expressed her strong support for women's rights and her 'trust and confidence in the depth of Jimmy Carter's commitment to women'.[84]

Feldman performed among other songs her signature tune *Angry Atthis*, whose lyrics about a lesbian's love and inability to publicly express it due to the state's oppression caused a stir among conservatives. The same was also caused by Tyler's 45-minute stand-up comedy act, which was mostly lesbian-themed; she said, 'My performance was totally political. I did about coming out, and about being an open lesbian'.* The performances of the lesbian artists represented the first time that openly lesbian artists appeared at a federally funded national event that also happened to be televised. Bunch said that the performances of the lesbian artists were 'very important for the lesbian community' as they 'played a *major* role in helping not only people to *see* these talented women who were lesbians, but also in helping many lesbians to come out because they wanted to identify with this. So, definitely, it contributed a lot to lesbian visibility'.*

Reflecting the increasing polarization on women's and family issues already visible in the preparatory stage, the Conference was largely divided between 'pro-family' women who opposed gay rights and other liberal ideals, and feminists who included a cadre of lesbian rights activists. Very soon, proceedings began to look like two conferences taking place rather than one. Feminist speakers would address a feminist audience in one hall while anti-feminists would address their supporters in another hall, often right next door.[85] Bunch, who attended the Conference as a delegate, said about the anti-feminist supporters: 'They created a very menacing atmosphere. On the floor of the conference we were literally fighting with them to get to the microphone all the time'. She said that it was then that the gay rights movement realized the strength of the right wing. Until then, they 'didn't have a sense that they were going to be that strong'.*

Over three days, delegates to the NWC debated and voted on twenty-six separate issues, ranging widely. Not only were there the hot-button issues of the ERA, abortion rights and sexual preference, but matters of insurance, health, home-making, child care, and the rights of minority, elderly and disabled women were all tabled for decision.[86] A highlight of the Conference was the series of lectures given by the women of the administration. In all of them, the aides clearly and strongly expressed Carter's and the administration's support for the ERA and all the items on the Conference's agenda, without however explicitly referring to the sexual preference plank. These women, along with other members of the administration, also extensively lobbied delegates to vote for the ERA.[87] At one point, Carter phoned Costanza to ask for an update on the conference, and she told him, 'It's so great here. I'm on such a high, I know the drug and alcohol council [*sic*] will declare it illegal'.[88]

Each plank was considered in alphabetical order and the ERA plank easily passed by Saturday midnight. The Sexual Preference plank, plank 23, was put to the vote

84 Ibid., 217–33.

85 Gabriner, 'International Women's Year'.

86 Anna Quindlen, 'Women's Conference Approves Planks on Abortion and Rights for Homosexuals', *NYT*, 21 November 1977.

87 Higgins, McKenna and Wales, author interviews.

88 Hays Gorey, 'That Woman in the West Wing', *NYT*, 22 January 1978. *NYT*'s interpolation.

around 8 p.m. on Sunday, during the plenary session of the day. Resolutions about minority women and reproductive freedom had already passed that day.[89] The plank, which was written mostly by O'Leary, read:

> Lesbian women are discriminated against by current laws and practices. For example, 32 states have sodomy laws which criminalize private sexual behavior between consenting adults. Discrimination on the basis of sexual preference in employment, housing, public accommodations, credit, public facilities, government funding and the military is not prohibited by existing federal civil rights laws. Lesbian mothers have been denied custody of their children solely on the basis of their sexual orientation. These conditions allow for persecution and abuse of individuals selected for harassment.
>
> Congress, State, and local legislatures should enact legislation to eliminate discrimination on the basis of sexual and affectional preference in areas including, but not limited to, employment, housing, public accommodations, credit, public facilities, government funding, and the military.
>
> State legislatures should reform their penal codes or repeal State laws that restrict private sexual behavior between consenting adults.
>
> State legislatures should enact legislation that would prohibit consideration of sexual or affectional orientation as a factor in any judicial determination of child custody or visitation rights. Rather, child custody cases should be evaluated solely on the merits of which party is the better parent, without regard to that person's sexual and affectional orientation.[90]

The plank was presented by O'Leary, Bunch and Smeal; its passage was the chief aim of the lesbian rights activists. It was preceded by jeers and tears, strong opposing arguments and radically polar speeches as apart from the religious conservatives, it was also opposed by conservative pro-ERA delegates.[91] Anne Taylor Fleming of the *New York Times* described the plank as 'the emotional focal point of the conference'.[92] After the plank's presentation by the three women, other delegates took the stage to debate it. One of those who spoke in favour of the plank was, unexpectedly, Betty Friedan, whose intervention turned out to be crucial.[93]

Costanza also went on stage and announced that she had a message to deliver on Carter's behalf: 'President Carter has said that he knew people who were taught by homosexuals and they were never negatively affected by that'. She then proceeded with a personal statement, 'I get very emotional about this issue because I feel very strongly

89 Gabriner, 'International Women's Year'.
90 Elenore G. Pred, 'IWY Proposes National Plan', *The Advocate*, 14 December 1977.
91 Faderman, *The Gay Revolution*, 314; Anna Quindlen, 'Women's Conference Approves Planks on Abortion and Rights for Homosexuals', *NYT*, 21 November 1977.
92 Anne Taylor Fleming, 'That Week in Houston', *NYT*, 25 December 1977.
93 Bunch, author interview.

that you should have the right to love whomever you want. I do'.[94] The delivery of Carter's message by Costanza was important as it was perceived by many delegates and attendees as an endorsement of the plank. As the time of the vote neared, Abram, Bunch, Costanza, O'Leary, the three lesbian rights organizations, feminist and lesbian delegates and activists, and several women from Carter's administration and the 51.3% Committee who were supportive of the plank relentlessly lobbied the delegates.[95]

Soon the balance of opinion began to swing towards the lesbian activists. The persistent attacks by religious conservatives helped convince many feminists that they could not reject lesbian rights, and they consolidated against the common enemy.[96] A move by conservatives to separate out the 'lesbian mother' segment and vote it down was easily defeated. When the resolution eventually passed overwhelmingly, lesbians in the galleries roared their approval: 'Thank you, sisters!' Pink and yellow helium-filled balloons were released with the message, 'WE ARE EVERYWHERE'.[97]

By the end of the Conference, all twenty-six planks had been debated and voted on, with the voting delegates approving twenty-five of them, including the resolution endorsing abortion. The only proposal to be rejected, plank 26, called for the creation of a Cabinet-level Women's Department. It was voted down due to feminists' fear that this would 'isolate women's concerns in a single agency'. However, the delegates then approved a new twenty-sixth resolution to establish a Continuing Committee of the Conference, which would continue the work of the NWC and ensure the implementation of all its recommendations.[98]

Impact and aftermath of the conference: 'Lesbian loud and clear'

That the National Women's Conference, arguably the largest single event in the history of the US women's movement, was a major victory for the lesbian cause goes without saying. Jo Delaplaine of *The Blade* called the passage of the sexual preference plank 'a decisive victory for lesbian rights'.[99] What prompted even greater rejoicing was the visibility which the event gave to lesbian causes, and to the existence of lesbians themselves. The wide coverage of the event in the press and on national TV brought for the first time discussions about lesbian rights and lesbianism, as well as performances by lesbian artists, to the forefront of public attention across the whole country. The activists now had an acknowledged position from which they could press their demands and respond to their conservative opponents. The lesbian victory was also particularly significant since it was achieved against committed and numerically

94 Faderman, *The Gay Revolution*, 314–15.

95 Bunch, Higgins and McKenna, author interviews.

96 Lucy Komisar, 'Feminism as National Politics', *The Nation*, 10 December 1977; Sally Quinn, 'The Pedestal Has Crashed: Pride and Paranoia in Houston', *WP*, 23 November 1977.

97 Gabriner, 'International Women's Year'; Anna Quindlen, 'Women's Conference Approves Planks on Abortion and Rights for Homosexuals', *NYT*, 21 November 1977.

98 IWY Commission, *The Spirit of Houston*, 169–70.

99 Jo Delaplaine, 'Victory in Houston: "We Are Everywhere"', *The Blade*, December 1977.

greater opposition by conservative women. Bunch told the author that the Conference was '*very* important' and a 'massive success' for lesbian rights and for lesbian visibility, and added, 'It was like a national coming out of feminism in support of lesbian and gay rights'.* Jeanne Córdova wrote in *The Lesbian Tide* shortly after the Conference,

> For lesbians, the significance of what happened in Houston stretches far beyond a report that goes to Congress and the President and may or may not get acted upon in piece meal over the next century. . . . It said the word lesbian loud and clear over the front pages of most major newspapers in this country. . . . We were front page stuff.[100]

In the view of the *Washington Post,* the Conference produced two significant results: the establishment of a place for women in mainstream politics and the positioning of lesbian and gay rights front and centre of American society.[101] In terms of American political culture, the Conference proved to be something of a flashpoint between conservatism and progressivism, with many on the right wing seeing social movements such as feminism and lesbian rights activism as part of the same general tendency towards the destabilization of what they believed to be the true American family and the bedrock of American civilization. For many on the religious right, feminists' embrace of the gay rights movement and acceptance of lesbians within their organizations was the final straw. Whereas many conservatives had remained largely quiet on the issue of feminism earlier, the fact that the women's liberation movement had lined up with gay rights activists meant that from now on, they would see all feminists as enemies. In fact, social conservatives would now always consider lesbianism and feminism to go hand in hand.[102] In retrospect, the Conference can be recognized as a pivotal moment in America's 'culture wars', very much setting the scene for Carter's White House Conference on Families, which followed it about three years later.

In March 1978, in accordance with the *Plan*'s 26th resolution, the IWY Commission created the Continuing Committee of the Conference. It consisted of about 470 members, including everyone who had been on the IWY Commission, women from leading national organizations and from the various caucuses that had been set up at the NWC, and a representative from each of the state and territorial delegations. Among the members there were thirteen open lesbians, including Bunch and O'Leary.[103]

On 22 March 1978, in the White House, the IWY Commission officially presented to Carter the Conference's official report, *The Spirit of Houston.* The report included the National Plan of Action as it had been voted on in Houston, including Plank 23, which contained exactly the same wording that had been read out by O'Leary.[104] In his speech, Carter acknowledged that the IWY programme was 'a potentially explosive situation and one that could have brought a great deal of disharmony and

[100] Jeanne Córdova, 'IWY. Those Lesbians Are Everywhere!', *LT*, January/February 1978.

[101] David S. Broder, 'The Real Significance of Houston', *WP*, 23 November 1977.

[102] Martin, *With God on Our Side*, 164.

[103] Bunch, author interview; 'Lesbians Named to IWY Conference', *LT*, May–June 1978.

[104] IWY Commission, *The Spirit of Houston,* 89–91, 264–71; Meeting with IWY Commission, 22 March 1978. MCSF, IWY, 1977 6/77-8/78 [O/A5773], JCPL.

discouragement to those who have been in the forefront of the fight for women's rights', but the work of 'Rosalynn, Judy, and Midge, three members of my family' and of the IWY Commission, as well as Abzug's 'superb leadership', had contributed to making the conference 'a complete success'.[105] Although he did not refer explicitly to any of the twenty-six resolutions in the Commission's report, Carter expressed his support for all of them and promised to 'redouble our efforts to keep the spirit of Houston alive'. Carter then announced in front of 300 cheering women that he was going to establish a new committee of women that will work with the White House, Cabinet officers and agency heads to further the aims of women, help with the implementation of the IWY Commission's recommendations and generally continue the work of the NWC.[106] Shortly afterwards, the government published and made available for sale *The Spirit of Houston*. Furthermore, it also published and made available for sale the nineteen Workshop Guides that the IWY Commission had produced. Among the guides was one about Sexual Preference, making it the first – and up to now, the last – work on lesbianism and lesbian rights to be published by the government of the United States.[107]

Subsequently, Carter began forming his new committee of women, which was named the National Advisory Committee for Women (NACW) and consisted of forty members. It came into being in April 1978 and its aim, apart from advancing the ERA, was to inform Carter about initiatives needed 'to promote full equality for women'.[108] On 20 June 1978, Carter announced the Committee's membership. Despite all the controversy caused by the appointments of O'Leary and Abzug to the IWY Commission and the fact that their efforts had been a controversial proposition for many Americans, Carter, at Costanza's suggestion, appointed both women to this new committee. He even appointed Abzug as co-chair.[109] O'Leary said that she was 'very pleased' with her appointment as it would give her the opportunity to advise Carter on lesbian and more generally women's concerns, and declared, 'we have a long way to go in removing barriers to full equality for women in this country, the establishment of a national committee which can advice the President on these matters is essential'.[110] The new committee again consisted solely of feminists and ERA supporters, with many of them, such as Koryne Horbal and Eleanor Smeal, who had previously served in Carter's IWY Commission, also being in favour of lesbian rights.[111] Naturally, conservative Christians were displeased. Schlafly alleged that by not including any opponents of the ERA, the NACW was flouting the Federal Advisory Committee Act, which mandated that such institutions should include a balanced range of opinions among their members.[112]

105 OWHPS, The President's Remarks at a Reception for IWY, 22 March 1978. MMSF, IWY, JCPL.
106 Janet Battaile, 'Carter Plans Panel to Aid Women', *NYT*, 23 March 1978.
107 US Department of State Archive, 'The President's Interagency Council on Women', US Department of State, https://1997-2001.state.gov/picw/archives/npa.html.
108 Executive Order 12050, 4 April 1978. WHCOF, SFE, FG300, JCPL; 'Mrs. Abzug Expected to be Named by Carter to Post on Federal Unit', *NYT*, 13 June 1978.
109 Abguz with Kelber, *Gender Gap*, 65; Letter, President Carter to Jean O'Leary, 20 June 1978. NGTFR, B.36, F.85, CU.
110 'O'Leary Appointed by President Carter to National Advisory Committee for Women', News from NGTF, 30 June 1978, NGTFR, B.36, F.85, CU.
111 Spruill, *Divided We Stand*, 266.
112 Terence Smith, 'Feminist Will Head Women's Panel', *NYT*, 17 January 1979.

On 17 September 1978, Carter sent a message to Congress regarding the IWY Commission's National Plan of Action, praising it as a 'national agenda to achieve women's full rights and equality'. He reported on the status of the actions his administration had taken and intended to take on the resolutions mentioned in it, while also reaffirming once again his dedication to eliminating discrimination against women.[113] Lesbian rights activists were 'pleased' with Carter's statement; although he had not explicitly referred to the sexual preference plank (nor did he mention any of the other individual planks), the fact that he had publicly praised the National Plan, which included the plank, in its entirety was seen by lesbian rights activists, and most likely by the attentive part of the public as well, as a clear statement of his acceptance of it and support for lesbian rights.[114]

However, in early 1979 a series of events occurred which resulted, not altogether justifiably, in a significant loss of support by Carter among the lesbian community. On 11 January 1979, a day before a scheduled meeting with Carter, the NACW sent to the White House Press Office a press release entitled 'President Carter Challenged on Social Priorities by National Advisory Committee for Women'. This document, which was meant to be released to the press immediately after the meeting with Carter the following day, was highly critical of Carter's economic policies.[115] Jody Powell shared it with Eizenstat, Jordan, Weddington, Wexler, and Mondale's top aide Richard Moe. They unanimously agreed to urge Carter to dismiss Abzug. On the same day, Carter, despite some reservations, but viewing the report as a betrayal, did so.[116]

As a result of Abzug's dismissal, some members of the NACW demanded that all members resign in protest; twenty-three of the thirty-nine remaining members resigned the following day.[117] One of those who resigned was O'Leary, despite the fact that she publicly acknowledged that the press release before the meeting with Carter was a 'premature tactic' and added, 'Never send out a press release before the meeting . . . that's not acting in good faith.'[118] In a public statement through the NGTF, O'Leary expressed her 'shock that a President who has given his strong support to women's issues . . . could have acted so callously in dismissing the Committee's very able and dedicated co-chair'.[119] O'Leary also warned Carter that 'he [would] pay a price for this injustice at the polls that he [had] not figured into his budget'.[120]

In the event, less than half of the twenty-six members who had announced their resignations actually resigned.[121] Nevertheless, Carter changed the structure of the NACW, renaming it the President's Advisory Committee for Women (PACW),

113 Abguz with Kelber, *Gender Gap*, 66–7; Letter, Marjorie Bell Chambers to President Carter, 27 March 1979. SWSF, [NACW] Correspondence, JCPL.

114 Apuzzo, Bunch and Higgins, author interviews.

115 Abguz with Kelber, *Gender Gap*, 69; Martin Schram, 'The Story Behind Bella's Departure', *WP*, 17 January 1979; Terence Smith, 'Bella Abzug's Ouster and Limits of Dissent', *NYT*, 16 January 1979.

116 Schram, 'The Story behind Bella's Departure'; Martin Tolchin, 'Salvaging the E.R.A. Remains a Carter Goal', *NYT*, 4 February 1979.

117 Richard Halloran, '23 Leave Committee over Abzug Dismissal', *NYT*, 14 January 1979; Terence Smith, 'Bella Abzug's Ouster and Limits of Dissent', *NYT*, 16 January 1979.

118 'Bella Abzug Exposes White House Double Standard', *LT*, March–April 1979.

119 'O'Leary Resigns from National Advisory Committee on Women in Protest of Abzug Dismissal', News from NGTF, 16 January 1978. NGTFR, B.36, F.66, CU.

120 'Statement from Jean O'Leary', NGTF press release, 14 January 1979. NGTFR, B.6, F.2, CU.

121 Terence Smith, 'Feminist will Head Women's Panel', *NYT*, 17 January 1979; Weddington, author interview.

extending its end date from March 1980 to 31 December 1980, and reducing its membership from 40 to 30.[122] A move which somewhat restored his standing with the gay community was his appointment, in July 1979, of Jill Schropp, a lesbian rights activist and open lesbian, to the PACW. The NGTF applauded the appointment and said it was 'a most positive sign that President Carter has again appointed a member of America's lesbian community to his Advisory Committee on Women'.[123] Carter had chosen Schropp as he wanted his new Women's Committee to include representatives of all the women in the country, including lesbians. Although Schropp was not as well known as O'Leary, her appointment was rightly perceived as another sign of Carter's commitment to gay rights.[124]

ɞ

While a feminist agenda might have been expected from a national conference on women in the late 1970s, even had Ford still been president, Carter's accession to the presidency allowed not only a radicalization of this tendency but also the emergence within it of the dimension of lesbian rights. For lesbian activists, the NWC played an important role in advancing their cause, especially with regard to public discourse. For the first time, lesbians were given a public platform from which they could discourse on who they were, what their needs were and what they hoped to achieve. Importantly, this took place at a government-funded event with the active (if guarded) approval of the president. The Conference gave lesbians unprecedented visibility.

Although Carter avoided participating in the Conference, his role in facilitating its achievements is indisputable. It was he who appointed Abzug as Chair of the IWY Commission and of the Conference, and Abram and O'Leary as Commissioners. Indeed, Carter accepted all of Costanza's Commission recommendations. The new slate was significantly more diverse and progressive than its predecessor appointed by President Ford. It is inconceivable that the newly enhanced lesbian presence and the passage of the sexual preference plank would have been achieved without Carter's appointees in place. Bunch acknowledged the 'huge difference' between Ford and Carter's commissions, and the fact that 'if Carter had not replaced Ford's Commission – or at least, added all these new people – it would have been very difficult to get the Sexual Preference thing included in the Houston Conference'.* But Carter did much more than just repopulate the IWY Commission. First, the administration provided funding for lesbian rights groups and workshops. Secondly, although Carter did not personally attend the NWC, he ensured that his administration would have a big and vocal presence in it; the lobbying and support of Carter's aides for the Sexual Preference plank significantly contributed to its passage. Thirdly, Carter's 51.3% Committee also played an important role, especially in the state conferences, and significantly

122 Memorandum, Sarah Weddington for President Carter, 9 May 1979, and OWHPS, Press release, 9 May 1979, both in WHCOF, SFE, BFG221, JCPL.

123 'NGTF Applauds Appointment of Jill Schropp to Women's Advisory Committee', News from NGTF, 10 May 1979. NGTFR, B.36, F.120, CU.

124 Apuzzo and Bunch, author interviews.

contributed to the cause by helping the organization of workshops on lesbian rights and in electing lesbian and pro-lesbian delegates.

However, the emergence of the lesbian dimension of the women's movement intensified the opposition that the feminist agenda, and its key issues of abortion and the ERA, had already evoked. The combination of all three made the threat to the family perceived by conservatives yet more vivid, and as this chapter has shown, this created reciprocal tensions, primarily of a tactical character, among feminists themselves. The political complexities were becoming more difficult to navigate, and even without the benefit of hindsight, the prospect of another White House Conference, on 'the family' itself, an aspiration of Carter's during his campaign, suggested even more treacherous political waters ahead.

6

Access

Federal employment and civil rights

The chapter brings together the Carter administration's efforts and reforms with regard to access to government employment and employment rights for gay people, as well as access to government-run voluntary and training programmes such as the Peace Corps. Eligibility and job security for gay people had been severely compromised by discriminatory language in place in numerous departments, agencies and programmes. Moreover, the use of statutory civil rights protections, and particularly their enforcement by the agencies with this responsibility, for the benefit of gay people was not yet established practice. A significant legislative achievement in this respect was the Civil Service Reform Act. Yet for many advocates, the agenda continued to evolve; as they put it, 'gay pride' had turned into a more complicated and challenging 'gay politics'.

Progress before Carter

Although gay people had been banned from federal employment throughout much of the history of the United States, it was not until the McCarthyite era of the 1950s that the presence of 'sex perverts' in the government came to be seen as a scandal that threatened both the nation's security and its morals. The FBI kept files on thousands of people who they believed to be gay and if they were found to be working in the federal government, they were fired.[1] An estimated seven to ten thousand people lost their jobs in the federal service on this ground during the 1950s,[2] which marked a high point, although not the only occurrence, of anti-gay sentiment and practice in relation to federal government employment.

1 Franklin E. Kameny, 'Government v. Gays: Two Sad Stories with Two Happy Endings, Civil Service Employment and Security Clearances', in D'Emilio et al., *Creating Change*, 188–203; Gregory B. Lewis, 'Lifting the Ban on Gays in the Civil Service: Federal Policy toward Gay and Lesbian Employees since the Cold War', *Public Administration Review* 57, no. 5 (1997): 387.

2 US Merit Systems Protection Board (MSPB), 'Sexual Orientation and the Federal Workplace: Policy and Perception', 16.

Several decisions in Federal District Courts in the 1960s and 1970s, culminating in *Society for Individual Rights, Inc. v. Hampton* of 1973,[3] led to a revision of policy by the Civil Service Commission (CSC), the agency responsible for personnel management in the federal government. In July 1975, it announced a new approach to determining the suitability of gay applicants. The announcement stated, 'A significant change from past policy – resulting from court decisions and injunctions – provides for applying the same standard in evaluating sexual conduct, whether heterosexual or homosexual'. People could no longer be disqualified from federal employment 'solely on the basis of homosexual conduct' or on the basis of 'unsubstantiated conclusions concerning possible embarrassment for the Federal service', but only 'where the evidence exists that sexual conduct affects job fitness'.[4] Some agencies, including the FBI and the CIA, remained outside the scope of the guidelines; other agencies, such as the Agency for International Development, had their own discriminatory policies and prohibited the employment of open gays.[5]

While this Ford-era change of regulations was important, with the *New York Times* commenting that 'its greatest impact is apt to be the influence it has on other public and private employers across the nation',[6] the circumstances of federal employment at the start of the Carter presidency remained far from ideal for gay people. One problem was that the administrative character of the change meant that no procedural recourse, other than an expensive court case, was available to those affected by violations of the new policy; it relied on complete compliance by all the relevant officials, obviously an unlikely prospect. And as this chapter will discuss, the exclusions created by the 1975 rule remained even in later reforms, exciting further protest by gay rights activists. Thus, due to the absence of legislation prohibiting discrimination on sexual orientation, gay people were often still harassed and discriminated against, since the regulations of the CSC were often ignored by the heads of the federal agencies. As a result, the federal sector remained uninviting to potential gay applicants, while it was common practice for several federal agencies to check up on alleged gay people and deny them employment or promotion either on 'moral' or 'security' grounds.[7]

Before 1977, the NGTF had written several letters to the CSC trying to address the issue. It had also repeatedly asked the US Commission on Civil Rights (CCR, created in 1957 and tasked with investigating civil rights violations and making recommendations in both the public and the private sector) and the Equal Employment Opportunity Commission (EEOC, created in 1964 and tasked with investigating and remediating cases of employment discrimination) to include discrimination on the basis of sexual and affectional preference within their jurisdiction. Both agencies had claimed that they had no power to do so.[8] On 17 January 1977, the CCR, still led by President Ford's appointees, voted unanimously 'not to accept a responsibility in the area of

3 63 F.R.D. 399 (N.D.Cal. 1973).

4 'Homosexual Hiring Is Revised by U.S.', *NYT*, 4 July 1975.

5 MSPB, 'Sexual Orientation and the Federal Workplace'; 'Shedding Blinders', *NYT*, 16 July 1975.

6 'Shedding Blinders', *NYT*, 16 July 1975.

7 Memorandum, Seymour Wishman to Midge Costanza, 14 February 1978. SWSF, [Gay] CR, JCPL; Bush and Kent, author interviews.

8 Clay, author interview; Correspondence between the NGTF and the CRC in SWSF, [NGTF: CHR], JCPL; See also documents in NGTFR, B.143, F.13, CU.

sexual orientation unless and until the Congress specifically authorizes it and provides funds for it'.[9] Furthermore, over the previous three years, Congresswoman Abzug had three times introduced federal gay rights bills, but none had even been brought for consideration by the Judiciary Committee.[10] In addition, the State Department, which according to Kameny was 'hardly noted for friendliness to gays',[11] considered them to be 'security risks'. Functions that required security clearances were therefore effectively closed to gay people. This issue had also been litigated in the courts, where some decisions were favourable to gay employees and others were not. The courts had ruled that if the State Department denied a security clearance based on the employee's homosexuality, it had to show that this person's homosexuality affected the security aspects of his or her job.[12] The NGTF had made multiple unsuccessful efforts to meet with representatives of the State Department, the CCR, the CSC and the EEOC to discuss the issues.[13]

These court cases, and the various administrative responses to them, undoubtedly represented progress. Activists nevertheless desired a wider-ranging legislative consolidation of employee protections. Carter entered office with a clear intention of eliminating the abuses of government personnel policy he considered to have developed especially under Nixon,[14] and was able to secure Congressional support for this agenda.[15] This effort could readily combine with the anti-discrimination agenda derived from Carter's interest in human rights, and in particular with his election campaign commitment to end discrimination on the basis of sexual preference.[16] During the March 1977 Meeting, the NGTF had raised all these issues and requested the administration's intervention with the respective agencies and departments.[17] The administration's response was swift and substantial.

The Agency for International Development and ACTION Programmes

The US Agency for International Development (USAID) was founded in 1961 and its main task was the administration of civilian foreign aid and development assistance. The agency since its creation had had a discriminatory policy against gays, who

9 Letter, John Buggs to James Harvey, 21 January 1977. SWSF, [NGTF: CHR], JCPL.
10 Leandra Ruth Zarnow, *Battling Bella: The Protest Politics of Bella Abzug* (Cambridge, MA: University of Harvard Press, 2019), 257.
11 Letter, Franklin Kameny to Jane Wales, 3 November 1979. ATSF, B.265, GR, JCPL.
12 Memorandum, Marilyn Haft to Margaret Costanza, 25 March 1977. SWSF, [Gay] CR, JCPL.
13 Clay, author interview.
14 Bert Carp and Eizenstat, author interviews; Martin Tolchin, 'Carter Seeks Change in Civil Service Law to Reward Efficiency', *NYT*, 3 March 1978.
15 Hugh Davis Graham, 'Civil Rights Policy in the Carter Presidency', in Fink and Graham, *The Carter Presidency*, 205.
16 'Write Letters to Carter', NGTF Action Report, December 1976. SWSF, NGTF F+P, JCPL.
17 Memorandums, Margaret Costanza to President Carter, 8 April 1977, and Marilyn Haft to Margaret Costanza, 25 March 1977, both in MCI.

were barred from working for it and were immediately dismissed when found out. For example, in 1972, L. M. Smith was dismissed from a Foreign Service position because he was gay. The NGTF had repeatedly asked the agency to reconsider its discriminatory policies against gay people but without any success, while USAID's top officials consistently refused to meet with gay rights activists.[18]

In March 1977, Carter appointed John J. Gilligan as Administrator of USAID. Gilligan immediately reversed his agency's longstanding anti-gay policy, and gay people were now permitted to work for the agency. Gilligan publicly announced this policy reversal, saying that 'homosexuals as a class are not unsuitable for employment in the AID Foreign Service' and that 'such a class-based determination would be fundamentally inconsistent with the due process rights'.[19] He also said in his public statement:

> This agency is dedicated to the principle that the suitability of each individual must be judged on his or her own fitness. Where, as here, an employee has a sound record, has a demonstrated ability to operate effectively in a foreign environment, and has no record of prior misconduct or of public behaviour which could or would impair the effectiveness of agency operations, private homosexual conduct will not be grounds for dismissal from employment.[20]

Furthermore, Gilligan ordered the immediate reinstatement of everyone who had been dismissed from the agency due to their homosexuality over the previous few years. One of those he reinstated was Smith, who on Gilligan's orders was given permanent Foreign Service status and received about four years of back pay. The gay community welcomed the development and Kameny expressed his wish that the policy change would '[signal] similar changes throughout the remainder of the State Department and in other federal agencies'.[21]

ACTION was an umbrella organization for federal agencies that organized volunteer work, the best known of which was the Peace Corps (established as an independent agency in 1961, and again made free-standing in 1979). The Peace Corps was set up by the Kennedy administration with the aim of providing American technical aid to further global social and economic development, and also to improve understanding between the participants and those they worked with. Its workers were volunteers; American citizens, mostly college graduates, who were sent abroad for two years after a three-month training course. It was a prestigious and much sought-after programme among many young Americans who saw it not only as an overseas adventure working for their government, but also as a way to gain valuable experience which was much desired by employers.[22] Since the Peace Corps' creation, gay people had been banned from participating, with the Peace Corps Manual stating that those engaged in 'sexual perversion', meaning homosexuality, were not allowed into the programme. If gay

18 'Government Agency Reverses Antigay Policy', *The Blade*, October 1977.
19 'Government Agency Reverses Antigay Policy', *The Blade*, October 1977; Bill Sievert, 'State Dept. "Aid" Clears Gay Workers', *The Advocate*, 2 November 1977.
20 Ibid.
21 Ibid.
22 Gerard T. Rice, *Twenty Years of Peace Corps* (Washington: Peace Corps, 1981), 1–15.

volunteers were detected while overseas, they were immediately returned home. Repeated appeals from gay rights organizations to the agency to change its policy had been unsuccessful.[23]

Seeking to end this discrimination and to revitalize the volunteer sector,[24] Carter appointed prominent anti-war activist Sam Brown as Director of ACTION, former Director of his 51.3% Committee Mary E. King as its Deputy Director, and Carolyn R. Payton, a Howard University psychologist, as Director (its first Black and female director) of the Peace Corps.[25] These appointments led rapidly to the ending of the discriminatory policy against gay people. Brown and King reformed not only the Peace Corps, but all the other programmes that were run by ACTION, which included the Foster Grandparents, the Senior Companions, and the Retired and Senior Volunteer programmes.[26]

The Foster Grandparents aimed to help people aged over fifty-five to remain active in their communities by helping the young. The volunteers were expected to act as 'foster grandparents': mentors, teachers and role models for children in need. Senior Companions was also targeted at over-55s, although in this case, the volunteers were expected to act as friends and helpers to fellow seniors who had difficulty with day-to-day activities, in order to aid them in remaining independent and reduce the burden on their families. The Retired and Senior Volunteer Program was another large-scale organization for seniors, who could apply the skills they had learned over their lifetimes, or else learn new ones, through taking part in a number of community activities such as tutoring and mentoring disadvantaged or disabled youth and teaching English to immigrants.[27] All three programmes had had discriminatory policies since their creation that prevented gay people from participating. Brown and King reversed these policies, creating in their agency specific job protection provisions governing non-job related behaviour for those who already work there or wished to be employed there.[28] ACTION and USAID became the first two agencies during Carter's administration to reverse their discriminatory policies against gay people, but this received rather limited coverage in the gay press.

The Job Corps and White House Fellowships

Two further instances of improvement in access to government-funded voluntary programmes can be mentioned here. The Department of Labor's (DoL) Job Corps,

23 Bush, Clay and McReynolds, author interviews.

24 Bourne and Eizenstat, author interviews.

25 Louie Estrada, 'Former Peace Corps Director Carolyn R. Payton Dies at 75', *WP*, 15 April 2001; *Peace Corps Times* 4, 1 January/February 1981: 9–10; 'Whatever Happened to … Peace Corps: Ready for a Comeback', *U.S. News & World Report*, 17 October 1977.

26 Letter, Anne Wexler to John Harris Burt, 13 February 1980. NGTFR, B.145, F.1, CU. WH memorandum: Talking points on gay issues, 5 August 1980. RMSF, G/L2, JCPL; Bourne and Bush, author interviews.

27 National and Community Service, 'Nationalservice.gov', https://americorps.gov/serve/americorps-seniors.

28 Letter, Robert Strauss to Charles Brydon and Lucia Valeska, 3 March 1980. RMSF, GH1, JCPL; Letter, Anne Wexler to John Harris Burt, 13 February 1980. NGTFR, B.145, F.1, CU.

formed in 1964, is a voluntary programme for 16–24-year-olds, offering free education and skills classes. According to Professor F. Ray Marshal, Carter's Secretary of Labor, it may be 'the most effective federal program for job training ever created', and its aim was to 'take unskilled recent high-school dropouts and give them the self confidence and skills they need to succeed in the job market'.[29] Carter said that the programme aimed to give the opportunity to 'young people who had grown up in poverty and frustration' to 'become responsible, employable, and productive citizens'.[30]

The programme was potentially very important for gay youngsters as a number of them were high-school dropouts and runaways, often due to bullying, and of course some had also grown up in poverty. However, since its creation the programme had had a discriminatory policy against gay people who were excluded from participating and dismissed if found out. The agency's Health Program Manual was aimed at the 'prevention and management' of homosexuality and contained phrases such as 'chronic overt homosexuality'; it warned against 'sexually deviant behaviour', prescribing 'medical discharges' for those perpetrating it, and recommended 'wholesome, supervised activities with members of the opposite sex'.[31] The NGTF had repeatedly complained to the DoL over the Job Corps' discriminatory policies, but the Department had taken no action to end them, and prior to 1976, requests for a meeting with officials from the DoL and the Job Corps had all been turned down.[32] In February 1976, Voeller and Kameny met with John Stetson, then Director of the Job Corps, and complained about the agency's Health Program Manual. Stetson promised that within the next few months a new manual without homophobic content would be issued and that the Job Corps would end its discriminatory policy against gay people. However, although Stetson was willing to amend the manual, the change did not materialize due to pressure from within the agency, as well as from the DoL.[33]

In late January 1977, Carter appointed Marshal as Secretary of Labor. Marshal immediately ended discrimination against gay people in all the agencies and programmes that fell within his department's jurisdiction. In April 1977, the 'Sexuality' component of the Manual was revised: all the homophobic references were removed, and it urged respect for differing sexual lifestyles, stating that 'a man or woman may not be excluded from participating in the Job Corps solely on the basis of his/her choice of sexual partner of the same gender. Therefore, homosexuality will be considered as one part of the total spectrum of sexuality'.[34]

A programme with a much narrower remit, but of symbolic importance as a sign of exclusionary norms, was the White House Fellows programme, established in 1964. It is a highly esteemed nonpartisan programme. Its inductees are normally given one-

[29] Ray Marshal and Marc Tucker, *Thinking for Living: Education and the Wealth of Nations* (New York: Basic Books, 1993), 224.

[30] Jimmy Carter, 15th Anniversary of the Job Corps Statement by the President. Online by Gerhard Peters and John T. Woolley, The American Presidency Project, https://www.presidency.ucsb.edu/node/248026.

[31] 'Job Corps Change Manual', *GN*, May 1977.

[32] Clay, author interview.

[33] 'Job Corps against Gays', *The Blade*, March 1976; 'Job Corps Won't Discriminate', *The Advocate*, 24 March 1976.

[34] 'Job Corps Change Manual', *GN*, May 1977.

year full-time salaried placements as assistants to high-ranking federal officials: the Vice President, members of the Cabinet, White House aides and so on. They also take part in discussion sessions with private- and public-sector delegations, and go on study visits both in the United States and overseas.[35] Many Americans believed the programme was just for the white elite, and people from minorities did not even bother applying. Furthermore, although there was no explicit policy barring gay people from participating in the programme, there was also no effort to say that it was open to everyone and that being gay was no barrier to being a White House Fellow; for this and because of the general attitude of the federal government towards gay people, there had been no openly gay Fellows before 1977.[36]

Carter established his own President's Commission on White House Fellows and appointed W. Landis Jones as its director, and Bourne as one of its Commissioners. The Commission campaigned to encourage people from all social backgrounds and ethnicities to apply for Fellowships, making it clear that the programme was open to all.[37] In 1979, the NGTF wrote to Jones asking him to include 'sexual orientation' in the Commission's brochure in the non-discrimination policy section, a request to which he acceded.[38] Although the exact number is unknown, several openly gay people became White House Fellows during Carter's presidency.[39]

The Civil Service Commission, the Commission on Civil Rights and the Equal Employment Opportunity Commission

Soon after the March 1977 Meeting, Haft and Costanza contacted the CSC, the CCR and the EEOC to discuss the issue of the three commissions expanding their jurisdiction to include discrimination on the basis of sexual orientation. Haft set up two meetings between the NGTF and the CCR for 15 and 16 May 1977,[40] the first time that a meeting had been arranged between gay rights activists and this Commission. At the same time, Costanza and Haft relentlessly lobbied the CCR, and especially its chairperson Dr Arthur Fleming, to include gay rights under its jurisdiction, highlighting Carter's support; this was despite the fact that only four months before, the Commission had unanimously voted against such a decision. Fleming had been Chair of the CCR since 1974.[41]

In May 1977, Carter appointed Dr Alan 'Scotty' Campbell as Commissioner of the CSC. Campbell was liberal and known for supporting equal rights for gay employees. Thus, he immediately opened his door to the NGTF and discussed with it and with

35 'White House Fellows', *The White House*, https://www.whitehouse.gov/get-involved/fellows/.
36 Bourne, author interview.
37 Ibid.
38 Letter, C.F. Brydon and Lucia Valeska to W. Landis Jones, 18 May 1980. RMSF, GTFN2, JCPL.
39 Bourne, author interview.
40 Marilyn Haft: Status report on NGTF meetings with Agencies, 28 April 1977. SWSF, [Gay] CR, JCPL.
41 Haft, author interview.

Costanza and Haft ways to completely eliminate discrimination in the federal sector.[42] In July 1977, Costanza and Haft facilitated a meeting between the CSC and the NGTF. Campbell and both women attended the meeting, and the Commission agreed quite readily 'for the first time to consider harassment cases against gays as within their jurisdiction'.[43] Around the same time, Malson, who had been assigned by Costanza to deal with the EEOC with regard to the NGTF's request to extend the agency's jurisdiction, got in touch with Eleanor Holmes Norton, recently appointed by Carter as Director of the Agency. Like Campbell at the CSC, Norton immediately agreed that the EEOC include within its jurisdiction cases of discrimination on the basis of sexual or affectional preference.[44]

Shortly afterwards, Fleming and the CCR also agreed, albeit after pressure from gay rights activists and especially from Costanza and Haft, to include gay rights under their jurisdiction despite the fact that the Congress had neither authorized it nor provided any funding. On 15 August 1977, Fleming issued a statement that gay people were included in the CCR's jurisdiction under the statutory language 'unequal administration of justice'; thus the Commission would investigate discrimination on the basis of sexual orientation in the area of the administration of justice, including the courts, prisons and law-enforcement agencies.[45] Furthermore, the CCR was at that time conducting a survey of the national civil rights community in an attempt to identify the issues expected to be of critical importance in the field during the next ten years. The CCR agreed to include in the survey questions regarding discrimination against gay people and included leaders of the gay community among those surveyed; the questions involved discrimination over housing, political participation and employment. This was the first time in its history that the CCR had included in a survey questions regarding discrimination against gay people.[46] O'Leary and Voeller declared that they were 'extremely pleased' that their effort had been 'successful', while a press release from the NGTF claimed that the Commission's decision was 'the result of urging' from itself and 'others'.[47] 'Others' meant Costanza and Haft, but the statement did not name them, thus leaving Carter's administration without any credit for the outcome. This was not the first or the last time that the NGTF attempted to claim sole credit for an achievement on a gay rights issue by omitting the role and efforts of Carter's administration (a topic discussed further in Chapter 13).

On 24 August, Fleming met again with Voeller and O'Leary. Although he stated that the CCR had no plans to conduct any study on sexual orientation in the fiscal years of 1978 and 1979, they discussed several other areas of study on a number of

42 Clay and Haft, author interviews.

43 OPL Records of Meetings, July 1977, and Letter, Midge Costanza to James Woodward, undated, both in MCI.

44 Malson, author interview; See also documents in NGTFR, B.143, F.13, CU.

45 'Civil Rights Commission Acknowledges Jurisdiction Over Anti-Gay Discrimination in Administration of Justice', News from NGTF, 27 August 1977. NGTFR, B.36, F.47, CU; Marilyn Haft Memorandums to Margaret Costanza, 7 October 1977 and 14 October 1977, both in SWSF, [Gay] CR, JCPL.

46 'U.S. Civil Rights Commission Includes Gay Issues, Leaders in Survey', News from NGTF, 15 August 1978. NGTFR, B.36, F.94, CU.

47 'Civil Rights Commission Acknowledges Jurisdiction over Anti-Gay Discrimination in Administration of Justice', News from NGTF, 27 August 1977. NGTFR, B.36, F.47, CU.

issues of concern for the gay community, for example police brutality, treatment of gay prisoners, the courts' handling of child custody cases involving gay parents and denial of legal-aid funds to gay-rights litigants.[48] Subsequently, Costanza and Haft organized another meeting between the CCR and the NGTF, which took place on 12 October.[49] Both women attended the meeting, along with O'Leary and Voeller, and four CCR Commissioners, including Fleming. Voeller and O'Leary discussed a number of areas of discrimination against gay people – the unequal enforcement of sodomy laws, discrimination in the military and in prisons, police brutality against gay people, and custody and visitation rights of divorced gay parents – and requested CCR studies into several of them. Finally, they asked that gay rights be the subject of an issue of the Commission's journal *Civil Rights Digest*.[50]

After the meeting, Costanza noted in a letter to Fleming that their offices shared many of the same interests, and that she was 'so impressed with the Commission's responsiveness' to the NGTF's requests.[51] The CCR moved quickly to address all of the activists' requests.[52] The Commission soon conducted an investigation and held hearings on police misconduct towards gay people in Houston and Philadelphia. Even more importantly, the Commission's reports on the allegations made in the two hearings made it clear that it would not tolerate police abuse and harassment towards gay people.[53] In early 1979, the CCR held a two-day conference on 'Police Practices and the Preservation of Civil Rights', and the NGTF was invited to participate in it. It was the first time that the CCR had invited the NGTF to participate in one of its conferences. O'Leary attended and told the CCR about the discrimination and mistreatment the gay community faced from the police, asking the Commission to conduct a national investigation of the issue.[54]

Finally, on 7 February 1978, Campbell and the CSC gave gay employees the same rights as heterosexuals by ruling that gay people should not be arbitrarily banned from federal jobs and could only be fired if it was proven that their actions were likely to affect job performance or the performance of the whole agency. The gay community hailed the news and praised Campbell for this change. Kameny characterized the CSC's ruling as 'a major victory' for gay people, although he also criticized the section allowing discipline for 'notoriously disgraceful conduct' by stating,

> Let the commission be warned that homosexual federal employees have no intention of being compelled to remain 'in the closet'. Having won in the Commission, the battle now will have to shift to the benighted agencies which still retain anti-gay personnel policies.[55]

48 Ibid.
49 Margaret Costanza schedule, 12 October 1977. SWSF, [NGTF: Agency Meetings], JCPL.
50 Memorandum, Marilyn Haft to Margaret Costanza, 14 October 1977. SWSF, [Gay] CR, JCPL.
51 Letter, Margaret Costanza to Commissioner Fleming, 19 October 1977. SWSF, [Gay] CR, JCPL.
52 Bill Sievert, 'U.S. Agency to Probe Some Gay Complaints', *The Advocate*, 2 November 1977.
53 Larry Bush, 'White House Claims Solid Record on Gay Issues', *The Sentinel*, 16 May 1980.
54 'Violence vs. Gays', *OOB*, February 1979.
55 Joseph Young, 'Homosexuals Given Equal Job Rights', *WS*, 8 February 1978.

The Civil Service Reform Act

In the meantime, California Democratic Senator Alan Cranston had put forward a bill that would prohibit discrimination in federal employment on the basis of sexual orientation. In mid-May 1977, Haft and Malson met with Gary Aldridge and Jonathan Fleming, Cranston's Legislative Assistants, to discuss the bill. Haft and Malson expressed Carter's 'full support' for the bill and offered help to promote it. Subsequently, Costanza, Haft and Malson frequently met and corresponded with both men to discuss the progress of the bill, offering assistance with its language and lobbying on behalf of Carter's administration for support. Aldridge sent Haft a 'thank-you' card.[56] However, despite the White House's support, Cranston's bill failed to gather support in Congress and died soon afterwards.

Shortly after taking office, Carter and his aides had began working on the Civil Service Reform Act (CSRA), the first large-scale revision of Civil Service laws in more than a century. The Act aimed to reward merit and efficiency, penalize incompetence, reduce bureaucracy, give women greater opportunities for federal employment, and to end what the administration saw as an abuse of the Civil Service system and the CSC under President Nixon, whom Carter accused of hiring and promoting federal employees for political reasons. Carter's legislation aimed to protect employees from such practices as well as from discrimination over issues such as political affiliation, race, colour, religion, national origin and sex. It also aimed to protect whistleblowers who had often been punished or even sacked when they pointed out abuses within the system. Carter intended to set up an Office of Personnel Management (OPM) and an independent Merit Systems Protection Board, for the over two million people employed by the federal government, to take on the quasi-judicial functions of the 95-year-old CSC, which would then be abolished.[57]

Despite pressure from conservatives who opposed the extension of civil rights to gay people, and a Congress that was not ready to even discuss gay rights, Carter was determined to fulfil his election promise to support legislation that would protect gay employees in the federal sector, apart from 'sensitive areas' such as the military and security.[58] Carter told his staff, 'We have to have civil rights not just for Blacks or for women, but for anybody'.[59] Carter, Campbell, Costanza and Eizenstat acknowledged that there was an opportunity to protect gay people in the federal sector by including in the new legislation such a provision, and began working for it. Carter was initially happy to include explicit language for the protection of gay people, but his advisers, including Eizenstat and Costanza, fully recognized the dangers of this position in

[56] Gary Aldridge's 'thank you' card to Marilyn Haft, undated. JWSF, [Gay Job Discrimination] [n.d.] [O/A 4458], JCPL; Haft, author interview; Marilyn Haft Weekly Staff Report, 9–14, 17 May 1977. MCI.

[57] Patricia W. Ingraham and James L. Perry, 'The Three Faces of Civil Service Reform', in Herbert D. Rosenbaum and Alexej Ugrinsky (eds), *The Presidency and Domestic Policies of Jimmy Carter* (Westport, Connecticut and London: Greenwood Press, 1994), 677–88; Martin Tolchin, 'Carter Seeks Change in Civil Service Law to Reward Efficiency', *NYT*, 3 March 1978.

[58] Bourne and Eizenstat, author interviews.

[59] Bourne, author interview.

the case of a Congressional bill.[60] Carter's difficulty is explained in a memorandum Wishman wrote to Costanza on 14 February 1978, contending that Carter 'cannot win' as 'either move he makes will inevitably involve him in controversy'. He added:

> If the President includes the category in his proposed legislation, he will be subjected to the enormous criticism such as that Midge has been subjected to over the year for defending the constitutional rights of gays. . . . If he does not make any reference to protecting gays the gay community will attack him for insensitivity.[61]

In a memorandum to Carter on 16 February 1978, Costanza wrote that 'the proposed Civil Service legislation may attract substantial public criticism from the gay community' because of the 'absence of explicit language' in 'protecting gays against employment discrimination'. However, she acknowledged that 'present Civil Service regulations do afford protection for gay and these regulations would be in force under the new legislation', and thus 'in effect, give gay people the same employment protection they would have if they were explicitly added to the new legislation'. Costanza outlined the pros and cons of including a specific reference to sexual preference in the bill.[62]

On 25 February Eizenstat 'strongly recommended ...against including explicit language protecting gays'.[63] Eizenstat told the author that the inclusion of the words 'gay' or 'lesbian' 'would just have raised red flags and endangered the passage of the entire legislation' which

> was a crucial piece of legislation for the whole civil service, professionalizing, encouraging whistle blowers, accountability, all part and parcel of the whole campaign that we ran in '76 against Watergate . . . we did not want to have one provision that would end up defeating this whole thing.*

Kameny agreed with the caution shown in 1978 by some of Carter's aides with regard to the language in the bill when he acknowledged in 2000 that 'at the time it was not considered politically practical to address the matter of employment of gays head-on, although in light of the events of the immediately preceding years, and the climate of opinion at the time, the issue had to be dealt with'.[64] The argument resembled that at the IWY Commission about the use of the word 'lesbian' in its resolutions (see Chapter 5).

The solution was the use of coded language: Carter's proposed legislation now prohibited discrimination on the grounds of 'political affiliation, race, color, religion, national origin, sex, marital status, age or handicapping condition'. Although it did not specifically mention sexual orientation, it barred discrimination 'on the basis of conduct which does not adversely affect the performance of the employee or applicant or the

60 Eizenstat, author interview; also see documents in OSS, Presidential Files, Folder: 2/27/78, [2], JCPL, and in SWSF, [Gay] CR, JCPL.

61 Memorandum, Seymour Wishman to Midge Costanza, 14 February 1978. SWSF, [Gay] CR, JCPL.

62 Margaret Costanza Memorandum to President Carter, 16 February 1978. SWSF, [Gay] CR, JCPL.

63 Memorandum, Stu Eizenstat and Steve Simmons to President Carter, 25 February 1978. OSS, Presidential Files, F.2/27/78, [2], JCPL.

64 Kameny, 'Government v. Gays', 194.

performance of others', which was meant to achieve the same effect.[65] In March 1978, Carter sent the CSRA to Congress. Despite the indirect language, some Congressmen were still not happy as they understood its real purpose. Subsequently, Carter, Campbell and the White House campaigned and lobbied with great commitment for the CSRA. Their efforts won them the backing of most of the country's leading newspapers. Eventually, in August 1978, Congress passed the bill.[66] Bert Carp, Carter's Deputy Assistant for Domestic Affairs, who campaigned and lobbied for the passage of the Act, told the author that it took 'a considerable effort' to convince Congress to support it.*

Finally, on 13 October, Carter signed the CSRA into law. As a result of the Act, 95 per cent of all federal positions covered by the civil service system were now made by law available to gay men and women. Some restrictions, however, continued to apply in the remaining 5 per cent, which included areas of national security such as the military and the intelligence services.[67] The State Department, which until then had been following a strict discriminatory policy against gay people, accepted that it had to follow the CSRA requirements. It issued the following policy statement, also known as the Harvard Doctrine:

> The Department considers each application on its own merits, in light of all relevant factors. Admitted or alleged homosexuality per se does not constitute a basis for denial of employment. However, within the context of the Department's responsibility for the conduct of foreign affairs, an applicant's personal traits or practices, including his/her sexual practices (either heterosexual or homosexual), may be relevant in evaluating his/her stability, character, discretion, and susceptibility to undue influence or duress.[68]

Carter hailed the CSRA for putting 'merit principles into statute' and very importantly for defining 'prohibited personnel practices'.[69] The White House stated, 'we believe that [the Act] is the most effective protection that gay federal employees can have. Unlike an executive order, it cannot be easily reversed'.[70]

Although the vast majority of the gay community appreciated the new legislation,[71] some gay rights activists were not entirely satisfied with the CSRA because of the lack of explicit language and on account of its remaining exceptions.[72] However, it should be recalled that both the policy and its exceptions were fully in line with what Carter had announced during his election campaign (e.g. in *The Advocate*, on NBC's

65 Rick Valelly, 'How Gay Rights Activists Remade the Federal Government', *WP*, 1 October 2018.

66 Jimmy Carter, Civil Service Reform Act of 1978 Statement on Signing S. 2640 into Law. Online by Gerhard Peters and John T. Woolley, The American Presidency Project, https://www.presidency.ucsb.edu/node/244000; Bert Carp and Eizenstat, author interviews.

67 Letter, Robert Strauss to Charles Brydon and Lucia Valeska, 3 March 1980. RMSF, GH1, JCPL; WH: Outline of Remarks on Gay Rights, undated. MCSF, GR, JCPL.

68 WH memorandums on gay issues, 5 August 1980, and undated, both in RMSF, G/L2, JCPL.

69 Rick Valelly, 'How Gay Rights Activists Remade the Federal Government', *WP*, 1 October 2018.

70 WH memorandum: Talking points on gay issues, 5 August 1980. RMSF, G/L2, JCPL.

71 Apuzzo, Bunch, Bush, Howell, Kent and McReynolds, author interviews.

72 NGTF, 'Federal Agencies that Discriminate Against Gay Citizens', October 1979. NGTFR, B.139, F.46, CU.

Tomorrow Show and his well-publicized response to Troy Perry's question; see Chapter 1). Conservatives were also unhappy with the CSRA. Carter received a large amount of correspondence from angry and 'worried' conservative Christians expressing outrage that gay people were now allowed by law to work in federal agencies and perceived the CSRA to be promoting homosexuality.[73]

The CSRA and the way it benefited gay employees received little attention from the mainstream media at the time, as was generally the case with Carter's efforts with regard to gay rights. More surprisingly, the gay press did not report it, and the NGTF, which had not been a prime mover behind the reform, did not mention it in its publications. But the gay rights activists who were interviewed for this book highlighted the significance and importance of the Act. For example, Bush said that it 'reversed a policy which denied employment based on sexual orientation. It was really a terrible effort to kick people out of their jobs for being gay. And the Civil Service Reform Act of 1978 changed that'.* Bunch said, 'It was a very important Act. . . . I knew *many* people who worked in the federal government and who were lesbian and gay, and it was *very* important that that Act, which made them not have to be afraid of being more open about their lives . . . it was *absolutely* important'.*

The NGTF's 'Petition the President' and the March on Washington: 'From gay pride to gay politics'

In April 1978, Robin Tyler brought to Harvey Milk the idea for a gay march on Washington, D.C.[74] During Gay Pride '78 in San Francisco, Milk urged the participants to march on Washington and tell Carter and the nation to 'wake up . . . no more racism, no more sexism, no more ageism, no more hatred'.[75] The NGTF overcame initial reservations and by August 1979 threw its support behind the initiative, which was entitled March on Washington for Gay and Lesbian Rights.[76] On 21 August, the NGTF launched its 'Petition the President' campaign in connection with the March. The petition which was circulated by the organization asked Carter

> to act on his campaign pledge of May 21, 1976 by 1) issuing an Executive Order barring discrimination against lesbians and gay men [in the remaining 5 per cent of the federal sector]; and 2) endorsing the bill before Congress (HR 2074) to extend the 1964 and 1968 Civil Rights Acts to include protection on the basis of sexual orientation.[77]

73 Various letters in JWSF, GI-HC, JCPL and in MCI.
74 Tyler, author interview.
75 'Gay Pride '78: Largest Gay Turnout in History', *The Advocate*, 9 August 1978.
76 'NGTF Endorses DC March; Announces "Petition the President" Campaign', *It's Time*, August–September 1979. ATSF, B.265, GR, JCPL.
77 Ibid. H.R.2074 was introduced in Congress by Representative Ted Weiss in February 1979. It would give the Attorney General the right to launch a civil action when someone was barred from a public facility over their sexual orientation. It would also prohibit discrimination against gay people in

The NGTF press release referred to comments Carter had made during his press conference at the Hilton Hotel in San Francisco on 21 May 1976 (discussed in Chapter 1), where he had stated, 'I don't think that the government at the local, state or federal level should single out homosexuals for special abuse or special harassment, or special prosecution under existing laws'. He had also stated that he would 'certainly sign' Abzug's bill to amend the Civil Rights Act of 1964, which was very similar to the bill referred to in the petition.[78] However, the NGTF had put words into Carter's mouth, as he had not promised then or at any other time during his 1976 campaign to issue an executive order over the issue, or to ban all exclusions. On the contrary, Carter had at least three times (in *The Advocate*, *The Tomorrow Show* and to Troy Perry) publicly declared that he supported an end to discrimination against gay people in the federal sector apart from the security sector. Far from going back on his promise, he had already fulfilled it, and not with an executive order that could have been easily reversed by the next president, but by legislation. Although one could argue that Carter's beliefs about the security sector were misguided or wrong, the NGTF's release was nevertheless inaccurate and misleading, though it was believed by the gay community, who were mostly not aware of all the facts regarding Carter's pre-election promises. Thus, thanks to the NGTF's release, the gay community was under the impression for the remainder of Carter's presidency, and also later, that Carter had failed to deliver on a promised Executive Order. This was even despite the fact that on May 1980, Larry Bush attempted to set the record straight on the matter with an article in *The Sentinel*. Bush attributed the alleged executive order claim to the 'gay grapevine', clarifying that Carter himself had been 'publicly putting the breaks on such speculation', and pointed the readers to Carter's interview in *The Tomorrow Show*.[79]

On 14 October 1979, the March on Washington for Gay and Lesbian Rights took place with the participation of between 25,000 and 250,000 people.[80] The marchers passed by the Washington Monument demanding a range of concessions for gay Americans, including an end to discrimination in employment and in the military and the repeal of all anti-gay laws.[81] Some of the speakers urged Carter to take a much stronger stance against anti-gay discrimination and warned that about twenty million American lesbians and gays were moving 'from gay pride to gay politics'.[82] It was clear that, for Carter, who was hoping to win the presidency in the upcoming re-election campaign, the position he took in response would have a huge impact on who would vote for him – and who would not. The religious right, led by Jerry Falwell, who declared 14 October to be a 'national day of prayer for homosexuals',[83] and Anita Bryant responded by organizing a press conference in protest and a prayer service at

employment, housing or access to federal programmes, allowing the Attorney General to set out penalties. However, it gathered little Congressional support and was not enacted.

78 Carter Presidential Campaign Press Release: 'Jimmy Carter Speaks Out on Gay Rights', 23 May 1976. RMSF, GR, B.7, JCPL; 'The Gospel According to Jimmy Carter', *GCN*, 26 June 1976.

79 Larry Bush, 'White House Claims Solid Record on Gay Issues', *The Sentinel*, 16 May 1980.

80 Estimates of attendance varied: the National Parks Service estimated 25,000 and the D.C. Police 75,000, while some of the participants suggested 250,000. Clendinen and Nagourney, *Out*, 408.

81 Thomas Morgan, 'National Gay Rights March, Counter Events Set Here', *WP*, 12 October 1979.

82 Quoted in Faderman, *The Gay Revolution*, 413.

83 'March on D.C. Signals Starts of Gay Politics', *Gaze*, December 1979.

the same time as the gay rights march.[84] A spokesman of the conservative Christian Voice announced, 'We are declaring war on homosexuals'.[85] Furthermore, the religious right organized its own march in Washington entitled 'Washington for Jesus' and promoting 'righteousness and morality' to be held on 29 April 1980, with more than 100,000 people making reservations well in advance to attend it.[86]

The day after the March on Washington, Jane Wales met in the White House with twenty representatives from the gay rights organizations who had participated in it, to discuss the reasons for it as well as the issue of immigration (see Chapter 8).[87] The activists had also invited the National Coalition of Black Gays to send a representative, but the organization turned down the invitation;[88] Gerald explained to the author, 'we withdrew from the meeting because, again, we thought we were being tokenized'.* On 29 October, Wales met with members of the GSDC and the main issue of the discussion was the federal employment areas that were not covered by the CSRA. Wales reiterated the administration's support for gay rights and its willingness to continue the dialogue with the activists to find ways to address this, but avoided committing Carter to issuing an executive order.[89] On 9 November 1979, the NGTF wrote to Wexler to let her know that they had already gathered 'over 70,000 signatures' for its petition and expressed their wish to come to White House and present it in what they described as a 'historical event'.[90]

In the meantime, the religious right was quickly intensifying its effort to halt the advancement of gay rights. On 21 November 1979, Mike Burns of the Moral Majority, Dot George of the National Christian Action Coalition and Gary Jarmin of Christian Voice presented to Allison Thomas in the White House a petition signed by 40,000 church ministers across the country asking Carter 'to resist efforts to legitimize homosexuality by giving special consideration under law to those who practice such acts'.[91] In late 1979, Senator Paul Laxalt (presidential hopeful Ronald Reagan's campaign manager) introduced, with the support of the religious right, the Family Protection Act.[92] The Act, among other restrictions, 'Prohibits the expenditure of Federal funds to any organization which presents male or female homosexuality as an acceptable alternative life style', 'Amends the Civil Rights Act of 1964 to provide that any action taken by an employer against a homosexual shall not be considered an unlawful employment practice' and 'Prohibits any instrumentality of the Federal Government from seeking to enforce nondiscrimination with respect to homosexuals'.[93] Despite strong support from conservatives, in the end the bill did not pass.[94]

84 Thomas Morgan, 'National Gay Rights March, Counter Events Set Here', *WP*, 12 October 1979.
85 Bill Roeder, 'Voice against Gay Rights', *Newsweek*, 30 July 1979.
86 '"Morality" March Blurs Church/State Lines', *Capitol Hill*, 2, 2. undated. RMSF, GTFN2, JCPL.
87 Letter, Paul Boneberg and DeeDee Knight to Jane Wales, 1 October 1979. ATSF, B.265, GR, JCPL.
88 Mailgram, NCBG to Jane Wales, 5 October 1979. ATSF, B.265, GR, JCPL.
89 Jane Wales's comments to the GSDC, 29 October 1979. ATSF, B.265, GR, JCPL; Wales, author interview.
90 Letter, Charles Brydon and Lucia Valeska to Anne Wexler, 9 November 1979. RMSF GTFN1, JCPL.
91 Courtland Milloy and Loretta Tofani, '25,000 Attend Gay Rights Rally at the Monument', *WP*, 15 October 1979; Allison Thomas's note for Bob Malson, 21 November 1979. ATSF, B.265, GR, JCPL.
92 Craig Howell, 'Senate Bill Pushes New Right Agenda', *The Blade*, 20 December 1979.
93 https://www.congress.gov/bill/96th-congress/senate-bill/1808.
94 Rosemary Ruether, 'Politics and the Family: Recapturing a Lost Issue', *Christianity and Crisis*, 29 September 1980: 262.

Although December 1979 was one of the administration's busiest and more crucial times, Wexler accepted the NGTF's request to present its petition at the White House. Thus, on 19 December the NGTF in the persons of Brydon, Carolyn Handy and Kay Whitlock, and another twelve gay rights activists (Adam DeBaugh, ABilly Jones-Hennin, Frank P. Scheuren, Steve Endean, Joseph Totten, Mary Spottswood Pou, Walter Lear, Margot Karle, Joyce Hunter, H. Gerald Schiff, Teresa DeCrescenzo and John C. Lawrence), presented it to Campbell, Chanin, Malson and Wexler in the Roosevelt Room.[95] Wexler chose the Roosevelt Room for the same reason Costanza had done in 1977.[96] The petition, however, contained not the promised 'over 70,000' signatures, but rather 51,000.[97]

Whitlock expressed warm appreciation for the attention being given to the petition and the issues it raised, and for Carter's efforts in areas of gay rights which she wished to 'recognize and acknowledge'. She referred specifically to the CSRA, to meetings between the administration and gay rights activists, to the fact that 'administration appointees' at the Internal Revenue Service had reversed the agency's discriminatory policy against gay organizations and granted them tax deductible status (see Chapter 7), to a new sensitivity about gay issues such as the ending of discrimination in the Peace Corps and to the appointment of known lesbians to certain presidential commissions. Whitlock accepted that these were 'important steps', but she claimed they had had 'only a minimal impact in the face of the institutionalized and entrenched prejudice that is rooted in government programs and in employment policies at agencies exempt from civil service rules'. She then explicitly compared the struggle of the gay rights movement with that of the civil rights movement, and stated: 'As was the case when President Truman acted to end institutionalized segregation within the armed services by executive order, so must President Carter act to reverse the government discrimination that places lesbians and gay men in the position of second class citizens'.[98]

The activists were told that Carter would be informed about the requests, and that the possibility of issuing the requested executive order would be explored. Campbell highlighted the fact that because of the CSRA 'there can be no discrimination on the basis of sexual orientation' as 'it protects 95% of all federal employees'. As for the other 5 per cent, Campbell assured the activists that he and Carter were going to look at this and examine all the available options, but cautioned that an executive order might not be the best option to reverse these policies and that other actions might be necessary. Wexler said that Carter's administration did not 'condone' the firing of gay federal employees because of their sexuality and admitted that 'there is discrimination that must be addressed. We cannot constantly be in a reactive position on this'.[99] However, Malson also reminded the petitioners that because of Congress's well-documented

95 'White House Receives Gay Rights Petition', News from NGTF, 21 December 1979. ATSF, B.271, NGTF, JCPL.

96 Apuzzo, author interview.

97 'White House Mulls Federal Ban on Bias toward Homosexuals', *WP*, 21 December 1979.

98 Statement of Kay Whitlock during the Presentation of the Petition in the White House on December 19, 1979. NGTFR, B.145, F.2, CU.

99 Claudia Moomjy, 'NGTF Parley at White House', *BAR*, 3 January 1980; 'White House Receives Gay Rights Petition', News from NGTF, 21 December 1979. ATSF, B.271, NGTF, JCPL; 'White House Mulls Federal Ban on Bias toward Homosexuals', *WP*, 21 December 1979.

unwillingness to support gay rights, 'some exemptions might be necessary with respect to intelligence agencies'.[100] The activists were pleased with what they heard and the attitude of Carter's aides. After the meeting, Whitlock hailed Carter's administration for taking 'important steps' to eradicate discrimination against gay people and said she was impressed with Carter's aides' 'genuine concern' on the issues the activists brought up: 'it was clear that some issues raised prompted genuine concern. And I was pleased to hear them say they will continue to work with us'.[101]

On 20 December, Thomas issued a press release concerning the gay rights activists' petition, making the public aware of it. On the same day, the NGTF through a press release also announced the news, and Brydon characterized the fact that Carter was considering issuing the executive order and that he was aware of the gay concerns as 'a significant forward step'.[102] The same day, Brydon also wrote to Malson to thank him for attending the meeting and for his 'continuing involvement' on gay rights issues. Brydon stressed that he 'recognize[d] the necessity for the intelligence community to have more discretion with employees than is the case with other agencies', but he believed that the issue was not this kind of 'discretion', but their 'anti-gay attitude' and the 'institutionalized prejudice'.[103]

Shortly after the 19 December meeting, Malson publicly stated that the demands of the gay rights activists had been brought to Carter's personal attention and that it was 'true' that an executive order was 'under consideration' by the administration.[104] The news, which made headlines in the mainstream press across the country, including *The New York Times* and *The Washington Post*,[105] received a mixed response from the public. Over the next few weeks the White House received a large number of letters from politicians and religious leaders in support of and against the petition.[106]

The revelation that Carter was contemplating issuing such an executive order outraged conservatives who rallied to denounce him.[107] In March 1980, Bob Jones III led a delegation of fundamentalist ministers to the White House where they met with Maddox. Jones told the reporters there, 'We are here to tell the president that homosexuality must not become a protected way of life; an alternate life style', and added that 'this so-called born again Christian President is not acting very born again' and is not fit to be president. Jones and his delegation presented several petitions that had been signed by 74,000 people opposing the extension of civil rights laws to gay people. The petitions, which were handed in to Maddox in a large grocery cart, urged Carter to 'resist all efforts' by gay rights groups 'to elicit an executive order legalizing homosexuality within the federal government and elsewhere in our American

[100] Letter, C. F. Brydon to Robert Malson, 20 December 1979. ATSF, B.265, GR, JCPL.

[101] 'White House Receives Gay Rights Petition', News from NGTF, 21 December 1979. ATSF, B.271, NGTF, JCPL

[102] Ibid.

[103] Letter, C.F. Brydon to Bob Malson, 20 December 1979. ATSF, B.265, GR, JCPL.

[104] 'White House Studying Homosexuals' Charges', *NYT*, 22 December 1979; 'White House Mulls Federal Ban on Bias toward Homosexuals', *WP*, 21 December 1979.

[105] Ibid.

[106] Maddox, author interview; see also letters in JWSF, GI and RMSF, GV 1980, B.8 in JCPL, and in NGTFR, B.145, F.1, CU.

[107] Ibid.

society'.[108] Maddox, who had discussed the issue of gay rights and of the ministers' visit with Carter, conveyed to Jones and to the other ministers a message from Carter which said that while the president did not endorse or promote homosexuality, he believed that gay people should have the same rights as other Americans and that he intended to continue to support equal rights for gays in all aspects of life. Maddox's admission of Carter's support for gay rights and of his intention to continue advancing them surprised and angered his guests. Jones was 'very angry' with Carter because of his stance on homosexuality and was in Maddox's words 'trashing' and 'levelling all kinds of biblical stuff, hellfire and brimstone, on the gay people'. He demanded that Carter should meet in person with him and that he should stop his efforts on gay rights, otherwise he and other evangelical leaders were going to urge all evangelicals to vote for Reagan. Carter refused Jones's repeated requests to meet with him and ignored his petition.[109] Carter, via Maddox, stood his ground on his beliefs, jeopardizing his evangelical support even further, at a crucial time in his presidency. His stance was praised by the NGTF shortly before the 1980 presidential election, which wrote in one of its press releases about Carter's accomplishments on gay rights that '[he] took on the rights wing evangelists [*sic*] who crusaded against us, telling them to their faces at a White House meeting that he would not abandon us'.[110]

Carter did investigate the alternative of issuing an executive order on federal employment. He asked Malson to obtain from Margery Waxman, OPM's General Counsel, a memorandum about the effects of the exclusion of intelligence agencies from the CSRA's discrimination provisions, especially the options that exclusion gave them, the reasons why they had been excluded, and the likely consequences if the exclusion was reversed by an executive order.[111] Waxman responded, 'it is a well-settled principle of law that an executive order may not overcome a statute' and that the law clearly excluded intelligence-type agencies from the scope of prohibitions against anti-gay discrimination. The heads of these agencies also had a good deal of legally backed autonomy over matters of hiring and firing. She concluded:

> Because statutory authorities take precedence over Executive Orders, I do not believe it would be either advisable or effective to include such intelligence-type agencies within an Executive order banning discrimination on the basis of sexual orientation or preference. . . . Heads of intelligence agencies would retain their authority to terminate employees for any reasons, within their discretion.[112]

The administration pointed out to the gay rights activists the weakness of the executive order strategy, and that the issuing of such an order at this time 'would be inviting confrontation with the Congress', a confrontation that 'would result in the passage of specific statutes prohibiting the hiring of gay people in the military. Such legislation

[108] Maddox, author interview; 'Ministers Oppose Rights for Homosexuals', *AP*, 21 March 1980; 'Rights for Homosexuals Denounced by Preachers', *NYT*, 23 March 1980.
[109] Maddox, author interview.
[110] NGTF, 'What Has Jimmy Carter Ever Done for Gays?', 1980. NGTFR, B.6, F.3, CU.
[111] Memorandum, Margery Waxman to Robert Malson, undated. RMSF, GTFN2, JCPL.
[112] Ibid.

would be a significant step backwards for gay civil rights'.[113] Carter and his aides continued exploring with the OPM other ways of improving and securing the rights of gay people in the sector.[114] Nevertheless, some gay rights activists were not entirely convinced by the administration's claim regarding the effectiveness of an executive order and continued asking Carter to issue it.[115]

The episode of the March, the petition and the executive order illustrate the rapidly changing political environment in which the Carter administration found itself, not only in spite of, but to a large extent because of, its own efforts in support of gay rights. The very access and legitimacy which had abruptly been won by gay rights activists prompted an increased focus on what had not yet been achieved, with the case of federal employment illustrating the dynamic vividly: with the radical extension of protection for gay federal employees, the issue soon became one not of glass 95 per cent full but rather of glass still 5 per cent empty. The discourse of rights does, of course, contain an implication of inviolability which encourages such maximalist demands,[116] but also relevant was the lack of full understanding by activists both of Carter's own well-established position and of the scope of presidential power. The March on Washington and the Petition the President campaign, moreover, evoked parallel responses from the religious right, further reducing the president's room for manoeuvre.

The Campbell Memorandum

In the meantime, the NGTF argued that the CSRA was not well understood among federal employees and that some heads of agencies were reluctant to apply it, and asked the administration and Campbell to address this. Eizenstat assigned Carp and Malson to work on the issue along with Campbell, who in January 1979 had been reassigned by Carter from chairman of the disbanded CSC to director of one of the agencies that replaced it, the Office of Personnel Management. Carp, Malson and Campbell worked closely with federal personnel officials, legal experts and gay rights activists to make the Act known to everyone, to oblige the agencies to enforce it and also to find a way to protect gay employees in the areas of the federal sector that were not covered by the CSRA.[117] A memorandum to this end was drafted by Campbell and was approved first by the gay rights activists, then by Eizenstat and finally by Carter himself,[118] and in May 1980 it was issued as a directive to the heads of 119 federal agencies, including security agencies like the FBI. It went beyond the wording of the

113 Background on Gay Issues, undated. RMSF, G/L2, JCPL.

114 Carp and Eizenstat, author interviews.

115 Lou Chibbaro Jr., 'Carter Statement Viewed as Retreat', *The Blade*, 20 March 1980.

116 Mary Ann Glendon, *Rights Talk: The Impoverishment of Political Discourse* (New York: Free Press, 1991).

117 Mike Causey, 'New Rule to Bar Query on Sex Habits', *WP*, 14 May 1980; Carp, Eizenstat and Malson, author interviews; Rick Valelly, 'How Gay Rights Activists Remade the Federal Government', *WP*, 1 October 2018.

118 Stu Eizenstat's notes on Bob Malson's memorandum, 8 May 1980. RMSF, GH1, JCPL; Eizenstat, author interview.

CSRA by including explicit language stating that discriminating against someone over matters not related to the conduct of their work, such as sexual orientation, was now banned across the whole of the federal sector. This was taken to mean that, in most cases, federal officials could no longer inquire about the sexual preferences of job applicants or current employees. The memorandum read, 'The privacy and constitutional rights of applicants and employees are to be protected at all times. Thus, applicants and employees are to be protected against inquiries into, or actions based upon, non-job related conduct, such as religious, community or social affiliations, or sexual orientation'.[119]

Furthermore, the memorandum warned agency heads that they would 'be held responsible for the prevention of prohibited personnel practices', and required them to:

1. Issue a strong management statement clearly defining the policy of the Federal Government as an employer with regard to discrimination on the basis of conduct which does not adversely affect the performance of an employee, an applicant for employment, or other employees.
2. Emphasize this policy as part of new employee orientation covering the merit principles and prohibited personnel practices; and
3. Make employees aware of the avenues for seeking redress, and the actions that will be taken against employees violating this policy.[120]

Finally, and very importantly, the memorandum stated that federal agencies had to treat voluntary work in gay-related civic projects, such as gay or lesbian community centres, or in gay legal or medical clinics, as work experience. Such experience would also be taken into account when deciding a new employee's grading and salary. Thus, for the first time in American history, work on a gay community project was recognized by the government as 'work experience' and was rewarded accordingly,[121] thus making another important contribution to the legitimacy of homosexuality in the country. Waxman told Larry Bush, 'We are making it clear that any agency that thinks it has the right to discriminate against homosexuals must come to us first. There will be no way that they can discriminate, because we don't believe that there are job-related grounds anyway in the civil service'.[122]

The Campbell memorandum was a significant development for gay people's employment in federal agencies as for the first time a ban on discrimination had been introduced as a standard government-sector protection rather than being imposed by the judiciary.[123] The *Washington Post* pointed out that the Carter administration had provided 'a major boost for gay rights'.[124] The memorandum was greeted 'enthusiastically' by the gay community,[125] with the NGTF hailing it as 'providing

119 Alan K. Campbell memorandum, 12 May 1980. RMSF, GTFN2, JCPL.
120 Ibid.
121 Robert Malson letter to Jerold A. Krieger, 30 July 1980 and White House memorandum: Talking points on gay issues, 5 August 1980, both in RMSF, G/L2, JCPL.
122 Larry Bush, 'The Carter Administration: More Done than Said?', *The Advocate*, 12 June 1980.
123 Larry Bush, 'White House Claims Solid Record on Gay Issues', *The Sentinel*, 16 May 1980.
124 Mike Causey, 'New Rule to Bar Query on Sex Habits', *WP*, 14 May 1980.
125 Bush, Howell, Kent and McReynolds, author interviews.

benefits to the gay community beyond the works and applicants directly affected'. Bush acknowledged in *The Sentinel* that as a result of Carter's policies, both in the FBI and the State Department there was 'a new openness in dealing with gay issues'.[126] Craig Howell, a member of the GAA who was described by Leonard P. Hirsch as 'one of the unsung heroes of the lesbian and gay movement',[127] told the author that the CSRA and Campbell's Memorandum were 'vital' for gay employees and added, 'We referred to the Campbell memo several times during subsequent Republican Administrations that tried to ignore that non-discrimination policy. All this counts very much in favour of President Carter's Administration'.* In December 1980, just a few months later, the first sign of this 'new openness' on the part of agencies in 'sensitive areas' appeared when it was discovered that a mid-level worker at the National Security Agency was gay. An in-depth investigation took place with the result that the employee was allowed to keep both his job and his government security clearance.[128]

ଔ

Progress in the employment area was one of Carter's greatest achievements in the advancement of gay rights; the CSRA was a major piece of legislation that dramatically changed the status quo for gay people. The NGTF eventually acknowledged that the administration had done more to advance gay rights than any other administration (see Chapter 13).[129] It said that Carter not only 'extended employment rights for gays to non-civil service agencies for the first time ever' but 'gave gay federal employees a firm guarantee of their rights . . . banning discrimination and holding the bosses to account'.[130]

Nevertheless, some gay rights activists continued pressuring Carter to issue an executive order. Only in December 1980, after Carter had lost the presidential election, did the NGTF admit that an executive order would have been 'easily overturned by the Congress', which would be a 'political setback' for gay rights.[131] Over the next thirty-three years, Congress rejected every bill that aimed to end discrimination in employment against gay people. It was only in 2013 that the Senate finally passed the Employment Non-Discrimination Act, but even this was a year later voted down by the House Rules Committee.[132] The significance and boldness of Carter's advances in this field stand out in stark relief against this later record of government quiescence.

126 Larry Bush, 'White House Claims Solid Record on Gay Issues', *The Sentinel*, 16 May 1980.

127 Leonard P. Hirsch, 'A Wheel Within a Wheel: Sexual Orientation and the Federal Workforce', in D'Emilio et al., *Creating Change*, 497 n12.

128 'Gay Analyst Keeps Job', *Gaze*, February 1981.

129 'Carter Appeals for Gay Support', News from NGTF, 6 March 1980. RMSF, GTFN1, JCPL.

130 NGTF, 'What Has Jimmy Carter Ever Done for Gays?', undated. NGTFR, B.6, F.3, CU.

131 Letter, NGTF to Judy Davenport. 11 December 1980. RMSF, G/L2, JCPL.

132 Chris Johnson, 'House Panel Rejects Last-ditch Effort to Pass ENDA', *The Washington Blade*, 3 December 2014.

7

Recognition

Tax exemption, federal funding and broadcasting

This chapter begins with an issue raised at the March 1977 Meeting which, although not the most rousing of political topics, was of vital importance for the gay community, namely the treatment of its organizations for taxation purposes. Its obvious financial implications were accompanied by symbolic ones which both gay rights activists and their opponents were keen to pursue, while in the Internal Revenue Service the activists had a staunch opponent. Success in this campaign unlocked others. More purely symbolic, but still vitally important, recognition was gained by the designation of the gay community *as* a community in the regulations of the Federal Communications Commission.

The 'abysmal depth of homophobia' at the IRS

A major practical issue for gay organizations during the 1970s was that of tax exemption. According to tax law, certain organizations – such as churches and charitable groups – were exempt from a range of taxes. For gay rights organizations, which considered their purposes to be charitable, tax exemption seemed a justifiable request, and would of course yield a considerable financial boost. But tax-exempt status would also provide them with legitimation, a recognition of their efforts by the government, and it would also make them eligible for federal funding. However, the Internal Revenue Service (IRS) was known for its anti-gay policies and attitude and had recurrently turned down the organizations' applications for tax-exempt status. Furthermore, dealing with the IRS was extremely difficult for gay rights activists; their requests for meetings with IRS officials were denied and the responses to their correspondence, whenever someone bothered replying, were extremely slow and written in an unprofessional manner that often verged on insulting.[1] Craig Howell told the author that gay rights organizations 'had been getting nowhere with the IRS homophobes'.* The unofficial policy of the IRS was to deny tax-exempt status to non-profit gay rights organizations unless they dropped the word 'gay' from their

1 Clay, Howell and Vida, author interviews.

title and agreed to clarify in their public advocacy that homosexuality is 'a sickness, disturbance, or diseased pathology'.[2] Given the particularly stark position of the IRS, it is relevant at this point to note that in March 1977 the American Psychiatric Association (APA) advocated in a letter to Carter, which it copied to the NGTF, 'the elimination of all discrimination against homosexual men and women that is based solely on the fact that they are homosexual', and pointed out that the Association had adopted a memorandum to that effect in 1973, when homosexuality had been declassified as a psychiatric disorder in its *Diagnostic and Statistical Manual of Mental Disorders*.[3]

Gay organizations had been attempting to achieve tax exemption for several years, but in 1973 they intensified their efforts after the ACLU asked Stanley Weithorn, a prominent attorney specializing in tax-exemption cases for non-profit organizations, to represent them. Weithorn suggested that the activists set up a not-for-profit group as party to its applications. The NGTF thus created the Fund for Human Dignity. Weithorn crafted its application for tax exemption to the IRS, which was denied. Weithorn then, as he put it, 'bombarded the IRS with memos and arguments' explaining why the Fund, as well as the other gay organizations whose applications had been turned down, had not been treated equally by the law. Still nothing came of it, and the IRS's replies to the activists' correspondence were particularly slow. Weithorn wrote that 'IRS bureaucrats in the Nixon Administration believed that whenever two or more homosexuals were in the same room, an orgy would break out'.[4] In 1975, encouraged by the APA's declassification (effectively the de-medicalization) of homosexuality, Weithorn applied once again to the IRS for tax exemption for the Fund. Weithorn had repeatedly requested a meeting with the IRS, and one was finally granted. According to Weithorn, the eight 'stone-faced bureaucrats of the IRS' who participated in the meeting opened the discussion by announcing, 'We are sticking to our position'. Despite Weithorn's legal arguments showing that the IRS was obliged to rule in the Fund's favour, the IRS officers kept on repeating, 'We'll stick to our position'.[5]

As a result of this kind of intransigence, alongside more general experience of governmental exclusion, many of the approximately 1,700 gay organizations did not even bother applying for tax-exempt status. Those that did apply typically reported substantial delays with their cases. On some occasions, when an organization fitted the tax-exemption criteria, the IRS would do everything possible to delay the application through bureaucratic means, and sometimes even through harassment. It appeared to gay rights activists that the IRS was finding excuses and creating as many problems as possible as an exercise in attrition. Nevertheless, there were some rare cases where gay organizations were granted tax-exempt status, even if only temporarily. Successful applicants were instructed not to engage in any activities that could be construed as 'promoting' homosexuality. Thus, the few groups that had been granted exemption,

2 'Fund for Human Dignity Receives Tax-Deductible Status', News from NGTF, 9 August 1977. NGTFR, B.36, F.44, CU.

3 Letter, APA to President Carter, 14 March 1977. MCSF, [GR: C], JCPL.

4 Stanley S. Weithorn, *Love, Death, and Taxes: My Life in Politics, Social Activism, and the Law* (Bloomington: Archway Publishing, 2013), xiii–xv.

5 Ibid., xiv.

given their purpose, were at risk of losing it.[6] An example is the Lambda Service Bureau, which, having gained tax-exempt status in July 1975, was informed in March 1976 that the status would be revoked because it had stated that it would advocate that homosexuality was 'normal', presenting to the IRS carried 'a serious risk of encouraging or fostering homosexual attitudes and propensities among minors and other impressionable members of society'.[7]

In 1976, after continued efforts, the IRS informed Weithorn that they were willing to grant tax exemption to the Fund under the conditions that it 'may never contend that homosexuality is not a disease'; it should include 'a foe of homosexuality' on each panel 'created for public discussions'; it 'must never use the broadcast media to present any of its views'; and it 'may not hold social events (i.e. dinners, dances, picnics, etc.)'.[8] Naturally, the Fund found the conditions unacceptable. Weithorn said about this, 'Although I had been working for homosexual rights for three years steadily, it wasn't until that moment that I saw the abysmal depth of homophobia in this Federal Agency'. He and the Fund abandoned arguing with the IRS and invested their hopes in a change of president. Weithorn said that when Carter won the election, 'I sat on my hands and waited until a new IRS commissioner and chief counsel were appointed'.[9]

Achieving unconditional recognition

A few weeks before the March 1977 Meeting, Haft, who was aware of the importance of tax-exempt status for the gay organizations, contacted the IRS to discuss the matter. However, she was told that the White House 'cannot intervene', and once again the agency stuck to its previous position. Haft and Costanza, though, vowed to continue lobbying over the issue.[10] On 21 March, five days before the meeting, Carter nominated Jerome Kurtz, a progressive tax lawyer, as the new Commissioner of the IRS. As expected, the tax issue was raised at the White House meeting by the activists. William B. Kelley presented on this topic, and submitted a detailed report about it to Costanza.[11] The NGTF asked Costanza to arrange a meeting with the IRS and assist in achieving a reversal of IRS's policy. Although the IRS was an independent agency and not under Carter's control, Costanza pledged on behalf of the administration to help, while she assured the activists that 'sensitivity to the rights of gay people will be very seriously considered' by Carter when considering nominees for vacancies on such

6 William B. Kelley, 'The Internal Revenue Service and Income Tax Exemption for Gay Organizations', 1977. NGTFR, B.144, F.25, CU.

7 Letter, IRS to Lambda Service Bureau, 25 March 1976. NGTFR, B.144, F.25, CU.

8 Weithorn, *Love, Death, and Taxes*, xiv–xv.

9 Ibid., xv.

10 Memorandum, Marilyn Haft to Margaret Costanza, 25 March 1977. SWSF, [Gay] CR, JCPL; Haft, author interview.

11 Letter, William B. Kelley to Marilyn Haft, 28 March 1977. MCSF, MCSF, [H-GRPH], JCPL; William B. Kelley, 'The Internal Revenue Service and Income Tax Exemption for Gay Organizations', 1977. NGTFR, B.144, F.25, CU.

agencies.[12] She suggested waiting to arrange a meeting between the NGTF and the IRS until after Kurtz had been confirmed as the new Commissioner and after Carter had appointed a new IRS Chief Counsel.[13]

The waiting game proved to be the right option. The Senate confirmed Kurtz's appointment and he began his term on 5 May. Furthermore, in April, Carter appointed Leon G. Wigrizer, another liberal lawyer, as the IRS's Acting Chief Counsel. Subsequently, Haft sent Kelley's report to Wigrizer, while she and Costanza arranged for the NGTF to meet in person with him and other IRS officials. It was the first time that the White House had facilitated a meeting between gay rights activists and the IRS, and the first time that activists would meet with the agency's Acting Chief Counsel. Seeing the changes in the IRS they had been waiting for, and assured by Costanza that this was the right time to make a move, Weithorn and the Fund resubmitted their application for tax exemption.[14] Simultaneously, Haft and Costanza conveyed to Kurtz and Wigrizer that Carter strongly favoured tax exemption for gay organizations. Both men turned out to be much more willing than their predecessors to discuss the matter and do something about it. Furthermore, Costanza and Haft arranged for Kurtz and Wigrizer to meet with Weithorn and gay rights activists.[15] Thus, in May 1977, Weithorn and activists held meetings with Kurtz and Wigrizer; it was the first time that gay rights activists had met in person with the IRS's Chief Commissioner.[16]

After Weithorn's application, Haft and Costanza maintained their contact with Kurtz and Wigrizer, lobbying them for a positive answer. The fact that the IRS leadership was considering granting tax exemption to gay organizations with the assistance and support of Carter's administration became known to conservative and homophobic IRS officials. These officials, strongly supported by religious and other anti-gay forces, mobilized and tried to convince Kurtz and Wigrizer not to grant tax exemption to gay organizations. Wigrizer's answer did not take long to come: in June, despite pressure from anti-gay IRS officials and religious leaders, he informed the White House and the activists that from then on all gay rights groups would be eligible for tax-exempt status. This meant that they were exempted from paying local, state and federal taxes, while tax payers who were making contributions to the groups were able to fully deduct these from their tax returns.[17] In July, the Fund for Human Dignity became the first gay rights organization to be granted tax-exempt status without all the self-abnegating restrictions previously imposed by the IRS.[18] The gay community hailed the reversed policy, the NGTF calling it 'a major breakthrough for gay organizations'.[19]

12 'NGTF-Federal Agency Meetings Set Second White House Conference in September', News from NGTF, 31 March 1977. NGTFR, B.145, F.47, CU.
13 Haft, author interview.
14 'Fund for Human Dignity Receives Tax-Deductible Status', News from NGTF, 9 August 1977. NGTFR, B.36, F.44, CU; Weithorn, *Love, Death, and Taxes*, xv.
15 Haft, author interview.
16 Weithorn, *Love, Death, and Taxes*, xv.
17 Haft, author interview; Jeffery St. John, 'Now Taxpayers Are Financing Homosexual Causes' (the newspaper title is unfortunately not visible in the archive record), MCSF, [H-GRPH], JCPL.
18 'Fund for Human Dignity Receives Tax-Deductible Status', News from NGTF, 9 August 1977. NGTFR, B.36, F.44, CU.
19 'IRS Grants GAA/DC Tax Exemption Status', *The Blade*, October 1977.

Numerous gay organizations all over the country followed this lead, and during Carter's presidency, hundreds of groups and facilities received tax-exempt status unconditionally, along with retrospective exemption to the date of their creation. Organizations labouring under the onerous conditions could now apply to the IRS for release from them.[20]

On 9 August 1977, the NGTF proudly announced the news in its newsletter and wrote, 'This important ruling is a major reversal of IRS policy'. The newsletter stated that it had been a two-year effort by the Fund, Weithorn, Voeller and ACLU's Aryeh Neier, but also misleadingly stated that the ruling was not the 'result of any intervention by Ms. Costanza or the White House' with the IRS.[21] In reality, the administration had not only complied with the NGTF's request to set up meetings with the IRS, it had arranged for the Chief Commissioner himself to attend, along with the Acting Chief Counsel; prior to this activists had been dealing in person only with low-ranking IRS officials. Also crucial, of course, was Carter's decision to appoint progressive men like Kurtz and Wigrizer to leading roles in the IRS. Furthermore, Haft and Costanza had relentlessly lobbied Kurtz and Wigrizer to grant the tax exemption.

Eventually, the NGTF acknowledged the Carter administration's contribution to the IRS decision. On 19 December 1979, Whitlock publicly acknowledged that 'administration appointees reversed the policy that had prevented otherwise qualified organizations from receiving tax deductible status'.[22] On 6 March 1980, the NGTF issued a public statement acknowledging the administration's contribution to the IRS's decision and citing this as one of the reasons why gay voters should vote for Carter again.[23] In August, the White House reminded the activists that the 'the IRS moved slowly until this Administration brought in a changed attitude towards gays'.[24] Shortly before the 1980 presidential election the NGTF again publicly acknowledged Carter's contribution to the IRS ruling and hence to all the benefits it had brought to the gay organizations.[25]

Clay, who had been actively involved with the issue of tax exemption at the time as a member of the NGTF's Board of Directors, said that Carter administration's contribution to the reversal of the IRS's decision was 'indisputable' as 'the White House helped us massively'. He also said, 'I know that Costanza and the White House pushed the IRS to make this decision. Anyone who was involved will tell you the same thing'.* Apuzzo, who became the Fund's Executive Director shortly after it was granted tax exemption, said that Carter administration's contribution to the IRS's decision was 'absolutely decisive, without a doubt', and made clear the magnitude of the financial implications:

20 Larry Bush, 'White House Claims Solid Record on Gay Issues', *The Sentinel*, 16 May 1980; Letter, Robert Strauss to Charles Brydon and Lucia Valeska, 3 March 1980. RMSF, GH1, JCPL.

21 'Fund for Human Dignity Receives Tax-Deductible Status', News from NGTF, 9 August 1977. NGTFR, B.36, F.44, CU.

22 Kay Whitlock's statement, 19 December 1979. NGTFR, B.145, F.2, CU.

23 'Carter Appeals for Gay Support', News from NGTF, 6 March 1980. RMSF, GTFN1, JCPL.

24 WH memorandum: Talking points on gay issues, 5 August 1980. RMSF, G/L2, JCPL.

25 NGTF, 'What Has Jimmy Carter Ever Done for Gays?', 1980. NGTFR, B.6, F.3, CU.

> This was an amazing step. It was an incredibly important thing, it enabled us to raise money, provide tax exempt status to the people who donated which is a must have if you're running a social education set of organizations, it's critical. All of our educational programs were able to then apply for tax exempt status which aids their funding, increases funding capacity tremendously. So, I think it was an incredibly important win for the community.*

But the ruling had far-reaching and unprecedented benefits for gay organizations beyond the avoidance of paying taxes. It offered legitimation and respect to gay groups at a time when a lot of people considered gay people to be 'child-molesters' and their organizations to be 'perverts' clubs that were promoting homosexuality and sodomy'.[26] It meant that these organizations were now officially recognized by the government, not just as interest groups but as charitable organizations attempting to help and educate people and to bring reforms to society. Carter's administration highlighted this by stating that 'the IRS action has practical benefits and indicates the increased legitimacy with which gay organizations are treated'.[27] Clay said, 'Yes, [the tax exemption] did contribute to the legitimacy of our movement; so many groups and their efforts were finally officially recognized by the government'.* In 1980, Larry Bush in *The Sentinel* emphasized the importance of the IRS's decision and highlighted the issue of legitimacy: 'Today, literally dozens of gay community organizations benefit from that ruling, not only in terms of tax relief but also in legitimizing their position in the community'.[28] Weithorn wrote about the IRS win:

> The scope of the victory cannot be overstated. . . . The victory was even more meaningful than we knew at the time. Within half a dozen years, AIDS descended upon the gay community with swift and deadly force. Had gays been unable to quickly organize new non-profits to deal directly with the crisis, and the federal government's shameful lack of response to it, the terrible death toll and the spread of the disease would be even worse than it is.[29]

The reaction of opponents

Soon after the IRS's decision, Jeffery St. John revealed in his column that the order for tax-exempt status for gay organizations had come to Wigrizer 'directly from the Carter White House', which was basically true. He continued, 'Taxpayer funding of lesbian groups within the International Women's Year organization and now White House approval of tax-exempt status for homosexual groups are a vivid contrast to the image of the Carter White House as a bastion of Southern Baptist religious faith'.[30] The IRS's decision outraged conservative Christians. What made it worse was that during this period, the majority of private Christian schools were losing their tax-exempt

26 Bush and Howell, author interviews.

27 WH memorandum: Talking points on gay issues, 5 August 1980. RMSF, G/L2, JCPL.

28 Larry Bush, 'White House Claims Solid Record on Gay Issues', *The Sentinel*, 16 May 1980.

29 Weithorn, *Love, Death, and Taxes*, xv–xvi.

30 Jeffery St. John, 'Now Taxpayers Are Financing Homosexual Causes' (the newspaper title is unfortunately not visible in the archive record), MCSF, [H-GRPH], JCPL.

status because the IRS was becoming stricter in enforcing compliance with federal anti-discrimination policies. These required schools to report the number of minority students they had in relation to the minority population in their region. Many such schools were de facto segregated by race with 'faith' serving as a proxy, and most of the others failed to meet the commitment to enrol a minimum quota of minority students. Falwell and his allies saw this as a deliberate attack on their attempts to set up a parallel educational system so that conservatives could escape the multiracial environment that had been introduced in the public schools and ensuring that their children were given an education based on supposed 'Christian' values. Having some of their privileges removed while benefits were extended to gay organizations was seen by religious conservatives as a slap in the face and increased their dissatisfaction with Carter.[31] Although the rescinding of tax-exempt status for Christian schools has began during Ford's Presidency, Paul Weyrich, co-founder of the Moral Majority, who had been trying unsuccessfully to mobilize evangelicals on conservative issues such as abortion, school prayer, the ERA and pornography, put the blame on Carter. He said, 'I was trying to get those people interested in those issues and I utterly failed. What changed their mind was Jimmy Carter's intervention against the Christian schools, trying to deny them tax-exempt status on the basis of so-called de facto segregation'.[32]

However, religious conservatives were not the only people who were dissatisfied with Wigrizer's decision, as a number of IRS officials continued their attempts to block it. One of them was Paul Byrne Haring, an IRS lawyer and tax law specialist in the department's Exempt Organizations Division. Haring filed a lawsuit against the federal government alleging that awarding tax-exempt status to gay organizations that publicly supported homosexuality 'encourages the destruction of the family and public morality and violates the criminal statutes against sodomy'. The lawsuit also asked that the IRS be permanently enjoined from granting tax-exempt to gay or pro-abortion organizations. Haring noted that Congress had not exempted gay and pro-abortion groups from taxation and that 'to require the IRS to recognize as exempt only organizations which Congress has exempted would violate no one's First Amendment rights'. The IRS, with the backing of Carter's administration, publicly stood by its decision and denounced Haring's actions. The case was heard in the US District Court for the District of Columbia in April 1979 by Judge Harold Greene, a Carter appointee. Greene dismissed Haring's lawsuit.[33]

Federal funding

In addition to the above benefits, and equally importantly, the IRS ruling made gay organizations eligible to receive federal funding for their programmes and their staff. This section discusses attempts to open up these funding streams under two headings.

[31] George J. Church, 'Politics from the Pulpit-Fundamentalists Take Aim at Carter', *Time*, 13 October 1980; Daniel K. Williams, *God's Own Party: The Making of the Christian Right* (Oxford: Oxford University Press, 2010), 163–4.

[32] Randal Balmer, 'Fundamentalism, the First Amendment, and the Rise of the Religious Right', *William and Mary Bill of Rights Journal* 18, no. 4 (2010): 898–9.

[33] Don Griffith, 'IRS Lawyer a Loser in Anti-Gay Suit', *The Blade*, 24 May 1979.

Employment and training

One of the most sought-after and largest government funding programmes at the time was that provided under the Comprehensive Employment and Training Act (CETA) whose goal was to train unemployed or low-income people through public or non-profit sector employment. Before Carter's presidency, the NGTF and numerous other gay organizations had had all their applications for CETA funding turned down.[34] However, the IRS decision had now opened the doors of programmes like CETA to gay groups. Ernest Green, who had been appointed by Carter as Assistant Secretary of the Department of Labor, had charge of the CETA programme. Green was very willing to meet with gay rights activists and listen to their requests.[35]

For the first few years of its existence, most of the NGTF's income came from 'benefit nights' that it ran in gay bars in New York City. Voeller had the idea that these bars would once a week charge a fee for entry and that this money would go to the NGTF. Its other sources of income at the time were donations and membership fees, but the combined yield nevertheless limited the NGTF's activities and ambitions.[36] In June 1977, as a result of the defeat of a gay rights ordinance in Dade County, Florida (see Chapter 11), the NGTF began an educational plan, entitled 'We Are Your Children'. This consisted of 'open dialogues', lasting for a week, in which gay men and women would try to talk to other people in their local area, to show the American people who they 'really are'. Simultaneously, the NGTF had launched a massive fundraising drive in order to finance the project, but despite a promising start, this had failed to meet the organization's target and the programme had not run as long and as widely as planned.[37] In early 1978, the NGTF was in serious financial trouble. It had expected its revenues to continue to soar after the White House meeting and had accordingly set out a very optimistic budget for the next two years. However, expenses had risen rapidly, eating into the group's 1977 surplus. The NGTF therefore sent out through its newsletters an 'urgent call for help' asking people to ensure the survival of the organization by making donations and recruiting three new members at $20 apiece by the beginning of 1980.[38]

In early 1978, the NGTF's future was under serious threat and its countrywide educational campaign project 'Open Understanding', which aimed to inform the American public of the many positive contributions that gay people had made to the country and to society, had been put on hold due to financial constraints. Costanza urged O'Leary and Voeller to apply to the DoL for CETA funding for the project. Costanza personally introduced O'Leary and Voeller to Green and later encouraged the two activists to apply for CETA funding, even offering to help them with their application. In April 1978, Green officially accepted the NGTF's application and the group became the first gay organization to receive funding from CETA. The funding of $48,000 was used to hire five staff – three gay men and two lesbian women – to work

34 Apuzzo, Bush and Clay, author interviews.

35 Larry Bush, 'White House Claims Solid Record on Gay Issues', *The Sentinel*, 16 May 1980; Bush, author interview.

36 Vida, author interview.

37 William Doubleday, author interview; 'National Gay Task Force Announces "We Are Your Children" Educational Campaign', News from NGTF, 13 June 1977. NGTFR, B.36, F.35, CU.

38 'NGTF in Trouble', *LT*, November–December 1979.

on its 'Open Understanding' project, and to produce educational pamphlets and other material.[39]

One of the five, Rev. William (Bill) Doubleday, an Episcopal priest, was assigned as the NGTF's first Education Officer, in charge of a new Educational Department also set up with the CETA funding.[40] Doubleday and the Educational Department shortly afterwards organized, with CETA funding, a Week of Dialogue with American Parents and Families (22–28 October 1978). This project aimed to 'promote greater communication among gay people, their parents, families and non-gay friends'; the NGTF considered it to be the most important project it had ever undertaken.[41] For the Week of Dialogue, and with the CETA funding, the NGTF published three educational pamphlets:

- *Twenty Questions about Homosexuality*, which answered questions about the nature of homosexuality, homophobia, gay people who wanted to come out, discrimination against gays, whether homosexuality was 'healthy', 'moral' and 'natural', and so on.[42]
- *About Coming Out*, which was about the process of 'coming out' to parents, family and friends.[43]
- *Answers to Parents' Questions about Homosexuality*, which was aimed at parents who might want to know more about gay people, their place within family groups, the influence they had on children, and so on.[44]

The Week of Dialogue with American Parents and Families was a massive success for the NGTF and attracted a lot of people. Among those attending was Sarah Weddington, Costanza's successor at the White House's OPL, who had been invited by the organization. Her presence lent additional credibility and visibility to the event and created a precedent for the NGTF; from then on the organization always invited a top White House aide to attend its events.[45] While this project did not receive any attention from the mainstream press, it was extremely important for the NGTF as it had never attempted to carry out an educational and awareness-raising campaign on such a scale. It was also an attempt to change people's mind directly, and not through government action. Doubleday described the importance of the pamphlets thus:

> It was the first time where they [NGTF] were involved less with celebrity leaders and talking to political leaders, and more trying to say, 'We have something we can offer to families, friends, parents, co-workers'. This was pretty novel. I mean,

39 Bush, Doubleday and Haft, author interviews; 'NGTF Education Project Begins this Month', *It's Time*, April 1978. NGTFR, B.153, F.10, CU; Letter, NGTF to its members, 1 June 1978. NGTFR, B.8, F.17, CU.

40 Doubleday, author interview.

41 'NGTF National Week of Dialogue Program Scheduled for Debut October 22', News from NGTF, 15 September 1978. NGTFR, B.36, F.98, CU; Doubleday, author interview.

42 NGTF, *Twenty Questions about Homosexuality*, 1978. NGTFR, B.8, F.16, CU.

43 NGTF, *About Coming Out*, 1978. NGTFR, B.8, F.17, CU.

44 NGTF, 'Week of Dialogue Guide Book', 1978. NGTFR, B.40, F.35, CU.

45 Weddington, author interview.

> today, you can go into a bookstore and there are hundreds of different things about sexuality, homosexuality and relationships. [At that time] it was easier to find pornography than it was to find anything constructive that might help people to understand gay people better . . . so [it was very important] to have developed that pamphlet and to distribute it.*

Encouraged by the CETA funding, and assured by Green and Wexler that they could find additional funding from the same source, the NGTF began planning two new projects, resulting in successful applications.[46] The first was the Week of Dialogue with the Media about Gay and Lesbian Concerns, taking place on 24–31 March 1979, which aimed to 'address several major concerns the gay community has about media coverage and treatment of homosexuality in the media' and to make contact with 'key media people'. The NGTF considered that the media determined to a large extent 'what gay and non-gay people believe about homosexuality'.[47] The programme was also important because at the time gay people were often presented in the media, including in films, in a negative light. For example, popular TV series of the time such as *Police Woman* and *Marcus Welby, M.D.* had homophobic episodes, and a newspaper headline might say 'homosexual robs bank' while the sexuality of a heterosexual robber would not be mentioned; this pattern both spread and perpetuated discrimination towards gay people.[48]

For this project, the NGTF created a series of workshops and published two new booklets, *The Media Manual for Gay Organizations* and *What Gay People Can Do about the Media*, in addition to a new edition of *Twenty Questions about Homosexuality*. The NGTF invited members of the media to its workshop and distributed its booklets to all the major media of the time. The project was a big success for the organization with representatives from major media outlets attending the workshops, including the *New York Times*, *Time* magazine, the *New York Daily News* and the *Washington Post*. After an invitation from the NGTF, Wexler, who had helped the organization with its CETA applications, attended the launch of the event.[49]

A second new CETA-funded initiative was Project Open Employment, which enabled the NGTF to hire professionals to conduct a study on discrimination in major American corporations in New York City. The NGTF's announcement of funding for Project Open Employment in its newsletter noted that it had happened 'at a time when many CETA programs have been curtailed and when many highly respected organizations have been denied CETA grants'.[50]

Green developed a good relationship with gay rights activists. Bush wrote in *The Sentinel* in June 1980, 'a major help to gay groups comes from the U.S. Department

[46] Apuzzo, Bush and Clay, author interviews.

[47] 'Media Week of Dialogue', *It's Time*, May 1979. NGTFR, B.145, F.2, CU; NGTF, 'Guide to the Week of Dialogue with the Media about Gay and Lesbian Concerns', 24–31 March 1979. NGTFR, B.40, F.35, CU.

[48] Doubleday and Vida, author interviews.

[49] Apuzzo and Doubleday, author interviews; 'Guide to the Week of Dialogue with the Media, March 24–31, 1979', NGTF. NGTFR, B.40, F.35, CU; 'Media Week of Dialogue', *It's Time*, May 1979. NGTFR, B.145, F.2, CU.

[50] 'NGTF Awarded CETA Grant', *It's Time*, August–September 1979. ATSF, B.265, GR, JCPL.

of Labor, through the office of Assistant Secretary Ernest Green'.[51] Green advised the NGTF on its applications for CETA funding and made the organization, as well as other gay organizations, aware of other federal funding opportunities. Furthermore, Green took the initiative and proposed to the activists that they cooperate with his department in examining ways to eliminate discrimination in the private sector, while indicating that the activists had to take the lead in formally requesting such a partnership. He said that this might lead to a requirement for all corporations to comply with anti-discrimination rules in order to win contracts with the federal government. However, while Green was in office no such formal request was made by gay rights activists.[52] Clay and Vida explained to the author that the NGTF's resources were not equal to the rapidly widening opportunities created under the Carter administration, having had during the first three years of its existence no access at all to federal agencies or federal funding. Despite the new funding, the NGTF remained seriously understaffed. It seems that Green's proposal was among those that had to be given lower priority.*

Federal government funding also encouraged other donors, such as *Playboy* and the Ford Foundation, to make money available to the NGTF. This and the CETA funding itself came at a time when the organization was in a difficult financial situation and was obviously of direct benefit to its activities and to expanding their range. However, in addition to its practical importance, the funding also had high symbolic value as basically the government paid a gay organization to conduct an educational campaign about homosexuality and thereby promote gay rights. Bush, Bunch and Clay argued that Costanza, Green and Wexler's contribution to the CETA funding for gay organizations was essential, as the unprecedented nature of the funding – and its cessation under President Reagan – evidences.[53]

During Carter's presidency, several other gay organizations, such as the Lambda Legal Defense and Education Fund, and gay community centres all over the country began to receive federal funding that enabled them to pay staff who had been working on a voluntary basis, to hire additional staff, and to run new projects and expand their programmes.[54] One beneficiary of federal funding was the Gay Community Services Center in Los Angeles. In 1978, it received for the first time funding from CETA and from the Department of Housing and Urban Development (HUD). The CETA funding of $187,000 enabled the Center to hire twenty-eight additional staff and to expand its seven programmes covering hotline crisis intervention, community education outreach, counselling, employment, prison probation and parole, housing for persons in poverty, and environmental design. As for the HUD funding, it enabled the Center to pay off the remaining $250,000 of its mortgage.[55]

The CETA workers programme in particular became a fixture in staffing gay community centres and in government contracts, which accounted for the bulk of

[51] Larry Bush, 'White House Claims Solid Record on Gay Issues', *The Sentinel*, 16 May 1980.
[52] Ibid.
[53] Apuzzo, Bunch and Clay, author interviews.
[54] Scott O. Anderson, 'Lambda Gets Funding', *The Advocate*, 1 November 1978; Bush and Clay, author interviews.
[55] Lillian Faderman and Stuart Timmons, *Gay L.A.: History of Sexual Outlaws, Power Politics, and Lipstick Lesbians* (Berkeley and Los Angeles: University of California Press, 2009), 207–8; Elenore G. Pred, 'L.A. Gay Center Gets Grant', *The Advocate*, 22 March 1978.

research that was then being done by lesbians and gays to assess the needs of their community; for example, various gay community centres all over the county, such as the San Diego Gay Center, were able to hire additional staff and to print out educational pamphlets with CETA funding. Furthermore, non-gay organizations and agencies throughout the country were for the first time able to receive CETA funding for programmes that aimed to benefit gay people; for example, the Commission on the Status of Women in San Francisco obtained money from CETA to employ an officer to provide outreach to lesbians. Her job focused on telling lesbian women about the help the Commission's could offer them, and raising consciousness on both sides.[56]

Health and community

Throughout Carter's presidency and for the first time, numerous gay organizations, gay health clinics and gay community projects received government research grants and other types of funding to support their work.[57] For example, several local and national gay and lesbian groups, such as the NCBG and the NGTF, received funding directly from Carter's administration to organize workshops on gay rights for their preparations for the White House Conference on Families (see Chapter 12).[58]

One of the gay organizations that benefited most from federal funding was the Fund for Human Dignity. The funding, which was received with Malson and Wexler's assistance, was characterized by Apuzzo, the Fund's Executive Director at the time, as being 'strategically important' as it enabled the organization to do three very important things:

- run numerous educational programs.
- gather data from fieldwork and surveys on issues like violence and discrimination against gay people in numerous areas, for example housing.
- set up the first national anti-gay violence hotline.*

The NGTF used the data it gathered to plan its goals and in its dealings with the White House and the federal agencies. However, what turned out to have the biggest impact on the gay community was the national anti-gay violence hotline. It provided a ready source of assistance for gay people and soon became a model for the rest of the country. It was also an important source of data, being modelled specifically on the Anti-Defamation League's data gathering on anti-Semitic attacks and incidents; it provided the first recorded homophobic violence dataset in the country. However, the hotline became even more important during the AIDS epidemic in the 1980s, when it became

56 Scott O. Anderson, 'San Diego Gay Center Gets CETA Funding', *The Advocate*, 15 November 1978; Larry Bush, 'The Carter Administration. More Done Than Said?', *The Advocate*, 12 June 1980; Larry Bush, 'White House Claims Solid Record on Gay Issues', *The Sentinel*, 16 May 1980; Bush, author interview; Elenore G. Pred, 'Notable and Quotable', *The Advocate*, 8 February 1978.

57 Larry Bush, 'The Carter Administration. More Done Than Said?', *The Advocate*, 12 June 1980; 'National Gay Task Force Directors Express Support for Carter', News from NGTF, 2 October 1980. NGTFR, B.6, F.3, CU.

58 Bus and Jones-Hennin, author interviews.

the first AIDS hotline, quickly becoming a model. Even the Reagan administration, when it was finally persuaded to have a national AIDS hotline, sent an official from the Public Health Service to learn how the Fund's hotline worked.[59]

Bush wrote in *The Sentinel* in 1980 that the biggest issue for most gay rights activists, aside from discrimination in the labour market, was obtaining help and recognition for their work in community building. In this area, HEW (split into the Department of Health and Human Services and the Department of Education in 1980) was the relevant funder.[60] One of the requests that the activists had made during the March 1977 Meeting was that they should receive funding from HEW for gay counselling and health problems, including funding for research on hepatitis. Subsequently, after researching the case, Malson informed the NGTF about a number of federally funded programmes that could be available to gay organizations, and HEW then provided the funding the activists wanted. For example, five gay health clinics, whose main aim was reducing the incidence of sexually transmitted diseases, obtained federal money for pilot programmes; this exceeded the support that had been provided to all other community health groups. Several other gay health clinics also received funds for hepatitis studies. Furthermore, with federal funding, seminars were set up to give guidance to health professionals on how to work with gay people and in gay environments, for example bathhouses. Meanwhile, the National Institute of Mental Health and the National Science Foundation funded studies on issues such as ageing in the gay community, gays and families and the affects of discrimination. Another of the activists' requests at the March 1977 Meeting was thus met.[61]

The generous funding the gay health clinics received continued throughout Carter's presidency, but was drastically reduced, and on some occasions stopped altogether, shortly after Reagan took office. The funding helped the clinics hire additional and expert personnel, buy essential equipment, improve their facilities, and carry out very important research on hepatitis and on sexually transmitted diseases. These enhancements proved to be extremely important in the clinics' battle with AIDS in the 1980s, despite the lack of federal funding during Reagan's presidency.[62] Bush argued that the funding was 'very important' because it contributed to the legitimation of the gay community and recognized it as 'not just a political entity, but a community service program, a larger community group. Because, as a community, people provided services and looked out for each other. President Carter was recognizing the LGBT as a community with community services that were provided by its own community'.*

Malson continued to inform gay organizations about new funding opportunities and personally helped them with their applications. In May 1980, he took the initiative, asking the NGTF for information about the 'experience of gay organizations with applications for federal funds' in an attempt to help further.[63] The government funding

59 Apuzzo, author interview.

60 Larry Bush, 'White House Claims Solid Record on Gay Issues', *The Sentinel*, 16 May 1980.

61 Larry Bush, 'The Carter Administration. More Done Than Said?', *The Advocate*, 12 June 1980; Heather Cassell, 'Activists Mark 30th Anniversary of White House Meeting', *BAR*, 28 May 2007; Malson, author interview.

62 Apuzzo and Bush, author interviews.

63 'White House Meetings', *It's Time*, May–June 1980. RMSF, G/L1, JCPL.

of gay organizations came under severe attack from conservatives, who used the funding of the Los Angeles Gay Community Centre as 'an example of outrageous use of taxpayer money'.[64] Naturally, they moved to stop it wherever possible. In 1979, the Congress publicly expressed its dissatisfaction with the Carter administration's funding for legal efforts to protect the rights of gay people. It was similarly irked by the National Science Foundation awarding money to projects studying gay couples. The third aim of the 1979 Family Protection Act was to deny federal funding to gay organizations. The Act also made specific reference to the banning of federal funding for educational material, like the booklets the NGTF and its Women Caucus had been publishing with government money. By a massive margin, the House endorsed the dismantling of the programme in a roll call vote. However, the Senate salvaged the situation; the funding was restored and gay organizations continued receiving federal funding throughout Carter's presidency.[65]

Throughout Carter's presidency, gay organizations had unprecedented access to federal funding; never before had such organizations received funding from the government. Carter's role and contribution to this becomes even clearer given the fact that after the end of his presidency and throughout the next ten years, the vast majority of applications by gay organizations for federal funding were turned down.[66] Gaining tax-exempt, tax-deductible status and becoming eligible to receive federal funding affected the resources of gay organizations in numerous ways. It meant that these organizations now had considerably more funds and, in some cases, could afford to hire and pay professionals rather than rely on volunteers. They also had more money to spend on advertising and mail-outs enabling them to reach out to the dispersed gay community and grow their membership. Overall, having a larger budget at their disposal meant that the organizations could become better organized, bigger, stronger and more influential. Finally, it also signalled to gay people that the person occupying the highest office in the land not only recognized their existence but also their right to continue their struggle.

The federal funding of gay organizations and programmes received at the time no coverage from the mainstream press and rather limited coverage from the gay press. Thus, it remained largely unknown even within the gay community, and even on the rare occasions when it was mentioned, there was no reference to the Carter administration's contribution. However, in October 1980, shortly before the presidential elections, the NGTF issued a press release which urged the gay community to vote for Carter because of his record on gay rights and among his achievements was listed 'the funding of gay health services'.[67]

64 Larry Bush, 'The Carter Administration. More Done Than Said?', *The Advocate*, 12 June 1980.
65 Craig Howell, 'Senate Bill Pushes New Right Agenda', *The Blade*, 20 December 1979.
66 Apuzzo and Bush, author interviews; Faderman and Timmons, *Gay L.A.*, 208.
67 'National Gay Task Force Directors Express Support for Carter', News from NGTF, 2 October 1980. NGTFR, B.6, F.3, CU.

Recognition by the broadcast media

In 1976, broadcasters were required to represent minorities, but they were not obliged to present the views of gay people because they were not included in the Federal Communications Commission's (FCC) checklist of groups that broadcasters had to contact.[68] The NGTF had written several times to the FCC to object and to request a meeting. The FCC not only denied or ignored these requests but when it did respond it sometimes used homophobic language or jokes.[69] In December 1976, the NGTF suggested that gay groups write to the FCC and complain about the way gay people were 'treated (or ignored) on radio and television'.[70] The NGTF had identified four areas of FCC policy in need of reform:

- **Ascertainment**: the absence of the gay community in the checklist of minorities whose interests broadcasters were required to 'ascertain' by regularly consulting community representatives.
- **Employment**: the lack of a non-discrimination policy in FCC employment, putting its gay employees at risk of losing their jobs if their homosexuality became known.
- **Public Service Announcements**: the reluctance of broadcasters to allow public service announcements from otherwise qualified charitable organizations in the gay community.
- **Programming/Fairness Doctrine:** the inability, thanks to their absence from the community ascertainment procedure, of gay advocacy groups to make complaints under the fairness doctrine against broadcasts which took a solely negative view of gay people.[71]

On 8 February 1977, the NGTF issued an alert to the gay media highlighting the fact that community broadcasting authorities were not required to interview gay people.[72] Given the huge battles taking place at both local and federal levels – and the apparent ease with which activists from the religious right, such as Anita Bryant, gained access to the airwaves of America – this was clearly a matter of considerable concern. If media outlets did not interview the very minority that was arousing so much ire among religious conservatives, the minority would risk being not heard at all.[73] Broadcasters were, however, reluctant to list gay people as a discrete group.[74]

These issues were discussed in the March 1977 Meeting, when the NGTF requested that Carter's administration 'smooth the way to a meeting with the FCC Commissioners', so that the organization could:

68 Caroline Mayer, 'FCC Orders Broadcasters to Heed Disabled, Gays', *WS*, 13 March 1980.
69 Clay and Vida, author interviews; 'FCC, Networks Hear Gay Case', *The Advocate*, 29 December 1976.
70 NGTF Action Report, 'Complaining to the FCC', February 1977. MCSF, MCSF, [H-GRPH], JCPL.
71 Letter, Ginny Vida to Belle O'Brien, 24 February 1978. SWSF, GR-FCC2, JCPL.
72 NGTF, 'Gay Media Alert', 8 February 1977. MCI.
73 Letter, Carol Jennings to Ronald Gold, 11 February 1977. MCI.
74 Letter, Wallace Johnson to Henry Waxman, 11 February 1977. MCI.

1) Obtain a commitment from the incoming FCC Chairman to equal treatment for gay people as a common element found in the communities served by all broadcast licensees – this commitment to include the addition of leaders of the gay community to the checklist of those required to be interviewed by broadcasters in their community ascertainment surveys.
2) . . . present [FCC Commissioner's staff] with the clear evidence that gay people constitute a common element in all U.S. communities, and request them to make the addition to the checklist without the delay and red tape necessitated by the filing of a formal petition for a change in rule-making.[75]

The FCC was an independent agency and not under the administration's control. The NGTF nevertheless highlighted the president's power to appoint its Chairman and Commissioners: 'The future direction of the FCC, despite its present overload of Nixon appointees, will depend on who is appointed by President Carter to the post of FCC chairman'.[76] As with the campaign for the IRS policy change, Costanza promised to help and reassured the NGTF that Carter was committed to appointing people who were sensitive to the rights and concerns of gay people.[77]

The organization took a different tack in June 1977: after noting that Anita Bryant and her husband had been given six hours of television time to air their anti-gay views, gay rights activists moved to seek equal access; along with the Council of Religion and the Homosexual, Inc., they petitioned the FCC to extend the broadcast fairness doctrine so that gay people could answer criticism on television. The petition charged that station KVOF had refused to let gay people have their say and asked that the Glendale, California station be required to air programming in response to the Bryant exposure. The FCC refused the request,[78] leading to a new and bigger effort by gay rights activists: in August 1977, the NGTF and another 143 gay organizations petitioned the FCC to amend its ascertainment policy to stipulate that broadcasters had to include the perspectives of gay people when performing their required activities to keep in touch with public opinion.[79]

A favourable response once again depended on new presidential appointments. Carter nominated Charles D. Ferris, a progressive lawyer who had played a key role in the enactment of the Civil Rights Act of 1964 and the Voting Rights Act of 1965, as Chairman of the FCC, and he took office in October 1977.[80] Ferris argued that the FCC should be committed to widening the range of perspectives that were portrayed in both news and entertainment programming, rather than shutting down minority views.[81] Carter also began replacing most of the FCC's Commissioners.[82] Soon after

75 NGTF, 'Needs of the Gay Community with Respect to the FCC and Community Ascertainment', 26 March 1977. SWSF, [NGTF: FCC1], JCPL.
76 Ibid.
77 'NGTF-Federal Agency Meetings Set Second White House Conference in September', News from NGTF, 31 March 1977. NGTFR, B.145, F.47, CU.
78 'Equal Time vs. Anita', *GCN*, 2 July 1977.
79 Bill Sievert, 'Gay Leaders Got to FCC', *The Advocate*, 21 September 1977.
80 Les Brown, 'Charles Ferris Named to Head F.C.C.', *NYT*, 14 September 1977.
81 Les Brown, 'Ferris Says F.C.C. Will Not Act as Censor of Controversial Issues', *NYT*, 23 July 1978.
82 WH memorandum: Talking points on gay issues, 5 August 1980. RMSF, G/L2, JCPL.

Ferris became Chairman, Costanza and Haft began lobbying the Commission on behalf of the NGTF and the administration, while Wishman was assigned by Costanza to check the legal aspects of the case. Ferris and the new Commission members turned out to be very willing to meet with gay rights activists and listen to their concerns. Within a few months, Costanza and Haft had set up two meetings between the NGTF and the FCC; one in February 1978 with Belle O'Brien, director of the Consumer Assistance Office, and another a month later with Ferris himself. Wishman attended both as the administration's representative. Prior to both meetings, Wishman met to discuss tactics with Ginny Vida, the NGTF's media director and editor of *It's Time* (the NGTF's monthly newsletter), who presented the organization's case to the FCC.[83] At the meetings, Vida presented the organization's position on the four issue areas noted above.[84] Separately, Costanza and Haft proposed for the FCC a new rule which would 'require broadcasters to ascertain the needs of significant community groups, including gay organizations, to determine community broadcast needs'.[85] Both women and Wishman continued lobbying the Commission to address all the issues raised by Vida.[86]

Ferris immediately pledged to the NGTF that the FCC would adopt a non-discrimination policy and a revised programming/fairness doctrine, and would work towards implementing the other two agenda items.[87] In July 1978, the FCC announced a proposed change of policy on community ascertainment, requiring broadcasters to seek input from gay leaders on community topics and needs. Ferris said:

> This is a very, very positive change. I think what we're trying to do is a positive contribution to every element of society. What we're trying to do is be fair and recognize a legitimate group. . . . I hope this item does give that sense to broadcasters that they *have* to consult with any significant group. Wouldn't you define ten percent of the population as significant?[88]

The NGTF welcomed the proposal as 'a major step forward' for the gay community, with Vida declaring that the ruling 'gives us official status as part of the public who interest must be served'.[89] Larry Bush, who a few months later began covering and reporting the issue in the gay press, highlighted the significance of Carter's new liberal appointments to the FCC as well as the White House's contribution to the decision, adding, 'that was, to my knowledge, the very first time any federal agency recognized LGBT people as a community'.* Vida commented to the author that Carter administration was 'very supportive' and added, 'The White House intervention on that was absolutely critical.

83 Letter, Ginny Vida to Belle O'Brien, 24 February 1978, and Ginny Vida note, 7 March 1978, both in SWSF, GR-FCC2, JCPL; Vida, author interview.
84 Letter, Ginny Vida to Belle O'Brien, 24 February 1978. SWSF, GR-FCC2, JCPL.
85 Haft, author interview; Letter, Robert Strauss to Charles Brydon and Lucia Valeska, 3 March 1980. RMSF, GH1, JCPL.
86 Haft, author interview.
87 Vida, author interview.
88 Larry Bush, 'FCC Boosts Gay Hopes for Media Access', *The Blade*, 1 August 1978.
89 Scott P. Anderson, 'Local Feedback Must Include Gays, FCC Says', *The Advocate*, 23 August 1978; Steve Martz, 'Pro-Gay Proposal in Trouble', *The Blade*, 8 November 1978.

In simple terms it was critical. I don't think it could have happened without that kind of support. These things were just not moving . . . and I think, once the White House had got involved, there were some big changes'.*

The religious right reacted angrily to Ferris's proposal, charging the Commission with 'giving queers a voice', while Falwell and Bryant set out to stop the proposal before it became policy. As a result of the conservatives' mobilization, the Commission began receiving letters at a proportion of 25–1 against the proposal. Ferris told Costanza of this public pressure, and she advised the NGTF to mobilize support, which it attempted to do. But by September 1978, Costanza, Haft and Wishman were no longer in their posts and the administration's involvement with the case was temporarily paused, and soon afterwards the NGTF also underwent changes with Brydon and Valeska replacing O'Leary and Voeller. Adoption of the policy was put in question by further pressure from conservative members of Congress and opposition by the National Religious Broadcasters Association, with some members of the Commission beginning to have second thoughts about it.[90]

Shortly after Brydon and Valeska took over as Co-Executive Directors of the NGTF, the organization resumed its efforts with the FCC and asked Weddington and Wexler for help. Weddington and Wexler, assisted by Thomas and Malson, began lobbying the FCC to proceed with its proposal,[91] while in the meantime Carter had continued appointing new liberal members to the Commission.[92] Eventually, in March 1980, despite relentless pressure from the religious right, the FCC, within which Carter appointees now constituted a majority, unanimously approved the new regulations, thus satisfying all the requests that had been made by the NGTF. The FCC's new regulations ordered radio and television broadcasters, including Christian broadcasters and networks, to listen to the concerns of the gay community, to ensure that they were adequately and accurately represented and to include them when they ascertained community broadcast needs. The FCC had ruled that while the broadcasters were not under an obligation actively to seek out such groups, when the latter identified themselves and showed that 'they are a significant element in the community', the broadcasters were then obliged to conduct community ascertainment. Under the fairness doctrine, the FCC committed to providing the public with an accurate portrayal of gay people and warned broadcasters that they would lose their licenses if they failed to comply with the new ruling. This also meant that an anti-gay message could not be broadcast unless the gay community was given an opportunity for rebuttal. Ferris stated after the decision, 'Our action today does acknowledge that groups constituting significant elements of the community', among which he mentioned 'gays', 'are part of our diverse American people' and 'deserve to be heard'.[93]

90 Scott P. Anderson, 'Local Feedback Must Include Gays, FCC Says', *The Advocate*, 23 August 1978; 'Anita Urges FCC to Reject Gay Plea', *BAR*, 9 November 1978; Haft, author interview; Steve Martz, 'Pro-Gay Proposal in Trouble', *The Blade*, 8 November 1978.

91 Weddington, author interview.

92 Larry Bush, 'The Carter Administration. More Done Than Said?', *The Advocate*, 12 June 1980; WH memorandum: Talking points on gay issues, 5 August 1980. RMSF, G/L2, JCPL.

93 'Federal Communications Commission Acts on NGTF Petition', News from NGTF, 14 March 1980. NGTFR, B.36, F.151, CU.

The NGTF announced the news of the FCC's decision in its newsletter, claiming that it was entirely a result of its August 1977 request and making no reference to the White House's role.[94] It enthusiastically hailed the Commission's new ruling: 'we see today's vote by the FCC as an affirmation of the fundamental principle that the nation's airwaves belong to all our citizens, the popular and the unpopular'.[95] In August 1980, the White House reminded the gay rights activists that 'though the FCC is an independent agency, it is worth remembering that its action came only after Carter appointees joined the Commission and formed a majority'.[96] This was an accurate description of the situation. Unlike the NGTF, *The Advocate* acknowledged that the FCC had 'shifted its stance remarkably since Carter was able to name a new majority of commissioners'.[97]

Both the ascertainment requirement and the fairness doctrine were to be dismantled by changes to FCC regulations in the 1980s, which moved them in the direction of a market-led broadcasting regime.

☙

Changes to the tax code are an unglamorous but consequential advance, in which organizations that pursued charitable purposes in relation to gay people were granted exemption due to this kind of purpose without a requirement, invented by the IRS, to make a public declaration of self-abnegation in order to become eligible. A wide range of organizational and community benefits were unlocked by this revision. Recognition of the gay community by broadcasters, with respect both to an assessment of their needs and interests as consumers of programming ('ascertainment') and to their representation as a legitimate interest in political debate ('fairness') created a more immediate kind of visibility, but again an obviously consequential one in terms of legitimation and normalization. In both areas, as this chapter has shown, the key to shifting the entrenched homophobia of the respective bureaucracies was President Carter's use of his appointment power, and his staff's prompt exploitation of the opportunities it created.

94 Ibid.
95 Caroline Mayer, 'FCC Orders Broadcasters to Heed Disabled, Gays', *WS*, 13 March 1980.
96 WH memorandum: Talking points on gay issues, 5 August 1980. RMSF, G/L2, JCPL.
97 Larry Bush, 'The Carter Administration. More Done Than Said?', *The Advocate*, 12 June 1980.

8

Admission

Ending discrimination at the border

Immigration was one of the most important issues for gay rights activists in the 1970s, as legislation prohibited gay migrants and tourists from entering the United States, and also allowed for deportation of those already admitted under certain circumstances. For a long time, Congress presented an insuperable challenge to any legislative resolution of the issue, and it was not until 1990 that it removed the statutory barrier; before then, 'the United States was the only country in the world with an explicit policy of excluding visitors and potential immigrants because of their sexual orientation'.[1] This chapter traces the arduous effort to revise or mitigate the anti-gay exclusion that was part of the Immigration and Nationality Act. Instead, an administrative solution which significantly mitigated the exclusion was found by Carter's aides and appointees, bypassing Congressional intransigence. The process of reaching this outcome is examined below, in a case study of reform efforts against the background of the constitutional separation of powers and Congressional intransigence. The crisis created by the 'Mariel boatlift' from Cuba, in which numerous gay refugees were involved, further demonstrates administration initiative in support of gay rights.

Traditional and modern exclusion

The legal basis for exclusion of gay people at the border was of two types: recent legislation aimed by design (though not necessarily in the statutory language) at excluding homosexuals, and broader and more antiquated legislative provisions which could be turned to that purpose. The focus of this discussion is the first type. The second type, expressed by provisions in immigration law regarding 'crimes of moral turpitude' and 'good moral character', had been present in US immigration law since 1790 (at first under the description 'good character'), and it was uncontroversial for most of that time for gay people, among other categories of people such as criminals, to fall under such descriptions for immigration and other legal purposes. However, in part thanks to challenges to the discriminatory use of the vague 'moral turpitude'

1 Shannon Minter, 'Sodomy and Public Morality Offenses under U.S. Immigration Law: Penalizing Lesbian and Gay Identity', *Cornell International Law Journal* 26, no. 3 (1993): 771.

and 'moral character' provisions in the courts, the main focus of concern for gay rights groups by the time of the Carter administration was the exclusion by legislative design which had been achieved through the Immigration and Nationality Act of 1952. This act (known also as the 'McCarran-Walter Act') contained in its Section 212(a) (4) a provision barring entry to 'aliens afflicted with a psychopathic personality, epilepsy, or a mental defect'.[2]

The Act, passed (over Truman's veto) at the height of McCarthyite anxiety about threatening or subversive aliens, 'legislat[ed] the most dramatic expansion of the grounds for exclusion in the nation's history'. While not mentioning sexuality directly, on the advice of the Public Health Service (PHS) which had suggested the less direct wording in preference to the formulation 'homosexuals or sex perverts' in the bill's draft, the intention to exclude homosexuals was clear from the legislative record, and the provision had been applied accordingly. The intention was in any case made clearer by an amendment in 1965, following a court case, that substituted 'sexual deviation' for 'epilepsy'.[3] Irrespective of this change, the Act had required the PHS to provide diagnoses to Immigration and Naturalization Service (INS) border officials when the latter suspected this disqualifying condition. The INS supplied a 'guide' to its officials on how to identify gay people, alerting them to clues such as makeup on men or an address book full of names of people of the same sex. Those who were suspected of being gay had to face humiliating and brutal treatment from the INS and PHS officials, similar to that inflicted on drug-smugglers and suspected foreign spies. They were held incommunicado for hours, subjected to strip- and body cavity searches, and interrogated at length about their sexual activities and attitudes, all under the constant observation of armed guards.[4]

The express prohibition had gained force from the agreement of the medical and psychiatric profession that homosexuality was a disorder. As already noted, in 1973 the APA had declassified homosexuality as a disorder, making it no longer a matter of medical concern. While legal and medical exclusionary classifications had previously lined up, the new psychiatric finding created a tension between them and eventually led to a conflict between the INS and the PHS. A further factor was a court case, *In re Brodie*,[5] which had found that private homosexual conduct did not on its own entail the absence of 'good moral character'. While this did not prevent all use of this traditional broad provision against gay people, the INS's eventual response would place the focus squarely on the more explicit 'sexual deviance' provision, intensifying the medical-legal conundrum just mentioned. Nevertheless, in 1977, the INS planned to appeal the court decision.[6] While many gay people had been excluded from the country under this discriminatory law, it was sometimes overlooked, especially when it came to the entry of celebrities such as Rudolf Nureyev.[7]

2 Ibid., 771–2, 791–2.
3 Ibid., 776–9.
4 Larry Bush, 'Borderline Homophobia', *Inquiry*, 9 and 23 June 1980; Bob Ingle, 'Harassing Gays at the Gate', *The Atlanta Constitution*, 1 July 1980.
5 394 F. Supp. 1208 (D.Or. 1975).
6 Memorandum, Seymour Wishman to Midge Costanza, 28 March 1978. SWSF, [NGTF] SG, JCPL.
7 Memorandum, Marilyn Haft to Margaret Costanza, 25 March 1977. SWSF, [Gay] CR, JCPL.

The 'sexual deviance' provision: The 'last stumbling block'

Carter's administration had from the beginning supported the elimination of the INS's policy of gay exclusion. The NGTF raised the issue of immigration during the March 1977 Meeting. The organization believed that 'action on this issue is considered by many gay leaders as the real test of [Carter's] intentions concerning the gay community and the sincerity of the Administration's human rights policies'.[8] Soon after the meeting, Costanza, Haft and Wishman began working on the issue. Haft arranged two meetings between senior INS officials and the NGTF, one in July and one in September,[9] and another meeting in September between the NGTF and the PHS.[10]

For the July meeting, Costanza and Haft managed to bring together Leonel Castillo, the INS's Commissioner and David Crosland, the INS's General Counsel (both Carter appointees), along with senior officials from the Justice Department (DoJ), and also Malson from the White House. In the meeting, the NGTF reminded the INS that the exclusion of gay people on the basis of their categorization as 'sexual deviants' by the PHS was not in line with the declassification of homosexuality as a pathology by the APA and the American Public Health Association.[11] Costanza and Haft expressed the administration's 'unequivocal' support for a change of policy that would allow gay aliens into the country and its disagreement with the INS's previous leadership's intention to appeal the federal court's ban on the use of the 'morally good character' provision for this purpose.[12] Crosland explained that the INS was simply 'following the lead' of the PHS in their classification of gays as 'sexual deviants',[13] and agreed to a joint meeting with the PHS to discuss a change. The INS admitted its previous use of the 'good moral character' provision had involved a double standard with regard to applications for entry by gay people but also pointed out that it had already modified this policy in light of the *Brodie* case (though at this time it was still planning to appeal the decision). It agreed to survey and reassess its policies and procedures affecting gay people and to determine whether a second double standard existed over the criteria applied to famous aliens entering the country. It further agreed to provide the NGTF with detailed data on the numbers of gay people who had been refused a visa to visit the United States or denied immigration and naturalization.[14] At another meeting with Costanza, Haft and the NGTF in September 1977, the INS agreed to drop its judicial appeal regarding 'morally

8 Memorandum, Marilyn Haft to Margaret Costanza, 23 June 1977. MCI.

9 Memorandum, Marilyn Haft to Margaret Costanza, 30 June 1977. SWSF, [NGTF: Agency Meetings], JCPL; Marilyn Haft, Staff weekly report, June 27 through July 1. MCI; Memorandum, Seymour Wishman to Midge Costanza, 28 March 1978. SWSF, [NGTF] SG, JCPL.

10 Marilyn Haft memorandums to Margaret Costanza, 31 June and 8 August 1977, both in SWSF, [Gay] CR, JCPL.

11 Memorandum, Marilyn Haft to Margaret Costanza, 8 August 1977. SWSF, [Gay] CR, JCPL; 'National Gay Task Force Meets with U.S. Immigration and Naturalization Service Officials', News from NGTF, 18 July 1977. NGTFR, B.36, F.39, CU.

12 Haft, author interview.

13 NGTF, 'Position Memorandum on Immigration Policy Regarding Homosexuals', 11 July 1979. RMSF, GR, B.7, JCPL.

14 Memorandum, Marilyn Haft to Margaret Costanza, 8 August 1977. SWSF, [Gay] CR, JCPL; 'National Gay Task Force Meets with U.S. Immigration and Naturalization Service Officials', News from NGTF, 18 July 1977. NGTFR, B.36, F.39, CU.

good character'. This was an important win for the activists as there was, in Wishman's view, 'an excellent chance that an appeal would have reversed the favourable lower court decision [whose implication] was to remove homosexuality from automatically being defined as failing to have good moral character'.[15]

For their meeting with the NGTF, the PHS had proposed sending a low-ranking official. However, the NGTF wanted three senior officials to attend: Dr Julius Richmond, the US Surgeon General and Assistant Secretary for Health (appointed to both positions by Carter),[16] Joyce Lash, Deputy Assistant for Health, and Bertram S. Brown, director of the National Institute of Mental Health. At the NGTF's request, Costanza called Richmond to say that she would be attending, and that 'it would be nice to see him and his deputy there',[17] and similarly persuaded the other senior officials to attend. At the meeting Richmond agreed to fully review the question.[18]

After the initial success in September, Wishman, who had been examining the legal aspects of the case, wrote to Costanza that the 'last stumbling block for freedom of gays into the country' was the 'sexual deviance' exclusion. At the NGTF's request,[19] Costanza set up a meeting for 4 April 1978, also inviting Dr Jules Masserman, President-elect of the APA, and Dr John Spiegel, its former President, who Costanza thought would strengthen the case for a change. As was often her practice, Costanza met in her office, continuing into dinner, with the reform-minded parties on the eve of the meeting to discuss strategy; both psychiatrists agreed to 'urge the redefinition'.[20] In the meeting, it was also made clear by Costanza, Malson and Haft that Carter strongly supported the change proposed by the NGTF's Voeller and O'Leary; Richmond immediately acquiesced. The activists also asked Crosland to appoint someone to serve as liaison between his agency and NGTF, and much to the activists' pleasure, he volunteered to take on this role himself.[21] In a memo to Costanza of 5 May 1978, Richmond stated:

> It is our feeling that the Public Health Service should no longer be administratively responsible for certifying to the United States Visa Consular posts abroad, as well as INS, aliens who are homosexuals without other mental abnormalities relating to their sexual orientation for exclusion under . . . Section 212 (a) (4).[22]

The NGTF announced in a press release, 'We believe that this far-reaching policy change will go a long way toward ending this country's exclusion of gay visitors and

15 Memorandum, Seymour Wishman to Midge Costanza, 28 March 1978. SWSF, [NGTF] SG, JCPL.

16 Up to 1968, the Surgeon General had been the administrator of the PHS. Since then, the role has been more public-facing and less directly managerial, though Richmond's joint appointment as Assistant Secretary of Health recombined the two roles, giving him line management of the PHS.

17 Memorandum, Marilyn Haft to Margaret Costanza, 8 September 1977. SWSF, [Gay] CR, JCPL.

18 Larry Bush, 'Borderline Homophobia', *Inquiry*, 9 and 23 June 1980; Haft, author interview.

19 Memorandum, Seymour Wishman to Midge Costanza, 28 March 1978. SWSF, [NGTF] SG, JCPL.

20 Haft, author interview; Memorandum, Seymour Wishman to Midge Costanza, 28 March 1978. SWSF, [NGTF] SG, JCPL.

21 Haft and Malson, author interviews; 'NGTF Wins Public Health Service Policy Change', News from NGTF, 6 April 1978, NGTFR, B.36, F.72, CU.

22 Memorandum, Julius Richmond to Midge Costanza. 5 May 1978. RMSF, GH1, JCPL.

immigrants'.[23] The press release presented the outcome as being entirely NGTF's achievement. Although it briefly mentioned that Costanza had been present at one of the meetings between the NGTF and the INS,[24] the considerable organizational effort of Costanza and Haft to set up meetings that were not only unprecedented for the respective parties but also successful was ignored. The *Bay Area Reporter* reported more accurately that Costanza 'was instrumental in arranging the sessions and was in attendance during the discussions'.[25]

Celebration was in any case premature. Surgeon General Richmond officially informed the INS that there was no medical basis for a 'diagnosis' of homosexuality, that gay people should not be barred any longer under the medical exclusion, and that the PHS would no longer carry out such 'investigations'.[26] However, Crosland, despite his not personally supporting the exclusion of gay aliens (other senior INS officials had a less accommodating view),[27] was now caught in the contradiction between Congress's intention to exclude gay entrants via the 'sexual deviancy' category and the evaporation of its diagnostic medical basis. He replied that it was 'clear that Congress had meant to exclude homosexuals', and it was hence 'a legislative rather than a medical determination'.[28] Hence the 'last stumbling block' remained stubbornly in place.

Throughout 1978 and 1979, Carter's administration kept working to find a solution that would end the exclusion of gay aliens from the country. Although the senior parties wanted to end the exclusion, they were also aware of the difficulties posed by the existing legislation and the unlikelihood of its being altered by Congress. Meetings continued between the NGTF and the relevant governmental departments and agencies.[29] In the meantime, people suspected of being gay were often still being denied entry.[30] Conservative pressure on Carter not to change current practice also continued.[31]

Richmond sought to force the issue by withdrawing PHS cooperation with the exclusion procedure, in a memorandum of 2 August 1979 which declared that since homosexuality 'will no longer be considered a "mental disease or defect" . . . Quarantine inspectors will no longer issue medical holds on aliens suspected solely of being homosexual'.[32] This would remove a key element of the INS's exclusion procedure. Unhappy with this intervention, which would produce a severe quandary for the INS, some senior officials from the Service sought assistance from the DoJ. Rumours of the inter-agency row got into the media, and the INS declared its intention of launching a lawsuit against Richmond. This forced Richmond to rescind the directive; meanwhile, the DoJ had reluctantly concluded that it had no choice but to enforce the statutory ban.[33]

23 'NGTF Wins Public Health Service Policy Change', News from NGTF, 6 April 1978, NGTFR, B.36, F.72, CU.
24 Ibid.
25 'Immigration Officials Drop Anti-Gay Policy', *BAR*, 27 April 1978.
26 Quoted in Larry Bush, 'Borderline Homophobia', *Inquiry*, 9 and 23 June 1980.
27 Bush, author interview.
28 Quoted in Larry Bush, 'Borderline Homophobia', *Inquiry*, 9 and 23 June 1980.
29 Bush and Weddington, author interviews; Several documents in RMSF, GTFN1, JCPL, for example Letter, Charles Brydon and Lucia Valeska to Anne Wexler, 9 November 1979.
30 Memorandum, GRA to the DoJ and John Shenefield, 1980. RMSF, G/L1, JCPL
31 Weddington, author interview.
32 Memorandum, Julius Richmond to the CDC Director and the HSA Administrator, 2 August 1979. RMSF, GH2 JCPL.
33 Larry Bush, 'Borderline Homophobia', *Inquiry*, 9 and 23 June 1980; 'Immigration Follies', *WP*, 8 July 1980.

Castillo, facing strong resistance to the easing of immigration rules from conservative senior officials within his agency, Congressmen and religious conservatives, admitted to gay rights activists that the situation, especially the Guide given to border officers about how to spot gay people, was ridiculous, and indicated that he was trying to find a way out.[34] Larry Bush, who had met with Castillo on several occasions and had participated in all of his meetings with gay rights activists, found him to be 'really quite wonderful' and responsive to the activists' requests, but with limited power due to the resistance he faced from within his own agency and beyond.*

On 10 August 1979, Castillo resorted to blurring the issue: he sent out a temporary directive to all customs officials stating that 'until the legal issues which have been raised by the General Counsel and others have been resolved', the cases of aliens who were suspected of being gay would be 'deferred for further examination';[35] gay people were allowed to enter the country in the meantime. This meant that the ban was effectively dropped, although gay people were only to be allowed in provisionally, 'on parole'.[36] The new approach acknowledged that the legal power to keep out aliens solely because they were gay rested on a certificate from the PHS.[37] Castillo explained to Larry Bush that he would have ended the exclusion altogether were it not for Crosland and the 'Anita Bryants around here' in the INS.[38] He also explained that the new policy meant that

> even if someone were to come to us and say 'I am homosexual. Exclude me', we will still allow them into the United States. . . . The less said, and the more done, the better. I've got enough crazies running around here. If the Anita Bryants found out what I'm doing, they'd lynch me.[39]

Despite its limitations, Castillo's directive pleased the gay community. The NGTF lauded the policy change, claiming again that it had resulted entirely from its 'six years of lobbying efforts'.[40] Bush, who attended all the meetings between the NGTF, White House aides, and officials from the relevant departments and witnessed the administration's efforts in the case, argued that Carter administration's contribution was 'undisputable'.*

The quandary continues: Amendment or workaround?

Castillo's 'parole' arrangement was by definition only a temporary solution to the quandary created by a statutory bar on 'sexual deviants' which now lacked any basis in expert diagnosis, and as a result any workable means of implementation. Moreover, violations of the temporary arrangement, such as the case of some Canadian

34 Larry Bush, 'Foreign Gays May Enter', *The Blade*, 16 August 1979; Bush, author interview.
35 Memorandum, Leonel Castillo on Homosexuality, 10 August 1979. RMSF, GH1, JCPL.
36 'Carter Supporting Change in Anti-Gay INS Laws', *GCN*, 5 July 1980; Robert Pear, 'Administration Opposing Ban on Homosexual Aliens', *NYT*, 24 June 1980.
37 Donald Knutson's testimony before the Select Committee on Immigration and Refugee Policy, 19 November 1979. RMSF, GH1, JCPL.
38 Larry Bush, 'Borderline Homophobia', *Inquiry*, 9 and 23 June 1980.
39 Quoted in Larry Bush, 'Foreign Gays May Enter', *The Blade*, 16 August 1979.
40 'Immigration Policy Change', *It's Time*, August–September 1979. ATSF, B.265, GR, JCPL.

women who were refused entry to the United States on account of their lesbianism, suffering a humiliating interrogation in the process – supposedly because border officials at the Port Huron crossing point had not received Castillo's directive – excited further controversy, and the NGTF continued to press for a permanent solution.[41] On 7 November 1979, three days after the hostage crisis started in Tehran, Brydon and Valeska met with Wexler in the White House to discuss, among other things, 'the conflict generated by INS and State Department exclusionary policies'. They thanked Wexler for her 'frank and open responses' to the questions raised.[42] In December, at the height of the Iran hostage crisis and the controversy regarding The Shah's stay in the United States, the administration met twice with gay rights activists with the immigration issue on the agenda.[43]

A solution seemed to recede later that month, when the Office of Legal Counsel (OLC), a unit of the DoJ whose function is to advise the president and the Executive Branch generally on legal questions, issued memorandums to the administration and the INS which stated that the existing legal prohibition of gay aliens, since it remained the prevailing law and had been upheld by the Supreme Court in 1967, had to be applied until Congress chose to alter it:[44] 'the INS is statutorily required to enforce the exclusion of homosexual aliens as long as the law remains unchanged . . . according to the intent of Congress at the time of enactment'.[45] This advice by the head of the OLC Assistant Attorney General John Harmon then came under review by Attorney General Benjamin Civiletti, who delegated the issue to recently appointed Associate Attorney General John Shenefield.[46]

A series of meetings took place at the White House and the DoJ, beginning on 3 January 1980, the first day that the White House opened for business after the New Year, less than ten days after the Soviet invasion in Afghanistan that created a new and massive crisis for the administration, and the same day that Carter withdrew the SALT II treaty from consideration by the Senate. On this occasion the activists informed both Carter's aides and (in a later meeting that day) Nelson Dong, Shenefield's deputy, of a proposal by the San Francisco-based Gay Rights Advocates (GRA), along with a number of immigration lawyers who specialized in gay rights cases, to revoke the prohibition on gay aliens not via new legislation but by revising the implementation of the existing law. As Dong characterized the problem, the DoJ 'was looking for a way through the situation, but had run out of ideas', and he was hoping to find a solution without having to turn 'the law upside down'.[47] On 7 January, Valeska and Brydon wrote to Malson to thank him for the time he had found to meet them four days previously,

41 Denise Sudell, 'Immigration Officials Exclude Women They Suspect Are Lesbians', *GN*, 5 October 1979; 'Justice Responds to NGTF Complaint', *The Blade*, 6 December 1979.
42 Letter, Charles Brydon and Lucia Valeska to Anne Wexler, 9 November 1979. RMSF, GTFN1, JCPL.
43 Letter, Charles Brydon and Lucia Valeska to Bob Malson, 7 January 1980, and NGTF's requests, 10 December 1979, both in RMSF, GH1, JCPL; 'White House Receives Gay Rights Petition', News from NGTF, 21 December 1979. ATSF, B.271, NGTF, JCPL.
44 Letter, Charles Brydon and Lucia Valeska to Bob Malson, 7 January 1980. RMSF, GH1, JCPL; Don Michaels, 'Immigration Decision Lauded', *The Blade*, 11 September 1980.
45 Memorandum, John Harmon to David Crosland, 19 December 1979. RMSF, GTFN1, JCPL.
46 Letter, Charles Brydon and Lucia Valeska to Bob Malson, 7 January 1980. RMSF, GH1, JCPL.
47 Ibid.

acknowledging that 'the events of that week created a particularly distracting context for everyone on the White House staff'.[48] Over the next few months, at least four meetings took place between activists, including Donald Knutson of the GRA, and the DoJ, and a White House aide, usually Malson or Thomas, was present at each one.[49]

At the same time that this 'workaround' for the sexual deviancy provision was being developed, a more frontal attack on the problem had been launched in Congress by Senator Alan Cranston. On 23 January Cranston observed in the Senate that the situation created by the standoff between the INS and the PHS, whereby 'inexpert' immigration officers had to make judgements about applying the 'sexual deviation' criterion, was 'absurd', and introduced legislation to remove the offending criterion from the Immigration Act's language.[50] The White House was immediately drawn into this strategy and during the first few months of 1980 had a series of meetings with activists and the DoJ over the matter.[51] Chanin, Malson and Thomas were now working on both strategies and regularly talked on the phone with the activists about progress.[52] Even Costanza was drafted again by the administration in order to provide some help because of her political contacts.[53]

After the Senate Judiciary Committee requested comment on Cranston's bill from the DoJ, Patricia Derian, Carter's Assistant Secretary of State for Human Rights, expressed (via Shenefield) the administration's 'firm support' for Cranston's bill. She also wrote that the White House acknowledged that the bill could 'have sensitive political repercussions', but that these could be 'minimized' by 'carefully basing our support for repeal on our human rights policy, our steady support for free movement of people, and the need to be consistent with what we have asked of other nations'.[54] At the same time, the DoJ, at the White House's urging, sent a letter to Senator Cranston expressing its support for his bill and offering to help with technical modifications such as its language.[55]

After returning from their meetings with the gay community in California (see Chapter 4), Malson and Thomas urged the administration to publicly express its support for Cranston's bill. They said that this was a matter of urgency for the community and that such an action 'would be greeted enthusiastically' and would also prove 'the community's legitimacy',[56] although Malson also acknowledged that such a move would not be popular with the majority of Americans and that 'the bill has only a small chance of passing'.[57] Carter agreed to this suggestion.[58]

48 Ibid.
49 Memorandum, Bob Malson for Stu Eizenstat, 19 April 1980. SESF, Gays [CF], JCPL; Jim Wood, 'Major U.S. Shift on Gay Aliens', *Examiner*, 12 September 1980.
50 *Congressional Record* 126, no. 1 (23 January 1980): 486–7.
51 Memorandum, Bob Malson for Stu Eizenstat, 19 April 1980. SESF, Gays [CF], JCPL.
52 Mike Chanin immigration calls; Bob Malson immigration calls; Allison Thomas immigration calls; all undated and in RMSF, G/L1, JCPL.
53 Mike Chanin immigration calls, undated. RMSF, G/L1, JCPL; Weddington, author interview.
54 Letter, Patricia Derian to John Shenefield, 8 April 1980. RMSF, GH1, JCPL.
55 Memorandum, Stu Eizenstat and Bob Malson to President Carter, 6 June 1980. RMSF, G/L1, JCPL.
56 Memorandum, Bob Malson to Ste Eizenstat, 8 May 1980. RMSF, GH1, JCPL; Memorandum, Allison Thomas to Anne Wexler, 8 May 1980. RMSF, GTFN2, JCPL.
57 Memorandum, Bob Malson to Ste Eizenstat, 8 May 1980. RMSF, GH1, JCPL.
58 Eizenstat, author interview.

A presentational stumble, however, occurred on 29 May when Wexler prematurely announced Carter's support of the bill to gay organizations and activists. She rescinded the announcement, but the episode went down poorly with Brydon of the NGTF, who called it a 'keystone cop's comedy' and deemed it 'typical' of his 'experience with the Carter people – a tremendous amount of uncertainty about handling any issue'. Bush, also initially misinformed by Wexler, took a more benign view, in *Gay Community News*, by noting the political stresses of the election year and observing, 'There is more staff time and work going on in the White House [on gay rights] than in any other campaign including Kennedy and Reagan'. He also claimed that Carter will officially announce his support for Cranston's bill 'within another week or so'.[59]

Chanin, in an interview with Bush for *The Sentinel* on the same day, said that the White House was still several weeks from arriving at a workable way of getting rid of the ban, but that they were 'working to resolve the problem either legislatively or administratively', alluding by the latter term to the 'workaround' strategy initially proposed by the GAA. Proponents of both strategies responded favourably: a Cranston aide told Bush that 'this is a very productive step and the President is to be commended', while Knutson of the GAA said publicly, 'I congratulate the Carter Administration for this action. I think that it is very good news, but I'll believe it when I see it'.[60]

Aside from the various discussions of substantive detail, attention was also being paid by the White House to gaining maximum political impact from the administration's position. Thomas proposed that support for the bill should be announced in the third week of June, which was Gay Pride Week in many cities across the United States. She suggested to Wexler that Carter should send to two events to which he and his wife had been invited a message or statement of 'a bland nature' but also including a statement of support for Cranston's bill.[61] Thus, on 18 June, the first day of Gay Pride Week, the announcement was made, and letters were simultaneously sent by the administration to the NGTF, Cranston and Edward Kennedy, chair of the Senate Judiciary Committee.[62] The announcement made big headlines, thanks to the timing, and constituted the first time that a president had publicly supported gay rights legislation.[63] The gay community rejoiced at Carter's endorsement of Cranston's bill and realized that its timing gave it tremendous symbolic significance.[64] After an interval, indeed shortly before the 1980 presidential elections, the NGTF acknowledged Carter's support for the bill and the fact that he was the first American president to support such legislation.[65]

A favourable legislative outcome was nevertheless still a remote prospect. Jonathan Fleming, Cranston's legislative assistant, and Brydon had both acknowledged that the

59 Bennett Klein, 'Carter and the INS Bill', *GCN*, 14 June 1980.

60 Larry Bush, 'White House Pledges End to Immigration Ban', *The Sentinel*, 30 May 1980.

61 Memorandum, Allison Thomas for Anne Wexler, 28 May 1980. RMSF, GH3, JCPL.

62 Letter, Anne Wexler to NGTF, 18 June 1980. RMSF, GH3, JCPL; Memorandum, Bob Malson to Mike Chanin, 18 June 1980. SESF, Gays [CF], JCPL.

63 'National Gay Task Force Directors Express Support for Carter', News from NGTF, 2 October 1980. NGTFR, B.6, F.3, CU.

64 Bush, DeBaugh, Kent and McReynolds, author interviews; 'Carter Endorses Bill to End Immigration Ban', The name of the newspaper is not visible, 27 June 1980, NGTFR, B.144, F.57, CU.

65 'National Gay Task Force Directors Express Support for Carter', News from NGTF, 2 October 1980. NGTFR, B.6, F.3, CU.

bill had little chance of passing in the near future. According to Fleming, Congress regarded anything to do with gay rights as 'touchy', and the impending elections would make garnering support even more difficult. There was also some disquiet among activists about the DoJ's delay in making a decision on the GRA's workaround proposal. Knutson threatened to challenge the Department in court if it refused to make the administrative changes.[66] However, Brydon and Valeska were more patient, acknowledging that 'our friends at the White House project a positive outlook when asked for an opinion'; they also acknowledged that the State Department's April letter to the DoJ supporting the remedy was 'helpful'.[67]

The White House continued to push Shenefield and Civiletti on the workaround. Eventually, on 8 September, Shenefield presented to Malson and Wexler the DoJ's new proposed immigration policy. Wexler immediately informed the activists about it.[68] The policy, announced publicly the following day, established a procedure of 'primary inspection', in which no question should be asked of an alien regarding sexual preference, and 'referral to secondary inspection' only after 'an unsolicited, unambiguous oral or written admission of homosexuality', specifically excluding indications such as 'buttons, literature or other materials referring to "gay rights" or describing or supporting homosexuality' (unsolicited statement of an alien's homosexuality by a third-party applicant would also entail secondary inspection, but this was expected to be a rare eventuality). 'Secondary inspection', conducted in private and without a search, would pose only a yes or no question about the alien's homosexuality, a 'no' ending the inspection, and a 'yes' resulting in referral to an immigration judge.[69]

This was in effect a 'Don't Ask, Don't Tell' policy, but unlike President Clinton's later policy of that name for gay servicepeople, it applied only to a unique interview situation at the point of entry; this made it a more viable defence of gay rights. The INS publicized the new rules in a 'priority' communication to institutions under its control. For its part, the State Department instructed foreign consular services to abide by the new procedure when it came to issuing travel visas. Furthermore, the DoJ declared that it would join the NGTF as plaintiff in any court case arising from an improper exclusion in terms of the new policy. On the day the policy went into effect, Shenefield met with Brydon and Knutson to explain it. He also told the activists that it was 'a priority for the coming year' for the DoJ to actively help in seeking passage of Cranston's bill, and expressed his hope that 'a year from now we would all sit down to talk and the issue would be moot'.[70] The *Los Angeles Times* accurately wrote that 'until Congress acts, the DoJ's policy means that a bad law will be enforced in the most civilized way possible'.[71]

The vast majority of the gay community was very pleased with the new policy. Brydon praised the DoJ for its 'sensitivity to the human factor involved' in the decision

66 Lou Chibbaro, Jr., 'White House Supports Immigration Law Change', *The Blade*, 26 June 1980; 'Immigration', *It's Time*, May–June 1980. RMSF, G/L1, JCPL.

67 Charles Brydon and Lucia Valeska, 'Notes from the Co-Execs', *It's Time*, May–June 1980. RMSF, G/L1, JCPL

68 Britt and Bush, author interviews; Uncompleted Gay Issues, undated. RMSF, G/L2, JCPL.

69 DoJ's press release, 9 September 1980, and Telegraphic Message from David Crosland, 8 September 1980, both in RCHTF, Homosexuals [File 2], JCPL.

70 Don Michaels, 'Immigration Decision Lauded', *The Blade*, 11 September 1980.

71 'Civilized Enforcement of a Bad Law', *LAT*, 15 September 1980.

it rendered, as well as its support of the Cranston bill. He said that the department had 'set an example other agencies should follow',[72] and described the new policy as 'an important practical victory for the gay rights movement'.[73] Brydon and Knutson wrote to Shenefield, 'this decision is a model in its concern for the human element, a consideration too often found lacking in government actions', and expressed their 'delight' that 'the vast majority of lesbian and gay aliens are now able to visit the United States'.[74] Bunch later judged, 'Well, it's never enough, but it was a very good thing. I mean, I think it's probably all he [Carter] could do'.* However, some gay rights activists were not entirely satisfied with Carter's efforts on immigration, and were pushing for the passage of Cranston's bill. Knutson expressed his disappointment that the DoJ had not abandoned 'enforcement of the obnoxious law altogether', though adding, 'As a practical matter, however, today's decision is very close to total victory'.[75] Knutson seemed to have forgotten that the DoJ had no power to abandon the law altogether; only Congress (or judicial review) could do that. Speaking to *The Blade*, an unnamed White House aide cautioned that, since Congress would probably not get around to debating the bill that year, the administration's efforts depended on Carter winning a second term.[76] Eventually, Cranston's bill was rejected by Congress. It would take another ten years for Congress to be convinced to pass legislation, the Immigration Act of 1990, that would end the legal exclusion of gay aliens from the United States.[77] However, Carter's new policy directive on immigration continued until then to mitigate the exclusion.[78]

The case of the gay Cuban refugees

The United States generally had a policy of accepting refugees from Communist countries; the approach became even more relaxed and welcoming during Carter's presidency. However, problems arose in regard to would-be refugees who were fleeing Cuba and who happened to be gay.[79] In April 1980, Fidel Castro announced that all Cubans who wished to leave the country would be allowed to do so via the port of Mariel. Seeing a chance to reunite themselves with their families and friends, Cubans living in Florida sent boats to collect them. Castro, somewhat vengefully, sent thousands of criminals and mental patients along with the would-be exiles. Between

72 Don Michaels, 'Immigration Decision Lauded', *The Blade*, 11 September 1980.
73 Robert Pear, 'U.S. Bars Exclusions of Homosexual Aliens in Most Circumstances', *NYT*, 10 September 1980.
74 Letter, Charles Brydon and Don Knutson to John Shenefield and David Crosland, 26 September 1980. RMSF, GH3, JCPL.
75 John Fogarty, 'U.S. Eases Policy on Gay Immigrants', *San Francisco Chronicle*, 10 September 1980.
76 Don Michaels, 'Immigration Decision Lauded', *The Blade*, 11 September 1980.
77 Faderman, *The Gay Revolution*, 303.
78 Bush, author interview; 'Immigration Reform Near', *OOB*, May 1988.
79 After the Cuban revolution, gay people in Cuba were sent to 're-education camps' or were fired or imprisoned. However, in 1979 Castro decriminalized homosexuality, and thirty years later he publicly apologized for the treatment of gay people, admitting that there were 'moments of great injustice against the gay community' and that 'if someone is responsible, it's me' ('Fidel Castro Takes Blame for Persecution of Cuban Gays', *BBC News*, 31 August 2010).

April and October 1980, about 125,000 Cuban refugees were allowed by Cuba to flee to the United States. This was known as the Mariel boatlift.[80] Among the refugees, there was 'a substantial gay group'.[81]

Though homosexuality was not at that point illegal in Cuba, it was still considered shameful by a few; despite this, some of the refugees had pretended to be gay in order to flee the country.[82] Carter publicly stated that he would welcome the Cuban refugees with 'an open heart and open arms'.[83] Although the policy described in the previous section was not yet in effect, Carter's administration assured the NGTF that the 'sexual deviance' exclusion in section 212(a) (4) of the Immigration Act would not be applied to the gay Cuban refugees, promising 'sanctuary' free from deportation based on sexual orientation.[84]

The White House worked closely with the INS to ensure that gay Cuban refugees would be able to enter and remain in the country. On 16 April 1980, Malson met with Crosland and both agreed that the best way to bypass the statutory exclusion was

> to say that the refugees paroled into the United States are subject to the exclusionary grounds contained in 212 (a) but these can be waived for humanitarian reasons in any particular case. This approach . . . makes it possible to insure no adverse decision will arise.[85]

Subsequently, on 2 May, Carter kept his promise to the NGTF and issued special immigration waivers on humanitarian grounds to the Cuban refugees. On Carter's order, the State Department created a Cuban Refugee Task Force (CRTF) and Ambassador Victor Palmieri, appointed by Carter as Coordinator for Refugee Affairs in the State Department, was put in charge in dealing with the refugees. Furthermore, Carter designated Eugene Eidenberg and Jack Watson, two of his most senior and trusted advisors and his assistants for Intergovernmental Affairs, to cooperate with Palmieri and coordinate the resettlement of the refugees in the United States.[86]

On 6 May, Carter declared a state of emergency in South Florida and directed the Federal Emergency Management Agency (FEMA) to coordinate the government response to the crisis, while he issued a $10 million budget for food, clothes and shelter for the refugees and for use by the non-state organizations that would help to resettle them.[87] The refugees were placed in various military bases. The Metropolitan

80 Felix Masud-Piloto, *From Welcomed Exiles to Illegal Immigrants: Cuban Migration to the U.S., 1959–95* (New York: Rowman & Littlefield Publishers, Inc., 1995), 83–8.

81 Robert Pear, 'Administration Opposing Ban on Homosexual Aliens', *NYT*, 24 June 1980.

82 Warren Brown, 'Cuban Boatlift Drew Thousands of Homosexuals', *WP*, 7 July 1980; Karen Dewitt, 'Homosexual Cubans Get Settlement Aid', *NYT*, 17 August 1980.

83 Milt Freudenheim and Barbara Slavin, 'Castro Divides Cuban Exodus in Three Parts', *NYT*, 11 May 1980.

84 'Carter Orders Marines Here', *Key West Citizen*, 7 May 1980; Karen Dewitt, 'Homosexual Cubans Get Settlement Aid', *NYT*, 17 August 1980.

85 Memorandum, Bob Malson for Allison Thomas, 16 April 1980. RMSF, GH1, JCPL.

86 Larry Bush, 'Gay Cubans Win Waiver', *The Sentinel*, 2 May 1980; Bush, author interview; Paul Heath Hoeffel, 'Fort Chaffee's Unwanted Cubans', *NYT Magazine*, 21 December 1980.

87 Stuart E. Eizenstat, *President Carter: The White House Years* (New York: St. Martin's Press, 2018), 873; CHTF: A Guide to Its Records, JCPL.

Community Church (MCC), aware of the presence of gay refugees, immediately mobilized to help them by setting up a Cuban Relief Fund, seeking sponsors and collecting clothes. The MCC then asked the White House for permission to visit the refugee camps and to seek out the gay population in an attempt to help them. The White House gave this permission and members of the MCC began visiting the camps. Sources inside the refugee camps had estimated that there were at least 2,000 and perhaps as many as 10,000 gay men and women. At a screening conducted by the MCC at Fort Chaffee, Arkansas, it was discovered that there were about 250 gay people, the vast majority of them men, among the 5,000 refugees, although it was believed that there were many more who were afraid to admit it.[88] The MCC discovered mistreatment of gays by other refugees and also by some guards.[89] Bill Traugh, a director at FEMA, said that among the refugees 'the homosexual group is shunned by the general population. Many of the Cuban men are very macho and don't take too kindly to the homosexuals'.[90] The MCC requested that the gay refugees be segregated for their protection, and the administration agreed.[91] For example, in Indiantown Gap, Pennsylvania, two hundred lesbians were moved into separate barracks from the other refugees.[92]

On 20 June, Carter gave Cubans and Haitians who had come to the United States over the previous few months a special classification, that of 'Cuban-Haitian entrant'.[93] This new designation allowed them to remain in the country, and after two years they would be able to become 'permanent resident aliens'. In the intervening time, they would be able to obtain medical treatment, income support and emergency benefits.[94] Carter did not stop there with the gay Cuban refugees and showed a genuine and humane concern for them. At the time, the administration had already initiated a financial package to encourage Americans to sponsor a refugee; each refugee received $50, plus travel expenses to the city of the sponsor, and then another $75 was given to the sponsor on behalf of the refugee.[95] Even so, and despite the MCC's efforts, there were not many who would agree to sponsor a gay refugee; thus the MCC was unable to get more than a tiny portion of them out of the camps and settled. DeBaugh, who had been in regular communication with Allison Thomas, informed her of the problems of these refugees. Carter immediately agreed to help. However, in order to avoid controversy, a joint operation with the MCC was arranged; the Church would do the

88 Arthur and DeBaugh, author interviews; 'Gay Cubans', *It's Time*, July–August 1980. RMSF, G/L2, JCPL; MCC press release, 'Lesbian and Gay Community Meets to Form Nationwide Network for Aiding Gay and Lesbian Cuban Refugees', 8 July 1980. NGTFR, B.144, F.1, CU.

89 B. Ruby Rich and Lourdes Arguelles, 'Homosexuality, Homophobia, and Revolution: Notes toward an Understanding of the Cuban Lesbian and Gay Male Experience, Part II', *Signs* 11, no. 1 (1985): 129.

90 Warren Brown, 'Cuban Boatlift Drew Thousands of Homosexuals', *WP*, 7 July 1980.

91 Arthur and DeBaugh, author interviews; David Morris, 'Gay Cuban Refugees Here: Where Do Feds Send Them?', *GCN*, 21 June 1980.

92 Letter, The MCC of New York to 'Dear Sisters and Brothers', 16 July 1980. NGTFR, B.144, F.1, CU.

93 Migration from Haiti had increased under the dictatorial regime of the Duvaliers (1957–86). Historically, and subsequently under the Reagan administration, they were treated much less favourably than refugees from Cuba.

94 Gil Loescher and John A. Scanlan, *Calculated Kindness: Refugees and America's Half-Open Door, 1945 to the Present* (New York: The Free Press, 1993), 186.

95 Letter, Steve Carson to members and friends of the MCC, undated. NGTFR, B.144, F.1, CU.

leg-work and be the public face of the operation, while the administration provided funding and any necessary logistical help.[96]

Subsequently, Eidenberg contacted the MCC in Los Angeles, which was already working with refugees, and with which the White House had already developed an effective relationship, and asked whether they were willing to cooperate with the State Department in setting up a joint resettlement programme for the gay Cubans. Troy Perry was pleasantly surprised at the unexpected proposal and immediately agreed to cooperate. The Church then created the UFMMC Lesbian/Gay Cuban Task Force, with the church's board of elders appointing Rev. Bob Arthur as its chair, in charge of the collaboration with Carter's administration.[97]

The State Department certified the MCC as a resettlement agency and the White House directed FEMA to cooperate with the Church and to provide it with funding for the resettlement programme; this included $300 for each refugee they resettled. The White House, FEMA and the State Department collaborated closely with the MCC in the Cuban relief programme, providing logistical and other financial support; whenever the Church needed additional money, for example for clothes or medical treatment for the refugees, it was provided through FEMA. It was the first time that the White House had taken the initiative to collaborate with a gay organization, and this initiative demonstrated a genuine concern for this constituency of disadvantaged gay people. Among the first requests that the Church made to the administration was that it provide translators, as most of the Cubans did not speak English, and that it also pay for the transportation of each Cuban to their assigned sponsor once they were matched up by the Church. Carter's administration accepted both requests. Carter's administration remained in close communication with the MCC throughout the duration of the operation and contributed significantly to its success.[98]

Over the following months, the MCC managed to raise on its own about $40,000 for the gay refugees,[99] but its joint resettlement programme with Carter's administration was not moving as fast as expected. The main issue was that there were still not many people who were willing to sponsor a gay refugee. The presence of the refugees was also proving unpopular as some Americans believed that their country was being invaded by gay people and criminals. In August 1980, according to a Harris poll, 70–80 per cent of Americans held a negative view of Cubans and Haitians, while 75 per cent of respondents to a Gallup poll thought that the situation was 'bad for our country'. Some in government feared that the high profile of the gay refugees was part of the reason for this. According to Arthur Brill, director of public affairs of the CHTF, 'homosexual' Cubans, along with other 'bad performers' such as 'hijackers, rioters, criminals, malcontents, and prostitutes' were responsible for this negative perception.[100] The MCC also wanted to ensure that those who had expressed an interest in sponsoring

96 DeBaugh and Weddington, author interviews.

97 Arthur and Perry, author interviews.

98 Arthur, Bush and DeBaugh, author interviews.

99 Susana Peña, *Oye Loca: From the Mariel Boatlift to Gay Cuban Miami* (Minneapolis and London: University of Minnesota Press, 2013), 53.

100 Memorandum, Arthur Brill to Christian Holmes, 22 August 1980. RCHTF, CHTF Public Affairs Files, JCPL.

someone were suitable to do so, so they conducted interviews with potential sponsors. Arthur said, 'We had to make sure that the people who were willing to sponsor a gay Cuban were doing so out of concern for them, rather than trying to find gay partners'.*

Meanwhile, the NGTF, as well as other gay organizations, had also been trying to find sponsors for the gay refugees, but with even less success than the MCC/White House programme. Observing the cooperation of Carter's administration with the MCC, the NGTF asked the Church if they could also join the programme. The NGTF and the MCC then worked jointly to mobilize the resources of the national gay community for the resettlement of gay Cuban refugees. They organized a Conference in the MCC's church in Washington, D.C. for 7 July, with the participation of another eight gay and other organizations: Dignity, Integrity, GRNL, GRA, the Pennsylvania Governor's Council for Sexual Minorities, the Dade County Coalition for Human Rights, the National Association of Business Councils and the American Council for Nationalities Services.[101] DeBaugh asked Thomas to attend the meeting as White House representative.[102]

Carl Harris, of the CRTF, and Thomas attended the Conference on behalf of the administration. Among the difficulties identified was confusion among potential sponsors regarding their obligations and responsibilities. Thus, the activists requested funding from Carter's administration for an information campaign to be conducted with leaflets and mailings to sensitize people about the plight of the gay refugees, inform them of how they could help by sponsoring one, and tell them the requirements to become a sponsor. Another request was that other gay organizations, in addition to the MCC, would be allowed to visit the refugee camps and speak to gay Cubans. Thomas and Harris did not make any promises, but stated that they would convey the requests to the administration.[103]

The same day, the *Washington Post* featured a front-page article entitled 'Cuban Boatlift Drew Thousands of Homosexuals' which stated that about 20,000 of the 40,000 Cuban refugees who were still in the camps awaiting resettlement were gay. The article also revealed that Carter's administration was cooperating with gay organizations to help the resettlement of the gay refugees. Furthermore, it contained a statement by Rev. Larry Uhrig of the MCC, who acknowledged that his Church had been contacted by the State Department to help with the resettlement of the gay refugees and that the two had been working together in this effort.[104] The story was immediately picked up by other mainstream media, including the CBS Evening News, which referred to the case in its newscast that night. The revelation that Carter had not only allowed gay refugees into the country but that he was cooperating with a gay church in resettling them and spending taxpayers' money to finance their stay led to outrage and strong protests by conservatives. However, the publicity about the story, which had grossly overestimated the population of gay refugees as in reality they numbered about

101 DeBaugh, author interview; 'Lesbians and Gay Community Meets to form Nationwide Network for Aiding Gay and Lesbian Cuban Refugees', NGTF press release, 8 July 1980. NGTFR, B.36, F.159, CU.

102 DeBaugh, author interview.

103 Bush and DeBaugh, author interviews.

104 Warren Brown, 'Cuban Boatlift Drew Thousands of Homosexuals', *WP*, 7 July 1980.

3,000, had some benefits too, as the MCC began receiving hundreds of phone calls from people who wanted to help and to sponsor gay refugees.[105] Despite the adverse response to the article, Carter's administration immediately accepted all the requests the gay rights activists had made at the Conference. The activists' visits turned out to be very beneficial for the gay Cubans as they had not been aware of what to expect in the United States and how to behave with regard to their homosexuality, and the activists provided them with counselling on a number of issues.[106]

Subsequently, several local and national gay organizations, such as the NGTF and the Dade Coalition for Human Rights, joined the White House and the MCC in their resettlement programme and also received federal funding for their efforts.[107] On 15 July, Carter established the Cuban-Haitian Task Force (CHTF), which aimed to 'manage the processing and resettlement of Cuban and Haitian arrivals', and appointed Richard Holmes as its director.[108] Holmes and the new Task Force collaborated closely with the MCC and the other gay organizations, providing them with funding and logistical support. An important part of this collaboration was the successful effort to locate relatives of the gay refugees in the United States.[109]

At one point, the MCC became worried about the mental state of around 150 gay refugees as they were struggling to cope with life in the camps. Thus, the Church requested funding from Carter's administration to take them out of the camps and into safe locations until they were resettled. Despite the controversy over the administration's involvement with the MCC and its financing of gay refugees, Carter agreed to provide the Church with a grant so that it could take these refugees out of the camps. Subsequently, the MCC, with federal funding, leased halfway houses in Chicago, Philadelphia and Baltimore and planned to move fift refugees into each one. Thus, the administration not only allowed the gay refugees into the country and financed a resettlement programme for them, but it also paid to ease their resettlement and keep them safe. However, this initiative also caused some controversy among local authorities and people who did not want gay Cuban refugees in their cities. Despite some protests from locals, the Church was able to move 100 refugees into two halfway houses in Chicago and Philadelphia. However, the City of Baltimore and local citizens fought against the resettlement and shortly before the refugees were moved there, the halfway house leased by the MCC was set on fire. The MCC informed the White House about the fire and the administration immediately agreed to provide the Church with additional funding to move the refugees into another location. Eventually the Church leased a halfway house in San Francisco and took the remaining fifty refugees there.[110]

In September, after repeated requests from Carter, Castro finally closed the port of Mariel to migrating Cubans. By October, a large number of refugees were still unsettled, so the administration increased the amount offered to organizations involved in the

[105] Arthur and DeBaugh, author interviews; Michael Massing, 'The Invisible Cubans', *Columbia Journalism Review* 19, no. 3 (1980): 49–50.
[106] Arthur, Bush and DeBaugh, author interviews.
[107] Bush, author interview; Mike Miller, *Out of the Past: Gay and Lesbian History from 1869 to the Present* (New York: Vintage Books, 1995), 493.
[108] CHTF: A Guide to Its Records, JCPL.
[109] Arthur and DeBaugh, author interviews.
[110] Ibid.

resettlement effort, including the gay organizations, from $300 to $1,000 for each refugee resettled.[111] This enabled the gay rights activists to attract more sponsors for the refugees and thus a large number of them were finally resettled. In the end, the MCC and other gay organizations received for their resettlement efforts a significant portion of the $10 million that Carter had provided for the Cuban refugees. Eventually, the joint resettlement programme by the MCC and Carter's administration turned out to be a significant and ground-breaking success, managing to find homes or to set up group homes for about 3,000 gay Cubans.[112] On 2 October, the NGTF publicly acknowledged and praised Carter's 'sensitive decision on enforcement of the immigration law and assistance and support of the resettlement of gay Cuban refugees'.[113]

The administration's response to the special plight of the gay Cuban refugees was noteworthy not only for its promptness and effectiveness but also for being largely spontaneous and not a response to sustained pressure from activists. Instead, the administration worked cooperatively and proactively with gay rights organizations, even when opposition to this policy, in which anti-gay sentiment combined with already powerful hostility to immigration, began to mount. This clearly shows Carter and his administration's real concern about these people, but also how much gay rights had progressed during his presidency.

Carter's efforts to end the exclusion of gay people from entry to the United States were sustained over much of his presidency; they illustrate the difficulties of policy-making in the separated institutions of American government. His administration met several times with gay rights activists over the issue while also facilitating many meetings between activists and the DoJ and the INS in an attempt to resolve it. Knowing that it would have been impossible for Congress to pass legislation to remove this exclusion, Carter supported and pushed for a new policy by the DoJ which achieved the same practical goal. Although in legal and formal terms gay people were still not allowed into the United States, the new directive prohibited the immigration authorities from questioning visitors about their sexuality or even making assumptions about it. This practical change, while in principle reversible by administrative order, was politically harder to reverse, setting the precedent that the government no longer considered gay entrants to be undesirable. It was Carter who made the first steps in the history of the United States to end the exclusion of gay aliens; ten full years would pass before another meaningful step was taken to permanently end this exclusion.

The administration's solicitous handling of the gay contingent of the Mariel boatlift, against opposition which even reached the level of acts of violence, is noteworthy as much for its spontaneity as its results. Arthur and DeBaugh described the administration was 'very helpful' and 'very supportive' in the gay Cuban refugees' resettlement programme, and said that without this help it would have been impossible for the MCC and the gay

111 'U.S. Offers $1,000 a Person to Resettle Cuban Refugees', *NYT*, 20 October 1980.

112 Arthur and DeBaugh, author interviews.

113 'National Gay Task Force Directors Express Support for Carter', News from NGTF, 2 October 1980. NGTFR, B.6, F.3, CU.

community alone to resettle the refugees.* Bush, who extensively reported on the case and attended the meetings between Carter's aides and gay rights activists regarding the matter, argued that the administration's initiative and its cooperation with the MCC was 'something that was unprecedented at the time. That was a very big change in American policy'.* Troy Perry found the Carter administration's contribution to the resettlement of the gay refugees to be 'incredible', considering it a 'shame' that this effort did not and still does not receive the appreciation it deserves.*

9

Honour and dishonour in the military

This chapter discusses efforts to address the exclusion and discriminatory treatment of gay people in the military. It is an area of federal government employment that has a very prominent symbolic dimension, especially in the post-war period, in which the United States had acquired a global military role. While by the time of Carter's presidency its defeat in the Vietnam War had brought the military's prestige into question, this question was itself a matter of severe disagreement between conservative and liberal opinion. Despite Carter's reluctance to extend his gay rights sympathies into the security and military field, his administration, partly through its attempt to deal with the fallout of the Vietnam experience, was nevertheless inevitably drawn into addressing it, as the severity of the symbolic affronts as well as the numerous material disadvantages suffered by gay military personnel and veterans became apparent. The chapter details the important steps which the administration, despite Carter's initial position, managed to take. It goes on to discuss the poignant issue of the official commemoration of gay people who had continued in military service despite the ban (usually by concealing their sexuality) and had given their lives in so doing.

'Traditions and suspicions'

The US armed forces had long held that gay people in uniform damaged discipline, morals and morale; they were banned from joining the forces and were dishonourably discharged if they were discovered. The Department of Defense (DoD) had set out a unified policy towards homosexuality in the services in 1949, stating, 'Homosexual personnel, irrespective of sex, should not be permitted to serve in any branch of the Armed Services in any capacity, and prompt separation of known gay people from the Armed Forces be made mandatory'. Four years later, President Eisenhower's Executive Order 10450 specified that 'sexual perversion' was sufficient reason for dismissing any federal employee. In 1959, the DoD issued a Directive on Administrative Discharges (Directive 1332.14) which specified 'sexual perversion', including homosexual acts and sodomy, as grounds for 'unfitness' leading to discharge. Revisions in 1965 improved matters by granting the right to present a case against discharge to an administrative discharge board, while a 1975 revision adopted the language 'homosexual acts or other aberrant sexual tendencies' as the basis for discharge.[1]

[1] National Defense Research Institute, *Sexual Orientation and U.S. Military Personnel Policy: Options and Assessment* (Santa Monica, CA: RAND Corporation, 1993), 1–7.

The NGTF felt that such discharges 'mark the recipient for life'.[2] In addition to the stigma of dishonourable discharges, they deprived veterans of access to numerous benefits.[3] Furthermore, the imperative to root out gay people from the military encouraged improper levels of surveillance.[4] The claimed incompatibility between gay people and the positive symbolic resonance of military service was a further important consideration, despite its intangibility.

The issue of gay people in the military was among the issues raised by the NGTF at the March 1977 Meeting. Carter's administration recognized both the concerns and the difficulty of addressing them: it was an area 'in which traditions and suspicions make changes very difficult. There is no magic formula in this area, or we would have used it already. The best chance for improvement will come from the movement in all areas of employment, not a frontal assault on the military'.[5]

Rectifying past dishonour

Carter wanted to end the trauma the Vietnam War had caused to American society by healing some of its remaining wounds.[6] During his presidential campaign he had characterized the Vietnam veterans as the 'nation's greatest unsung heroes' and had signalled his intention to grant 'a blanket pardon' to those who had non-violently 'violated Selective Service laws'. This would succeed and expand upon President Ford's clemency programme for Vietnam War deserters. Carter's first step, once in office (indeed on his first full day), was to grant an unconditional pardon to most draft evaders (though not to deserters).[7] In February 1977, a group of pro-amnesty activists met with Charles Kirbo, Carter's advisor, to discuss the possible expansion of Carter's programme to include deserters and others with dishonourable discharges. Among them was David Addlestone who proposed the inclusion of veterans discharged for homosexuality in the programme.[8] In March 1977 Carter ordered the Department of Defense to create the Special Discharge Review Program (SDRP), which would review 'Vietnam-era' discharges of military personnel in categories other than honourable; it offered 433,000 veterans of the Vietnam War who had received dishonourable discharges but had not been convicted of serious crimes by court-martials the opportunity to apply to upgrade their discharges.[9]

Haft had been involved in the issue of dishonourable discharges of gay veterans long before she began working in the White House; she had not only defended Leonard

2 Memorandum, Marilyn Haft to Margaret Costanza, 25 March 1977. SWSF, SWSF, [Gay] CR, JCPL.

3 Peter Slavin, 'The Stigmas of Discharge', *WP*, 18 April 1978.

4 Memorandum, Marilyn Haft to Margaret Costanza, 25 March 1977. SWSF, SWSF, [Gay] CR, JCPL.

5 WH memorandum: Talking points on gay issues, 5 August 1980. RMSF, G/L2, JCPL.

6 James Reston, 'Carter's Ends and Means', *NYT*, 23 January 1977; 'Those who Served', *WP*, 9 January 1977.

7 Myra MacPherson, *Long Time Passing: Vietnam and the Haunted Generation* (Bloomington and Indianapolis: Indiana University Press, 2002), 350; James T. Wooten, 'Legionnaires Boo Carter on Pardon for Draft Defiers', *NYT*, 25 August 1976.

8 David Addlestone, author interview; 'Carter Program to Affect Gays', *Out Front*, February 1977.

9 MacPherson, *Long Time Passing*, 350.

Matlovich (see Chapter 2) but had also assisted Vernon E. Berg, a Navy ensign, who like Matlovich had been dishonourably discharged because of his homosexuality.[10] After Haft's appointment was confirmed and Carter had announced his intention to re-examine Vietnam-era dishonourable discharges, Voeller asked her to press the idea that the programme would take in the case of gay veterans. Haft accordingly began working on the case and informed Costanza and Eizenstat about it. Carter immediately agreed to the suggestion.[11] Haft mentioned the programme and the prospect of the inclusion of gay veterans in it during a speech on 14 February 1977 at a New York Bar Association symposium on sexual orientation and the law. The proposal took gay veterans and activists completely by surprise.[12] On 18 February, Berg, who was another of the speakers in the symposium, also wrote to Haft to thank her for her efforts and for her concern over the case, stating that gay veterans 'cannot stress enough our gratitude for your part in the opening of discussions on these sorely neglected areas of discrimination'.[13]

At the March 1977 Meeting at the White House, the NGTF requested that the administration end discrimination against gay people in the military and that gay veterans who had received dishonourable discharges be included in the new SDRP.[14] The first of these was the only issue on the gay rights agenda at the meeting whose political viability Costanza had questioned, given the likely resistance of not only conservative politicians and voters, but also the military establishment. Nevertheless, she promised that the administration would work on it.[15] After the meeting, Costanza and Haft recruited Wishman to the cause and they began by examining the Army discharge guidelines and consulting with military officials. Shortly afterwards, the White House informed the DoD of its intention to include in the SDRP veterans who had received dishonourable discharges because of their homosexuality.[16]

Clifford Alexander Jr, recently appointed by Carter as Secretary of the Army, was very willing to include gay veterans in the SDRP, but as anticipated he faced strong resistance from senior Army staff and from conservative politicians who were already unhappy with the SDRP in relation to its principal focus on Vietnam veterans. The White House insisted, and the Army eventually agreed,[17] stating in a letter to the NGTF, 'individuals separated from the Armed Forces on the basis of homosexuality may qualify for upgrading . . . providing the circumstances of their service and separation meet the criteria of the programme and do not constitute a bar for upgrading'.[18] Gay veterans and activists were ecstatic, especially since Carter had acted so early in his

10 David Addlestone had also been on the legal team in Matlovich and Berg's cases.

11 Haft and Eizenstat, author interviews.

12 'Sexual Orientation, Society and the Law', Association of the Bar of the City of New York, 14 February 1977. MCSF, [H-GRPH], JCPL; Haft, author interview.

13 Letter, Vernon E. Berg to Marilyn Haft, 18 February 1977. SWSF, GHD, JCPL.

14 Memorandum, Margaret Costanza to President Carter, 8 April 1977. SWSF, [Gay] CR, JCPL.

15 Haft and Perry, author interview.

16 Marilyn Haft, Weekly Staff Report 16–20 May 1977. MCI; Haft, author interview. See also documents at JCPL, e.g., Vietnam Veterans Lacking Honorable Discharges. MCSF, B10, and SWSF, GHD.

17 Eizenstat and Haft, author interviews.

18 Letter, Paul Phillips to the NGTF, 8 June 1977. MCSF, [H-GRPH], JCPL.

presidency;[19] Voeller said, 'This policy statement is a major breakthrough by the Armed Forces on matters concerning gays in the military', and credited the White House for this 'important step'.[20]

The SDRP began on 5 April 1977, and was to run until 4 October.[21] In the Navy, the first upgrades of dishonourable discharges took place through the personal intervention of W. Graham Claytor Jr, the Secretary of the Navy recently appointed by Carter. On 7 April, Claytor upgraded to honourable the dishonourable discharge of Kenneth L. Pittman Jr,[22] and shortly afterwards did the same for Berg after he had personally evaluated his case.[23] Claytor went on to upgrade to honourable several other dishonourable discharges that had been given to gay servicemen, among them Robert A. Martin Jr, who in 1971 was ousted from the Navy because of his homosexuality.[24] The Navy's letter to him explained the practical and financial implications of the discharge upgrade,[25] but Martin spoke of its symbolic importance: 'What an honourable discharge means to me is that it is the nation's way of saying that it is proud of gay veterans and by extension that it is proud of millions of gay veterans and current service people. We've come a long way'.[26]

Initially, however, the SDRP's impact was limited by the paucity of information available about who was eligible to apply, and by its limited duration.[27] The programme required veterans to take the initiative, and some, especially deserters, were afraid to apply, fearing that they could still be court-martialled and sent to prison. The initiative factor was especially problematic for gay veterans, as neither the mainstream press nor indeed the gay press (which in any case was far from widely read by the gay population) dedicated much space to it.[28] On 24 May, seven weeks after the programme had begun, the NGTF requested to Haft that the Army clarify 'whether a person separated from the Armed Forces on the basis of homosexuality may be upgraded through participation' in the SDRP.[29] Haft passed on the request to Army Secretary Alexander, and a letter then went to the NGTF giving an affirmative answer and confirming eligibility for veterans' benefits upon upgrade.[30]

Carter's SDRP immediately came under massive attack from conservatives, the military establishment, veterans and several military organizations who felt that it rewarded cowardice and brought shame to the military. They also believed that the inclusion of gay discharges in the SDRP was a concession to gay people in the

19 Hallman, Kent, McReynolds and Sandifer, author interviews.
20 'Gay Veterans may Qualify for Upgraded Discharge', News from NGTF, 17 June 1977. NGTFR, B.36, F.37, CU.
21 '29,528 of the 433,000 Eligible Apply for Upgrading Military Discharges', *NYT*, 15 May 1977.
22 Letter, David Addlestone to Kenneth L. Pittman, Jr. 7 April 1977. MCSF, [H-GRPH], JCPL.
23 Peter Kihss, 'Discharge by Navy of Homosexual Raised to Honorable by Secretary', *NYT*, 28 April 1977.
24 Bob Martin, David Addlestone and Franklin Kameny Press Release, 'Gay Vet Wins Honorable Discharge', October 1979. FGJP, UC.
25 Letter, Department of the Navy to Robert Martin, 26 September 1977. FGJP, UC.
26 Bob Martin, David Addlestone, Franklin Kameny Press Release, 'Gay Vet Wins Honorable Discharge', October 1979. FGJP, UC.
27 Charles Mohr, 'Upgraded Veterans Face Aid Loss in Bill Signed by President', *NYT*, 9 October 1977; MacPherson, *Long Time Passing*, 350.
28 Kent and McReynolds, author interviews.
29 Letter, Marilyn Haft to the Secretary of the Army. 24 May 1977. MCSF, [H-GRPH], JCPL.
30 Letter, Paul Phillips to the NGTF, 8 June 1977. MCSF, [H-GRPH], JCPL.

military that would lead to more (plausibly, since nothing substantially distinguished gay dishonourable discharges in the Vietnam era from those at other times). In June, three bills were introduced into Congress that, if passed, would have hobbled Carter's programme by decreeing that anyone who upgraded their discharge would not gain automatic eligibility for GI Bill or other federal benefits.[31] On 15 June, the House voted to deny Veterans Administration funds for benefits to deserters and any others who might have their dishonourable military discharges upgraded to honourable under the SDRP.[32] Carter announced that he intended to veto any bill with this effect and continued his SDRP as planned.[33] By 4 October, the end of the six-month period, Carter's programme had reviewed the cases of only about 10 per cent of the 433,000 eligible veterans,[34] and only 16,227 discharges had been upgraded, while another 8,600 cases were pending.[35] The exact number of gay veterans whose discharges were upgraded to honourable remains unknown.

Carter's veto threat forced conservative Congressmen to take a middle road. On 8 October, four days after the conclusion of the SDRP, Congress approved a bill that granted benefits to veterans with upgraded discharges only if a discharge review board affirmed the SDRP's decision, thereby creating a new but potentially surmountable hurdle for the upgraded veterans. Carter thought seriously about vetoing the new bill, but decided against on the grounds that he did not want his first presidential veto to be over an issue that had whipped up such intense controversy among reactionaries in Congress and the military.[36]

Due to the lack of clarity over the regulations of the SDRP and its limited duration, many veterans, including some who were gay, had not managed to apply. Carter was asked to extend the programme. Acknowledging these limitations, he asked the Army to set up military 'travelling panels', basically discharge review boards, to tour the country and hear petitions from veterans in person. The travelling panels were slated to hear such cases until 1 January 1980. They turned out to be very useful for veterans, who had to travel less far to state their case. Due to the high volume of applications, in January 1980 Carter extended the programme once again, taking it, including the travelling panels, to 1 April 1980. Although the exact number remains unknown, thousands of gay discharges were upgraded through the travelling panels.[37]

The significance of the upgrade of the previous gay discharges was not necessarily registered by the public at large as the issue did not receive widespread media coverage.

31 Warren Brown, 'Bills Would Deny Benefits for Upgraded Discharges', *WP*, 1 June 1977; 'Carter Authorizes Pentagon to Review 432,000 Discharges', *NYT*, 29 May 1977; Sharon Herbaugh, 'Christians Urged to Get Involved in Politics', *AP*, 22 August 1980; Mary Russell, 'Taking "Joy Rides" on the Floor', *WP*, 16 June 1977.

32 Mary Russell, 'Taking "Joy Rides" on the Floor', *WP*, 16 June 1977.

33 Eizenstat, author interview; Charles Mohr, 'Upgraded Veterans Face Aid Loss in Bill Signed by President', *NYT*, 9 October 1977.

34 MacPherson, *Long Time Passing*, 350.

35 'Pentagon Ends Drive on Discharge Review', *NYT*, 5 October 1977.

36 Eizenstat, author interview; Charles Mohr, 'Upgraded Veterans Face Aid Loss in Bill Signed by President', *NYT*, 9 October 1977.

37 Scott P. Anderson, 'Gay Vets Can Upgrade Discharges', *The Advocate*, 4 October 1978; Hallman, Kent, McReynolds and Sandifer, author interviews; Joseph P. Fried, 'Traveling Panel Hears Discharge Appeals by Veterans', *NYT*, 25 July 1979; 'More Time for Vets to Change Discharges', *The Advocate*, 21 February 1980.

Anti-war and civil rights activist Tom Hayden told the author that Carter 'deserves credit' for the review programme, which he described as 'a marker' in the evolution of gay rights.* Donald Hallman, who was dishonourably discharged from the Army in 1955 for being a 'Class II homosexual', was 'so scared of being an outcast that he burned all his military records, save for a single dog tag he hid away'.[38] He said to the author about Carter's efforts,

> The Army is very important in the minds of most Americans, and that soldiers and veterans might be gay was not something that was ever publicly discussed. Society did not believe, or did not want to believe, that there were gay soldiers in the Army. What Carter did was to render visible a body of Americans who hitherto were unseen and ignored, a very brave thing to do. Carter's ground-breaking initiatives on behalf of gays in the military were massively important, not only in according respect to such servicemen and women, but in changing the attitude of the wider public.*

Preventing future dishonour, and other interventions

The benefit of the SDRP, while considerable, was mainly felt by those directly affected by it. On its own, the programme did nothing to prevent the imposition of future dishonour by the same means, even though it sent a signal of the administration's intent – an intent that was shortly put into action. In 1978, a new DoD policy declared that gay people discharged from the military because of their homosexuality could not be automatically denied an honourable discharge if they had a clean service record. This meant that although gay people were still discharged from the military if found out, they were now able to receive an honourable discharge.[39] This was a major breakthrough and extremely important for gay soldiers as it took a huge weight off them. As a result, numerous gay soldiers voluntarily came out in order to quit the Army with an honourable discharge.[40] One example was that of Master Sgt. Bill Douglas, serving in the US Army at Fort Carson in Colorado Springs. He was given an honourable discharge and even the option to re-enlist in two years.[41]

In 1979 alone, 1,624 soldiers were discharged for gay conduct or gay tendencies. However, 539 of the discharges were for 'unsuitability', providing for automatic honourable status, while the other 1,085 were for 'misconduct' involving homosexuality; these could have led to a non-honourable status.[42] The following year there was an increase in the number of discharges; the biggest such rise since the McCarthy era.[43]

38 Dave Phillips, 'Ousted as Gay, Aging Veterans Are Battling Again for Honorable Discharges', *NYT*, 6 September 2015.
39 Bridget Overton, 'Short Currents: Change in Defense Department Policy', *LT*, November–December 1978.
40 Hallman, Kent, McReynolds and Sandifer, author interviews.
41 Scott P. Anderson, 'Sergeant in Full Drag Discharged', *The Advocate*, 18 October 1978.
42 Larry Bush, 'Federal Court Strikes at Homophobia in Army', *The Sentinel*, 30 May 1980; 'Homosexual wins Air Force Case', *NYT*, 14 September 1980.
43 Shilts, *Conduct Unbecoming*, 356.

This was attributable to the DoD's new policy regarding gay soldiers and their new ability to obtain an honourable discharge.[44]

Meanwhile, having noted inconsistencies in standards, documentation and procedures and in response to several challenges in the courts, notably *Matlovich v. Secretary of the Air Force* (in which the court objected that 'it is impossible to tell on what grounds the Service refused to make an exception or how it distinguished this case from the ones in which homosexuals have been retained'),[45] the DoD began a review of the rules and processes over discharges. The upshot was that a new edition of Directive 1332.14 was released on 16 January 1981. It sought to avoid the risk of legal action by making mandatory the discharge of anyone serving in the armed forces who was found to be gay, removing all discretion over the matter by explicitly stating that 'Homosexuality is incompatible with military service'.[46] Valeska described the now more explicit exclusion rule as 'a reactionary move on the part of the Department of Defense to counteract recent progress made through the courts in challenging discrimination against Gay men and Lesbians in the military'. However, as she also somewhat grudgingly noted, 'the new policy has some positive aspects: (1) all exclusions and discharges solely on the basis of sexual orientation will now be classified as HONORABLE, and (2) "homosexual identity" will no longer be determined by so-called homosexual mannerisms or through guilt by association'.[47] Thus, gay personnel, although still prohibited from serving, would now (barring aggravating circumstances) consistently be honourably discharged.

Elsewhere, Claytor not only continued upgrading gay discharges during his time as Secretary of the Navy (1977–79), but in March 1978, he issued a new regulation, 1900.9C, for the Navy which now permitted (though did not guarantee) the retention of gay personnel. The regulation stated that separation from the service for those who engaged in gay acts was customary rather than essential, and removed the definition of gay people as persons 'who cannot be tolerated in a military organization'. Thus, under Claytor's regulation, enlisted gay people could now have their cases reviewed by him before being discharged, a right that until then was afforded only to officers. Berg called the regulation 'a significant change and a substantial victory. It takes away the Pentagon's ability to hand out dishonourable discharges arbitrarily', but he also warned that the regulation fell short of removing all impediments to gay people's service in the Navy.[48] Indeed, gay people in the Navy could still be prosecuted because of their sexual preference; for example, eight lesbian women were prosecuted in 1980.[49] While serving as Deputy Defense Secretary (1979–1981), Claytor persuaded the Department to adopt the policy of honourable discharge across all the services.[50]

Through 1979 and 1980, the White House, mainly in the persons of Malson and Thomas, continued working with the gay rights activists to review the military's anti-

44 Hallman, Kent, McReynolds and Sandifer, author interviews.

45 591 F.2d 855 (D.C. Cir.1978).

46 Craig Howell, 'Total Military Ban on Gays Proposed', *The Blade*, 1 August 1979; Shilts, *Conduct Unbecoming*, 376–80.

47 Quoted in 'Defense Directive Targets Legal Forces of Gay Movement', *Gaze*, February 1981.

48 Jim Marko, 'Navy Changes Stance on Those Accused of 'Homosexual Acts', *GCN*, 18 March 1978.

49 Jeff Britton, 'U.S. Navy vs. The Lesbian Eight', *The Blade*, 7 August 1980.

50 Don Phillips, 'W. Graham Claytor Jr., 82, Ex-Amtrak President, Dies', *WP*, 15 May 1994.

gay policies, with a number of meetings taking place between them.[51] Furthermore, Kameny, who voluntarily counselled several gay soldiers who had been dismissed, contacted the White House and asked for its assistance with such cases. Malson and Thomas always responded to Kameny's requests.[52] One beneficiary of these efforts was Richard Melchionno, who had been dismissed by the DoD's Defense Mapping Agency. His attorney, Norman Elliot Kent, got in touch with Kameny, who in turn advised him to seek assistance from Thomas in the White House. Kent phoned Thomas and she immediately agreed to help.[53] On 6 December 1979, Kent sent to Thomas confidential information about Melchionno and asked for clarification on the laws on the subject and a copy of the Civil Service Regulations.[54] On 17 December, Thomas sent to Kent the section from Carter's Civil Service Reform Act which prohibited the dismissal of gay people from civil service jobs but cautioned that she was not sure whether the Defense Mapping Agency was among the 5 per cent that was exempt from these provisions. Thomas advised Kent to contact the Special Counsel's office of the OPM; she also got him in touch with other lawyers who could help his case, and invited him to write to her again if she could 'be of further assistance'.[55] Thomas remained in touch with Kent until the end of the case, whose outcome was 'favourable' for Melchionno.[56]

Another case was that of William Getz Jr, who in January 1980 was informed by his superiors at the Groton Naval Submarine Base that he was going to be dismissed by the Navy with a general discharge because of his 'homosexual attitude'. Thomas Kidd, Getz's lover, wrote to Brydon of the NGTF and asked for his help, arguing that the less-than-honourable discharge was inconsistent with the Navy's policy at the time, which awarded honourable discharges to gay people with a good service record such as Getz's.[57] At Brydon's request, Thomas contacted John Fugh, the legal advisor to the Assistant Secretary of Defense, about the case, and less than two weeks later Getz was honourably discharged.[58] Although it is not known to the author whether Thomas's intervention played a role in this upgrade, certainly she had responded promptly to the request for assistance.

Carter also attempted to satisfy one of the requests of feminist, predominantly lesbian activists: to advance equality between men and women by conscripting women into the Army. Jean O'Leary was among those who had pitched the idea to Carter.[59] For many years, women had joined up on a voluntary basis, making up as much as a tenth of the personnel in some parts of the Army. At the time, a large number of lesbian women were already working in the military or seeking to work there as the Army was seen by many of them as a very good employer.[60] Thus, Carter proposed a single draft for both men and

51 For example, see Letters, C. F. Brydon to Robert Malson, 20 December 1979, and C.F. Brydon to Allison Thomas, 12 August 1980, all in ATSF, B.265, GR, JCPL.
52 Kent and McReynolds, author interviews.
53 Kent, author interview.
54 Letter, Norman Elliot Kent to Allison Thomas, 6 December 1979. ATSF, B.265, GR, JCPL
55 Letter, Allison Thomas to Norman Elliot Kent, 17 December 1979. ATSF, B.265, GR, JCPL.
56 Kent and Melchionno, author interviews.
57 Letter, Thomas Kidd to Charles Brydon, 5 February 1980. ATSF, B.265, GR, JCPL
58 Letter, C.F. Brydon to Allison Thomas, 15 February 1980 and Memorandum, John Fugh for Mr. Gilliat, 2 April 1980, both in ATSF, B.265, GR, JCPL
59 Higgins and Weddington, author interviews.
60 Bunch and Higgins, author interviews.

women. Carter's decision divided the women's movement, with some criticizing it on the basis that it might confirm a longstanding contention of anti-feminists that the ERA would lead to the drafting of women. Peace activists in the women's movement opposed the draft completely. However, the vast majority of the lesbian community supported Carter's proposal; it was endorsed by several lesbian organizations and lesbian rights activists, as well as the leadership of NOW, much to the dismay of many of its members.[61]

On February 1980, Carter presented his proposal to Congress under the rubric of equal rights for women. He did not propose to open all roles in the armed forces to women, but only to open more of them, and he clarified that women would not be involved in close combat. Rather, he was proposing both a symbolic change and another step towards equality between men and women in all aspects of life, as he had promised.[62] Conservatives were deeply angered at Carter's attempt to conscript women. Schlafly denounced him in public, condemning him for giving in to women's rights activists, and even accused him of having 'stabbed the women of this country in the back'.[63] Eventually, in June 1980, both the House and the Senate turned down Carter's proposal and the draft remained open only to men. The ACLU, supported by feminist and lesbian organizations, immediately filed a lawsuit against the decision, claiming that a draft only for men was unconstitutional. However, the Supreme Court upheld the male-only draft.[64] Nevertheless, Carter and his administration initiated policies that expanded opportunities for women in the military by opening jobs that were previously reserved only for men, thus making available to women 94 per cent of all Army jobs and all but four combat-related jobs in the Air Force.[65] These efforts were hailed by the lesbian community and contributed to making the military an even more sought-after employer for many lesbians.[66]

Honouring the gay fallen

Since the early 1960s, until they gave up in the face of the Army's intransigence, Frank Kameny and gay war veterans had sought to lay a wreath in an official ceremony at the Tomb of the Unknown Soldier at Arlington Cemetery in order to honour gay soldiers who had died in combat. In July 1979, the Gay Activists Alliance (GAA) wrote to Army Secretary Alexander requesting that he publicly renounce this discriminatory position.

[61] Bunch, author interview; Linda J. Malin, 'N.O.W.: E.R.A. Missionaries', *OOB*, November 1981; Vickie Leonard, 'Draft – This Time There Are Feminists', *OOB*, March 1980; Sarah Weddington, Presidents of National Women's Organizations meeting with President Carter, 28 February 1980. BASF, B.58, ERA 1, JCPL

[62] President Carter's Statement on the Registration of Americans for the Draft, 8 February 1981. PPPUS: Jimmy Carter: 1980–81, [Book 1], 290–1.

[63] Carol Felsenthal, *Phyllis Schlafly: The Sweetheart of the Silent Majority* (Chicago: Regnery Gateway, 1981), 317–18.

[64] Felsenthal, *Schlafly*, 317; Mansbridge, *Why We Lost the ERA*, 73–5.

[65] The Record of President Jimmy Carter on Women's Issues, December 1979. BASF, B.58, ERA 1, JCPL.

[66] Bunch and Higgins, author interviews.

Alexander did not respond to the letter.[67] In October 1979, an effort to lay a wreath was made without prior approval from the Army. Bob Kunst's Congress United for Rights and Equality had requested the Pentagon to allow an official ceremony, a request that was initially accepted, but then turned down. Kunst and two other activists nevertheless arrived at the cemetery and attempted to proceed to the wreath-laying, only to be turned back by cemetery officials and forcibly removed from the cemetery.[68]

Learning of another fruitless appeal by the GAA to participate in an official wreath-laying ceremony at the Tomb, Kameny became so angry that he was willing to have himself 'arrested or shot by a sentry in order to lay the wreath'. On further reflection, he called Allison Thomas and asked her to intervene. Thomas called Alexander 'to make sure the [gay] group's rights were being upheld'. As a result, Alexander issued a direct order giving permission for gay veterans and activists, along with Reverend Larry J. Uhrig, a gay pastor of the MCC in Washington, D.C., to conduct an official wreath-laying. Alexander even assigned three currently serving high-ranking military officers to preside over the ceremony.[69] This permission caused outrage among conservatives and within the military, and Alexander came under huge pressure to rescind it, resulting in the ceremony being delayed. However, Malson and Thomas insisted, assuring Alexander that the administration supported the initiative, so he upheld his decision.[70]

Thus, on 28 May 1980, about five months before the presidential election and at a time when Carter was under increasing pressure from the religious right, for the first time in history gay veterans and activists were allowed to lay a wreath at the Tomb in an official ceremony. Several dozen gay veterans and activists took their place in the official ceremony alongside Uhrig, Lt. Col. Robert Faxon of the Office of the Secretary of the Army, and three high-ranking military officers. The Army had also provided another half dozen soldiers as a military honour guard, and 'to avoid trouble' from objectors who might seek to disrupt it.[71]

Indicative of the importance of the official ceremony for gay veterans and activists, as well as of how crucial the administration's intervention was, is the letter Charles Brydon wrote and sent to Thomas, which he wrote on the same day as the ceremony. Brydon's letter was very personal and quite different in tone from his previous correspondence with the Carter White House (Figure 5):

> We write and call often, bringing problems to the attention of you and other helpful White House staff, usually asking for something or being critical. This is not one of those letters.
>
> Rather, I want to thank you for the special effort you and Bob [Malson] made to make it possible for the Gay Activist [*sic*] Alliance of Washington to hold a wreath-

[67] 'Army Chief Alexander Rebuffs Gays', *The Blade*, 27 November 1979.

[68] Larry Bush, 'Federal Court Strikes at Homophobia in Army', *The Sentinel*, 30 May 1980; Nick Maklary, 'Honoring Unknown Gay Vets', *The Blade*, 25 October 1979.

[69] Robert Meyers, 'Gays Pay Honor to War Dead at Arlington Tomb', *WP*, 29 May 1980.

[70] Letter, C.F. Brydon to Allison Thomas, 28 May 1980. RMSF, G/L1, JCPL; Lou Chibbaro, Jr., 'A Solemn Commemoration', *The Washington Blade*, 21 November 1980; Malson, author interview.

[71] Larry Bush, 'Federal Court Strikes at Homophobia in Army', *The Sentinel*, 30 May 1980; Lou Chibbaro Jr., 'Carter Backs off Immigration Bill', *The Blade*, 12 June 1980; Robert Meyers, 'Gays Pay Honor to War Dead at Arlington Tomb', *WP*, 29 May 1980.

laying ceremony at the Tomb of the Unknown Soldier at Arlington Cemetery today.

Having served nearly 10 years in the military and seen first hand the personal pain and trauma the uniformed services can inflict on gay people whose primary interest is to serve their country, this event has a special meaning for me. I realize there was resistance to this particular ceremony and that you had to fight for the GAA request. But it is important for me to say how significant it is to me and to the many, many women and men who willingly served their country. To you, Bob,

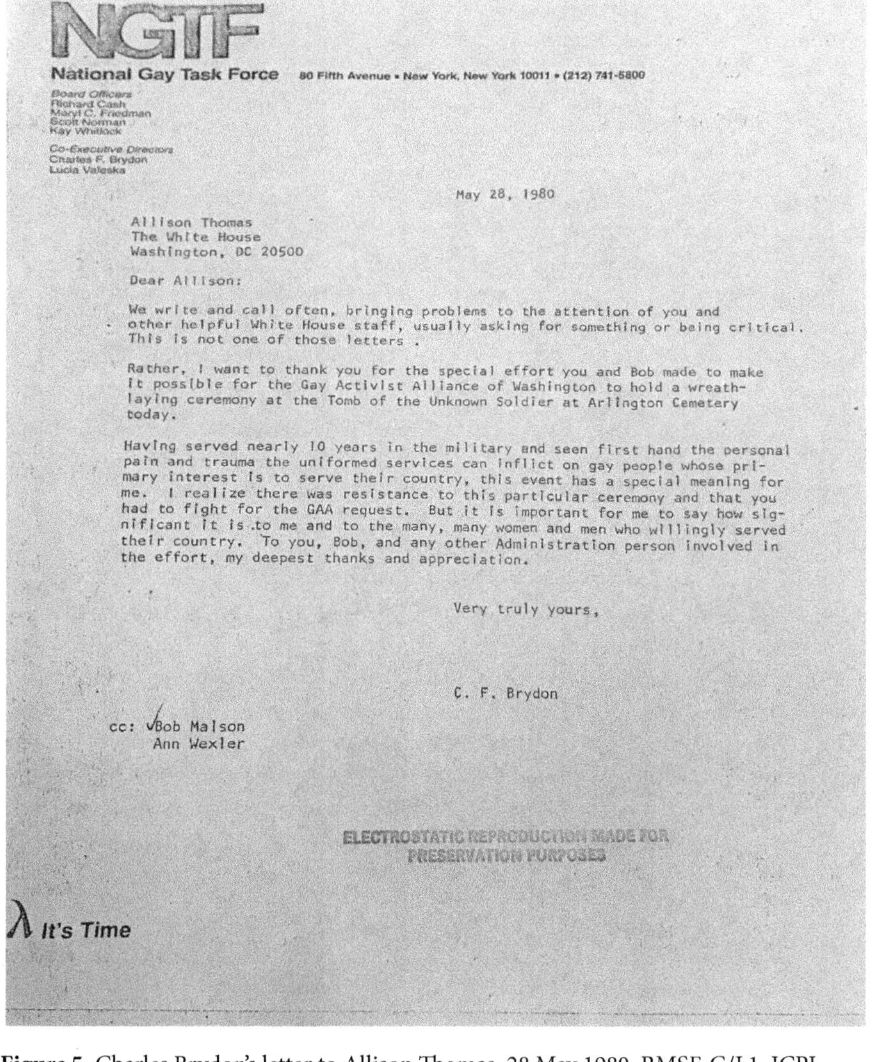

NGTF

National Gay Task Force 80 Fifth Avenue • New York, New York 10011 • (212) 741-5800

Board Officers
Richard Cash
Maryl C. Friedman
Scott Norman
Kay Whitlock

Co-Executive Directors
Charles F. Brydon
Lucia Valeska

May 28, 1980

Allison Thomas
The White House
Washington, DC 20500

Dear Allison:

We write and call often, bringing problems to the attention of you and other helpful White House staff, usually asking for something or being critical. This is not one of those letters .

Rather, I want to thank you for the special effort you and Bob made to make it possible for the Gay Activist Alliance of Washington to hold a wreath-laying ceremony at the Tomb of the Unknown Soldier at Arlington Cemetery today.

Having served nearly 10 years in the military and seen first hand the personal pain and trauma the uniformed services can inflict on gay people whose primary interest is to serve their country, this event has a special meaning for me. I realize there was resistance to this particular ceremony and that you had to fight for the GAA request. But it is important for me to say how significant it is to me and to the many, many women and men who willingly served their country. To you, Bob, and any other Administration person involved in the effort, my deepest thanks and appreciation.

Very truly yours,

C. F. Brydon

cc: ✓Bob Malson
Ann Wexler

λ It's Time

Figure 5 Charles Brydon's letter to Allison Thomas, 28 May 1980. RMSF, G/L1, JCPL.

> and any other Administration person involved in this effort, my deepest thanks and appreciation.[72]

The *Washington Post* reported on the ceremony, mentioning its unprecedented character but also noting that 'the White House intervened to get the activists permission for the ceremony after the Army turned down their request'.[73] This revelation led to an outcry against Carter's administration from religious conservative leaders and politicians, but mostly from within the Army itself. Some angry Army officials contacted North Carolina Senator Jesse Helms. Helms then released a statement condemning the administration's intervention. The spokesman of the Veterans of Foreign Wars described the ceremony as a violation of 'common decency', while William Dickinson, Alabama Congressman and ranking Republican member of the House Armed Services Committee, described it as a 'nauseating spectacle'.[74] Several Congressmen complained to the White House while some expressed their belief that the current Military Chief of Staff was 'too responsive' to White House directives.[75] Jerry Falwell used his huge direct mailing list to warn that

> we are losing the war against homosexuals . . . gays were recently given permission to lay a wreath on the Tomb of the Unknown Soldier at Arlington Cemetery to honor any sexual deviants who served in the military. That's right – the gays were allowed to turn our Tomb of the Unknown Soldier into THE TOMB OF THE UNKNOWN SODOMITE![76]

The day after the ceremony, Kameny wrote to Thomas to express 'our appreciation to you individually, and to our White House [a phrase he used twice more], for your efforts in helping us to bring to successful (if slightly flawed) completion our wreath-laying ceremony'. The 'flaw' he referred to was the ostentatious scrutiny that the three senior Army officers had given to the prayer before permitting it to be read; he called it 'as squalid a display of governmental bigotry and paranoia as I have ever seen'.[77]

Later that year, Kameny made a request to Paul Miller, director of Ceremonies and Special Events of the US Military District of Washington, to lay another wreath at a ceremony on 11 November, Veterans' Day, notifying Thomas of this request, but hoping that her intervention to facilitate it would not be necessary.[78] Permission was indeed granted, and hence for the first time a gay organization participated in an official ceremony at the Tomb of the Unknown Soldier on Veterans' Day.[79]

Aware of the GAA's first ceremony, the Gay Ex-Marines (GEMS), a recently founded gay veterans' organization, expressed its interest in performing its own

[72] Letter, C.F. Brydon to Allison Thomas, 28 May 1980. RMSF, G/L1, JCPL.
[73] Robert Meyers, 'Gays Pay Honor to War Dead at Arlington Tomb', *WP*, 29 May 1980.
[74] Shilts, *Conduct Unbecoming*, 334.
[75] Larry Bush, 'Federal Court Strikes at Homophobia in Army', *The Sentinel*, 30 May 1980; Lou Chibbaro Jr., 'Carter Backs off Immigration Bill', *The Blade*, 12 June 1980.
[76] Martin, *With God on Our Side*, 204–5.
[77] Letter, Franklin Kameny to Allison Thomas, 29 May 1980. ATSF, B.265, GR, JCPL.
[78] Letter, Franklin Kameny to Allison Thomas, 15 September 1980. ATSF, B.265, GR, JCPL.
[79] Lou Chibbaro, Jr., 'A Solemn Commemoration', *The Washington Blade*, 21 November 1980.

official ceremony at the Marine Corps War Memorial in Arlington. Due to the short notice, Kameny advised Nick Maklary, the president of GEMS, to get in touch with Thomas to avoid bureaucracy and to secure a quick authorization. Maklary did this, and following Thomas's intervention, the GEMS wreath-laying ceremony took place on 10 November.[80] Maklary's request came shortly before the 4 November presidential election, not only a busy but also a politically sensitive time. It seems logical to assume that Maklary and Kameny's requests were accepted by the services due to White House intervention, while Kunst's was rejected because there was no such intervention.

ꕤ

A theme of this chapter has been the personal significance that questions of honour and dishonour, and the Carter administration's attempt to rectify undeserved military classifications of these, had for many gay veterans, and for people who wished to honour those who did not survive to be veterans. These mitigations alone, given the prevailing lack of sympathy and the strong hostile responses that raising the issue could provoke, are to the administration's credit. While the military ban on homosexuality was in fact reinforced under Carter, with the aim of ending the arbitrariness that had previously entered into the process of administrative discharge, it was a substantial step, both symbolically and practically important, to rescind the classification of dishonour that that had accompanied it, both for gay veterans and for current servicepeople. The visceral responses it provoked have also been described; these reflect the emotional depth of the resonance of military service to many people, as well as the popular imagery of the American forces and their personnel. For many, the prospect of gay people serving in the forces, to which Carter's reforms seemed to point, evoked a particularly strong homophobic response and led to vilification of Carter.[81] This response extended to service personnel themselves, doubtless in part a reflection of values instilled in their training. According to Holman and Sandifer, Carter's efforts for gay soldiers made him at the time by far the most unpopular serving American president ever among Army personnel.[82]

Carter, in fact, told Eizenstat and Wexler, in mid-1980, that he would if re-elected force the military to review its policies towards gay people.[83] In the event, the battle for gay rights in the military continued for years after Carter's presidency, and even the most liberal presidents who succeeded him struggled to reconcile the competing responses it evoked. This struggle is epitomized by Bill Clinton's 'Don't Ask, Don't Tell' policy, which enabled gay soldiers to remain in the armed forces provided they did not reveal that they were gay; a policy which satisfied nobody and did little to further the cause of gay rights. Only in December 2010 was the debate finally resolved when the Don't Ask, Don't Tell Repeal Act was passed by Congress and signed by President Obama. It finally established that gay people could serve in the military on

80 Lou Chibbaro, Jr., `A Solemn Commemoration', *The Washington Blade*, 21 November 1980; McReynolds, author interview; 'The Unknown Soldiers', *GCN*, 13 December 1980.

81 'Carter Aide Assails Moral Majority', *AP*, 9 October 1980; McReynolds, author interview.

82 Hallman and Sandifer, author interviews.

83 Larry Bush, 'The Carter Administration. More Done Than Said?', *The Advocate*, 12 June 1980, citing Eizenstat and Wexler.

the same terms as heterosexuals.[84] The fact that it took more than thirty years after his presidency to end discrimination against gay people in the military puts Carter's actions in this area, as incomplete as they were, in a positive light. Denny Meyer, Public Affairs Officer for the American Veterans for Equal Rights, said of Carter's efforts that 'all of these early actions were extremely important in setting the stage for our rights, for awareness, for the fact that Gay Lives Matter'.* And Sandifer told the author,

> Symbolically, the difference was huge. A dishonourable discharge is a disgrace. It's no exaggeration to say that removing this penalty probably saved the lives of hundreds of gay veterans. We have moved on since then and Carter deserves much of the credit. Although it might be forgotten today, I think every gay solider at the time was very grateful to President Carter for his efforts.*

[84] Greg Sargent, 'It's Official: "Don't Ask Don't Tell" Is History', *WP*, 19 September 2011.

10

'The power of the White House'

Miscellaneous mitigations

This chapter collects a variety of further Carter administration interventions whose discussion does not require an entire chapter, or in some cases an entire page, but which each illustrate further steps to extend protections to or to remove disadvantages from the gay community, in terms of concrete conditions and equally of symbolism and legitimation. The effort to end discriminatory treatment of gay inmates of federal prisons is another case of 'two strategies', as found in the discussion of the immigration issue in Chapter 8; the unsuccessful strategy in this case was not legislation but litigation. The successful strategy is again the use of the president's authority in relatively informal ways to break through resistance elsewhere in government. This 'power to persuade', in Richard Neustadt's famous phrase,[1] is in practice almost always exercised by White House staff, people such as Midge Costanza. Further miscellaneous examples of White House interventions are discussed in no particular order, except that the final one illustrates not just the breadth but also the occasional absurdity of anti-gay prejudice in federal government bureaus prior to the Carter administration.

Correcting corrections: Litigation and intervention

At the start of the Carter presidency, gay prisoners faced numerous forms of discrimination in the federal prison system. They were often segregated from other prisoners, in what amounted to solitary confinement, ostensibly for their own protection. Assaults against them, up to and including rape, were often reported as 'homosexual rape' – giving the impression that the assailant, rather than the victim, was gay when assailants were in fact identified primarily as heterosexuals. There was also discrimination against gay people in decisions about parole and furloughs.[2] Matters for lesbian detainees were no better. They faced similar dangers from other prisoners,

1 Richard E. Neustadt, *Presidential Power and the Modern Presidents: The Politics of Leadership from Roosevelt to Reagan* (New York: Free Press, 1991).

2 Memorandum, Marilyn Haft to Margaret Costanza, 25 March 1977. SWSF, [Gay] CR, JCPL; 'Prison Rapes No Longer Labeled "Homosexual Rape"', News from NGTF, 19 April 1978. NGTFR, B.36, F.74, CU.

although to a lesser extent.[3] Less dramatic infringements of rights included the fact that while heterosexual prisoners were allowed to access a wide range of publications, including magazines like *Playboy* or *Hustler*, gay prisoners were routinely denied the right to read gay magazines of any kind, including political publications with no sexual content such as the NGTF's *It's Time*, the Metropolitan Community Church's *Cellmate* and *The Advocate*. Prison authorities believed that such publications would expose the prisoners' homosexuality, making them liable to assault by others.[4] This was a major issue for the NGTF, which characterized its effort as a 'long-standing battle to get gay literature into federal prisons'.[5] Another matter of concern was that gay prisoners were denied access to ministers from the MCC, while other prisoners had access to spiritual counsel and support. Again, prison authorities claimed that visits from the MCC 'would tend to identify and open to attack the homosexual prisoner'.[6]

Before Carter became president, the NGTF and the MCC had contacted Norman Carlson, director of the Federal Bureau of Prisons (BOP), on several occasions, but he had been, as Arthur and Clay put it to the author, 'uncooperative', refusing multiple requests to meet, and hardly ever responding to correspondence.* A response was however forthcoming after the NGTF asked Congressman Edward Koch to intervene about the issue of publications.[7] Carlson responded on 10 December 1976 that he and the BOP's Executive Staff had 'unanimously agreed that such publications should not be permitted in Federal institutions', and continued,

> We agree with the philosophy of limiting an offender's access to literature or publications only in cases where there is a clearly overriding institutional interest. In this case, we believe that such is the case, as publications advocating or supporting homosexuality exacerbate a major problem. Publications which call attention [to] or identify inmates who accept homosexuality can, in our opinion, be detrimental to their safety as well as to the safety of others. For that reason, we have concluded that such publications should be prohibited.[8]

The NGTF, in cooperation with Lambda Legal, then began exploring the possibility of taking Carlson and the BOP to court.[9] They judged, however, that Carlson was the main barrier, and for a while invested their hopes in the prospect of his replacement by Carter when he entered office.[10]

The issue of gay prisoners was brought to the White House's attention at an early stage by E. Carrington Boggan, an attorney and one of the founders of Lambda Legal.

3 Bunch, author interview; Janis Kelly, 'Congress Looks at Women Prisoners', *OOB*, November 1979.

4 Letter, Norman Carlson to Bob Arthur, 23 December 1976. SWSF, NGTF: PCC3, JCPL; 'Prisoner Fights Homosexual Magazine Ban', *WP*, 14 May 1977.

5 'Bureau of Prisons', *It's Time*, May–June 1980. RMSF, G/L1, JCPL.

6 Robert Arthur, 'Gays in Prison. Position Paper', 9 February 1977. MCSF, Gays-Prisons Background Information, JCPL.

7 Letter, Edward Koch to Norman Carlson, 27 September 1976. RMSF, GV, JCPL.

8 Letter, Norman Carlson to Edward Koch, 10 December 1976. SWSF, NGTF: PCC3, JCPL.

9 'Bureau of Prisons Bans Gay Publications', News from NGTF, 14 December 1976. NGTFR, B.36, F.9, CU.

10 Clay, author interview.

He was a close friend and former colleague of Haft; two years earlier they had (with two others) co-authored the ACLU handbook *The Rights of Gay People*. On 1 February 1977, following up on Carlson's reply to the NGTF, Boggan wrote to the BOP asking for an official document stating its policies regarding access to 'sexual orientated publications'.[11] Failing to receive a reply,[12] he contacted Haft, who began to investigate. She came to believe, and to fear, that the BOP 'do not like any interference and they may take it out on the gay prisoners'.[13] She therefore advised Costanza to bypass the Bureau and arrange a meeting between the NGTF and the Department of Justice (DoJ), the BOP's parent department, without the presence of Carlson or any other Bureau officials.[14]

On 9 March, Boggan wrote again to Carlson.[15] On 16 March, perhaps also prompted by inquiries from the White House on the same matter, Carlson sent a letter to all prison wardens, directors and superintendents, claiming that his letter to Koch, apparently outlining a policy applicable across the federal prison system, had been 'misinterpreted'. He explained that 'our policy statement provides that wardens make the final determination regarding publications based on the content of the issue' and that the Executive Staff decision reported in the Koch letter 'merely supported a particular decision made by several wardens on a given publication'.[16] At the same time, Carlson sent to Boggan the documents he had requested,[17] each containing the following policy:

> The head of each institution is responsible for making decisions regarding incoming publications, and applying guidelines of the Policy Statement . . . Caution will be exercised before declaring a publication unacceptable because of its religion, philosophical, social or sexual views. . . . The decision not to forward a publication to an inmate under this Policy Statement must be based on a showing that doing so will clearly compromise the security, discipline and good order of the institution.[18]

Issues involving gay prisoners were on the agenda of the March 1977 Meeting. There, Costanza informed them that Carter was not planning to replace Carlson but that she would intervene and help them with their case. Costanza expressed her belief that lawsuits against Carlson would be 'counter-productive' and that a solution could be found with the BOP through the White House's intervention. The activists nevertheless agreed with Haft's suggestion of a meeting between the NGTF and the DoJ, without the BOP's presence.[19] It took place on 28 April. This marked the first time that gay rights

11 Letter, E. Carrington Boggan to BOP Director, 1 February 1977. RMSF, GV, JCPL.
12 Letter, E. Carrington Boggan to BOP Director, 9 March 1977. RMSF, GV, JCPL.
13 Memorandum, Marilyn Haft to Margaret Costanza, 25 March 1977. SWSF, [Gay] CR, JCPL.
14 Haft, author interview.
15 Letter, E. Carrington Boggan to BOP Director, 9 March 1977. RMSF, GV, JCPL.
16 Letter, Norman Carlson to wardens, directors and superintendents, 18 March 1977. SWSF, NGTF: PCC1, JCPL.
17 Letter, Norman Carlson to E. Carrington Boggan, 16 March 1977. RMSF, GV, JCPL.
18 Federal Prison System Policy Statements regarding Incoming Publications, 2 September 1975, and 4 May 1976, both in RMSF, GV, JCPL.
19 Haft and Perry, author interviews.

activists were able to present the issue of discrimination against gay prisoners to the relevant authorities.[20]

O'Leary and the other activists were, however, not convinced by the suggestion that they drop their litigation strategy. On 18 July 1977, the NGTF, along with Calvin Keach, a gay prisoner in El Reno, Oklahoma, and the publishers of *Gay Community News*, *Off Our Backs* and *Join Hands*, filed a lawsuit against Carlson and the BOP.[21] Involvement in the lawsuit brought problems for Keach; prison authorities told him to withdraw the suit or he would be segregated or sent to another facility.[22] The same month, the MCC also filed a lawsuit against Carlson (Keach was a plaintiff in this case as well) over both the BOP's denial of access to MCC publications and its refusal to allow the Church to minister to federal prisoners.[23]

The NGTF case was that the exclusion of gay publications was, contrary to the BOP's regulations, 'not based on any showing of detriment to the security, discipline, or good order of the institutions involved, but, rather, [was] based solely on the political, social, and sexual views of the said publications'. The policy was, hence, 'arbitrary and capricious' and violated various constitutional rights as well as the law of administrative procedure.[24] Carlson and the BOP's brief in response reiterated the earlier 'clarification' of policy, whereby prison wardens were responsible for decisions to exclude 'homosexually oriented publications', so that no 'total exclusion' was in effect and instead decisions were 'based upon [wardens'] determinations that said publications were detrimental to the good order of the institutions involved'.[25] The MCC's case was instead based primarily on religious freedom and religious establishment grounds. It had the advantage of its argument having been previously successful in a suit by the MCC against the California prison system.[26]

The NGTF, continuing to pursue a dual strategy of litigation and working through the Carter administration, again requested help from Costanza, who asked Wishman to look at the legal aspects of the NGTF case. He concluded that the case was weak and would probably fail. Costanza then suggested setting up a meeting between the activists, herself and Carlson.[27] Aware that Carlson had up to then rejected repeated requests from activists to meet with them, Costanza personally phoned him to request such a meeting. Carlson immediately accepted, and Costanza scheduled the meeting to take place on 16 March 1978, at the DoJ.[28] The build-up to this meeting was, however, somewhat fraught, mainly because of interference between the two strategies that were then running in tandem. Lower officials in the BOP were concerned about the legal complexities of meeting with parties pursuing legal action against them, a concern shared by Robert Keuch, Deputy Assistant Attorney General at the DoJ, who

20 Marilyn Haft: Status report on NGTF meetings with Agencies, 28 April 1977. SWSF, [Gay] CR, JCPL.
21 *NGTF et al. v. Carlson*, Complaint, undated. SWSF, NGTF: PCC1, JCPL.
22 Memorandum, Marilyn Haft to Doug Huron. 6 June 1977. MCSF, [GR: MECOCL], JCPL.
23 *Metropolitan Community Church v. Carlson, Benson and Bell*, 14 July 1977. RMSF, GV, JCPL.
24 *NGTF et al. v. Carlson*, Complaint, undated. SWSF, NGTF: PCC1, JCPL.
25 *NGTF et al. v. Carlson*. Answer to Complaint, 18 July 1977. SWSF, NGTF: PCC1, JCPL.
26 Arthur and Perry, author interviews.
27 Arthur, Clay and Haft, author interviews.
28 Haft, author interview.

recommended to the Bureau and to Deputy Attorney General Patricia Wald, who was going to attend the meeting at Costanza's request, that the meeting be postponed, or otherwise, that someone from the Department's Special Litigation Section attend to help avoid problems.[29] Carlson and the BOP themselves had second thoughts on the same account. Wald then intervened and convinced Carlson and the BOP to attend, assuring them that the issue of gay publications would be excluded from the discussion at the meeting.[30] In one more twist, shortly before the meeting Carlson found out that Haft would replace Costanza there, and withdrew. Costanza then announced she would be there, whereupon Carlson also reversed himself. Recalling the episode in 1980, Costanza said 'He would not have been in that room if I had not personally said that I was going to be there. . . . You understand that in almost every single instance, as long as I was there, the head of that department was there. That's the power of the White House'.[31]

On 16 March, shortly before the meeting, some of the activists who were going to attend it, including Jean O'Leary of the NGTF and Bob Arthur from the MCC, met with Costanza, Haft and Wishman at Wishman's office in the White House to discuss their tactics and (a regular practice of Costanza's) to help them prepare their answers. Costanza also advised requesting that the BOP appoint someone to serve as its direct liaison with the activists. In further preparation, Haft and Wishman had gathered a large number of legal and academic documents that supported the activists' demands.[32] The meeting was notable for the fact that the activists were greeted and welcomed upon arrival at the White House by Carter himself, who expressed his support for their agenda. This left a strong impression on the visitors. Arthur commented, 'He knew why we were there. He knew what our agenda was. And he welcomed us . . . it was just a very brief meeting. I mean, he welcomed us and made it known to us that he was in support of what we were there for'.*

Costanza conducted the meeting with Carlson. She began by endorsing the activists' concerns, repeatedly emphasizing that Carter supported them.[33] The activists then presented their concerns in detail, requesting that the BOP

- cease using terms such as 'homosexual rape' and 'homosexual assault' to describe prison sexual assaults
- include members of the gay community among those conducting sensitivity-training sessions for prison staff at upcoming seminars in Atlanta, Dallas and Denver, so that the concerns of gay prisoners could be adequately represented
- provide the NGTF with copies of all the Bureau's guidelines and statistics regarding gay prisoners

29 Memorandum, Robert Keuch to Patricia Wald, 6 March 1978. SWSF, NGTF: PCC2, JCPL.

30 Memorandums, Marilyn Haft to Midge Costanza, 15 March 1978, and Patricia Wald to George Calhoun, 10 March 1978, both in SWSF, NGTF: PCC2, JCPL.

31 Mattingly and Boyd, 'Bringing Gay and Lesbian Activism to the White House', 369.

32 Arthur, Haft and Perry, author interviews; Memorandum, Marilyn Haft to Midge Costanza, 15 March 1978. SWSF, NGTF: PCC2, JCPL.

33 Ibid.

- appoint, as Costanza had suggested, an official to liaise between the Bureau and the NGTF in order to 'deal directly with complaints about prison practices from lesbian and gay inmates'.[34]

Costanza then repeated her, and more importantly Carter's, support for these requests. Carlson remained quiet throughout. The activists found Costanza's contribution to be very forceful; Arthur commented that they had the impression that she would not let Carlson leave the room unless he agreed to all of their demands.*

Carlson turned out to be much more willing to work with the activists than they had expected, taking everyone by pleasant surprise. He emphasized that the BOP and the NGTF had a 'mutual goal, to eliminate violence in prisons'. He expressed agreement with the activists' concerns, promised to take action in response, and even went beyond what had been requested by suggesting that sensitivity training involving representatives of the gay community might be extended to all federal prisons. O'Leary commented about the meeting, 'we account it among the most productive sessions we've had with Federal agencies to date'.[35] Shortly afterwards Carlson implemented the suggestion of appointing a liaison officer and issued a policy statement to prison staff prohibiting the use of language that attributed sexual assaults in prisons to homosexuality.[36] This apparent shift of position was later attributed by activists present to Costanza's moving and convincing speech.[37] Arthur said that Costanza was 'really instrumental' in convincing Carlson to accept their demands and that obviously she had 'the authority to insist'.* In its press releases at the time, however, the NGTF, while briefly referring to the presence of Costanza, Haft and Wishman, did not mention Costanza's contribution or the fact that the White House had facilitated the meeting,[38] though in private O'Leary and Voeller sent a letter thanking Wishman for his 'participation and contributions'.[39] For his part, on 10 April Carlson wrote to the NGTF thanking them for meeting and stated that he 'looked forward to a cooperative working relationship'.[40]

As its contribution to this improved relationship, the NGTF launched the Prison Project, headed by Carolyn Handy, which aimed at monitoring and improving the conditions of gay prisoners.[41] One of the most important benefits that resulted from the activists' meeting and their new relationship with Carlson was the 'sensitivity

[34] 'NGTF Holds Meeting with Bureau of Prisons', News from NGTF, 22 March 1978. SWSF, NGTF: PCC3, JCPL; 'Prison Rapes No Longer Labeled "Homosexual Rape"', News from NGTF, 19 April 1978, NGTFR, B.36, F.74, CU (author's bullets).

[35] 'NGTF Holds Meeting with Bureau of Prisons', News from NGTF, 22 March 1978. SWSF, NGTF: PCC3, JCPL.

[36] 'Prison Rapes No Longer Labeled "Homosexual Rape"', News from NGTF, 19 April 1978. NGTFR, B.36, F.74, CU.

[37] Arthur and Perry, author interviews.

[38] 'NGTF Holds Meeting with Bureau of Prisons', News from NGTF, 22 March 1978. SWSF, NGTF: PCC3, JCPL.

[39] Letter, Jean O'Leary and Bruce Voeller to Seymour Wishman, 22 March 1978. SWSF, NGTF: PCC3, JCPL.

[40] Letter, Norman Carlson to Jean O'Leary and Bruce Voeller, 10 April 1978. NGTFR, B.145, F.36, CU.

[41] 'NGTF Holds Meeting with Bureau of Prisons', News from NGTF, 22 March 1978. SWSF, NGTF: PCC3, JCPL.

training' seminars for prison staff that were carried out in most, if not all, federal prisons, as Carlson had proposed. With Wald's intervention, the DoJ even provided gay rights activists with funding to carry out the seminars. The seminars were carried out by gay people and were organized by the NGTF and the MCC in cooperation with local gay organizations. Their aim was to make prison staff aware of the issues and concerns faced by gay inmates and to help them better understand homosexuality and overcome stereotypical beliefs.[42] Clay, who participated in some of these seminars in Atlanta, explained that for many guards, in common with many Americans at the time, homosexuality was 'a disease, something abnormal'; gay prisoners were seen as perverts and often treated appallingly by some of the prison staff. The programme helped them to understand that gay prisoners were ordinary people, just like them, and deserved some respect. Clay said that gay prisoners were asking not for preferential treatment but for 'for equal rights, for respect, to be treated like the other prisoners and not be harassed and ridiculed. . . . I think that this program played an important role in changing the minds and attitudes of many warders'.*

Although the relationship between Carlson and the activists had changed for the better and they were now in continuous dialogue, the issues of access to gay-oriented publications and to MCC ministers remained in contention. Several senior BOP officials were unhappy with the Bureau's concessions to gay prisoners, the more so since, despite them, the NGTF and the MCC had not yet dropped their lawsuits, desiring assurances that the BOP would allow gay publications before dropping them. On the other hand, the BOP, aware that its defence in the lawsuit was a strong one, refused to discuss the issue unless the lawsuits were dropped.[43] Hence the remaining part of the litigation strategy continued to impede progress.

While the lawsuits were awaiting resolution, Costanza and Wishman left the White House, and the administration's involvement with the issue was brought to a temporary halt. Not confident of victory, the NGTF began exploring an out-of-court resolution. In December 1979 it asked again for the administration's intervention, raising the issue with Wexler, who agreed to help.[44] Brydon of the NGTF told the press, 'They are going to be moving very quickly on the issue'.[45] Subsequently, the *Washington Post* revealed that the activists' demands 'had been brought to Carter's attention' and that his 'administration will intervene with the Federal Bureau of Prisons to lift a ban against a homosexual church holding services in the institutions'.[46] Wexler directly asked the BOP to review its policies regarding gay publications, emphasizing Carter's support for a reversal of the policy. In January 1980, the BOP's Executive Staff reviewed the issue once again and agreed that from then on all prisons, including the maximum security ones, would allow access to gay non-pornographic publications, while it also agreed to allow the ministers' visits on a trial basis at low and medium security prisons

42 Clay and Perry, author interviews.

43 Haft, Perry and Weddington, author interviews.

44 Bush, author interview; Letter, Robert Strauss to Charles Brydon and Lucia Valeska, 3 March 1980. RMSF, GH1, JCPL.

45 'White House Mulls Federal Ban on Bias toward Homosexuals', *WP*, 21 December 1979.

46 Ibid.

for a year, extending them to maximum security facilities if no problems arose.[47] No problems did arise, and a year later the policy was duly extended.[48] The NGTF and the MCC were delighted with the development and dropped the lawsuits.[49] That it was the White House that had cut this Gordian knot was not mentioned in any of the NGTF's statements or press releases.

While lack of access to gay publications had not been the severest of privations suffered by gay inmates, it, along with religious ministry from the MCC, was the first to be taken up by gay rights activists in a strategy of litigation. The strategy was however unproductive, and Costanza might have been right to argue that it was indeed *counter-*productive. But whatever adverse effect the MCC and the NGTF's dogged pursuit of this strategy had, it was easily outweighed by the dramatic beneficial effect of White House intervention, spearheaded by Costanza and Wexler with Carter's full support.

Commemorating gay victims of the Holocaust

Until the late 1970s, the Nazi persecution of gay people remained largely unexplored and publicly unacknowledged in the United States and generally around the world. In order to increase the public understanding of the Holocaust, Carter in November 1978 created the President's Commission on the Holocaust which aimed to recommend an appropriate way to publicly remember the victims. The Commission consisted of thirty-four members, including Holocaust survivors, historians, scholars, Congressmen and Jewish and Christian religious leaders.[50] The appointments were characterized by Eizenstat as 'a very contentious issue. We felt it should be broad-based, Jews and non-Jews, other groups killed during the Holocaust. This was necessary to get a broad base of American support and get it through Congress'.[51] Among the Commission's members appointed by Carter was Bayard Rustin, another appointment of a high-profile openly gay person to a presidential commission.[52] Eizenstat told the author that his reference to 'other groups killed during the Holocaust' included gay people and that this was one of the reasons that Rustin was appointed.*

In September 1979, the Commission submitted its report to Carter, which recommended the creation of a Holocaust memorial in Washington, D.C. and contained a list of categories of people who had been persecuted by the Nazis. Despite Rustin's presence on the Commission, and to the disappointment of the gay community, gay people were not listed as a persecuted group. Congress approved the recommendation for the memorial and established the US Holocaust Memorial Council in order to implement the Commission's other recommendations and oversee the creation of the

47 Letter, Norman Carlson to Robert Kastenmeier, 1 February 1980. RMSF, GTFN1, JCPL; Weddington, author interview.
48 Arthur, author interview.
49 'Bureau of Prisons', *It's Time,* May–June 1980. RMSF, G/L1, JCPL; Perry, author interview.
50 Jimmy Carter, United States Holocaust Memorial Council Appointment of the Membership. The American Presidency Project, https://www.presidency.ucsb.edu/node/249927.
51 Phil McCombs, 'The Politics of Creating the Holocaust Memorial', *WP*, 13 April 1983.
52 D'Emilio, *Lost Prophet*, 491.

memorial. Carter was tasked to appoint the members of the Council and chose Harvard Law Professor Monroe H. Freedman as its executive director. Freedman was a former chair of the National Capital Area of the ACLU and a strong supporter of gay rights, having voluntarily served as General Counsel of the Mattachine Society; he was also a very good friend of Kameny.[53] Freedman's appointment pleased the gay community.[54] Kameny characterized Freedman after his appointment as 'an outstanding advocate of civil liberties in general, and gay rights in particular'.[55]

Gay rights activists mobilized to ensure that gay victims would not be neglected. On 15 January 1980, Craig Howell wrote to Carter asking him to 'to appoint at least one openly gay man or woman' to the Council 'to focus public attention on one of the most serious gaps in public understanding of the Holocaust: the fact that the Nazis carried out an intensive campaign to exterminate homosexuals'.[56] On 31 January, Melvin Boozer, president of the GAA, and Clint Hockenberry, American liaison to the International Gay Association, also wrote to Carter asking him for 'a commitment to help end the long silence about the gay victims' of the Holocaust and to appoint an openly gay person to the Council.[57] Prompted by the GAA's letter to Carter, Freedman wrote to the organization on 1 February and asked them for information and evidence regarding the Nazi persecution of gay people. On 14 March, Freedman wrote again to the GAA and assured them 'that the memorial will appropriately honour the memory of all those who were the victims of Nazi oppression' and once again requested 'documented materials' 'relating to the homosexual experience during the Holocaust'.[58]

Meanwhile, the White House organized an official ceremony in Washington, D.C. on 15 April and proclaimed 13–19 April as Days of Remembrance of Victims of the Holocaust. Gay rights activists were very keen to be represented in the ceremony as it would provide them with a unique opportunity to publicize the Nazi persecution of gay people. The GAA asked the White House to allow Boozer, as a representative of the gay community, to speak on this subject at the event. The White House agreed. Boozer's presence at the ceremony and his speech were of major importance for the gay community. It marked the first time that the persecution of gay people by the Nazis had been publicly mentioned and acknowledged by the US government.[59]

In May 1980, Carter announced the members of the Holocaust Memorial Council; Rustin was among them, thus fulfilling the activists' request for an openly gay person to be on it. Rustin played an active role in the Commission, and in the summer of 1980 he travelled along with other members to Europe to visit Holocaust memorials and Nazi death camps to gather precedents and impressions for the proposed memorial

53 Craig Howell, 'Behind the Exhibits: The Campaign to Memorialize Gay Victims of Nazi Persecution', Paper Presented to The Rainbow History Project, 3 November 2003; 'Holocaust Staff Calls for Input', *The Blade*, 6 March 1980'; Phil McCombs, 'The Politics of Creating the Holocaust Memorial', *WP*, 13 April 1983.

54 Howell, author interview.

55 'Holocaust Staff Calls for Input', *The Blade*, 6 March 1980.

56 Howell, 'Behind the Exhibits'.

57 'Gays Want Inclusion on Holocaust Panel', *The Advocate*, 1 May 1980.

58 Howell, 'Behind the Exhibits'.

59 Steve Martz, 'Holocaust Ceremony Notes Gay Victims', *The Blade*, 17 April 1980; Howell, author interview.

in Washington.[60] Meanwhile, in response to Freedman's request, the GAA assembled documentary evidence, and in May 1981, it submitted to the Council a study by Professor Ruediger Lautmann of the Nazi persecution of gay people. In April 1983, Elie Wiesel, the chair of the Council, announced that all victims of Nazi persecution, including gay people, would be included in the Memorial. Since then, every official US commemoration of the Holocaust has included the history of the Nazi persecution of gay people, during which thousands were beaten or imprisoned and a great many were killed.[61]

Same-sex couples' adoptions and gay youth peer counselling

A major issue for gay organizations throughout the 1970s was runaway gay youths; gay children who had left their homes because their parents or the wider milieu they lived in did not accept their sexuality. Most gay runaways were aged between 12 and 18; many had been disowned by their families, and many had been forced to abandon their homes by fear that they would be, if 'found out'. Many had turned to prostitution in order to survive.[62] Shortly after it was formed, the NGTF in conjunction with child welfare agencies in various cities, for example New York, developed a national network of gay foster homes to provide placements for gay teens who had left home and were not doing well in existing group accommodation. The law on fostering was uncertain: in the state of Washington in 1974, a judge had allowed a gay teenager to be placed with gay foster parents, but a year later, another Washington judge denied such a placement. Government and judges were also not ready to allow adoption by same-sex couples. Thus, there are no official records of any adoption by an openly gay or lesbian parent during this period, although of course gay men and lesbians who were not open about their sexuality were still able to adopt.[63] Gay rights activists, aware of the political climate of the time, had not even raised the issue with Carter's administration, believing that nothing would come of it.[64]

In November 1979, while his administration was preparing for the White House Conference on Families (see chapter 12), Carter created the Office for Families. It was placed within the Department of Health and Human Services and its aims were to ensure a follow-up on Conference recommendations and to support family needs through government policy.[65] Shortly after its creation, the Office published a new model adoption code which placed no restrictions on same-sex couples' adoptions, but instead suggested that 'non-traditional' family environments should be considered

60 Phil McCombs, 'The Politics of Creating the Holocaust Memorial', *WP*, 13 April 1983.; Naegle, author interview,

61 Craig Howell, 'What We Owe Elie Wiesel', *The Washington Blade*, 14 July 2016.

62 Bush and DeBaugh, author interviews; 'Young Gay Runaways', *The Blade*, 7 February 1980.

63 Nancy D. Polikoff, 'Lesbian and Gay Couples Raising Children: The Law in the United States', in Robert Wintemute and Mads Andenaes (eds), *Legal Recognition of Same-Sex Partnerships: A Study of National, European and International Law* (Oxford and Portland, OR: Hart Publishing, 2001), 157.

64 Bush and Clay, author interviews.

65 WHCF, *Listening to America's Families, Action for the 80's* (Washington, DC: The White House Conference on Families, 1980), 5.

equally and on their particular merits. The Office expressed its hope that this new model adoption code would be accepted by state authorities. This was a highly important, and completely unexpected, development for the gay community as the government recognized that a family could also consist of same-sex couples and for the first time declared that there should be no discrimination against such families in adoptions; thus, same-sex couples should be allowed to adopt children.[66] However, this adoption code remained largely unknown among members of the gay community until Bush wrote about it in *The Sentinel* in May 1980.[67] Although the Office for Families' model adoption code was not well received by most state authorities, it was nevertheless a first step by the government in recognizing the right of same-sex couples to adoption.

Furthermore, aware of the issue of gay runaways, Carter's administration directed the Office for Families' office in Atlanta, Georgia, to begin a pilot programme which would make use of group peer counselling when dealing with gay youth runaways.[68] For this reason, the Atlanta office began recruiting openly gay qualified experts from the Atlanta Gay Center and Louie Clay's Integrity to provide counselling for gay runaway youths, but also to find them permanent accommodation.[69] The success of the programme in Georgia led to its implementation all over the country and prompted the Office to urge state officials to adopt it. The programme was very important for the gay community and helped numerous gay runaway youths, saving many of them from exploitation, prostitution, abuse and even suicide.[70] Finally, the programme signalled one more collaboration between the government and gay organizations, another sign of the growing acceptance of gay people by the government and authorities.

Fair housing

One of the requests made by gay rights activists during the March 1977 Meeting was that the Department of Housing and Urban Development (HUD) should amend its regulations to require all federal housing grants to include a policy forbidding discrimination against gay people and that it should provide equal access to housing opportunities for gay citizens.[71] Until 1976, only low-income, heterosexual couples who were either married or had met state tests for a common-law relationship had been allowed to obtain public housing.[72] In December 1976, HUD began a consultation on a new Housing Authorization Act, which would open up public housing to single persons, who up until then had been excluded. Priscilla Banks, HUD's housing programme specialist and author of the proposed regulations, included a provision

66 Larry Bush, 'White House Claims Solid Record on Gay Issues', *The Sentinel*, 16 May 1980; Robert Malson memorandum on gay issues, 20 May 1980. DTSF, GI, JCPL.

67 Larry Bush, 'White House Claims Solid Record on Gay Issues', *The Sentinel*, 16 May 1980.

68 Larry Bush, 'White House Claims Solid Record on Gay Issues', *The Sentinel*, 16 May 1980; WH memorandum: Talking points on gay issues, 5 August 1980. RMSF, G/L2, JCPL.

69 Clay, author interviews.

70 Larry Bush, 'White House Claims Solid Record on Gay Issues', *The Sentinel*, 16 May 1980; Bush and Clay, author interviews; WH memorandum: Talking points on gay issues, 5 August 1980. RMSF, G/L2, JCPL.

71 Memorandum, Margaret Costanza to President Carter, 8 April 1977. SWSF, [Gay] CR, JCPL.

72 'H.U.D. Will Accept Unmarried Couples for Public Housing', *NYT*, 29 May 1977.

that made same-sex couples eligible for housing subsidies, although this was written in coded language rather than being explicitly stated. Banks had also redefined family as 'two or more persons sharing residence whose income and resource are available to meet the family's needs and who are either related by blood, marriage, or operation of law, or have evidence of a stable family relationship'. This meant that a gay couple living together in a stable relationship qualified for housing subsidies. Little opposition came forward in this consultation: only two responses out of forty-nine commented adversely on the implications of the family definition.[73]

In January 1977, Carter appointed Patricia Roberts Harris, who was a supporter of gay rights, as HUD's new Secretary.[74] Harris immediately accepted Banks's policy. On 9 May 1977, Harris initiated a new housing policy which aimed to increase 'the effectiveness of the low-rent housing program' for people who were previously excluded and to establish 'a uniform definition of family'. HUD had rewritten its regulations defining who qualified for rental and mortgage subsidies; in addition to the standard qualification of poverty, it included anyone showing a 'stable family relationship', the definition that Banks had used in her policy. Thus, although the regulation did not explicitly include gay couples, the definition meant that any couples or families showing a 'stable' relationship were eligible for housing subsidies. The regulation did not define 'stability'; it was up to each Public Health Assistant or the private housing owner to determine whether applicants were in a 'stable family relationship'.[75]

Although the policy had gone into effect from 9 May, it was only publicly announced on 28 May. Banks publicly stated that the expanded concept of the family was 'very brand new' and liberalized the country's housing policy with the aim of eliminating discrimination against unmarried persons who lived together. Banks also publicly and explicitly admitted that gay couples were eligible as long as they were in a stable family relationship, which meant having pooled their resources and lived together for some time. Banks expressed her hope that 'the PHAs [Public Housing Authorities] out there are liberal enough to interpret it generously' and added that an applicant who was denied eligibility may appeal the local decision to her department.[76] The new policy was subject to approval by the local housing authorities, some of which moved immediately to allow gay couples into HUD housing; for example, HUD's officer in Charlottesville, North Carolina.[77]

Unlike the consultation process, the policy announcement caused a furore and created headlines across the country; the day after Harris's announcement, *The New York Times* reported, 'The Government is opening public housing to unmarried couples living together and to homosexual couples if they can show a "stable family relationship"'.[78] The *Washington Post*, in an article entitled 'HUD to Allow Gays, Unmarried Couples in Public Housing', wrote that 'The federal government has opened

[73] Judy Burke, 'HUD to Allow Gays, Unmarried Couples in Public Housing', *WP*, 28 May 1977.
[74] Peter Perl, '15,000 Parade, Picnic and Politick on Gay Pride Day', *WP*, 21 June 1982.
[75] 'Gay Couples Eligible for Housing', *GN*, July 1977: 4; Office of the Federal Register, *Federal Register* 42, no. 84–90 (1977): 23582–3.
[76] Judy Burke, 'HUD to Allow Gays, Unmarried Couples in Public Housing', *WP*, 28 May 1977; 'Gay Couples Eligible for Housing', *GN*, July 1977.
[77] Randy Shilts, 'Public Housing for Gay Couples', *The Advocate*, 27 July 1977.
[78] 'H.U.D. Will Accept Unmarried Couples for Public Housing', *NYT*, 29 May 1977.

the doors of public housing to unmarried couples living together and to homosexual couples'.[79] The announcement of HUD's new policy caused immediate outrage among conservatives, with Harris and Carter coming under severe attack by both Republican and Democratic politicians; for example, Representatives Tom Hagedorn (R-MN) and Edward Boland (D-MA). Hagedorn proposed to the House an amendment that would nullify HUD's new regulation so that gay people would be excluded from housing benefits and subsidies.[80] Mike O'Neil, Boland's legislative assistant, proposed an amendment that 'would allow HUD to re-think the whole area of regulation'. Hagedorn also made a similar statement declaring that housing aid was 'an issue that should be voted upon by Congress, not regulated by HUD'.[81]

Hagedorn's amendment, however, did not go forward, because the floor manager of the bill (Boland) had already put forward a nullifying amendment. Eventually, Hagedorn and Boland agreed a 'compromise', setting out an amendment that annulled the new rule without making explicit mention of gay people. Gay rights activists stated their preference for this proposal over the Hagedorn amendment, since while it was plainly directed at them, it did not enshrine in law a rule that same-sex couples could not receive housing benefits. On 15 June, just over two weeks after the announcement of HUD's new policy, the House of Representatives by voice vote passed the Boland amendment, which made it public policy to close public housing projects to 'gay families' by denying housing aid to unmarried couples living together.[82]

Despite the ultimate failure, Carter's administration had attempted to address another of the issues raised by gay rights activists. The quick Congressional response to HUD's new policy and the speedy attempt to nullify the policy were further proof of Congress's hostility to gay rights.

Welcoming the gay press

Before Carter's presidency, no administration had ever invited the gay press, or accepted its representatives, into the White House, while all requests for interviews or even comments from gay publications to senior White House staff had been turned down or ignored. No senior aide had even agreed to publicly discuss gay rights with a gay journalist. By the mid-1970s, gay rights activists had given up requesting accreditation to the White House, to attend White House events or to interview administration aides; the only information the gay press was able to get from the White House was from anonymous sources, mostly low-level staff.[83]

The exclusion of the gay press from the White House completely changed during Carter's presidency; now, for the first time the gay press had access to the White House and to the administration, both to events and to senior staff who agreed to

79 Judy Burke, 'HUD to Allow Gays, Unmarried Couples in Public Housing', *WP*, 28 May 1977.
80 Lou Romano, 'House Passes Antigay Bill', *The Blade*, August 1977; Mary Russell, 'Taking "Joy Rides" on the Floor', *WP*, 16 June 1977.
81 'House Nullifies Housing Aid for Gay Couples', *GCN*, 2 July 1977.
82 'House Nullifies Housing Aid for Gay Couples', *GCN*, 2 July 1977; Lou Romano, 'House Passes Antigay Bill', *The Blade*, August 1977.
83 Bush, author interview.

be interviewed and to publicly speak about gay rights. For example, Costanza and Haft were often interviewed by various gay magazines and newspapers such as *The Advocate* and *The Blade*, while Chanin, Eizenstat, Malson, Weddington and Wexler were interviewed by *The Advocate* and *The Sentinel*.[84] Furthermore, the gay press could now call the White House at any time to discuss issues of concern with an aide, to ask for a comment on a case or to make inquiries about the progress of gay rights issues; the administration would always openly comment. Malson and Thomas in particular were in constant communication with the gay press, including over the phone, especially with Larry Bush.[85]

In 1978, Bush left his job at the Department of Agriculture to become a full-time journalist for *The Blade*.[86] It was a very difficult time to be an openly gay journalist, and it was even more difficult to be working for a newspaper that was largely unknown to the public. In late 1978, Bush made a request to the White House to become an accredited reporter there. Bush's application was immediately accepted, and he became the first openly gay reporter and the first reporter from a gay publication to be accredited at the White House. Subsequently, Bush was given unrestricted access to staff in the White House and Carter's administration. Bush said that Carter's aides made him feel 'very welcome' in the White House; there was never even a hint of discrimination against him, and he was treated like any other accredited White House journalist. He said about his relationship with Carter's aides, 'There was a mutual respect for a core sense of values'. Bush not only had constant and direct access to Carter's aides, but he attended a number of meetings between the administration and gay rights activists, as well as meetings between federal agencies and activists that the White House had facilitated. Furthermore, Bush's credentials as a reporter accredited at the White House opened the doors of federal agencies to him. For the first time, a reporter for a gay publication had access to Cabinet members and heads of federal agencies. Bush said that 'one of the reasons why people were willing to meet with me' was 'because the White House had blessed it'. Bush established a very good relationship with some of Carter's aides, especially Malson, with whom he communicated regularly over the phone and in person. Bush was also personally invited by Carter's administration to the White House on election night in 1980, when for the first time he met with Carter and spoke to him.[87]

Furthermore and very importantly, immediately after Carter was sworn in as president, the White House, through Costanza, spontaneously took out subscriptions to a number of gay newspapers and magazines, including *The Advocate*. This was the first

84 For example see: Larry Bush, 'The Carter Administration. More Done Than Said?', *The Advocate*, 12 June 1980; Larry Bush, 'White House Claims Solid Record on Gay Issues', *The Sentinel*, 16 May 1980; Jim Marko, 'Midge Costanza: Gay Rights Proponent at the White House', *GCN*, 9 July 1977.

85 Bush, author interview; also see: Allison Thomas' note to Bob Malson, 10 December 1979, Letter, Charles Brydon and Lucia Valeska to Bob Malson, 7 January 1980, both in RMSF, GH1, JCPL; Bob Malson immigration calls and Allison Thomas immigration calls, both undated and in RMSF, G/L1, JCPL.

86 In 1980, *The Blade* was forced to change its name to *The Washington Blade* due to registration conflict with another newspaper called the *Blade*, a daily in Toledo, Ohio ('Blade Forced to Change Name Due to Registration Conflict', *Gaze*, October 1980).

87 Bush, author interview.

time that the White House had taken out a subscription to a gay publication, obviously a highly important symbolic gesture that nevertheless did not become widely known at the time.[88] Throughout Carter's presidency, every edition of *The Advocate* was delivered to the White House. Reagan cancelled *The Advocate*'s subscription within four months of being sworn in as President.[89] Reagan's win also ended the constant and unrestricted access to the White House that the gay press had enjoyed during Carter's presidency.[90]

Another issue regarding the gay press that was raised during Carter's presidency was that of *Gaysweek*, a gay magazine whose application to the United States Patent and Trademark Office (USPTO), part of the Department of Commerce, to have its name registered as a trademark had been rejected. In June 1978, Michael Lavery, the General Counsel of the USPTO, explained that *Gaysweek*'s registration was refused 'because the mark is considered to contain or be comprised of material that is of an immoral or scandalous nature'.[91] The NGTF asked for Costanza's help in the matter. She immediately wrote to Secretary of Commerce Juanita Kreps and less than a month later the decision was reversed and the *Gaysweek* registration accepted.[92]

Even so, the NGTF sought further progress, requesting in December 1979 that Carter would personally speak to the gay press.[93] Carter did not do this; it would be another seventeen years before an American president met such a request, when President Clinton was interviewed by *The Advocate* in June 1996.[94] As for Carter, he would be interviewed by *The Advocate* in January 2006, with the magazine's cover announcing the interview under the title 'Jimmy Carter Bashes the Antigay Right'. In the interview, Carter repeated his longstanding support for equal rights for gay people and attacked the religious right for its attacks on gay rights.[95]

Honouring openly gay people

Among the more symbolic elements of the administration's inclusive attitude towards gay people, of course with special implications for the individuals concerned, were the explicit gestures of recognition made towards prominent gay rights activists or cultural figures. An example of the former was Gary Mundt, a veteran who in the early 1970s, after leaving the Air Force, had become a leading organizer of the Vietnam Veterans Against the War in Denver. Since 1973, Mundt, who was by then openly gay, had been working at the office of Colorado Congresswoman Pat Schroeder on veterans' and other military casework. He was also actively involved with gay rights activism. By 1979, Mundt was one of the most prominent and outspoken gay rights activists in

88 Ibid.
89 'For the Record: Maybe Nancy Dislikes the Pink Section', *The Advocate*, 14 May 1981.
90 Bush, author interview.
91 Scott P. Anderson, '*Gaysweek* Patent Denied', *The Advocate*, 23 August 1978.
92 Letters, Midge Costanza to Juanita Kreps, 28 June 1978, and D. Banner to Midge Costanza, 14 July 1978, both in MCI.
93 NGTF's requests, 10 December 1979. RMSF, GH1, JCPL.
94 J. Jennings Moss, 'Bill Clinton: The Advocate Interview', *The Advocate*, 25 June 1996.
95 Sean Kennedy, 'Q&A: Jimmy Carter', *The Advocate*, 17 June 2006.

Figure 6 President Carter and Andy Warhol at the White House in June 1977. WHSPC, nlc01726. JCPL.

Colorado. In June 1979, he was presented by Carter with a citation for 'Outstanding Community Achievement of Vietnam Era Veterans'.[96]

Among cultural figures, Robert Rauschenberg and Andy Warhol, both openly gay, visited the White House in June 1977 (Figure 6), having been invited to a special reception hosted by Carter to honour them for contributing to his inauguration and his election campaign (see Chapter 2).[97] Tennessee Williams, one of America's greatest playwrights, had had his homosexuality publicly revealed in *Time* magazine. Subsequently, Williams, who lived in Key West, Florida, was often a target of well-publicized homophobic attacks in which he was harassed and sometimes even physically assaulted. For example, between January and April 1979, he was physically assaulted, his house was hit by firecrackers and beer cans, and even his dog was abducted from his house, never to be seen again.[98] On 9 June 1980, in a White House ceremony, Carter awarded Williams with the Medal of Freedom, the nation's highest civilian honour. Williams became the first openly gay person to receive the award.[99] Carter's honouring of Williams was a major public statement at the time, especially due to the recent homophobic attacks on him (Figure 7). Not only did it indicate Carter's respect for and acceptance of an openly gay man; it also demonstrated to the public that gay people could make and had made significant contributions to the country and that they deserved respect and recognition.

96 Phil Nash, 'Gays in Politics: Gary Mundt', *Out Front*, 2 May 1980.
97 Bockris, *Andy Warhol*, 305.
98 Leigh W. Rutledge, *The Gay Decades: From Stonewall to the Present: The People And Events That Shaped Gay Lives* (New York: Plume: 1992), 134–5.
99 'Carter Honors Tennessee Williams', *The Blade*, 12 June 1980.

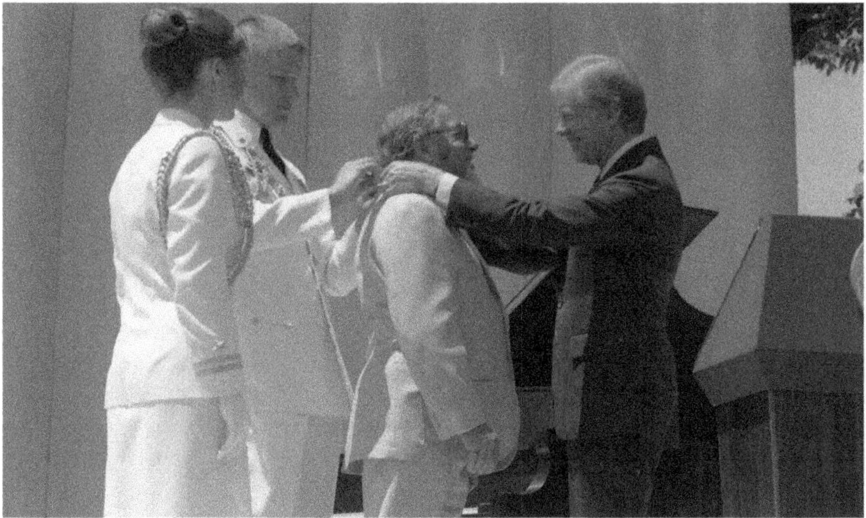

Figure 7 President Carter awarding Tennessee Williams the Medal of Freedom, 9 June 1980. WHSPC, nlc017424.6. JCPL.

Gay awareness training begins at DHR

Sometime in 1977, it was revealed that a Black gay adolescent had been grossly abused by staff of the Department of Human Resources (DHR) at the Children Center in Laurel, Maryland. The Department was part of HEW, and in early 1978 Joseph Califano, who Carter had appointed as HEW Secretary, accepted a request by the GAA to provide its staff with gay awareness training. Thus, in April 1978, about twenty-five DHR employees received training aiming to help them understand how to deal with young gay people who were under their supervision.[100] This was the first time that a federal agency had allowed such training to take place; as discussed earlier in this chapter, Carlson later allowed the same training for BOP staff.[101]

Incendiary lesbians

Carter's administration paid attention to anachronisms such as the inclusion in the National Fire Academy's training course manual of an allegation that homosexuality and arson went hand in hand and that arsonists were frequently lesbians: the manual said of an arsonist, 'she is often thought to be homosexual'.[102] The issue was raised with Allison Thomas by Brydon and Valeska in February 1980.[103] Thomas contacted Gordon Vickery, Administrator of the US Fire Administration, and asked if there

[100] 'DHR Staff Receives Gay Awareness Training', *The Blade*, 1 June 1978.
[101] Bush and Clay, author interviews.
[102] 'Gay Pyromaniacs a Natural?', *Montrose Star*, 14 February 1980.
[103] Letter, C.F. Brydon and Lucia Valeska to Allison Thomas, 22 February 1980. RMSF, GTFN1, JCPL.

was any statistical evidence to support the controversial statement.[104] After Vickery did not find sufficient evidence to support the claim, Thomas asked him to excise the unsubstantiated statement from the training manual, which he immediately did.[105]

☙

The case of federal prisoners was a complex one but illustrates again the effectiveness of a committed White House operating with the full support of the president, something, as demonstrated above, that even the activists of the NGTF had not expected, resulting in their abortive and arguably counter-productive strategy of litigation. White House intervention eventually achieved all of the aims regarding the prison system set out by activists at the March 1977 Meeting, including those put in limbo by the litigation effort; indeed they were exceeded in some respects. Prison sexual assaults ceased to be classified as 'homosexual rape', prison libraries began to hold non-pornographic gay literature, MCC ministers were allowed to extend pastoral care to federal prisoners at all security levels, the BOP established a system-wide programme of sensitivity training in which gay people participated, and the NGTF obtained a direct line of communication to the top levels of the BOP through a liaison officer.

The other examples discussed in this chapter, which still do not exhaust all the cases that could be presented, are notable for their range, extending from small but telling mitigations such as changing the homophobic national firefighters' training manual to the incorporation of gay people and gay concerns into the administration's substantial effort to enhance official and public memorialization of the Holocaust, and also extending from primarily symbolic issues such as these to interventions with direct implications for gay people's material welfare, such as assistance for gay runaways. White House intervention, of various kinds, made the difference in all cases, a fact unfortunately further demonstrated by the fate of some of these initiatives under Carter's successor.

[104] Allison Thomas memorandums to Gordon Vickery, 3 March 1980 and 8 April 1980, both in RMSF, GTFN2, JCPL.

[105] 'Homophobic National Fire Academy Manual Revised', News from NGTF, 29 April 1980. NGTFR, B.36, F.154, CU.

11

Gay rights in the incipient culture wars

Despite attracting a vast amount of scholarly attention, the dynamics of cultural change are poorly understood. Theories of 'socialization' in childhood or a slightly later 'formative period', most consistently advanced in recent decades by the late Ronald Inglehart and his collaborators,[1] suggest that change is slow and its main mechanism is generational replacement. Much can be said in favour of this view, as generational differences in cultural norms are often readily apparent even to the casual observer. But other processes obviously enter in as well. It is, of course, an assumption of this book that cues from a 'bully pulpit' such as the presidency of the United States can themselves be powerful factors promoting a change in 'cultural framing', as students of social movements term it.[2] Changes in the visibility and, hence, the perceived normality and legitimacy of derogated groups can be effected by this means, as this book has argued, and further examples will be presented in this chapter.

But people who notice cultural change can also resist it. Hence the phenomenon of 'cultural backlash' occurs. Inglehart himself made this mechanism central to the argument of his last major work,[3] and more generally the much discussed phenomenon of 'culture wars', even though some have argued that the phrase is an exaggeration,[4] points to a dramatic contest between cultural change and its resisters. This chapter will discuss further the bestowal of visibility and legitimacy on the gay rights cause by the administration's words, and by the appearances at gay events of members of the presidential family, and administration officials. The chapter also documents some key episodes in the growth of cultural resistance. As these moments include a political assassination, the thesis that 'culture war' is a mere over-dramatization cannot be wholly right.

[1] Ronald Inglehart, *Culture Shift in Advanced Industrial Society* (Princeton, NJ: Princeton University Press, 1990).

[2] Robert D. Benford and David A. Snow, 'Framing Processes and Social Movements: An Overview and Assessment', *Annual Review of Sociology* 26 (2000): 611–39.

[3] Pippa Norris and Ronald Inglehart, *Cultural Backlash: Trump, Brexit, and Authoritarian Populism* (Cambridge and New York: Cambridge University Press, 2019).

[4] Rhys H. Williams (ed.), *Cultural Wars in American Politics: Critical Reviews of a Popular Myth* (Hawthorne, NY: Aldine de Gruyter, 1997).

Words and appearances for gay rights

As president, Carter spoke explicitly in favour of gay rights, making him the first sitting American president to ever do so. He did this in June 1977 during an interview with the Associated Press, and in January 1980 in a televised interview on NBC, while in November 1978 he publicly urged the people of California to vote against the anti-gay Proposition 6 (all examined later in this chapter). Furthermore, Carter also spoke about the changing nature of family, which he acknowledged was not limited to just the classic American white Christian nuclear family; he said that modern families were 'pluralistic', including those with 'alternative lifestyles', which included gay families (see Chapter 12).

On 27 November 1978, Harvey Milk was assassinated. Following the murder, Carter described Milk as 'a leader of San Francisco's gay community who kept his promise to represent his constituents . . . As supervisor, Milk had come to be widely regarded as a symbol of the aspirations of gay people to participate openly in mainstream politics and society at large'.[5] These comments were important and pleased the gay community. First, Carter publicly acknowledged the community and spoke about it as a legitimate group of people in American society who should openly participate in it and in politics, providing for the community both visibility and legitimation. Secondly, Carter became the first American president to publicly acknowledge an openly gay elected politician and his contribution to gay rights.[6]

It is, on the other hand, true that Carter did not use the words 'gay' and 'lesbian' as readily as gay rights activists wished him to. A contentious debate over this wording in relation to the Gay Rights Plank of the 1980 Democratic platform is discussed in Chapter 13. In December 1979, NGTF activists at a White House meeting proposed, among a range of other requests (also discussed in Chapter 13), that in the forthcoming State of the Union address, where it would deal with 'American goals for the 1980, the language discussing the goal of a just society should specifically refer to lesbians and gay men'.[7] Carter did not include this language, although in his speech he reaffirmed his commitment to 'the protection of human rights'.[8] It would in fact take another thirty-six years for an American president to use the words 'lesbians' and 'gay men' in a State of the Union address; President Obama did so in 2015.[9] However, on 7 January 1980, just two weeks before his address, Carter made a clear and strong public statement in support of gay rights in his NBC interview with John Chancellor; he said, 'I don't think there ought to be any discrimination against a person because of their sexual desires and beliefs'.[10]

5 Scott Anderson, 'Murder and Mourning in San Francisco', *The Advocate*, 11 January 1979.
6 DeBaugh, Hayden, Kent and Schockman, author interviews.
7 NGTF's requests, 10 December 1979. RMSF, GH1, JCPL.
8 Jimmy Carter, 'State of the Union Address 1980', 23 January 1980. JCPL, https://www.jimmycarterlibrary.gov/assets/documents/speeches/su80jec.phtml.
9 Alexandra Jaffe, 'Obama Makes Historic "Transgender" Reference in SOTU', *CNN*, 21 January 2015.
10 Don Leavitt, 'Latest Carter Move Termed "A Step Forward"', *The Washington Blade*, 10 October 1980.

Furthermore, in October 1980, a month before the presidential election, Carter's campaign team released a packet that contained detailed reports – 'issue papers' – detailing the administration's main achievements so far and briefing the public about the president's positions on a number of issues. There were thirty such papers included in the packet, covering topics ranging from national defence to housing. One of the papers was about gay rights. It started with Carter's statement on NBC and then listed some of his accomplishments on gay rights, such as the CSRA, tax exemption for gay organizations, the federal funding that gay establishments and organizations had been receiving, the immigration issue, his support for Cranston's bill and the reversal of anti-gay policies in agencies like the Peace Corps and USAID. This was the first time that a president had released an issue paper on gay rights, again expressing his support for equal rights for gay people. The gay community was thrilled with the paper, with some gay leaders calling it 'a step forward'. Also very important for them was the fact that Carter had taken the initiative to issue it without being asked by gay rights activists to do it; a signal that he really valued the subject and sought to contribute to it.[11]

Carter could certainly have spoken more often and more forcefully about gay rights during his presidency, but actions often speak louder than words. Wales's comment about how public statements could 'often be counter-productive', and that 'in some instances it is far better to act than to make public statements',[12] seems clearly to have been apt in this case. While strong or numerous public statements by Carter would have had a positive effect in terms of legitimation, the likelihood of backlash had to be considered, as evident as it already was, and this could jeopardize the advance. Not only were religious fundamentalists becoming more prominent and visible, but Congress still contained a powerful anti-gay bloc which had been in the ascendancy for decades and had achieved legislative advances (such as replacing 'epilepsy' by 'sexual deviance' in the Immigration Act) as recently as the 1960s. It often acted to limit Carter's reforms, as in its attempt to block the new HUD policy that recognized gay couples as families and provided them with housing benefits (see Chapter 10), or its attempt to strip gay veterans of their benefits after their dishonourable discharges had been upgraded to honourable via Carter's SDRP (see Chapter 9). On the other hand, whenever Carter attempted to do something about gay rights without much fanfare, he succeeded; the CSRA is an example. Even the IWY Commission had acknowledged the backlash that a resolution containing the word 'lesbian' would have caused and had therefore avoided using it (see Chapter 5). Charles Brydon admitted in May 1979 about Carter's reluctance to speak more forcefully about gay rights that 'actions sometimes speak louder than words' and acknowledged that 'what has happened under this administration has been very important and has affected the lives of many gay people. Not dramatically perhaps, but we're light years ahead of where we were five years ago'.[13]

Throughout Carter's presidency, members of his administration received numerous invitations from gay organizations to attend gay events or events about gay rights; as far as this research can establish, they accepted almost all, if not all, of them. It

11 Ibid.

12 Ernie Acosta, '3rd World Gays Take Issues to White House', *The Blade*, 7 June 1979.

13 Mark Hansmann, 'New Leader, New Vistas for National Task Force', *The Advocate*, 3 May 1979.

was the first time that presidential aides had been invited to attend such events. Previously, no gay organizations had even contemplated inviting presidential aides as they knew what the answer was going to be.[14] At all the gay events they attended, Carter's aides were ready to publicly express their personal support, as well as that of the president and his administration. The NGTF in particular frequently invited senior Carter administration aides, such as Costanza, Wales, Weddington and Wexler, to attend its events, as the organization was well aware that their presence would provide visibility and legitimation for the event. Wales said that all the members of Carter's administration always happily agreed to attend gay events, acknowledging the symbolic power that their presence had for the gay community. She added that 'It was important for us to make very clear that this is part of a human rights agenda and this belongs way up high it also belongs in our conversations with other governments, but it belonged here too'.*

Gay organizations began inviting presidential aides to their events shortly after Carter's inauguration, with Costanza and Haft receiving many invitations to such events. Whenever their commitments in the White House permitted, both women would attend and express support.[15] Haft was the first aide to be invited to speak at an event about gay rights. On 26 January 1977, just a few days after she had been appointed to the White House's OPL, Haft was invited by the Association of the Bar of the City of New York to speak at a symposium about homosexuality and the law (see also Chapter 9). Haft accepted the invitation and presented a paper entitled 'The Current State of the Laws Affecting Gay Men and Lesbians'. She received huge applause when she expressed her commitment, as well as that of the administration, to gay rights, promising to work to advance the issue.[16] Another invitation for Haft came from the only one-year-old GSDC in Washington, D.C. The Club invited Haft to attend an event on 20 June 1977, at the Martin Luther King Jr. Memorial Library, and she happily agreed to participate. At the event, Haft publicly stressed the administration's 'strong commitment' to gay rights and that Carter knew and approved of White House facilitation of meetings between gay rights activists and federal agencies.[17] In May 1979, Costanza, who by then was no longer employed by the White House, and Haft, now Mondale's Deputy Counsel, were invited to and attended a benefit dinner in New York City organized by the NGTF to honour O'Leary and Voeller who were retiring as Co-Executive Directors of the organization.[18]

Costanza also attended and spoke at numerous gay events. For example, she was invited to speak about lesbian rights at an event organized in September 1977 by the Southern California Women for the Whitman-Radclyffe Foundation, a lesbian rights organization. Costanza happily agreed to do so, and personally called the organization to make arrangements for her talk and visit.[19] Costanza also attended several events in Washington, D.C. organized by local gay organizations such as the GAA and the

14 Apuzzo, Bunch, Bush, Clay, Perry and Vida, author interviews.
15 Haft, author interview.
16 Letter, E. Carrington Boggan to Marilyn Haft, 16 February 1977. MCSF, [H-GRPH], JCPL.
17 Lou Romano, 'Aide Clarifies Carter Views', *The Blade*, July 1977.
18 Haft, author interview.
19 Letter, Myra Riddell to Margaret Costanza, 28 July 1977. MCSF, [H-GRPH], JCPL.

GSDC. In 1977, just a few months after she had been appointed to the White House, she travelled to Dade County to actively support the county's gay rights ordinance, attending rallies and giving speeches (discussed in the next section). Shortly afterwards, she and Haft had attended an NGTF fundraiser for its We Are Your Children campaign.[20] In January 1978, Initiative 13 was launched in Seattle, Washington, aiming, among other things, to repeal the city's gay rights ordinances, which prohibited discrimination based on sexual preference on employment and housing; local gay rights activists invited Costanza to campaign in their city. In October, Costanza, no longer employed at the White House but using her status as a former special assistant to the president, campaigned against the Initiative, and local activists printed leaflets referring to her former position as well as a number of Carter's statements in support of gay rights and against discrimination.[21] In November, the Initiative was defeated. O'Leary phoned Weddington in the White House and suggested she send a brief telegram to Brydon on behalf of Carter's administration congratulating Costanza for her contribution to the 'tremendous victory'. Weddington sent the telegram which read, 'We share a respect for Midge Costanza's deep caring about human rights issues. Her sensitivity to people and their concerns is an example to all of us'.[22]

Malson and Thomas were also invited by gay rights activists to a number of gay events, including fundraisers, and they attended several of them. For example, in May 1980, they attended a fundraiser at the Los Angeles Gay Community Services Center and another in San Francisco (see Chapter 4), while Thomas, invited by Kameny, attended a fundraiser for the GAA in Washington, D.C.[23] Another White House aide who attended several gay events, mostly in Washington, D.C., was Mike Chanin. For example, on 27 November 1979, he attended the kick-off gala and fundraiser for Gay Vote 1980: The National Convention Project, at The Pier, a gay disco in Washington, D.C. (see Chapter 13).[24] Wexler also attended several functions and events organized by gay organizations and activists; for example, the NGTF's Week of Dialogue with the Media about Gay and Lesbian Concerns (see Chapter 7), while another evening she had accompanied Kameny's mother to a Parents of Gays event in Washington, D.C.[25] Wales also attended several gay events and talks organized by the GSDC, the NGTF and the GAA.[26] For example, on 29 October 1979 she met with members of the GSDC at the Club's office in Washington, D.C. In her speech, Wales characterized gay rights as a human rights issue that the whole administration strongly supported, and offered to help advance the cause in any way she could.[27] Finally, Weddington also attended several gay events; for example, the official launch on 22 October 1978 of the NGTF's Week of Dialogue with American Parents and Families (see Chapter 7).[28] Several other

20 'Anita Bryant Interview', *Playboy*, May 1978; Haft, author interview.
21 Britt, author interview.
22 Telegram, Sarah Weddington to Charles Brydon, 17 November 1978. CPP, HU 1, 7/1/78-12/31/78, JCPL.
23 McReynolds, author interview.
24 Elizabeth Bamiller, 'Gay Rights, Laser Lights & Jerry Brown', *WP*, 28 November 1979.
25 Apuzzo, McReynolds and Weddington, author interviews.
26 Wales, author interview.
27 Letter, Franklin Kameny to Jane Wales, 3 November 1979. ATSF, B.265, GR, JCPL.
28 Weddington, author interview.

members of Carter's administration on numerous occasions publicly expressed their, as well as the administration's, support for gay rights, for example Joseph Califano, Benjamin Civiletti, Stuart Eizenstat, Patricia Robert Harris, Mary E. King, Juanita Kreps, Margaret McKenna, Walter Mondale, Eleanor Holmes Norton, Jody Powell, Andrew Young and Patricia Wald.

Although Carter did not personally attend any gay event, members of his immediate family did, and they spoke in favour of gay rights. On 27 January 1978, O'Leary wrote to Chip Carter asking him to attend an NGTF ceremony and to present Costanza on behalf of the organization with an award for her 'outstanding contributions to the human rights of gay people'. O'Leary wrote in her letter, 'Chip, it would mean so much to the gay community and to our non-gay supporters if you would attend'. The importance of Chip's presence for the gay community is evident from the fact that O'Leary told him that they had not set a date and venue for the ceremony yet and first wished to know his availability.[29] Chip accepted the invitation and attended the ceremony, which took place on 15 June 1978 at Les Mouches discotheque in New York City.[30] The gay community was thrilled with Chip's presence in the ceremony. Activists interviewed for this book remembered his presence and its legitimating force.[31] For example, Bunch said:

> I think it was a *major*. . . . I mean, it's *very* important that his son attended the ceremony. Because I think that his son would symbolize that Carter really had a support and a comfort level with the issue, that even though he might not be willing to be there himself or to speak himself, I think the fact that he was okay with – and probably gave permission to – his son to go there is very important.*

Chip was not the only member of Carter's family who attended gay events and gay establishments and spoke out for gay rights: Carter's mother Lillian did so too. In mid-1978, Ms Carter was interviewed by Henry Mitchell of the *Washington Post* and took a public stand in support of gay rights and against Anita Bryant after the latter's anti-gay crusade (see later in this chapter). Ms Carter told Mitchell that initially she was 'crazy about her – the sweetest little singer'. However, after Bryant's anti-gay crusade, she had a change of heart and said that she now felt 'absolute disgust' for her because of her 'position against homosexuals'. When Mitchell told her she should tell Bryant to 'shut up and mind her own business', she replied, 'Oh, I did'.[32] Naturally, Ms Carter's public stand against the gay community's number one enemy delighted the community and turned her overnight into a sort of hero for gay rights activists. This led to numerous invitations from gay organizations to attend their events.[33] In addition to attending a fundraiser for Integrity in Georgia (mentioned in Chapter 4), she also attended fundraisers for the Atlanta Gay Centre and the Atlanta Lesbian

29 Letter, Jean O'Leary to Chip Carter, 27 January 1978. NGTFR, B.152, F.46, CU.
30 'Lining Up for "Humankind"', *NYP*, 16 June 1978.
31 Apuzzo, Bunch and Clay, author interviews.
32 Grant Hayter-Menzies, *Lillian Carter: A Compassionate Life* (Jefferson, NC: McFarland & Company, Inc., 2015), 193–4; 'Miss Lillian Puts the Squeeze on Anita', *The Blade*, October 1978.
33 Clay and Perry, author interviews.

Feminist Alliance Centre. At all these events, she expressed her, and her son's, support for gay rights. In Atlanta, when she was asked about Bryant's anti-gay crusade, she repeated that she must 'shut up and stop her hate campaign'. The crowd went wild at her comments and almost lifted her up in their arms.[34] On another occasion, in December 1977, she accompanied Andy Warhol to a charity event at Studio 54 in New York.[35]

However, her most famous appearance at a gay event came on 25 October 1979, when she was a guest speaker at the Los Angeles Gay Community Service Center's $150-per-plate black-tie dinner at the Beverly Wilshire Hotel, which aimed to raise funds for the construction of a gay community bath clubhouse. It was Troy Perry who had the idea of inviting her as a drawing card after her public comments in favour of gay rights and her presence at other gay events.[36] Arriving at the hotel, which was packed with journalists, one of them asked her, 'Miss Lillian, how does it feel to be at a gay and lesbian dinner?' Carter replied, 'Oh my. Is this what this is?' and made her way inside.[37] Ms Carter spent most of the evening talking and dancing with Sheldon Andelson's father; she also addressed a crowd of 800 people, expressing her support, as well as her son's, for gay rights. The event was a great success and raised over $100,000. Asked by a reporter whether she was embarrassed to raise funds for the gay community, she said, 'no, not at all'.[38] The following day, accepting a last-minute invitation issued the previous night by Sheldon Andelson, she visited the local Gay Community Service Center.[39] It goes without saying that Lillian Carter was the first mother of a sitting president to attend gay events and to publicly support gay rights.

Rosalynn Carter also had no problem with talking publicly about gay rights. For example, in January 1977, she was interviewed by the *Ladies Home Journal*. She was asked about the 'family chats' that she, Carter and their children had at home. She replied, 'marijuana, gay liberation and things like that', adding that her husband always listened and 'encouraged the boys to have their own opinions'.[40] This made her the first First Lady to publicly acknowledge the issue of gay rights.

Throughout Carter's presidency, gay rights activists made widespread use of two of Carter's quotes: 'I favor the end of discrimination against homosexuals' from his 1976 presidential campaign, and 'human rights are absolute' from his inauguration speech, inscribing them on placards and printing them on stickers, T-shirts and fliers. On most occasions, the quotes were accompanied with Carter's face;[41] for example on 26 June 1977, during the Gay Freedom Day Parade in San Francisco,[42] and the same event the following year.[43] The public statements of support for gay rights members of Carter's family and of his administration, and their presence at gay events, played an important

34 Clay, author interview.
35 Hayter-Menzies, *Lillian Carter*, 193.
36 Perry, author interview.
37 David Mixner, *Stranger Among Friends* (New York: Bantam Books, 1996), 155.
38 Hayter-Menzies, *Lillian Carter*, 194; Mixner, *Stranger Among Friends*, 155; Perry, author interview.
39 Perry, author interview.
40 'What Carter's Discuss at Home', *The Blade*, June 1977.
41 Britt, Clay, DeBaugh and Kent, author interviews.
42 Les Ledbeter, '40,000 Join Peaceful March for Homosexual Rights in San Francisco', *NYT*, 27 June 1977.
43 Randy Shilts, *The Mayor of Castro Street: The Life and Times of Harvey Milk* (New York: St. Martin's Press, 1982), 223.

role in bringing the gay rights issue to the attention of the public and in changing the cultural frame with regard to homosexuality. But this necessarily changed the terms of public debate and provoked opposition. Two major state battles over gay rights took place during Carter's presidency, in California and in Florida. Carter was asked by both sides in these battles to publicly take a stand and support their cause. These two important events in the emerging culture wars are examined below.

The Dade County Gay Rights Ordinance

In 1976, Ruth Shack, a member of the Board of Commissioners of Dade County, Florida (called Miami-Dade County since 1997), introduced an amendment which banned discrimination in areas of housing, employment and public accommodation based on *sexual orientation*.[44] The Commission voted to enact Shack's ordinance, but Anita Bryant, a singer and well-known personality of the 1960s, and other religious conservatives launched a campaign to have it overturned; they formed a coalition named 'Save Our Children' and voted Bryant to be their president.[45] Save Our Children claimed that the new law would force private and religious, as well as state, schools to hire gay people. Bryant implied that gay people were paedophiles[46] and called the ordinance a 'homosexual recruitment bill', stating that 'since homosexuals cannot reproduce, they must recruit'.[47] During a massive campaign, in which she also received substantial support from the local Cuban anti-Castro community,[48] Bryant and her supporters managed within only a few weeks to easily surpass the 10,000 signatures needed to force a referendum by gathering over 60,000, while also raising about $200,000 to fund the campaign. A referendum for the ordinance was set for 7 June 1977.[49] Bryant issued a statement asking why the White House was 'dignifying these [gay rights] activists for special privilege with a serious discussion on their alleged "human rights"', and why Carter was allowing himself to be pushed unto endorsing a way of living that violated the laws of both God and nature.[50]

The ordinance became a rallying point for conservative activists who answered Bryant's call for help and joined her anti-gay crusade. One of them was Falwell, who later recalled that it was his first taste of political advocacy.[51] Gay rights activists in Florida also got organized to fight for the preservation of the ordinance; for example, Robert (Bob) Kunst and Dr Alan Rockway formed the Miami Victory Campaign.[52] The gay rights activists publicly quoted Carter's inauguration speech claim that 'human

44 Clendinen and Nagourney, *Out*, 294–7.
45 John Arnold, 'Gay Rights Battle Lines Are Drawn', *Miami Herald*, 27 March 1977.
46 Arthur Lubow and Lucy Howard, 'The Homosexual Teacher', *Newsweek*, 18 December 1978.
47 Adam DeBaugh, 'Florida Gay Rights Battle Rages', *The Blade*, April 1977.
48 Rich and Arguelles, 'Homosexuality, Homophobia, and Revolution, Part II', 126–7.
49 Jonathan Steele, 'Miami Puts Gay Rights on Test', *The Guardian*, 6 June 1977.
50 Clendinen and Nagourney, *Out*, 291.
51 Randall Balmer, *Redeemer: The Life of Jimmy Carter* (New York: Basic Books, 2014), 98.
52 Fejes, *Gay Rights*, 136.

rights are absolute', while the Miami Victory Campaign printed out stickers, fliers and T-shirts with the same slogan.[53]

Both gay rights activists and their opponents actively sought Carter's endorsement prior to the referendum; Carter avoided taking a position, despite strong pressure from both sides.[54] On 18 March 1977, Kunst wrote to the White House calling for 'the President's help'.[55] The same month, Kameny wrote to Haft that 'support for gays is needed in Miami' and that 'someone from the White House' should go there and help.[56] Gay rights activists from Florida requested a meeting in the White House with presidential aides to discuss the matter. The White House accepted the request, and sometime between 11 and 14 April, Haft and Richard Reiman met in the White House with gay rights activists, including DeBaugh and Kunst. The activists asked for the administration's help to save the ordinance; like Kameny, they suggested that the presence of a senior White House aide on their side would boost their chances of winning. Haft expressed the administration's support for their cause and stated that she and Costanza were trying to find a way to help in the matter. She also informed them of pressure on Carter from prominent conservatives, including many Democratic politicians, indicating that he would probably avoid taking sides in a local matter.[57] On 15 April, Haft wrote to Kunst and assured him of Carter's commitment to gay rights and of her intention to help; she wrote, 'As you know, this Administration is very anxious to do all it can to help eradicate sources of discrimination against gays as against other groups'.[58]

Meanwhile, the Dade County Coalition for Human Rights attempted to take out an ad in *The Miami Herald* supporting the ordinance and quoting Carter as saying 'I don't think that the government at the local, state or federal level should single out homosexuals for abuse or harassment or prosecution under existing laws. I favor the end of harassment or abuse or discrimination against homosexuals'. The newspaper sought to confirm that the quotation was genuine, and Haft responded to its inquiry that it was.[59] The *Herald* accepted the ad and printed it.[60]

Costanza and Haft discussed at length how to help the activists. Costanza initially had doubts about going to Dade County, believing that a male White House official should go. Hamilton Jordan argued against on 'local issue' grounds.[61] Costanza discussed the possibility with Carter, who did not raise any objection and left it up to her to decide. Pleased with this reaction, Costanza decided to go to Dade County,[62]

53 DeBaugh and Kent, author interviews.

54 'The Gay Issue: Whose Rights Prevail?', *Miami Herald*, 4 April 1977; Haft, author interview; Jim Marko, 'Midge Costanza: Gay Rights Proponent at the White House', *GCN*, 9 July 1977.

55 Letter, Bon Kunst to Tim Kraft, 18 March 1977. MCSF, [GR: MECOCL], JCPL.

56 Memorandum, Marilyn Haft to Midge Costanza, 31 March 1977. SWSF, [Gay] CR, JCPL.

57 DeBaugh and Haft, author interviews; JCPL; Richard Reiman, Weekly Activity Report, 11–15 April 1977. MCI.

58 Letter, Marilyn Haft to Bob Kunst, 15 April 1977. MCSF, [H-GRPH], JCPL.

59 Letter, Marilyn Haft to John Kosanke, 3 June 1977. MCSF, [H-GRPH], JCPL.

60 Gillian Frank, '"The Civil Rights of Parents": Race and Conservative Politics in Anita Bryant's Campaign against Gay Rights in 1970s Florida', *Journal of the History of Sexuality* 22, no. 1 (2013): 151–2.

61 Mattingly, *A Feminist*, 114.

62 Haft, author interview.

where she attended three fundraisers and several public meetings. The local activists made the most of Costanza's presence by highlighting the fact that she was Carter's personal and trusted assistant. In every meeting Costanza attended, she was asked about Carter's opinion on the matter. She maintained and emphasized Carter's personal support for the ordinance and for gay rights in general. Asked why Carter was not speaking out, Costanza said that he was unwilling to take a public stand on a local issue that had caused such controversy. On many of her appearances, Costanza was accompanied by Leonard Matlovich, who had travelled there to act as co-chair and spokesperson of the Dade County Coalition.[63] Her presence was 'a big boost' for the gay rights cause and was perceived by the local population as Carter's endorsement of the ordinance.[64] DeBaugh, who actively participated in the campaign in Dade County, argued that Costanza's presence there was '*very* important. Costanza was *very*, very much a part of that, and very supportive of our work'.*

Conservative Christians and other opponents of course made the same observation. John Conlan, a former Congressman, said that Carter 'sent Midge Costanza down to Florida to fight Anita Bryant on the anti-gay ordinance'.[65] George Hansen, a Republican Congressman, wrote to Carter, 'My concern is that what began as a local fight is now being billed as a national battle where the gays have the support of the President, members of the Cabinet, of the Congress and other high officials of government'.[66] Bryant, who had supported Carter in the 1976 presidential elections, publicly criticized him now, not only for not helping her efforts but for allowing Costanza to go to Florida and speak 'for the administration' in support of gay rights.[67] A year later Bryant was still infuriated with Carter:

> I looked at Carter as a hero, as one who had caught the eye and the heartbeat of the grassroots in America. I really had great expectations of him . . . and yet he allows Midge Costanza to go down to Dade County on a local issue and campaign for homosexuality.[68]

On 7 June, Bryant and her supporters easily prevailed with 202,319 to 89,562 votes.[69] However, the defeat in Dade County proved to be a rallying call to gay rights activists as, largely in response to Bryant's efforts, the membership of the NGTF and the level of political activity in the gay community increased dramatically. O'Leary said that the anti-gay campaign had resulted in the NGTF's budget and membership being doubled while individual gay groups had found a new sense of solidarity and common cause; indeed she characterized Bryant as 'the best thing that ever happened to us'.[70]

63 'Carter Adviser Causes Bryant Grief on Gays', *Miami Herald*, 22 May 1977; DeBaugh and Kent, author interviews.
64 DeBaugh and Kent, author interviews.
65 'Reagan Backed', *The Desert Sun*, 3 December 1979.
66 Letter, George Hansen to President Jimmy Carter, 8 April 1977. SWSF, [Gay] CR, JCPL.
67 Allen Murray, 'Anita Bryant Raps Against Carter for Failing to Help', *Atlanta Constitution*, 13 June 1978.
68 'Anita Bryant Interview', *Playboy*, May 1978.
69 Bill Peterson, 'Gay Rights Law Loses 2-1 in Miami', *WP*, 8 June 1977.
70 Eileen Keerdoja, 'Anita and the Gays', *Newsweek*, 13 March 1978.

O'Leary even defended Carter for not coming out in support of the ordinance, telling the audience of the National Gay Leadership Conference in Denver on 29–30 July that it was not wise to 'push President Carter for a broad statement on gay rights, because, despite his silence, he is allowing governmental departments to meet with gay leaders in order to resolve gay problems with various bodies'.[71]

California's Proposition 6

In 1977, the Southern Baptist General Convention of California passed a resolution asserting that homosexuality was sinful and that gay people should not be employed in a range of jobs, including public education.[72] The same year, also in California, John Briggs, a Republican State Senator, filed a petition to enable the state to fire or refuse to employ any gay person or any advocator, solicitor or promoter of homosexuality as a teacher, teaching assistant, counsel or educational administrator. State laws required the signatures of 312,303 registered voters to get a petition onto the ballot; Briggs managed to get more than 520,000 signatures, and the petition qualified for the general election ballot on 7 November 1978. If it passed, gay teachers, or those who discussed homosexuality in a way that 'condoned' it, would be dismissed or not hired.[73] Briggs considered homosexuality to be 'the hottest issue in the country since Reconstruction' and the proposal was known as Proposition 6 or the Briggs Initiative.[74]

At the time there were about 2.4 million elementary and secondary school teachers in the United States, and it was estimated that 120,000 to 240,000 were gay.[75] Briggs cited a recent nationwide Gallup Poll where 65 per cent had said that they opposed gay teachers.[76] Furthermore, although a Harris poll earlier that year had shown that 54 per cent of those surveyed were in favour of legislation banning job discrimination against gay people, when asked about specific professions, 55 per cent supported the idea that gays should not be allowed to teach. Louis Harris, the pollster, observed that 'despite public feeling that discrimination against homosexuals isn't justified, most Americans are opposed to hiring them for jobs that might bring them into contact with the young'.[77] The NGTF had also admitted that 'the public still finds homosexuality to be "abnormal" and is not ready to accept such things as gay teachers'.[78]

Immediately after the launch of Proposition 6, Carter again came under pressure from both conservatives and gay rights activists to express his support for their respective causes. On 17 June, Mondale appeared at a reception for Democratic fundraisers in San Francisco's Hall of Flowers. Some 500 gay rights activists demonstrated outside

71 George Mendenhall, 'Denver Conference', *The Advocate*, 7 September 1977.
72 Russell Chandler and John Dart, 'Many Church Leaders Oppose Prop. 6', *LAT*, 3 November 1978.
73 'More Cities Face Battles over Homosexual Rights', *NYT*, 28 May 1978.
74 Shilts, *The Mayor*, 219–31.
75 Gene I. Maeroff, 'Issue and Debate: Should Professed Homosexuals Be Permitted to Teach School?', *NYT*, 24 June 1977.
76 Grace Lichtenstein, 'California Homosexuals Prepare for Schools Battle', *NYT*, 8 August 1977.
77 Victor F. Zonana, 'California Is Roiled by a New Initiative over Homosexuals', *WSJ*, 10 October 1978.
78 'Does Support for Gay Civil Rights Spell Political Suicide?', GRNL, n.d. RMSF, G/L1, JCPL.

the building, demanding that the administration commit itself more firmly to working for gay rights. About seventy-five of these activists managed to enter the building and interrupted Mondale's speech, demanding to know when Carter was going to 'speak out on gay rights', while others were chanting 'gay rights now'. Mondale left the stage.[79] The following day, Carter was interviewed by Ann Blackman of the Associated Press and was asked whether 'homosexuality is a threat to the family. Should they be able to adopt children and teach school? And marry?' Carter replied,

> I don't see homosexuality as a threat to the family. What has caused the highly publicized confrontations on homosexuality is the desire of homosexuals for the rest of society to approve and to add its acceptance of homosexuality as a normal sexual relationship. I don't feel that it's a normal interrelationship. But at the same time, I don't feel that society, through its laws, ought to abuse or harass the homosexual. I think it's one of those things that is not accepted by most Americans as a normal sexual relationship. In my mind it's certainly not a substitute for the family life that I described to you.

Carter was then asked, 'Do you think they should be able to adopt children or teach school? Would you be upset if you knew Amy were being taught by a homosexual?' Carter replied,

> That's something I'd rather not answer. I don't see the need to change laws to permit homosexuals to marry. I know that there are homosexuals who teach and the children don't suffer. But this is a subject I don't particularly want to involve myself in. I've got enough problems without taking on another.[80]

Naturally, gay rights activists were unhappy with Carter's comments; they had expected him to take a stronger and more clear-cut stand on the issue. Voeller and O'Leary stated that 'when the nation is concerned, the president should not intentionally avoid the issue'.[81] Despite the fact that Carter's statement was not as strong as gay rights activists had hoped for, he was still the first American president to declare that the laws should be enforced equally for gay people and that they should not be discriminated against.[82] Two days later, Haft was the keynote speaker at a GSDC meeting in Washington, D.C., where she reaffirmed Carter's commitment to equal rights for gay people. Kameny then asked her about Carter's comments to the AP which he characterized as 'a rather disdainful and cavalier dismissal of the problems of 20 million of his citizens'.[83] Haft replied:

> I cannot defend President Carter, nor will I attempt to. I will just tell you what I read and what I understand. When he said 'I don't really what to get involved in this

79 'Mondale Driven Out', *GCN*, July 1977.
80 Quoted in, 'Carter Speaks Out on Homosexuality', *AGN*, 24 June 1977.
81 'Carter Takes Stand: Gay Is Not Normal', *Out!* 29 July 1977.
82 Memorandum, Marilyn Haft to Dick Pettigrew, 28 November 1977. MCSF, GRJCV, JCPL.
83 Lou Romano, 'Aide Clarifies Carter Views', *The Blade*, July 1977.

> question', I think he was talking about whether gay people are accepted sexually or not. I think what he said in the centre of his statement was the key issue, and what the President should be doing. Which is, he does not believe the laws should be used to discriminate against gay people or to harass gay people.[84]

Costanza publicly defended Carter's statement in an interview with *Gay Community News*:

> Sure, his comment on gay teachers should bother some of you, but have you ever heard any president speak openly on this issue? Especially after the massive defeat of the referendum in Miami? Here's a president who says he doesn't see 'homosexuality as a threat'. That to me is . . . well, have you ever heard Ford say that? President Carter, even during the campaign, did not say anything about supporting or understanding the gay life-style. He did say that he would sign a gay rights bill into law. That's an incredibly positive statement for a president to make.[85]

Rosalynn Carter also made a public statement on the issue. After attending the President's Commission on Mental Health in San Francisco, she was asked by journalists about her opinion generally on gay people. She said, 'I think they deserve to be heard by society. I don't think they should be harassed'. Asked if she would mind if their daughter Amy was taught by a gay teacher, she replied, 'I think Jimmy answered that question very well!'[86]

Meanwhile, in California, gay rights activists were preparing for the ballot and had received large sums of money for their campaign from various celebrities like Rock Hudson, Burt Lancaster, Donna Summer and John Travolta.[87] The most well-known gay rights activist in the state at the time was Milk, who had also gained the attention and support of Costanza.[88] Milk co-founded the Fund to Defeat the Briggs Initiative to help raise funds for the anti-Proposition 6 campaign. He took part in a series of public debates with Briggs over the initiative, featured frequently as a gay rights advocate on network TV, and became a totemic figure for the anti-Proposition 6 campaign.[89] On 25 June 1978, in a speech at Gay Freedom Day in San Francisco, Milk railed against the hypocrisy of anti-gay rights campaigners such as Bryant and Briggs. He called on lesbian and gay rights activists to rally behind the cause of gay rights and insist that Carter start to deliver on the human rights initiatives that they demanded. Milk also addressed Carter directly:

> I am tired of the silence from the White House. Jimmy Carter: You talk about human rights a lot. In fact, you want to be the world's leader for human rights. Well, damn it: lead. There are some 15–20 million lesbians and gay men in this

84 Ibid.
85 Jim Marko, 'Midge Costanza: Gay Rights Proponent at the White House', *GCN*, 9 July 1977.
86 'Names/Faces: Where Others Fear to Tread', *WS*, 22 June 1977.
87 Faderman and Timmons, *Gay L.A.*, 227.
88 Letter, Midge Costanza to Harvey Milk, 30 July 1978. MCSF, [GR-HMSL], JCPL.
89 Shilts, *The Mayor*, 240–50.

> nation listening and listening very carefully . . . now the time has come for you to speak out. When are you? . . . When you do speak out, then and only then, will some twenty million lesbians and gay men be able to say that Jimmy Carter is our President too. . . . And now, before it becomes too late, come to California and speak out against Briggs.[90]

Three days later, Milk sent his speech to Carter, along with a letter asking him to speak out against Proposition 6:

> Though it is a state ballot issue, it is also of great national importance and we hope you will strongly oppose it. I would very much appreciate a response to our call for your support and I would be honored to work with you to protect the human rights of all Americans.[91]

Milk also wrote to Costanza urging her to provide any help she could give to defeat Proposition 6.[92] Costanza replied with a warm and personal note stating her view that the battle against Proposition 6 was very important and 'a telling vote' for gay rights. She expressed her admiration for his speech, which she characterized as 'one of the best defenses for human rights' she had 'read or heard in a good while'. She also urged him to stay in touch and expressed her willingness to help defeat Proposition 6; she felt that 'efforts should step up right away'.[93]

Meanwhile, a number of prominent religious conservatives came to Briggs's support, including Bryant, Falwell, Tim LaHaye and Robert Grant who set up the American Christian Cause to campaign for the Briggs Initiative. Falwell and Bryant publicly and repeatedly asked Carter to come out in support of Proposition 6.[94] In mid-1978, Carter had still not taken a public stand on the issue despite the activists' repeated requests to do so: 'How many lives must be destroyed before you speak out?' Milk asked him.[95] Carter continued to ignore the appeals of both sides.

Despite the backlash that her presence in Dade County had caused to his administration, Carter did not object to a proposal by Costanza to go to California and campaign against Briggs. Determined to avoid another backlash, Costanza now took some precautions. To find an excuse to travel to California, she organized a series of meetings there with local interest groups that had nothing to do with gay rights, over a two-week period. However, while in California, she embarked on a massive campaign against Proposition 6, speaking against it in all her meetings with non-involved interest groups, as well as at several anti-Briggs events, including fundraisers, always expressing the president's opposition to the Initiative and quoting Carter's comments about ending discrimination against gay people. The anti-Briggs organizers and Costanza always used the title 'Assistant to the President' at the events, as well

90 Harvey Milk's speech at Gay Freedom Day, 25 June 1978. MCSF, [GR-HMSL], JCPL.
91 Letter, Harvey Milk to Jimmy Carter, 28 June 1978. MCSF, [GR-HMSL], JCPL.
92 Letter, Harvey Milk to Midge Costanza, 28 June 1978. MCSF, [GR-HMSL], JCPL.
93 Letter, Midge Costanza to Harvey Milk, 30 July 1978. MCSF, [GR-HMSL], JCPL.
94 Maddox, author interview; Williams, *God's Own Party*, 152, 164.
95 Shilts, *The Mayor*, 244.

as in leaflets promoting them, to add more weight to her appearance and to the events. Costanza's appearances caused a major stir in California. Notwithstanding her precautions, it soon became obvious that the real reason for her visit was Proposition 6. Costanza's presence and her stand on the Briggs Initiative led journalists to ask her whether and when Carter was going to speak out on the subject, questions she was not able to answer. Even so, Costanza's campaign in California against Proposition 6 delighted the local gay community and represented a major boost for their cause.[96] Among the fundraisers Costanza attended, one was organized by the Fund to Defeat the Briggs Initiative and another by the No on 6 Committee. The latter took place at Sheldon Andelson's home and made headlines as a male guest offered $4,000 to the campaign if Costanza would swim naked. A woman counter-offered with $4,000 if she did not do it. In order to gain both donations, Costanza swam in her bathing suit. In the end, the event raised $12,000 for the cause.[97] Schockman, who actively campaigned against the Initiative, said about Costanza's presence in California: 'As a staff person you don't do anything unless your boss endorses it. It's not like she was going to go as a private Midge Costanza, she was going as the White House assistant to Jimmy Carter, so there was a direct umbilical cord and everyone knew it.'*

Gay rights activists continued to believe that a personal public statement by Carter would turn the tide in their favour, but like the campaigners of Dade County they printed numerous T-shirts, stickers and pamphlets with Carter quotes and his picture. This merchandise, which was widely seen in California, contributed to convincing heterosexual people in the state that Carter was against Proposition 6 and that he supported gay rights.[98] The gay community received an additional boost when Andrew Young, whom Carter had appointed as Ambassador to the United Nations, publicly spoke against Proposition 6 and also revealed that he had hired an openly gay man as nanny for his children.[99]

Two months before the vote, polls put Proposition 6 ahead by 61 to 31 per cent. However, things began to change after a massive campaign by gay rights activists and sympathizers, but mostly after several influential politicians such as Gerald Ford and Ronald Reagan, and Catholic Church leaders, publicly opposed the Proposition.[100] Particularly important to the turnaround was Reagan's contribution, which somewhat overshadowed Carter's later support. Reagan's aides admitted that it was 'a close call' whether he would support or oppose the Proposition,[101] and it was later revealed that he had opposed it only after he was assured by Evelle Younger, California's Attorney General, that the state had already adequate laws to protect children from teachers who were 'seeking to indoctrinate them into homosexual conduct'.[102] On 6 October, the American Psychiatric Association issued a statement that suggested that teachers 'should be judged only on the basis of professional competence, not on the basis

[96] Britt, Higgins, Perry and Schockman, author interviews; Don L. Volk, 'Community Interview: Midge Costanza', *L.A. Edge*, 15–29 June 1983.
[97] Don L. Volk, 'Community Interview: Midge Costanza', *L.A. Edge*, 15–29 June 1983.
[98] Britt, Higgins, Perry and Schockman, author interviews.
[99] Bush, author interview.
[100] Faderman and Timmons, *Gay L.A.*, 227–8.
[101] Rutledge, *The Gay Decades*, 128.
[102] 'Candidates Take Stand on Gay Rights', *Gaze*, April 1980.

of personal lifestyle or sexual preference'.[103] Despite all this, three weeks before the election, polls still showed strong support for Proposition 6, which had an even chance of passing.[104] In mid-to-late October, Costanza, who was no longer working for the administration, appeared at a series of events in support of the campaign to defeat it.[105] During an interview with the *San Francisco Chronicle*, she was asked whether Carter would make a forceful statement for gay rights. She replied, 'The President doesn't understand the gay issue. He has trouble with it. He's a wonderful guy and supports human rights, but personally, I just think he's uncomfortable with the issue'.[106]

When November came, Carter had yet to take a stand on the subject. The same month he endorsed the re-election of Democratic Governor Jerry Brown in California. Brown opposed Proposition 6 and was popular among California's gay community. On 3 November, just four days before the ballot, Carter appeared at one of Brown's rallies in Sacramento. In the audience there were some gay rights activists who were shouting 'No on 6' and holding placards with the same message. Finally, Carter publicly expressed his opposition to the Initiative; at the end of his speech, he said, 'I also want to ask everybody to vote against Proposition 6'. For this statement, Carter received the loudest applause of his speech.[107] The *Sentinel* hailed Carter with the headline 'A President Makes History',[108] while Randy Shilts characterized Carter's statement as 'a big boost for gays'.[109]

However, shortly afterwards it emerged thanks to an unexpectedly open microphone that Carter had spoken only after Brown had reassured him, 'You'll get your loudest applause if you do. It's going to be defeated and Ford and Reagan have already come out against it, so I think it's perfectly safe'. Only then did Carter turn back to the crowd and ask them to vote against it.[110] The revelation disappointed some in the gay community.[111] Religious conservatives were also unhappy with Carter's statement, for the obvious opposite reasons. Guy Archer Weniger, president of the Fundamental Baptist Fellowship, said that Carter's actions had 'cast grave doubt over the credibility of his confession of being born again by associating himself on the side of moral perversion and homosexual wickedness'.[112]

On 7 November, Proposition 6 was easily defeated by 3.9 million to 2.8 million votes (58 to 42 per cent).[113] Although Carter's public opposition to Proposition 6 came very late and under the circumstances described above, it could be regarded as 'better late than never'; his statement made him the *first* sitting president to publicly support a gay rights ordinance. Although it is not possible to calculate Carter's

103 APA, News Release, 6 October 1977. SWSF, [NGTF: Agency Meetings], JCPL.
104 Faderman and Timmons, *Gay L.A.*, 228.
105 Scott P. Anderson, 'Prop. 6 News', *The Advocate*, 29 November 1978; 'Fonda and Costanza to Speak Anti-Prop 6', The name of the newspaper is not visible, 13 October 1978. NGTFR, B.152, F.49, CU.
106 Clendinen and Nagourney, *Out*, 406.
107 Harry Kelly, 'Carter Risks Ire of Gay Foes', *Chicago Tribune*, 4 November 1978.
108 'A President Makes History', *The Sentinel*, 17 November 1978.
109 Shilts, *The Mayor*, 247.
110 Harry Kelly, 'Carter Risks Ire of Gay Foes', *Chicago Tribune*, 4 November 1978.
111 Britt, author interview.
112 Robert Freedman, 'The Religious Right and the Carter Administration', *The Historical Journal* 48, no. 1 (2005): 242.
113 Clendinen and Nagourney, *Out*, 389.

contribution to the vote turnaround, the fact is that three weeks before the election, and after Reagan, Ford and Brown had spoken publicly against the Proposition, the polls showed that the result could go either way. Despite the lateness and hesitancy of his intervention, gay rights activists at the time praised it and considered it to be crucial to the defeat of Proposition 6.[114] The NGTF sent him a letter thanking him for his support and his contribution to the defeat of the Proposition, but also asked him to be bolder: 'while we applaud your past interest as well as your recent statement against the Briggs Amendment, we nevertheless feel it is imperative that you speak out forcefully and specifically in the near future in favor of equal rights for gay citizens'.[115] Britt suggested that the T-shirts and pamphlets the activists had printed with Carter's face and statements were perhaps more helpful to the Proposition's defeat than Carter's belated statement.* Clay argued that Carter's contribution to the Initiative's defeat was 'decisive'.* Higgins praised the contribution of both Carter and Costanza: 'Midge was much more vocally supportive than he was, of course, but he did come out in support of a "No" vote, and this was all that mattered to us. It was actually more than enough and yes, it certainly played an important role in defeating Proposition 6'.* Sandifer told the author 'Polls showed there was an even chance [as to the outcome] and we were all very concerned about it. I believe Carter's intervention turned the tide. The opinions of governors and other politicians are important, but the most important contribution certainly comes from the president'.*

From the disappointed supporters of Proposition 6, the White House received numerous protest letters. For example, William Hann, President of the Southern Baptist Convention of California, wrote to Carter that they had 'worked hard to pass Proposition 6 and your 'statement hurt us'. Robert Hughes, of the same Church, also wrote to Carter to inform him that the Convention had passed a resolution which expressed the Church's 'grave disappointment' over his 'public opposition to an issue so strongly supported by his fellow Christians and Baptists'.[116] While the defeat of Proposition 6 was a major win for gay rights activists, it also left them no better off than before. Finally, almost two years later, Carter would take a much stronger stand on the issue of gay teachers and would publicly support their right to teach in federally operated classrooms such as on Army bases.[117]

☙

This chapter has particularly explored the public face of President Carter's administration's engagement with gay rights issues – the face in large measure of Margaret Costanza. Of course many of the changes explored in this book had a symbolic and legitimating aspect that was vitally important, but it is an intervention

[114] Britt, Clay, Higgins, Kent, Perry and Schockman, author interviews.

[115] Letter, Jean O'Leary and Bruce Voeller to President Carter, 26 December 1978. NGTFR, B.152, F.46, CU.

[116] Neil J. Young, 'Worse than Cancer and Worse than Snakes', *The Journal of Policy History* 26, no. 4 (2014): 490.

[117] Moral Majority report, 'Religious Leaders Join Task Force in 10-hour Meet', undated. RLMSF, GI, JCPL.

of a different order when the president or his close adviser actually speaks. That is the more true when the issue becomes conflicted, inspiring both stronger advocacy in its favour and stronger and more overt resistance, as this of course brings the president's future electoral prospects into question. Hence this chapter has traced an ambiguous record, with numerous important firsts and the display of clear signals from Carter, most obviously in his permission for Costanza to campaign in two high-profile local gay rights debates, but also some hesitancy on his part to make positive public statements. He was evidently aware of the likelihood that positive statements would provoke further questions, pressing for bolder answers, and both his own thoughts about sexuality and family, which he tried to shelter behind his version of the wall of separation, and his concern for electoral viability, set off warnings. Even so, Carter's negotiation of the rapidly burgeoning cultural conflict of the late 1970s, to which of course he significantly contributed, presents a creditable record, in which his abhorrence of discrimination still shines out amid the forces converging on him.

12

The White House Conference on families

Few single words could better express the rapid changes in the terms of political debate during Carter's presidency than the word 'family'. The issue of the family and the need to strengthen it was pointed out by Carter during his 1976 election campaign.[1] On 4 October 1976, Carter had announced in a speech at the National Conference of Catholic Charities that, were he elected, he would convene a White House Conference on the American Family.[2] He believed that the family was in 'trouble' because of the government's 'confusion or insensitivity', that its policies had 'weakened our families, or even destroyed them', and that the level of family breakdown had reached 'dangerous proportions'. He argued that it was the role of government to do everything it could to 'support and strengthen the American family'.[3]

However, by the end of his presidency, the term 'family' had come to encapsulate much that the growing forces of cultural conservatism and religious fundamentalism were finding abhorrent about political and cultural change, and increasingly about the Carter administration. The very anxieties about family that he had expressed in 1976 had become the prerogative of Carter's bitterest opponents and of the Republican Party, and while much of this reaction was provoked by feminist advances to which Carter was also sympathetic, an increasingly important element was the emerging visibility of the gay rights cause. The idea of having a conference on the family had probably seemed relatively uncontroversial when it was first mooted, but it was quickly evident that it was likely to be a highly contentious event and a flashpoint for the culture war that was steadily heating up.

A 'flawed beginning' and a relaunch

As incoming president, Carter considered the state of the family to be one of his priority issues. Thus, he took the idea of the Conference very seriously, and shortly after he was sworn in, he sent a $3 million budget recommendation for planning and

1 Michael Novak, *The Spirit of Democratic Capitalism* (Lanham, New York: Madison Books, 1982), 157.

2 Leo P. Ribuffo, 'Family Policy Past as Prologue: Jimmy Carter, the White House Conference on Families, and the Mobilization of the New Christian Right', *Review of Policy Research* 23, no. 2 (2006): 311.

3 WHCF, *Listening to America's Families*, 56.

development to Congress, which approved it.[4] On 30 January 1978, he announced that the Conference would be held on 9–13 December 1979 in Washington, D.C.,[5] and would 'examine the strengths of American families, the difficulties they face, and the ways in which family life is affected by public policies'.[6] Carter immediately signalled his intention for the Conference to be diverse and open to everyone. Mike Grant, public affairs specialist for the Conference, said, 'We are simply trying to involve everybody. We are giving citizens a vehicle to talk about issues that adversely affect families. We hope to hear from as diverse groups as possible'.[7] In order for the Conference to recognize diversity in the different types of families, Carter changed the word 'Family' in its title to 'Families'. Conservatives, like Phyllis Schlafly, interpreted the term 'diversity' as coded language for gay families.[8]

Carter designated Joseph Califano, his HEW Secretary, to organize the White House Conference on Families (WHCF). He then set up an Advisory Council to help plan the Conference, consisting of forty-two religious and service organizations such as the Red Cross, the National Council of Churches and Planned Parenthood. Among them was the NGTF.[9] He also appointed Wilbur Cohen, former Secretary of HEW, as chairman of the WHCF, and Patricia Fleming, his special assistant at HEW, as the WHCF's Executive Director. The fact that Fleming was a divorcee prompted widespread criticism from Catholics. Within two months of her appointment, Fleming resigned after Califano insisted she accept Francis Butler, a Catholic married man and director of social policy for the US Catholic Conference, as her co-director, a move designed to appease Catholic objectors to Fleming. In June 1978, Cohen also resigned for health reasons.[10] Further controversy arose when Califano, who supported gay rights, invited Jean O'Leary to participate in the planning of the WHCF and when the Advisory Council recommended that 'same-sex couples' be included in the Conference.[11] Meanwhile, there were fears in the administration that a December 1979 conference would provoke pre-election conflicts about abortion and homosexuality. Already facing the organizational problems mentioned above, Carter decided to postpone the WHCF.[12]

In summer 1979, Carter revived his plan for the WHCF and again began planning for it, but this time without Califano whom he had dismissed. The news of the revived Conference mobilized gay rights activists and the religious right, and the two sides prepared for another battle. However, they were not the only ones with an interest in the Conference as a wide range of bodies was quick to jump on board the train; every demographic in the US seemed to have a stake in the WHCF, so a number of coalitions

4 USCSCHR, *WHCF 1978* (Washington: U.S. Govt. Print. Off., 1978), 1–2.
5 OWHPS, Press Release, 30 January 1978. RWHPO, WHCF, JCPL.
6 Ribuffo, 'Family Policy Past', 321.
7 Victoria Irwin, 'Factions Seek Control of Family Conference', *The Christian Science Monitor*, 13 February 1980.
8 Ruth Murray-Brown, *For Christian America: A History of the Religious Right* (Amherst, NY: Prometheus Books, 2002), 143–4.
9 'Carter's Family Conference Controversy Spreads', *BAR*, 17 August 1978.
10 Spencer Rich, 'Strife, Touchy Issues Sank Conference on Families', *WP*, 24 June 1978.
11 'Carter's Family Conference Controversy Spreads', *BAR*, 17 August 1978.
12 Spencer Rich, 'Old Conflicts Buttoned Down, Family Conference Looking Up', *WP*, 21 August 1979.

were formed. Most influential among them was the Coalition for the White House Conference on Families (Coalition for the WHCF) which consisted of fifty national religious, advocacy and social service organizations and aimed to monitor and encourage participation. Its component groups had a centrist or liberal orientation, embracing organizations such as the NGTF, a number of Catholic charities, the Red Cross, the National Council of Jewish Women and other church and welfare bodies. The founder and chairman of the Coalition was Robert M. Rice, director of Policy Analysis and Development for the Family Service Association of America. Rice was very liberal and a supporter of gay rights; he had personally invited the NGTF to join the Coalition and had turned down an application for membership by Schlafly's Eagle Forum. The Coalition, although unofficial, became an integral part of the planning of the WHCF and collaborated closely with the White House and Carter's advisory committee for the Conference.[13] The Coalition's vice-chairman was Joseph Giordano, director of the Center on Group Identity and Mental Health, Institute on Pluralism and Group Identity.[14]

In April 1979, Carter appointed Jim Guy Tucker, former Congressman from Arkansas, as chairperson of his intended National Advisory Committee (NAC) and of the Conference itself. Carter also appointed John Carr, coordinator for urban issues of the US Catholic Conference, as the WHCF's executive director. Carter and Tucker began appointing members to the forty-member NAC.[15] The Federal Advisory Committee Act of 1972 required 'the membership of [such an] advisory committee to be fairly balanced in terms of the points of view represented',[16] and gay rights activists and conservatives both sought to gain representation in the NAC and hence, more importantly, the Conference. For gay rights activists this was an important occasion to present themselves as part of the mainstream of American society and not just a fringe group, while conservatives wanted to make their opposition known and to avoid a repeat of their marginalization at the National Women's Conference in Houston two years earlier (see Chapter 5). On 29 May 1979, Ira Glaser, the ACLU's Executive Director, wrote to Tucker to ask him to recommend the appointment to the NAC of 'at least one person representing same sex families'.[17] The NGTF also asked Carr and Tucker to appoint a representative from their organization.[18] The religious right was far more persistent than the gay rights activists and used political connections and lobbying in an effort to have one of its representatives selected for the Committee. For example, James Dobson, founder of Focus on the Family, urged his followers to conduct a write-in campaign to secure him a place on the NAC. As a result the White House received about 80,000 letters requesting Dobson be selected to the Committee.[19]

13 Eagle Forum, 'WHCF Material', undated, and Cynthia Miller, 'Homosexuals!! An Official American Family Unit', undated, both in RLMSF, GI, JCPL.

14 USCSCHR, *WHCF 1978*, 489.

15 WHCF, *Listening to America's Families*, 57–8.

16 5 U.S. Code 1004 (Public Law 92-463, s. 5).

17 Letter, Ira Glasser to Jim Guy Tucker, 29 May 1979. NGTFR, B.142, F.5, CU.

18 Ribuffo, 'Family Policy Past', 322.

19 Dan Gilgoff, *The Jesus Machine. How James Dobson, Focus on the Family, and Evangelical America Are Winning the Culture War* (New York: St Martin's Press, 2007), 31.

In the end, in order to avoid internal conflicts in the NAC, Carter and Tucker did not appoint to it either any openly gay people or activists, or members of the religious right.[20] The NAC consisted of forty members, twenty-one men and nineteen women.[21] Although there were no openly gay people or gay rights activists, the majority of the appointments were politically progressive. Among them were Mario Cuomo, a long-time gay rights supporter who had appointed several openly gay people, including Apuzzo, to high-level positions while serving as Governor of New York; Coretta Scott King (who served as deputy chairperson); Rice, chairman of the Coalition for the WHCF; and Eleanor Smeal, the president of NOW. In order to balance the Committee and to comply with the law, it included some conservative religious leaders, though no members of the religious right, such as Harry Hollis, a Southern Baptist, and Barbara Smith, General President of the Mormon Relief Society.[22]

Despite persistent calls by prominent conservatives for Schlafly's appointment to the NAC, Carter and Tucker refused to appoint her. Schlafly, aggrieved also at the earlier denial of her application to join the Coalition for the WHCF, filed a lawsuit against the NAC claiming that it was going to use federal funds to lobby for interest groups.[23] Falwell did not even bother applying, saying that 'we probably would have been rejected'. Nevertheless, under pressure, Tucker agreed to appoint some additional conservatives, such as Dobson, Connie Marshner and Jerry Regier, as at-large delegates to the Conference. But conservatives continued to believe that the NAC was 'stacked with liberal, social welfare, government types'.[24] The Eagle Forum argued that, contrary to the balanced membership requirement, only 'a few token pro-family' members had been appointed to the NAC.[25]

The NGTF was also not happy with the NAC because it did not include anyone representing same-sex couples.[26] An unnamed member of the NGTF argued that the Conference organizers were afraid that if they had included a gay representative, the religious right would have accused them of destroying the American family. A disappointed Valeska commented, 'We tried desperately to get a seat on the Advisory Committee. There is representation of every group under the sun on the committee, but there is no gay representative'.[27]

Carter, Tucker and Carr agreed to a new format for the Conference. Carr felt strongly that the Conference should be 'decentralized', so instead of a single gathering in Washington, D.C., which was the customary location for White House conferences,[28] there would be three conferences – in Baltimore, Minneapolis and Los Angeles – in the

20 Weddington, author interview.
21 WHCF, *Listening to America's Families*, 6.
22 Eagle Forum, 'WHCF Material', undated. RLMSF, GI, JCPL; Report from the WHCF, 'Diverse Group of 40 Leads Conference', August 1979. LBP, B.5, F.43, CU.
23 Murray-Brown, *For Christian America*, 108.
24 Flippen, *Jimmy Carter*, 266.
25 Eagle Forum, 'WHCF Material', undated. RLMSF, GI, JCPL.
26 Letter, Lucia Valeska and C.F. Brydon to the Coalition for the WHCF, 22 August 1979. NGTFR, B.142, F.14, CU.
27 'Homosexuality & Abortion', *OOB*, December 1979.
28 The IWY Conference was not technically a White House conference.

summer of 1980.[29] It was also agreed that each event would last for forty-eight hours and would include a variety of different sessions and events. The format also specified a series of public regional hearings in seven different cities, between September 1979 and January 1980. Their purpose was to 'reach out, not only to scholars and to experts, but to many thousands of Americans around this country who know from their own experience what makes a family strong', to enable them to describe their families' 'concerns, ideas, successes and problems about contemporary life'. The results of these hearings would provide data for the three final conferences to analyse and develop into recommendations. In addition to the regional hearings, each state and territory was to conduct from November 1979 to May 1980 its own state conference, a forum-type event in which members of the public could discuss family-related issues and choose delegates. Delegates elected from each state conference would attend one of the regional conferences, bringing with them ten topics drawn from the concerns expressed by the attendees of their state conference. Each state conference would lay out a platform, which would be sent to the White House. Tucker assigned liaisons to all states and territories, making them responsible for organizing the local conferences.[30]

After a 'flawed beginning', as Eizenstat characterized it in November 1979,[31] referring to the delays and the postponement, organization of the Conference was now well underway. However, the bottom-up and decentralized structure of the process would prove to be vulnerable to well-organized conservative forces, threatening Carter's original conception of the Conference. It would eventually be modified, causing further political strife. And an even more difficult problem quickly became visible, which had not been solved but merely highlighted by renaming the conference a Conference on *Families*. The grammatical change scarcely addressed the suddenly visible political difficulty of agreeing what a family was.

'What is a family?'

Even before preparations for the White House Conference on Families got underway, everyone involved had run into a fundamental problem, a problem that probably had not even occurred to Carter as a possibility until then: there was no consensus on what the word 'family' meant. Merely replacing the singular with the plural had not solved the problem, since the lack of consensus it signalled was experienced by many on the religious right as an attack on values that they held very dear personally and that they believed were hugely important for the well-being of the American nation: they wanted to restore what they saw as a consensus under threat, and to promote a singular and

29 Spencer Rich, 'Old Conflicts Buttoned Down, Family Conference Looking Up', *WP*, 21 August 1979; WHCF, *Listening to America's Families*, 60. The elaborate structure creates some problems of reference, which sources often exacerbate rather than resolve: 'Conference' can refer to the whole process, from delegate selection to final report, to one or all three of the main regional events, or to the numerous prior state conferences. Below, clarifications will be given where necessary.

30 Report from the WHCF, 'NAC Establishes Conference Goals', August 1979. LBP, B.5, F.43, CU; WHCF: Guide for National Organizations, undated. NGTFR, B.142, F.13 CU.

31 Memorandum, Stuart Eizenstat to Fran Voorde, 5 November 1979. F.TR96, B.TR33, JCPL.

traditional conception of family, not a plural and diverse one.[32] They wanted the state to endorse their conception of a family as a set of persons bound together by ties of blood, marriage or adoption; 'two unmarried, unrelated people are not a family', they argued.[33] The centrist and left-leaning delegates took a broader view, seeing a family as including anyone in a relationship of mutual love and caring, even if they were unmarried or gay.[34]

The NGTF had expressed its view on this matter of definition in the first, abortive, phase of preparation for the WHCF, in which Congressional Joint Hearings on the WHCF had been organized to review the plans for the Conference. The NGTF was invited to testify by the Coalition for the WHCF. In its testimony of 3 February 1978, it said that in order to 'strengthen and support' the American family, people needed first to ask, 'what is a family?' Its answer was that a family involves 'two basic human needs': 'The need of each individual to share love and caring with other human beings and to take responsibility in other people's lives' and 'The need of children to depend on adults during their formative years, not only for their safety and survival but for the experience, love and caring that will enable them to make rewarding relationships with other human beings as independent adults'. It concluded, 'We believe that a working definition of "family" is any constellation of two or more individuals which meets one or both of these basic human needs'.[35]

The White House did not want to cause further controversy and avoided adopting an official definition of family.[36] However, it was impossible to avoid being drawn into this debate, in part because of Carter's existing and strong stance against discrimination, and also because of decisions that would need to be made about the procedures for selecting delegates. In July 1979, Carter held a reception in the White House for the WHCF and the NAC, essentially a relaunch of the Conference programme. He attempted to strike a progressive note while also evoking traditional family themes of filial and marital affection and generational change:

> We often feel nostalgic about a past that seems to be simpler and sometimes seems to be better, and we can learn from the past, but we must not limit our vision of what a good family is just to what a family was in the past. Instead, we must find meaning in today's challenges, and today's realities, which we cannot change, honestly, creatively, with courage and with compassion. . . . Families, as you well know, are more than just households. They are a network of relationships rooted not just in kinship based on blood, but a kinship based on shared experiences, shared joys and sorrows, and I think most of all, in shared love that crosses vast distances and also crosses very easily the barrier of generations.[37]

32 Tony Campolo, author interview.
33 Nadine Brozan, 'White House Conference on the Family: A Schism Develops', *NYT*, 7 January 1980.
34 Bush, author interview; Victoria Irwin, 'Factions Seek Control of Family Conference', *The Christian Science Monitor*, 13 February 1980.
35 Testimony from the NGTF, Hearings on the 1979 WHCF, January 1978. NGTFR, B.142, F.5, CU.
36 Eizenstat and Weddington, author interviews.
37 OWHPS, 'Remarks of the President at Reception for WHCF, undated. NGTFR, B.142, F.5, CU.

These somewhat general but heart-warming pronouncements provoked a rather direct question from a member of the NAC: whether 'two people of the same sex living together in the same household' should be considered to be a family. Carter replied 'yes', and that all types of families should be included (this reply was not however disseminated outside the meeting).[38] Carter's commitment to anti-discrimination entailed, for him, inclusiveness, a reluctance to exclude anyone; he did not mention gay people directly, but he could not exclude them, and Tucker and the NAC echoed this ineffectively evasive pattern by speaking frequently of the 'pluralistic' nature of the American family and its 'diversity', as well as of families with 'different structures and lifestyles'.[39]

The gay community was on the whole satisfied with Carter's definitions, mostly on account of the fact that he and Tucker had not yielded to pressure from the religious right to adopt *its* definition.[40] For its part, the religious right condemned Carter and Tucker's position; Beverly LaHaye, of Concerned Women of America, said that the WHCF was 'geared up toward changing the definition of the family' to legitimize homosexuality, divorce and children born outside of wedlock.[41]

The NAC began its work of establishing the goals of the WHCF, in particular trying to determine which families the Conference would consider and involve. It was agreed that specific attention should be paid to poor families, single-parent families, the handicapped, the elderly, and members of ethnic, racial and religious minorities. Smeal suggested that gay families should also be included, giving rise to a debate. Another member suggested, 'we want to talk about homosexuality somewhere along the line, but we don't want to make it a goal'.[42] Eventually it was agreed that gay families should be included among the Conference's themes, thus recognizing the existence of such families, but that this should be done in a way that avoided explicitly mentioning them.[43] The Committee thus referred to the diversity and pluralistic nature of families and acknowledged the need for families with 'differences in structure and lifestyles' to receive 'understanding and respect'.[44] Furthermore, it was agreed that rules for the regional conferences would contain a clause barring discrimination on the basis of sexual orientation for participants of the conferences as well as potential delegates. Tucker told the NAC that more direct action and explicit language regarding gay people would threaten the Conference's overall objectives.[45] The Committee eventually adopted six themes for the Conference: Family Strengths and Supports, the Changing Realities of Family Life, the Impact of Public and Private Institutional Policies on Families, the Impact of Discrimination, Families with Special Needs and Diversity of Families. The

38 Weddington, author interview.

39 Bush, Jones-Hennin, Maddox and Weddington, author interviews; Clendinen and Nagourney, *Out*, 422; Ann Hulbert, 'The Baltimore Bust', *The New Republic*, 28 June 1980; 'White House Conference on Families: Goals', NAC, n.d. LBP, B.5, F.41, CU.

40 Bush and Jones-Hennin, author interviews.

41 Quoted in Ribuffo, 'Family Policy Past', 325.

42 Quoted in Letter, C.F. Brydon and Lucia Valeska to the NAC, 22 August 1979. NGTFR, B.142, F.14, CU.

43 Bush, author interview.

44 WHCF, *Listening to America's Families*, 59.

45 Larry Bush, 'Family Conference Drops Gays', *The Blade*, 13 September 1979; Bush, author interview; Eagle Forum, 'WHCF Material', undated. RLMSF, GI, JCPL.

last contained the following explanation: 'American families are pluralistic in nature. Our discussion of issues will reflect an understanding and respect of cultural, ethnic and regional differences as well as differences in structure and lifestyles'.[46]

The 'Diversity' theme and its description were perceived by both the gay community and conservatives as a veiled allusion to gay families,[47] correctly in the recollection of Robert Maddox and Sarah Weddington;* as was already apparent, veiled language was no longer any defence against the predictable reactions by gay rights activists and the religious right. Unlike most gay rights activist groups, the NGTF, which learnt, presumably from Smeal, all the details of the NAC's meeting establishing goals and themes, was not satisfied with the language of diversity, pluralism and different lifestyles and wanted an explicit reference to gay families. Thus, on 22 August, Brydon and Valeska wrote to the NAC to complain. The letter pointedly asked the NAC, 'can the "impact of discrimination" be seriously approached if the Conference itself is a discriminator?' Clearly frustrated by the exclusion of a representative of gay families, they wrote (and underlined the text for emphasis): 'We do not intend to remain invisible. We will demand the right to open participation in deliberations that affect our lives. We will seek representation, according to our numbers in this society, at the state and regional family conferences. And in order to do that, we need your help'. At the end of their letter Brydon and Valeska said they had been 'impressed' by Carter's statement to the NAC about not limiting its vision of what a good family was and asked the Committee 'in the name of that broad vision' that gay families 'be openly included in the Conference process'.[48]

The same day, Valeska and Brydon wrote to the NGTF's members to inform them that planning for the state conferences was underway and urged them to contact conference coordinators in their state to ensure gay participation at the state level and to help elect gay people as delegates.[49] Also, they wrote to the members of the Coalition for the WHCF to ask for support for their request to give a presentation to state conference directors on the need for gay family participation. The NGTF argued that such a presentation was necessary if gay delegates were to be included at the state level.[50] In response, the Coalition wrote to the NAC and requested that the recognition of 'diverse family forms' should be made more specific and should explicitly mention that gay families were included.[51] Tucker ignored this request.

As the NGTF's letter makes clear, at issue was not only the language of the agenda but also the procedures for selecting delegates, which would directly impact the scope of discussion at the Conference. In order to meet the aspiration for diversity, which originated with Carter, the NAC established rules which included an open process for selection, including public balloting and selection at random. In each state, a minimum of 30 per cent of the allotted delegates were to be elected by popular vote, another 30 per

46 WHCF, *Listening to America's Families*, 59.

47 Bush and Jones-Hennin, author interviews; Report from the WHCF, 'Themes Cite Family Strengths, Diversity', August 1979. LBP, B.5, F.43, CU.

48 Letter, C.F. Brydon and Lucia Valeska to the NAC, 22 August 1979. NGTFR, B.142, F.14, CU.

49 Letter, Lucia Valeska and C.F. Brydon to State Contacts, 22 August 1979. NGTFR, B.142, F.14, CU.

50 Letter, Lucia Valeska and C.F. Brydon to the Coalition for the WHCF, 22 August 1979. NGTFR, B.142, F.14, CU.

51 Letter, Virginia Martin to the NAC, 7 September 1979. NGTFR, B.144, F.58, CU.

cent to be selected by the state's governor, and the other 40 per cent to be chosen by the state's steering committee and the NAC, with a small number also being drawn from a lottery barrel. The NAC's guidelines regarding the selection of delegates included a clause which prohibited discrimination against gay people,[52] meaning that gay people and gay families were allowed to participate in the conferences and to be elected as delegates. Tucker repeatedly reinforced this inclusive message to the coordinators of state conferences.[53] The religious right objected strongly and repeatedly called upon Carter and the NAC to exclude gay people, but to no avail,[54] while Tucker received numerous protest phone calls.[55]

Conservatives, whose outrage had not diminished since the NAC's assertion that 'American families are pluralistic in nature' and had 'different structures and lifestyles', were angered even further when Tucker met with the Liberty Court Group, a coalition of leaders and financiers of the religious right led by Paul Weyrich, to explain to them the goals of the Conference. Among the participants was Connie Marshner, who asked Tucker whether his definition of the family was 'the traditional one of people related by blood, marriage or adoption'. Tucker bluntly answered in the negative; he said that he believed that a family could consist of any set of at least two people living with each other and committed to their mutual well-being.[56] This was not all; Tucker excited further hostility when he later publicly characterized some pro-family advocates as 'extremists' and admitted that his definition of a family included 'homosexuals' and 'cohabiting unmarrieds'.[57]

Marshner and Weyrich then demanded, unsuccessfully, to meet Carter to discuss the issue of the family and the conference more generally. Robert Maddox instead agreed to meet them, but not in the White House. In the meeting, Maddox restated Carter's stance on the inclusion of gay people and of gay families in the Conference. To the question of whether a gay couple could be called a family, he said, 'Sure, yes. They call themselves a family, they are a family'. He clarified, against their objections, that Carter did not want to 'promote homosexuality', and that he simply wanted 'all Americans to have equal rights' irrespective of their sexual preference. To Maddox, it seemed that Marshner and Weyrich had 'their knives out to trash and destroy Carter'.[58]

The definition of 'family' continued to be an issue of constant debate and conflict at the state conferences. For example, in March 1980 during the state conference in Atlanta it was agreed that gay people should be included within the definition. However, when the proceedings of the conference were released this definition was

52 JoAnn Gasper, 'White House Conference on Families: Stacking the Deck', *Conservative Digest*, May/June 1980, and Eagle Forum, 'WHCF Material', undated, both in RLMSF, GI, JCPL; WHCF, *Listening to America's Families*, 68.

53 Nadine Brozan, 'White House Conference on the Family: A Schism Develops', *NYT*, 7 January 1980; Bush, author interview; Eagle Forum, 'WHCF Material', undated. RLMSF, GI, JCPL.

54 Bush, Maddox and Weddington, author interviews; Eagle Forum, 'WHCF Material', undated. RLMSF, GI, JCPL.

55 Ellen Goodman, 'Family Feud', *WP*, 27 February 1980.

56 Clendinen and Nagourney, *Out*, 422.

57 Eagle Forum, 'WHCF Material', undated. RLMSF, GI, JCPL.

58 Maddox, author interview.

excluded. It turned out that the definition had been removed by Georgia Governor George Busbee on the basis that sodomy and gay marriages were illegal in Georgia.[59] The issue gained yet further prominence when a permissive policy on adoption by same-sex couples was announced by the Office for Families (see Chapter 10), created by Carter as part of the Conference initiative.

The Houston battle revived: 'Not this time'

After Carter announced the rescheduling of the WHCF for the summer of 1980, the NGTF, the NCBG and other gay organizations began their efforts to ensure gay participation and visibility at the conferences. Several of these groups requested and received federal funding for the preparation of material to be used to advertise and promote the event in the gay community.[60] The NGTF urged the community to participate at all levels of conference preparations, become or support delegates at the state and then regional conferences and ensure the raising of gay issues at the workshops.[61] Naturally, conservatives mobilized too, in massive numbers. For them, the conference was an important opportunity to voice again their opposition to gay rights, abortion and the ERA. Some conservatives, especially the religious right, wanted to avoid a repeat of the Houston Conference where they had been outnumbered and defeated by feminists and lesbians; they saw the WHCF as an ideal opportunity to avenge this defeat. An unnamed conservative told *The Christian Science Monitor*, 'We were shut out at the International Women's Year Conference. We're not going to be shut out this time'.[62] Schlafly felt the same and declared her readiness for the struggle: 'we were excluded there [the IWY Conference] because the commission was entirely pro-ERA and the rules were rigged. Now we know what to look for, and we're prepared'. Their mobilization led to the creation of the National Pro-Family Coalition on the White House Conference on the Family. The coalition, whose chairman was Marshner, consisted of more than 150 Christian conservative organizations, including the Eagle Forum and the Moral Majority.[63] Carr admitted, 'It's clear the conservative groups are making this a real priority'.[64] A number of prominent conservatives and religious right leaders continued to demand from Carter that he exclude gay couples and gay people in general from regional hearings, the state conferences, and of course the WHCF. Carter refused all these requests, and the NAC again instructed its state coordinators that there should be no discrimination against participants and potential delegates on account of sexual orientation.[65]

59 Letters, Dianne Stephenson to Randy Humphrey, 23 May 1980, George Busbee to Dianne Stephenson, 29 May 1980, Dianne Stephenson to the delegates to the WHCF, 3 June 1980; Press Release from Atlanta Gay Centre, 2 June 1980; all in NGTFR, B.142, F.13, CU.

60 Bush and Jones-Hennin, author interviews.

61 'Families Conference: Getting Involved', *It's Time*, November–December 1979. RMSF, GV, JCPL.

62 Victoria Irwin, 'Factions Seek Control of Family Conference', *The Christian Science Monitor*, 13 February 1980.

63 Nadine Brozan, 'White House Conference on the Family: A Schism Develops', *NYT*, 7 January 1980.

64 Helen Dewar, 'Conference on the Family is Rallying "New Right" Activists', *WP*, 18 June 1980.

65 Bush, Maddox and Weddington, author interviews; Eagle Forum, 'WHCF Material', undated. RLMSF, GI, JCPL.

On 11 September 1979, the White House organized an event at which 250 national organizations would be briefed on participation in the WHCF. Adding to the grievances of conservatives, the NGTF was invited to participate, while representatives of the religious right were not. The NGTF's invitation and presence at the event were important for the gay community as it effectively meant that the administration recognized the existence of gay families. Valeska, who represented the NGTF, made a point to Carter about the inclusion of gay families at the conferences; he assured her that there would be no discrimination against any American, including gay people.[66]

On 28 October 1979 in Kansas City, Rosalyn Carter opened and gave a keynote address to the first of the seven regional hearings.[67] Openly gay people gave testimony in most, if not all, of these.[68] For example, in Washington, D.C., six openly gay people – Melvin Boozer, Clint Hockenberry, Carolyn Handy, ABilly Jones-Hennin, Frank Kameny and Mayo Lee – testified before the NAC at the hearings that took place on 30 November and 1 December. Hockenberry testified on the right of gay people to marry, Handy on the problems conventional families faced with a gay child, and Boozer and Kameny spoke about the problems of gay families. But despite the strong urging of local gay rights activists and the fact that about 70,000 gay people lived in the city, very few open gays turned up to the hearings, much to the activists' disappointment.[69]

Openly gay people also had active and visible roles in most of the state conferences, if not in all of them. Despite strong protests by conservatives, gay people were allowed to participate and raise their concerns, as well as to organize their own workshops and hearings. Most of the workshops by the gay community focused on education on homosexuality and on gay rights. After lesbian women had been given, for the first time, a forum by the government to present their situation and their concerns to the American public at the IWY state conferences, it was now the gay men's turn. The process was very simple: whoever wanted to lead a workshop had to make a proposal to the state coordinators, who could accept or reject it. Workshops on homosexuality and gay rights took place in most, if not all, states, with the majority of them being held in Washington, D.C., Los Angeles and New York. For example, Dana Naparsteck,[70] a lesbian rights activist, led a workshop on the 'Diversity of Families' in Washington; Nancy Higgins led a workshop in Los Angeles on 'Gay Parents', and how gay parents could retain custody of their children; ABilly S. Jones-Hennin, who was also chosen as representative of Ward 1 of the District of Columbia, chaired one of the Conference meetings of his Ward and led a workshop on 'The Changing Realities of Family Life', where he recalled to the author highlighting 'the importance of including – or expanding the definition of – "families," and including the LGBTQ families'. The activists received

66 Eagle Forum, 'WHCF Material', undated. RLMSF, GI, JCPL; Weddington, author interview.

67 WHCF, *Listening to America's Families*, 76.

68 Bush, Higgins, Howell and Jones-Hennin, author interviews.

69 Craig Howell, 'Witnesses Speak Out for Gay Families', *The Blade*, 6 December 1979.

70 In one of the state conferences, Naparsteck and her partner Susan Silber met ABilly S. Jones and his partner Cris Hennin. In 1983, Naparsteck and Silber had their first baby with Hennin being the biological father; it was one of the first children born to open/out lesbian parents (Naparsteck, author interview).

federal funding to organize and promote their workshops.[71] Furthermore, Valeska was invited by the NAC to present to state coordinators a workshop on new lifestyles, but this was cancelled at the last minute due to 'scheduling conflicts'.[72]

The workshops on homosexuality and gay rights were extremely important as they allowed gay people to learn about their rights and their opportunities. Equally important was the fact that they provided an unprecedented visibility to gay men, as for the first time ever, gay people all over the country were able to approach and talk about their concerns with other members of their community. This was particularly beneficial in states like Utah, Wyoming and Arizona, where there was strong anti-gay sentiment and gay people had limited access to organized groups; the conferences created a much-needed 'sense of belonging' among them. What also made the conferences significant was the fact that they were organized by the White House, a clear sign for all Americans that Carter's administration considered gay people to be equal members of society.[73]

As with the IWY state conferences, the WHCF state conferences turned into battlefields between conservatives and progressives who fought over the definition of 'family' and the participation of same-sex couples. The mobilization of the anyway much smaller gay community was not a match for that of the religious right. The latter's effort bore fruit, helping them secure some early important wins. The first came in Virginia in November 1979, where they elected twenty-two of the twenty-four state delegates. The conference had not even been advertised to potential liberal participants, some of whom were only made aware of it by the NGTF. In this exceptionally hostile environment, the few gay rights issues that were raised were met with heckles and booing. More wins followed for the conservatives: Oklahoma, in December 1979, where they secured all eight available spots, and Minnesota in January–February 1980. Throughout this time, the moderates and liberals managed to elect a majority only in South Dakota.[74] Up to that point, about 80 per cent of the workshops had passed resolutions rejecting the ERA and acknowledging only 'traditional heterosexual families', while none of the openly gay candidates had been elected as delegates and the gay workshops were not well attended.[75]

On 7 January 1980, the *New York Times* ran an article headlined 'White House Conference on Families: A Schism Develops'. The article discussed the increasingly organized efforts of the religious right to gain representation and the fact that 150 organizations had come together to fight their corner.[76] The perceived attempt by the religious right to hijack the WHCF and use it for their own ends alarmed not only gay

71 Bush, Jones-Hennin and Higgins, author interviews; J.K., 'Family Conference', *OOB*, March 1980; Don Leavitt, 'Family Topics Paper Stirs More Controversy', *The Blade*, 15 May 1980.

72 Thomas J. Burrows, 'Family Values: From the White House Conference on Families to the Family Protection Act', in D'Emilio, et al., *Creating Change*, 342.

73 Bush and Jones-Hennin, author interviews.

74 Nadine Brozan, 'White House Conference on the Family: A Schism Develops', *NYT*, 7 January 1980; Helen Dewar, 'Conference on the Family is Rallying "New Right" Activists', *WP*, 18 June 1980; Eagle Forum, 'WHCF Material', undated, RLMSF, GI, JCPL.

75 See Workshop's resolutions in LBP, B.5, F.41, CU.

76 Nadine Brozan, 'White House Conference on the Family: A Schism Develops', *NYT*, 7 January 1980.

rights activists and other liberals but also Carter and the NAC.[77] A number of liberal organizations, such as the National Council of Jewish Women, wrote to the White House and the NAC to warn them.[78] Giordano of the Coalition for the WHCF also sent a warning to Carr that the 'New Right' groups posed 'a threat' to the WHCF, as they had the power to 'derail the event' because their 'tactic and militancy on the state level has succeeded in almost capturing of delegates [*sic*] in two of these states that have held preliminary state conferences and threaten other state conferences'. He urged Carr and the NAC to act by monitoring and exposing the actions of these groups and 'carefully' reviewing the guidelines for the state conferences, as well as the conferences' structure, in order to stop the religious right from monopolizing them.[79]

Meanwhile, the conservative pressure to exclude gay people and gay families increased, and there were protests outside and inside some state conferences against their inclusion. Carter and the NAC not only did not give in to this pressure, but they hired security to protect the gay and pro-abortion workshops and the presence of gay and pro-abortion activists.[80] Furthermore, in response to the early success of the religious right in rallying delegates and in order to protect the diversity and pluralism of the WHCF and prevent a conservative takeover, Carter directed Tucker and the NAC to change their own rules. The number of elected delegates was limited, and 'at-large' delegates would also be appointed to enable an overall balance which included all constituencies, including gay people. Now, instead of a minimum of 30 per cent elected delegates, a maximum of 13.8 per cent could be peer elected from each state, while the new regulations explicitly called for the inclusion of all constituencies, including gay people. In Los Angeles, out of the 613 delegates only 85 were peer elected, 75 were chosen by lottery, with the other 453 being appointed by the NAC and Governor Jerry Brown. This turned the tide in favour of the progressive forces.[81]

The NAC's appointments were crucial and helped to balance out the delegations in most of the states. In Baltimore, after a majority of pro-family delegates were elected, the state organizers and the NAC organized a 'supplemental election' which conservatives thought, probably correctly, was intended to get liberal delegates elected. The Virginia delegation was deemed by the NAC a 'non-representative, predominantly white, middle-class delegation with one or two major interests'. This led the Committee to balance it by appointing more diverse delegates, including openly gay people. After similar adjustments in a number of other states, the Governors of Alabama and Indiana refused to participate in their state conferences.[82] Conservatives accused the NAC of wielding its power to annul elections when they did not result in an appropriately 'diverse' mix of delegates.[83]

77 Eagle Forum, 'WHCF Material', undated. RLMSF, GI, JCPL; Maddox and Weddington, author interviews.
78 NCJW Press Release, 23 January 1980. NGTFR, B.142, F.14, CU.
79 Letter, Joseph Giordano to John Carr, 31 January 1980. NGTFR, B.142, F.14, CU.
80 Bush, Jones-Hennin and Weddington, author interviews.
81 Eagle Forum, 'WHCF Material', undated. RLMSF, GI, JCPL; JoAnn Gasper, 'White House Conference on Families: Stacking the Deck', *Conservative Digest*, May/June 1980; Edward J. Lynch, 'White House Family Feud', *Policy Review*, No. 13, 1980: 125.
82 JoAnn Gasper, 'White House Conference on Families: Stacking the Deck', *Conservative Digest*, May/June 1980.
83 Eagle Forum, 'WHCF Material', undated. RLMSF, GI, JCPL.

The state conference in the District of Columbia took place between 2 and 9 February 1980 and gave rise to the most protests by conservatives. Marion Barry, the District's Mayor, and the two state coordinators, Audrey Rowe Colom and Karl Banks, were liberals and supporters of gay rights. They appointed four openly gay people, Eugene Baker, Boozer, Hockenberry and Jones-Hennin, to the state's planning committee. Subsequently, the committee organized and the NAC provided funding for several workshops on gay rights to take place during the state conferences. Gay rights activists had a visible presence, and several of them, like Naparsteck and Jones-Hennin, led a series of workshops on gay rights and homosexuality. Meanwhile, gay candidates ran to be delegates in five of the eight wards. Despite calls from the local gay leaders for a strong gay presence at the state conference, the gay community's turnout was minimal and gay people were vastly outnumbered by conservatives. Thereafter, all gay rights activists were easily defeated in their attempt to be elected as delegates. The activists were so disappointed, mostly at the very low turnout of the gay community, that they considered dropping out completely from the state's conference, seeing that there was no chance of electing a delegate.[84] Instead, they recommended that Barry and the NAC appoint Ngina Lythcott, a lesbian, gay rights activist and member of Planned Parenthood, as chairperson of the District of Columbia delegation to the Baltimore Conference. Much to the dismay of conservatives, Barry and the NAC accepted the recommendation. However, the final blow to the conservatives was struck when Barry, Banks, Rowe Colom and the NAC unanimously appointed Jones-Hennin, despite the fact that he had been overwhelmingly defeated in the election process, as a delegate for the District of Columbia. The appointments of Jones-Hennin and Lythcott caused substantial controversy and Banks, Barry, Rowe Colom and the NAC came under severe criticism from conservatives. Despite these protests, they stood firmly by their decisions. They cited Carter's regulations, which required the selection of representatives from all constituencies, including gay people, prompting a protest by Catholics and Muslims at the White House against the regulations. Openly gay delegates were also appointed and elected in several states across the country, for example California, Illinois, New York and Pennsylvania.[85]

The religious right began to complain about a number of what they considered to be irregularities at the state conferences, citing the rigging of regulations to outnumber and exclude them, and alleging the threatening and intimidation of pro-family participants. They made claims of a conspiracy by pro-ERA and gay rights activists to replace an elected majority of delegates by a majority chosen by the states' steering committees and the NAC who were pro-ERA, openly gay or supporters of gay rights.[86] Some conservatives and the religious right believed that the WHCF was, in fact, rigged against them, with a selection process that explicitly favoured liberals. The conference, they said, was 'contaminated by the liberal Carter machine', creating a 'national pattern

[84] Jones-Hennin and Naparsteck, author interviews; Don Leavitt, 'Apathy and Right Wingers Doom Family Confab', *The Blade*, 21 February 1980.

[85] Jones-Hennin, author interview; Craig Howell, 'Witnesses Speak out for Gay Families', *The Blade*, 6 December 1979; Don Leavitt, 'Jones Appointed as Family Delegate', *The Blade*, 3 April 1980; Don Leavitt, 'Family Topics Paper Stirs More Controversy', *The Blade*, 15 May 1980.

[86] Eagle Forum, 'WHCF Material: Of Interest to Texans', undated. RLMSF, GI, JCPL.

of secrecy, deception, and changing rules' aimed at the family values movement.[87] Dan Richey, Senator from Louisiana, said, 'This entire WHCF has been stacked and rigged from the very start to promote Jimmy Carter's views on gay rights, abortion, and more federal government in our lives'.[88] Carr defended the selection process, stating that 'Diverse points of view are represented in the delegates selected thus far. No single ideological point of view will be able to overwhelm the Conferences'.[89] While it was not true that the process had been 'rigged from the very start', the decision to radically decentralize the conference process had left a large opening for the growing mobilizational capacity of the religious right, already a large constituency; it was to prevent this that moves were made by organizers to prevent its being completely overwhelmed. The administration was caught off-guard by a process that it had itself initiated.

The conservatives' suspicion of a conspiracy gained additional fuel when a number of delegates who were selected by lottery turned out to be openly gay or gay rights activists. For example, in Texas, Ginny Cleaver, Chair of the programme committee of the Austin Lesbian/Gay Political Caucus, and Blandina Cardenas Ramirez, a feminist and pro-gay Civil Rights Commissioner who had also worked on Mondale's staff, were selected as delegates by the lottery.[90] Another complaint was that although the NGTF was allowed to circulate internal memoranda urging participation at the state conferences, Carr had formally complained about the 'tactics' of the editor of the pro-family *Right Women* newsletter, which urged the same thing.[91] The Southern Baptist Convention (SBC) passed resolutions denouncing the WHCF along with pornography, homosexuality and human evolution.[92] The Church alleged that the conference represented 'an undermining of the biblical concept of family'.[93] With these resolutions, the SBC was now at odds with almost all of Carter's views on important social issues. The Moral Majority referred to the WHCF as 'the Anti-Family Conference'[94] and called for a state boycott of the Conference on grounds that it was 'stacked against family life'. Members of the group in Alaska attended the state's Republican convention and succeeded in passing a resolution in support of a state boycott.[95]

Ultimately, state conferences and activities to select delegates for the conference took place in forty-eight of the fifty states and in seven territories.[96] In total, 500 state forums were held and 125,000 people voted for 2,000 delegates, who would attend the three major regional meetings; about 1,600 were chosen at the state level, 310 were

87 Ann Hulbert, 'The Baltimore Bust', *The New Republic*, 28 June 1980.

88 Celia W. Dugger, 'Political Momentum Is Sought for Families Conference Goals', *WP*, 21 August 1980.

89 Lynch, 'White House Family Feud', 124.

90 Eagle Forum, 'WHCF Material: Of Interest to Texans', undated. RLMSF, GI, JCPL.

91 JoAnn Gasper, 'White House Conference on Families: Stacking the Deck', *Conservative Digest*, May/June 1980.

92 Williams, *God's Own Party*, 158.

93 Kevin Phillips, *American Theocracy: The Peril and Politics of Radical Religion, Oil, and Borrowed Money in the 21st Century* (New York: Viking, 2006), 185.

94 Seth Dowland, '"Family Values" and the Formation of a Christian Right Agenda', *Church History* 78, no. 3 (2009): 606.

95 Wallace Turner, 'Group of Evangelical Protestants Takes Over the GOP in Alaska', *NYT*, 9 June 1979.

96 Letter, Jim Guy Tucker to President Carter, 11 March 1980. F.TR96 1/20/77–1/20/81, B.TR33, WHCF, JCPL.

appointed at large, 55 were state coordinators and 40 were members of Carter's NAC.[97] The pro-family forces had managed to elect a majority of delegates only in nine of the forty-eight states and in two of the lotteries[98] and only about 250 were theologically conservative Christians.[99] During a Housing Workshop, the delegates had passed a Homosexual Rights in Housing resolution which prohibited discrimination against gay people in housing; when the NAC met for its Plenary Session, it adopted the resolution, which meant that the topic would be discussed in the WHCF.[100] As the WHCF approached, leaders of the religious right once again demanded that Carter not allow gay people to be a part of the Conference, and once again he ignored them.[101]

Ahead of the first Conference in Baltimore, debate arose over whether Carter should open it. On 11 March, Tucker wrote to Carter and officially invited him to give a keynote address to the Conference's opening session, claiming that his presence 'would firmly establish the commitment of the White House to the Conference and set a positive tone for the remaining two meetings'.[102] However, some of Carter's aides disagreed and did not want to risk Carter being caught up in the acrimonious disputes between conservatives and liberals over such issues as abortion and gay rights. In May, Tucker called Weddington and pleaded with her that Carter should attend, assuring her that the conference 'will be a good one with no disasters'.[103] On 31 May, Eizenstat argued that absence would suggest cowardice on Carter's part, while his presence would signal his support for a strong family life and 'very strongly' recommended that he should open the Conference. Eizenstat reminded Carter that 'key constituencies' who supported the Conference such as Catholics and other religious organization whose vote would be needed in a few months would be disappointed with his absence. Moreover, this was a Conference Carter had himself proposed, and although Eizenstat agreed that it had 'been more controversial than other White House Conferences', he concluded that 'the advantages of attending far outweigh any possible criticism for your continued commitment to the Conference'.[104] Eizenstat's intervention was crucial; Carter agreed to attend and deliver the keynote in Baltimore, announced by the White House three days before the opening of the Conference.[105]

The depth of hostility to Carter among the religious right was demonstrated just before the Baltimore event at a press conference held jointly by Marshner and Weyrich. Both described Carter's record on family issues as 'abysmal', while Weyrich accused Carter of having 'the worst record for family issues of any president in history'. They accused him of stacking the Conference in favour of liberals and claimed that Tucker had manipulated delegate selection to ensure that policies which conservatives

97 WHCF, *Listening to America's Families*, 18, 56.

98 Murray-Brown, *For Christian America*, 150.

99 Ribuffo, 'Family Policy Past', 326.

100 Eagle Forum, 'WHCF Material: Plenary Session', undated. RLMSF, GI, JCPL.

101 Eizenstat and D. Michael Lindsay, author interviews.

102 Letter, Jim Guy Tucker to President Carter, 11 March 1980. F.TR96 1/20/77–1/20/81, B.TR33, WHCF, JCPL.

103 Flippen, *Jimmy Carter*, 267–8.

104 Memorandum, Stuart Eizenstat for the President, 31 May 1980. F.TR 96, 1/20/77–1/20/81, B.TR 33, WHCF, JCPL.

105 'Carter Is to Travel to Baltimore for Family Conference Thursday', *NYT*, 3 June 1980.

favoured would be excluded. Finally, the Weyrich-Marshner alliance announced that it would hold its own conference, the American Family Forum, in Washington, D.C. on 30 June to 2 July.[106]

The conferences take place: 'Getting a little closer'

Baltimore, 5–7 June

The first WHCF opened at the Baltimore Convention Center with more than 700 delegates from Eastern states taking part.[107] The NGTF was represented by Barbara Weinstock and Tom Burrows.[108] Although only seven of the delegates were openly gay at the beginning of the conference, among them Jones-Hennin,[109] in comparison to the forty conservative delegates,[110] as many as thirty 'came out' during the course of the conference.[111] From the beginning, conservatives picketed the entrance to the venue, claiming that Carter had packed the delegations with left-wingers.[112] They also distributed a paper with their main concerns, with homosexuality prominent among them, which stated, 'The entire WHCF amounts to a covert attempt at shifting community standards away from the traditional concept of the heterosexual family'.[113]

Carter's opening address lauded the diversity, pluralism and solidarity to be found among families, noted the progress made in the battle for racial and gender equality and praised single parents. He sought to widen the definition of the family by stating that families were 'based on more than blood' and that

> they are a kinship of shared experiences, shared dreams, shared joys and sorrows. Most of all, they are based on love that can span vast distances and the barrier of generation. . . . We have made great progress against racial, religious, sexual and age discrimination – and we are fighting to make more.[114]

Affirming that 'we do not want the government in our kitchens, bedrooms, and living rooms', Carter observed that it affects the lives of families with its policies, such as the tax system, and its programmes, such as housing and social security. Finally, he promised to do all he could to ensure that the WHCF's work 'does not end just as a report on the shelves in Washington'.[115] The gay participants in the conference took heart specifically from Carter's comments about government interference in the bedrooms and the

[106] Spencer Rich, 'Carter Opens Conference on Families', *WP*, 6 June 1980.
[107] WHCF, *Listening to America's Families*, 63.
[108] 'White House Conference on Families: Baltimore', *It's Time*, July–August 1980. RMSF, G/L2, JCPL.
[109] 'Conference Acknowledges "Alternative" Families', *GCN*, 21 June 1980.
[110] Murray-Brown, *For Christian America*, 150.
[111] Don Leavitt, 'Family Conference Results a Surprise', *The Blade*, 12 June 1980.
[112] Spencer Rich, 'Carter Opens Conference on Families', *WP*, 6 June 1980.
[113] Don Leavitt, 'Family Conference Results a Surprise', *The Blade*, 12 June 1980.
[114] OWHPS, 'Text of the President's Address to the WHCF in Baltimore', 5 June 1980. LBP, B.5, F.44, CU.
[115] Ibid.

basis of family in 'more than blood' as they perceived them as veiled references to gay families and gay rights.[116] Among them was Don Leavitt who explicitly referred to them as a 'veiled reference to Gay issues' in his article in *The Blade*.[117]

The conference debated numerous proposals and on many, such as the elimination of the marriage tax, there was wide agreement. As in Houston, tempers flared and neither the gay rights proponents nor the conservatives behaved particularly well. It quickly became apparent that the workshops were dominated by liberals and moderates.[118] Marshner and her allies attempted to raise their opposition to abortion and homosexuality in every workshop, regardless of their relevance. Workshop leaders, prepared for this, acted strongly to limit discussion to the matters at hand, infuriating the conservatives.[119] The D.C. delegation led by Lythcott had a lively presence and Jones-Hennin repeated his workshop on 'The Changing Realities of Family Life'. To ensure the successful completion of his workshop the organizers had allocated extra security in the room where it took place, doing the same for all the workshops regarding homosexuality and gay rights. Attempts by Marshner and her followers to disrupt these workshops were thus unsuccessful.[120] After the first day of meetings, Marshner complained about the way the conference was being run.[121]

Early work saw the drafting of one pro-gay proposal after another followed by their rejection one after another. Although openly gay people were allowed to make proposals and run workshops, the conservative and moderate participants held the majority and thus were able to vote down the gay proposals. In Proposal 49, a multi-topic resolution, gay rights activists in collaboration with liberals set out five clauses they described as legal and human rights. The main demand was for the elimination of discrimination, and encouragement of respect, for differences based on various criteria, including sexual preference. It also expressed support for the ERA and the right to abortion. Tucker, although he supported gay rights and abortion, told the press that he would not vote for it, as he believed that relating gay rights and abortion to the ERA would hurt the chances of having the amendment ratified. He admitted that he had asked some delegates to do the same.[122] Lythcott, despite being a supporter of gay rights and a lesbian, publicly also urged delegates to not vote for it for the same reasons, arguing that 'it is not politically positive at this time for the three issues (ERA, abortion, gay rights) to be associated with each other because that is what the Right wants, and I believe that is how they want to conquer us'.[123] Proposal 57 stated that community institutions should provide services which take into account individual preferences and differences in the makeup of families. Both proposals found support from workshop members and efforts were made in the 'Challenges and Responsibilities' workshop to

[116] Bush and Jones-Hennin, author interviews.
[117] Don Leavitt, 'Family Conference Results a Surprise', *The Blade*, 12 June 1980.
[118] Ibid.
[119] Flippen, *Jimmy Carter*, 269.
[120] Jones-Hennin, author interview.
[121] Martin, *With God on Our Side*, 182.
[122] 'Conference Acknowledges "Alternative" Families', *GCN*, 21 June 1980; Jones-Hennin, author interview; Don Leavitt, 'Family Conference Results a Surprise', *The Blade*, 12 June 1980.
[123] Don Leavitt, 'Family Conference Results a Surprise', *The Blade*, 12 June 1980.

include a general non-discrimination clause. It did not pass and efforts to include 'gay families' in a statement which listed types of families lost 64 to 57.[124]

Returning to the conference on day two, gay rights advocates sought to craft a definition of family that would include gay families, but lost 20–18. However, an attempt by conservatives to state that only heterosexual families should be considered true families was also defeated, 22–15. The result was that the final recommendations did not contain a precise definition of the family. However, many losses gay rights advocates sustained, the conservatives suffered the same with regard to their causes. The key delegates were the moderates, who were effectively swing voters. A subcommittee, in endorsing the ERA, referred to persons with 'special preferences', meaning gay households, and argued that there should be no discrimination against them. The language in favour of the ERA and against discrimination for 'special preferences' was included in the 73–24 vote.[125]

The conservatives were upset by the organizers' decision to provide gay participants with what they perceived as 'special treatment' by assigning security guards to protect the gay-themed workshops.[126] As a result of this and their inability to shut down their opponents, many conservatives walked out of the conference. Lawrence Pratt, a Virginian Republican Congressman, in a dramatic scene on the platform, seized the microphone from Tucker and declared, 'We have decided this delegation is stacked and we should walk out'. Pratt then led the contingent of conservatives, which included about fifty delegates and Marshner, out of the room.[127] Marshner claimed that she walked out as she wanted to demonstrate that the conference had lost its 'credibility' because it was 'pro-ERA, pro-abortion, pro-sexual preference . . . in some workshops ideas like freedom of sexual preference were approved. This is equivalent to an endorsement of homosexuality'.[128] The walk-out proved to be an act of self-destruction by the conservatives.

The final day was crucial for both sides, but particularly for gay rights advocates because the recommendation to end discrimination on the basis of sexual preference (Proposal 49) was up for the vote. The recommendation regarding sexual preference read,

> We support policies which preserve and protect basic legal and human rights of all family members. To guarantee these rights we support:
>
> Elimination of discrimination and encouragement of respect for differences based on sex, race, ethnic origin, creed, socio-economic status, age, disability, diversity of family type and size, sexual preference or biological ties.[129]

124 Burrows, 'Family Values', 347–8; 'Conference Acknowledges "Alternative" Families', *GCN*, 21 June 1980; Jones-Hennin, author interview; Don Leavitt, 'Family Conference Results a Surprise', *The Blade*, 12 June 1980.

125 Spencer Rich, 'Band of Conservatives Walks Out of Conference on Families', *WP*, 7 June 1980.

126 Bush and Jones-Hennin, author interviews.

127 Spencer Rich, 'Band of Conservatives Walks Out of Conference on Families', *WP*, 7 June 1980.

128 Nadine Brozan '2nd Day of Family Conference: Workshops and a Walkout', *NYT*, 7 June 1980; Spencer Rich, 'Band of Conservatives Walks Out of Conference on Families', *WP*, 7 June 1980.

129 'Families and Major Institutions Recommendations', WHCF, undated. LBP, B.5, F.45, CU.

In the event, the recommendation was passed by a single vote, 292 to 291.[130] Lythcott had eventually voted in favour of the resolution.[131] Crucial for the win was the support the gay rights activists received from various participating organizations, including NOW, the Black Caucus, the Hispanic Caucus and various other groups not specifically aligned with their cause. Furthermore, if the conservative delegates had not walked out, they would have won the vote easily. However tiny the margin was, for gay rights advocates a victory was a victory. Burrows and Weinstock highlighted the importance of the result in itself which 'shows the increasing recognition that gay people are a significant and vital part of the American family'.[132] Reporting on the conference proceedings, *Gay Community News* wrote that openly gay and lesbian delegates were 'absolutely delighted' by the passage of the recommendation.[133] By the end of proceedings, the conference had voted on fifty-seven recommendations, including controversial ones like the right to abortion, the ratification of the ERA and civil rights protections for gay people.[134]

Finally, and very importantly, the conference enabled several closeted gay people to 'come out' on their own terms and not because they were forced to. The visible and vibrant gay presence created the right environment for the thirty closeted gays to come out.[135] Furthermore, homosexuality and gay rights were now becoming major news and a political issue. The media for the first time sought to hear the concerns of the gay community by speaking to the gay delegates. Although the conference had focused mainly on economic matters, such as national health insurance, the *Los Angeles Times* and the *Washington Post* included 'nondiscrimination against homosexuals' in the first paragraph of their reports on the conference.[136]

Minneapolis, 19–21 June

Wexler opened and keynoted the Minneapolis Conference where 600 delegates from thirteen Southern and Mid-Western states participated.[137] There were about 150 pro-family delegates,[138] in comparison to only one openly gay delegate, William B. Kelley from Chicago, a member of the NGTF board and its representative there. There were also a few closeted gay delegates, but they were outnumbered by the pro-family delegates.[139] The opening and subsequent debates were generally quieter than in Baltimore, but when conservative delegates failed to get their platform included in conference recommendations, about ninety of them walked out, including Marshner,

130 'Conference Acknowledges "Alternative" Families', *GCN*, 21 June 1980.
131 Burrows, 'Family Values', 347.
132 'White House Conference on Families: Baltimore', *It's Time*, July–August 1980. RMSF, G/L2, JCPL.
133 'Conference Acknowledges "Alternative" Families', *GCN*, 21 June 1980.
134 Nadine Brozan, 'Conference on Families Produces a 57-Point Plan', *NYT*, 9 June 1980.
135 Bush and Jones-Hennin, author interviews.
136 Burrows, 'Family Values', 348.
137 'Family Conference Rejects Antiabortion Amendment', *NYT*, 22 June 1980.
138 Murray-Brown, *For Christian America*, 150.
139 'White House Conference on Families: Minneapolis', *It's Time*, July–August 1980. RMSF, G/L2, JCPL.

citing the same reasons as in Baltimore.[140] However, the walk-out was short-lived, lasting less than an hour, as having learnt their lesson, they returned in time for the voting on their main issues. The conservatives seemed this time to be more concerned about abortion than gay rights, but despite strenuous efforts, their anti-abortion amendment was rejected.[141]

The main issues discussed were financial matters, social justice, drugs and alcohol, and violent or sexual TV programmes. In the end, the Conference endorsed almost identical recommendations to those of Baltimore, including abortion rights and the ERA. However, the Conference proved significant as the only one of the three to agree on a definition of the family, a conservative one of 'two or more persons related by blood, heterosexual marriage, adoption or extended families', approved on a vote of 297 to 259.[142] Nevertheless, two small wins for gay rights were achieved: a resolution to ensure 'equity and social justice for all individuals regardless of race, sex, age, handicap, religion and cultural traditions and values' contained in its last clause a veiled reference to the rights of gay people; and a resolution was passed on the issue of housing which included a reference to stopping discrimination on the basis of sexual preference, the wording quoting verbatim the NGTF's Memorandum on Family Issues that Impact on Gay Families.[143] Meanwhile, the strong support of the Coalition for the WHCF for gay rights and abortion led to the withdrawal of two of its Catholic group members, the National Conference of Catholic Bishops and the United States Catholic Conference, from the Coalition.[144]

After the Minneapolis Conference, the NGTF hailed the outcome of the first two conferences as 'a clear victory for the rights of gay men and lesbians. We are getting a little closer to being recognized as integral aspects of the American family'.[145]

Los Angeles, 10–12 July

The Los Angeles conference was opened by Patricia Roberts Harris, Carter's Secretary of Health and Human Services, who also delivered the keynote address. The Conference brought together 613 delegates from nineteen states and four territories, with about fifty of them being pro-family and about ten being openly gay, who debated the fifty-seven recommendations that had resulted from the Conference's twenty workshops. Although overall the Conference focused mostly on economic issues, two topics dominated the opening session: the definition of the family and the role of government in personal affairs.[146]

140 Michael W. Fedo, 'Second Parley on Family Opens Quietly', *NYT*, 20 June 1980.
141 'Family Conference Ends in Agreement in 10 Goals', *NYT*, 23 June 1980; 'Family Conference Rejects Antiabortion Amendment', *NYT*, 22 June 1980.
142 Ibid.
143 'White House Conference on Families: Minneapolis', *It's Time*, July–August 1980. RMSF, G/L2, JCPL.
144 J. Brooks Flippen, 'Carter, Catholics and the Politics of Family', *American Catholic Studies* 123, no. 3 (2012): 48–9.
145 'Notes from the Co-Execs', *It's Time*, July–August 1980. RMSF, G/L2, JCPL.
146 Bush, author interview; Sharon Johnson, 'After Heated Debates, Family Parley Ends Quietly', *NYT*, 14 July 1980; Murray-Brown, *For Christian America*, 151.

Several workshops on homosexuality and gay rights took place at the Conference, with the gay community having an active and visible role. Gay rights activists and the religious right cancelled each other out as all their respective recommendations were voted down. Although no resolution either supporting or condemning gay rights was passed, the Conference was seen as very beneficial for the gay community due to its visibility in it, the many workshops it organized, and the fact that several closeted gay men and women 'came out' during the proceedings.[147]

At the same time as the WHCF in Los Angeles, conservatives organized another extramural protest meeting, a pro-family gathering, at Long Beach, California, with Tim LaHaye and Schlafly among the speakers. The meeting called for the Senate to investigate the process of delegate selection for the WHCF. LaHaye was furious with Carter whom he accused of having 'falsely used his born-again image to hoodwink people into thinking he is one of us' and said that the WHCF 'does not represent the more traditionalist viewpoint of the family, but instead favors the feminist and pro-homosexual viewpoints espoused by the liberal establishment'.[148]

Outcome

In October, Carter received the official report on the whole Conference process. It stressed the Conference's pluralistic nature and the open spirit which had animated Carter's original call for it. Very importantly for gay rights, the report included same-sex families among the list of possible families, without however adopting an official definition.[149] Among the proposals for housing was that of outlawing discrimination on the basis of sexual preference. Finally, listed among the 'minority concerns' was a section using the following explicit language: 'Gay Rights: Three reports urged an end to discrimination against homosexuals'.[150]

Carter stressed that if re-elected, he would be best placed to make changes based on the recommendations from the conferences.[151] He directed all units within the federal government to conduct a full review of their work, taking into account the report's recommendations, and to set out a strategy for implementing them. Clearly perceiving the WHCF as a success, he stated, 'I am proud of the way this Conference listened to and involved so many American families, of the way it has put families at the center of national discussion, of the way it has found consensus and agreement where many predicted only conflict'.[152]

The final report, entitled *Listening to America's Families: Action for the 80's*, was published in December, by which time Carter had lost the presidential election. It included twenty recommendations, to be implemented within six months, but only two were carried out. One was to create the Office for Families, which Carter had

[147] Bush and Higgins, author interviews.
[148] Clendinen and Nagourney, *Out*, 422–3.
[149] Flippen, *Jimmy Carter*, 306.
[150] WHCF, *Listening to America's Families*, 10–12, 37, 48, 96.
[151] OWHPS, Kansas, 15 October 1979, RWHPO, GR, JCPL.
[152] WHCF, *Listening to America's Families*, 4–5

already done; the other was the marriage tax reduction, which was included in the 1981 Economic Recovery Tax Act. Much of the work of implementing the report was put in the hands of state authorities with the federal government tasked with very little.[153]

ଔ

Carter said that he considered the WHCF 'a great success'.[154] But the reality was that the Conference in its entirety had become more of a battleground for activists on two opposing sides in the culture wars than a forum for the positive and healthy exchange of views. The impact of the WHCF on the religious right and the gay rights movement alike was considerable, both being deeply affected by the results. Carter attended only the first Conference, but his decisions played an extremely important role in the outcome and the aftermath.

The WHCF proved hugely important for gay rights and contributed to changing public discourse on the topic. Carter had allowed openly gay people to participate and express their views publicly, including in front of the TV, in a federally funded event of his own creation, thus bringing gay rights and homosexuality to the attention of every American. Equally important was that Carter, by his efforts in support of diversity, had effectively admitted that gay families existed. The NAC, and subsequently the state conferences and the three regional conferences, had promoted 'diverse family forums' and 'plurality' that included families with 'different lifestyles'. This theme was very prevalent throughout the year-long proceedings, even though in the end the Conference did not adopt any formal definition of 'family'.[155] Another big win was Conference support for an end to discrimination on the basis of sexual preference. Finally, a number of closeted gay delegates 'came out' during the conference, signalling that the climate was becoming increasingly accepting of the gay community. Sandifer said:

> Certainly people would not have come out if the environment was not welcoming. And I know that it was despite the attacks against us. . . . For us, the important thing was that we had the acceptance of the president himself. He was the one who had allowed us to express our views and concerns at a Conference organized by him. The important thing was not to talk and convince people about our rights; the important thing was to change a president's mind about us and Carter showed with his stance in the Conference and generally that he recognized us and accepted us. Since he did that, then it was a matter of time until most of the nation did.*

Bush, who followed and covered all the state conferences and the subsequent WHCF for the gay press, said:

153 'White House Conference on Families', n.d. The James Guy Tucker, Jr. Papers, University of Arkansas, https://ualrexhibits.org/tuckerblog/2016/02/10/white-house-conference-on-families/.

154 OWHPS, Kansas, 15 October 1979, RWHPO, GR, JCPL.

155 Bush and Jones-Hennin, author interviews; Moral Majority Report, 'Religious Leaders Join Task Force in 10-Hour Meet', undated. RLMSF, GI, JCPL.

> One of the things that I felt that Carter did not get enough credit for was for including gay and lesbian families in the WHCF. It was more important for the lesbian and gay families than it was for the White House, because it was the first affirmation that [such] families were valuable, and that they provided assets to both the members of the families and to the community. This was not very long after Anita Bryant had been campaigning on 'save the children'. So Carter, to be doing this in 1980 [an election year], just less than two years later, is a statement in itself.*

As for the religious right, the Conference had a big impact on its relationship with Carter. Although Carter had made no explicit reference to gay people and was rather circumspect on the topic of homosexuality in his speeches regarding the WHCF, he had refused to exclude gay people from participating, insisting that they should be included, while his references to different 'lifestyles', 'diversity' and 'pluralism' were perceived as veiled references to gay families. There appears to have been no doubt in the minds of the religious right that the WHCF had been an attempt to widen the definition of the word 'family' to include gay couples. The *Blade* wrote shortly after the end of the WHCF that the White House believed that 'evangelicals are frustrated and disillusioned with the President over his unprecedented promotion of homosexuals and gay rights during his administration'.[156] Despite suffering several defeats to gay rights campaigners, the religious right emerged galvanized from the conferences. Several of the right-wing evangelical organizations that were created around this time, such as the Christian Voice and the Moral Majority, remained influential for many years to come. Conservatives had also learnt about the importance of making alliances to combat the threat of gay rights activism.

Carter had sensed problems for the American family, making the issue a theme of his election campaign in 1976 and seeking to press on with a conference on the subject, despite some difficulty getting it off the ground. In the event, it was an enormous own goal with regard to his relationship with religious conservatives, which was going to cost him dearly a few months later in the presidential election. Instead of strengthening the idea of the traditional American family, Carter seemed, to conservative Americans, to have threatened it like no one else before. It is among the greatest ironies of his presidency that he, who had sounded a sincere alarm about the health of the family which seemed to resonate with the public, ended up being perceived by a growing body of opinion, and an increasingly active conservative movement, as the principal threat to it. As Tony Campolo said, 'The chaotic WHCF was what brought the homosexual issue to the fore in American political discussion'.*

[156] Quoted in 'Religious Leaders Join Task Force in 10-Hour Meet', Moral Majority Report, undated. RLMSF, GI, JCPL.

13

The beginning of the end

Gay rights and the 1980 nomination battle

As the story in Chapter 12 of the White House Conference on Families showed, Carter and his administration were increasingly trapped in the jaws of a vice composed of the rising demands of gay rights activists and the even more rapid burgeoning of organized resistance from religious and more generally cultural conservatives. The poor state of the economy and the abrupt onset of several crises in the realm of foreign policy, notably the Iran embassy hostage crisis, added to the difficulties of Carter's final year. The resulting bruising primary battle – unusual for a sitting president seeking re-nomination from his own party – with Edward Kennedy had an important gay rights dimension, as Kennedy felt able to promise more. Carter's own achievements were also under-reported and under-appreciated, arguably a self-inflicted harm by both activists and the administration.

Results, reporting and resistance

In mid-July 1979, a *New York Times*/CBS News poll showed that thanks to gasoline shortages, the worsening economy and doubts about his judgement under pressure, Carter's public approval rating had reached a historic low of 26 per cent. Despite the fact that Senator Edward Kennedy had insisted that he was not running for the Democratic nomination for the 1980 election, the poll showed that he was the preferred candidate of 53 per cent of Democrats, with Carter receiving only 16 per cent, while California Governor Jerry Brown got 7 per cent.[1] Furthermore, 36 per cent of registered Democrats and 41 per cent of independent voters declared that they would not consider voting for Carter in the next presidential election.[2] Among those who were not happy with Carter were some members of the gay community. In view of the advances made by the Carter administration, charted in preceding chapters, this fact requires some explanation.

When describing pioneering efforts, it is important to remember the conditions of the pioneer, which differ considerably from conditions in the new era created by the

1 Adam Clymer, 'Gas Shortages Spurs Carter Decline in Poll', *NYT*, 13 July 1979.
2 Stanley, *Kennedy vs. Carter*, 96.

pioneer. It is an entry into new territory, where resources may be scarce and unexpected resistance may arise, so that it is necessarily somewhat tentative. The territory of gay rights was not only relatively unexplored, it was actively avoided and feared in mainstream politics, culture and media. As already suggested, creating visibility for what had previously been invisible, if not forcibly suppressed, also brings the risk of exciting opposition to the new affront. As it happens, it was the conservative forces of the late 1970s that most rapidly and effectively mobilized support, in part because of their early turn towards new methods of communication, notably computerized direct mail. The pioneer was entering not a primitive environment, but one with an increasingly sophisticated capacity to resist.

Despite the growing visibility of the gay community, there was still some reluctance in the mainstream press to take its concerns seriously. The media of the time rarely gave much coverage to the issue of gay rights. Some journalists believed that they might be seen as not serious enough or lose their credibility if they reported such news. Larry Bush said in 1980 that at the time gay news was not 'legitimate national news. Each new story involving gay people has to be proved to be a legitimate story'.[3] This applied, he said to the author, even to White House reporters, otherwise best placed to report on the administration's achievement: 'most of the White House press corps, who were the ones who would have covered it, thought that anything to do with gays was nuts'.* But while this was a reason for relative neglect in the mainstream media, for the burgeoning media environment of the religious right and the new right, it was a strong energizing factor.

For its part, the gay press was small and had limited resources. Especially during the first two and a half years and before Bush became accredited to the White House, it is clear from reading it that the gay press was not fully aware of the administration's efforts on gay rights, despite its improved access. An example of this ignorance is that after an April 1980 White House meeting between Maddox and gay religious leaders (see Chapter 4), the *Bay Area Reporter* reported that this was the fourth time gay rights activists had visited the White House since Carter became president;[4] in fact it was the sixteenth. Except for the March 1977 Meeting, none of the White House meetings with gay rights activists received any attention from the mainstream press. Even the gay press reported only very few of these meetings. The NGTF publicized every White House meeting it attended on the front page of *It's Time* and it also released press statements specifically about these meetings and their outcomes. However, it failed to mention any meeting between Carter's administration and other gay rights activists or organizations; for example Malson and Thomas's meetings with the local gay community in California or Maddox's White House meeting with the gay religious leaders (see Chapter 4 for both). Evidently the gay press was also not fully aware of the scope of the White House's efforts or of its collaboration with gay rights activists. Some of the resulting achievements were also neglected, for instance the administration's success in securing permission for gay rights activists to conduct an official wreath-laying ceremony in the Tomb of the Unknown Soldier was not mentioned at all, even

[3] Massing, 'The Invisible Cubans'.

[4] 'Gay Religious Leaders Visit White House', *BAR*, 22 May 1980.

though Charles Brydon had sent a 'thank you' letter to Thomas acknowledging her and the administration's efforts (see Chapter 9). Paul Kuntzler, co-founder of the GSDC and of the GAA, admitted shortly before the 1980 presidential election that Carter had 'a remarkably good record on gay rights' and that the gay rights activists had failed 'to demonstrate how much we've gained in the past four years'.[5]

The readership of the gay press, and membership of gay community organizations, was also limited. While a major part of Carter's achievement was to make the gay community more aware of itself, the starting condition of relatively low self-awareness must not be forgotten, and helps to account for the community's incomplete knowledge of Carter's accomplishments and efforts on gay rights. Important accomplishments like the upgrading of dishonourable discharges for gay veterans and the federal funding gay organizations received did not make it into the gay press or were not publicized by the activists. Furthermore, the positive effects on gay people of some of Carter's broader initiatives, such as the CSRA, were not emphasized by the gay press or by gay organizations.

Gay publications could not reach many gay people as they were not widely available for sale, while most gay people were closeted and avoided taking out subscriptions to such publications. Important in the lack of acknowledgement of Carter's achievements was the absence of coverage by *The Advocate*, the only gay publication with national distribution at the time. This was a result of the feud between Goodstein, *The Advocate*'s publisher, and the NGTF and Costanza (see also Chapter 3). In consequence, *The Advocate* almost completely avoided reporting on the accomplishments of the NGTF and Carter's administration. Things began to change after Costanza left the staff, and especially when Bush became the first openly gay reporter to be accredited to the White House. Bush experienced first-hand the administration's efforts. He described a number of its accomplishments in two articles that provided the first and most comprehensive overviews of Carter's record on gay rights: in *The Sentinel* in May 1980 ('White House Claims Solid Record on Gay Issues') and in *The Advocate* in June ('The Carter Administration: More Done than Said?'), commenting also on how little they had been discussed.

Ironically, Carter's efforts on gay rights regularly received prominent coverage in the much larger conservative press, occasionally even more than they received in the gay press.[6] Conservative columnists in the mainstream media and publications such as *Reader's Digest*, *Conservative Digest* and *The National Enquirer* relentlessly attacked Carter for his efforts on gay rights. In June 1980, *The Advocate* admitted that although Carter constantly took heat from those who were opposing gay rights for his efforts on the subject 'virtually no support came from the gay community to salve the wounds'.[7] But this ironic pattern is not surprising when the starting point is considered. After decades of invisibility and exclusion, it had to take time for the community's media, the infrastructure of cultural change, to develop. Some new media of the opposition to gay rights, as already noted, developed much more quickly. The dynamism and expansion

5 Lou Chibbaro, Jr., 'Carter Committee Formed', *The Blade*, 25 September 1980.

6 See documents in RLMSF, GI, JCPL.

7 Larry Bush, 'The Carter Administration. More Done Than Said?', *The Advocate*, 12 June 1980.

of the novel techniques of political direct marketing and televangelism easily outpaced the poorly funded and sparsely distributed efforts of the gay press.

Conflicts within the gay rights movement, such as the Goodstein–NGTF feud, also played their part. Such tensions are an inevitable part of a growing political movement, but can be especially destructive in its nascent phase. The NGTF tended to highlight its own contribution to an accomplishment at the expense of the efforts of Carter's administration, while it often avoided giving timely acknowledgement to Carter's contribution to an achievement, instead claiming sole responsibility. For example, the organization publicly acknowledged Carter's contribution to the tax exemption for gay organizations only a few weeks before the 1980 elections, three years after the exemption was granted.[8] Steve Endean, the NGTF's Co-Chairman of the Board of Directors in the 1970s, wrote in his biography about the organization's tendency to credit itself without acknowledging others' contributions: 'Over time, I came to believe the Task Force would take credit for the sun rising if they could get away with it, which was a painful reality for a former cochair of the board!'[9] Clay, also on the NGTF's Board of Directors at the time, said that he 'totally agreed' with Endean's comment and attributed the organization's tendency to overhype its efforts and downplay Carter's to its attempt to increase its 'appeal, visibility and prestige'.*

Finally, the pioneer's own trepidation must be understood. The White House failed to adequately promote its own efforts and accomplishments. In part this has to do with Carter's personal qualities: he had a lack of interest in 'politics' or what might be called 'politicking', conceived as persuasion, presentation, rhetoric and coalition-building. Failure to build a good relationship with the press was an aspect of this,[10] and his outsider status, however electorally effective it might have been in 1976, fed into it too. In the context of gay rights, which was not central to his policy agenda, but was an implication of something that was, namely human rights, both his achievements and the ineffective promotion of them can be understood as effects of this style of governing and communicating. Tactical concerns about conservative religious opposition were undoubtedly a factor, stemming primarily from his advisers.[11] Bert Carp admitted that 'certainly there was an attitude of caution' when publicly speaking about the administration's efforts on gay rights as they could not risk 'having the thing blow up, which wouldn't have been helpful to anyone'.* But a degree of inconsistency even about these tactical questions, preventing them from rising to the level of strategy (exemplified by the prolonged stumble into lose-lose scenarios such as the Conference on Families) was also in evidence.

Even the administration's attempt to present its accomplishments to gay rights activists was incomplete. Bush's two articles mentioned above contained a far more detailed overview of the administration's accomplishments on gay rights than any

8 NGTF, 'What Has Jimmy Carter Ever Done for Gays?', 1980. NGTFR, B6, F3, CU.

9 Steve Endean, *Bringing Lesbian and Gay Rights into the Mainstream. Twenty Years of Progress* (New York and London: Routledge, 2006), 231.

10 Mark J. Rozell, *The Press and the Carter Presidency* (Boulder and London: Westview Press, 1989); Mark J. Rozell, 'President Carter and the Press: Perspectives from White House Communications Advisers', *Political Science Quarterly* 105, no. 3 (1990): 419–34.

11 Larry Bush, 'Exit Interviews with the Carter Administration', *The Sentinel*, 20 February 1981; Carp, Eizenstat, McKenna and Weddington, author interviews.

of the administration's own reports on the issue, although they too were incomplete. In this context, all the above contributed to a largely inaccurate portrayal of Carter's efforts and accomplishments on gay rights, as many accomplishments remained largely unknown to the vast majority of the gay community at the time, while tangible gains for gay Americans were easily overlooked. These conditions explain the difficulties Carter began to face from gay rights activists in 1979 and 1980.

Great expectations and short memories

While factors described in the preceding section limited the full recognition by its beneficiaries of the Carter administration's achievements in gay rights, the wider environment also encouraged the growth of expectations on the part of activists (who, to a greater extent than the gay community at large, had evidence of what could be achieved with sustained effort by a sympathetic administration).

On 7 November 1979, three days after fifty-two Americans were taken hostage in Tehran, a new factor came into the equation for Carter when Kennedy announced that he would seek nomination for the 1980 presidential election. Two days after that, the NGTF sent a questionnaire to all presidential candidates asking for their positions on gay rights issues. In the version sent to Carter, the questions were:

- Will you continue the precedent you established of an 'open door' to White House and administration officials for lesbian and gay representatives?
- Will you reaffirm your commitment to nominate people who are sensitive to lesbian and gay concerns and make a commitment to appoint open lesbians and gay men who are qualified to administration positions, regulatory bodies, judicial seats, and Presidential advisory groups? Will you solicit suggestions and comments on prospective nominees?
- Will you support a plank in your party's platform for lesbian and gay rights?
- Will you sign an Executive Order ending discrimination in Federal employment and services?
- Will you commit your administration to the passage of the Federal gay rights bill (H.R. 2074)?[12]

Meanwhile, gay rights activists formed Gay Vote 1980: The National Convention Project (NCP), which aimed to elect openly gay delegates to the two major parties' conventions and to secure gay rights planks on both parties' platforms. The NCP's two Co-Directors were Tom Bastow and Mary Spottswood Pou. On 3 November, Bastow and Pou wrote to all the Democratic and Republican presidential candidates inviting them to the organization's kick-off gala on 27 November, at The Pier, a gay disco in Washington, D.C.[13]

12 Letter, NGTF to President Carter, 9 November 1979. RMSF, GH1, JCP (author's bullets).

13 Dan Daniel, 'National Convention Project Launched', *GCN*, 10 November 1979; Letter, Mary Spottswood Pou and Thomas Bastow to President Carter, 3 November 1979. AWSF, B.34, NGTF,

Mike Chanin, a Deputy Assistant and Wexler's close confidant, attended on Carter's behalf. Only Jerry Brown accepted the invitation to personally attend the event; Kennedy sent an aide, while none of the Republican candidates attended or sent a representative. Brown was very popular in the gay community due to his actions as Governor of California and was the star speaker of the event, which was attended by about 600 people. Kennedy expressed his support for gay rights in a letter which was read out by his aide. In contrast, Chanin was booed by the crowd, who expected a more senior presidential aide, and he struggled to make an impression. To his comment, 'I came tonight prepared to make a lot of remarks on what Jimmy Carter has done in the way of issues', members of the crowd shouted, 'What? What's he done?' Chanin pressed on, you have 'a President who is meeting with you, a President who respects you. I think we've made progress . . . we've begun to change the attitudes of people'. He then stated that the administration was giving 'serious consideration' to issuing the desired executive order and listed some of the administration's achievements, for example regarding gay veterans, and the employment protections secured by the CSRA, much of which was unknown to the crowd. A heckler indicated what they did know by yelling, 'What happened to Bella Abzug? What happened to Midge Costanza?' Chanin realized that the audience had already made up their minds about Carter.[14]

After the event, the NGTF and the GRNL publicly acknowledged the importance of the presence of a Carter aide at the event, describing it as an act of 'recognition of legitimacy' of gay rights.[15] Pou and Bastow wrote to Chanin and expressed their 'regret' about the 'rude treatment' he had received from some of the audience, but then they went on to defend their actions. First, they said the crowd was disappointed because they were expecting a 'senior representative' of the administration and because they found some of Chanin's remarks to be 'inconsistent'; finally, they cited the general disappointment among the gay community that Carter had failed to fulfil his campaign promises. The letter quoted – actually, misrepresented – Carter's remarks from his 1976 campaign that he 'opposed all forms of discrimination' and that as president he would work to ensure 'that all policies of the federal government will reflect this commitment', observing that there was still discrimination in 'many elements of the federal government'.[16] But, as discussed earlier, Carter had always made a national security exception to his promise on federal employment access. He had in fact fulfilled his campaign promise on federal employment precisely.

The White House was concerned at Chanin's reception. Although December 1979 was perhaps the most crucial month for the Carter administration and although a White House meeting had already been arranged for later in the month for the presentation of the gay rights activists' petition from its 'Petition the President'

JCPL.

14 Elizabeth Bamiller, 'Gay Rights, Laser Lights & Jerry Brown', *WP*, 28 November 1979; Bastow, author interview; 'Governor Brown Attends Project's Kick-off Gala', *Capitol Hill*, 2, 1, undated. RMSF, GTFN2, JCPL; Bill Peterson, 'Brown's Support for Gays Brings Cheers', *WP*, 28 November 1979.

15 'Does Support for Gay Civil Rights Spell Political Suicide?', GRNL, n.d. RMSF, G/L1, JCPL.

16 Letter, Mary Spottswood Pou and Tom Bastow to Michael Chanin, 3 December 1979. ATSF, B.265, GR, JCPL.

campaign,[17] nevertheless, the administration invited gay rights activists to the White House for talks in order to understand the problem of limited awareness of the administration's achievements.[18] On 10 December, Chanin, Malson, Rock and Thomas met with Brydon, Valeska and Bush. The activists expressed their gratitude for what Carter had done so far, acknowledging that he had fulfilled by then almost all the requests that had been made to his administration during the March 1977 Meeting. On the other hand, they expressed their dissatisfaction with slow progress on the immigration issue, the only outstanding one. They also made a series of seventeen new requests of the president and the administration. These ranged from appearances by Carter at suggested events, for instance that Carter and his family should attend an MCC service in Washington and that he personally receive the forthcoming Petition in order to 'express his appreciation for input received from meetings since 1977, state a specific accomplishment, and express commitment to further progress', to various actions regarding named individuals whose cases the NGTF was pursuing, or nominations of gay or lesbian people to specified positions, and finally to actions associated with the forthcoming campaign, notably the endorsement of a gay platform plank at the Convention.[19] It was a mixture of easily achievable symbolic gestures, some flattering primarily to the NGTF, symbolic gestures which were potentially far more controversial, detailed interventions, and recurrent demands which the administration was still wrestling with.

During the meeting, the activists admitted that a large portion of the gay community was unaware of most of the administration's efforts and accomplishments and discussed ways to address this. The activists requested a letter containing all of the administration's accomplishments so far and Bush committed to researching the issue for the gay press (the results of which have already been mentioned). Carter's aides maintained that they were still 100 per cent committed to advancing gay rights and eager to prove the administration's sincere intentions they offered additional federal funding for gay organizations and gay programmes. The activists were very pleased with the discussion and later privately acknowledged that the administration was not getting the credit it deserved for its accomplishments on gay rights and agreed to work to correct this.[20] The following day, Brydon sent a letter to Chanin acknowledging that it was 'the best meeting we have had with the White House staff since the original March 1977 meeting with Midge Costanza' and that they perceived 'a genuine interest in moving forward beyond the "meeting" stage on the various issues of concern to our community' – although this was something of a misrepresentation, as things had already moved well beyond the 'meeting' stage. The letter added another request for Carter: to appoint an openly gay attorney as general counsel or deputy counsel of a department or agency.[21]

17 As discussed in Chapter 6, this petition, like the NGTF's candidate questions, expressed the demands for an Executive Order on federal employment and for White House support for H.R.2074.

18 Larry Bush, 'The Carter Administration. More Done Than Said?', *The Advocate*, 12 June 1980.

19 NGTF's requests, 10 December 1979. RMSF, GH1, JCPL.

20 Larry Bush, 'The Carter Administration. More Done Than Said?', *The Advocate*, 12 June 1980; Bush, author interview.

21 Letter, C.F. Brydon to Michael Chanin, 11 December 1979. ATSF, B.271, NGTF, JCPL.

These new demands are evidence of the progress that had been made on gay rights since Carter became president; to see this one has only to compare them with those that were made in the March 1977 Meeting, which had all been successfully addressed, with the exception of immigration, still in the process of an administrative resolution (see Chapter 8). They were evidence of raised expectations and hopes. But they also indicate an underestimation of the progress that had in fact been made and an overestimation of its scope for rapid acceleration. Even until now, no American president, or his immediate family, has ever attended an MCC service,[22] other than Carter's mother, who attended one in 1980. Carter did not appoint an openly lesbian delegate to the US delegation to the UN, and neither has any other President; however, Carter appointed Koryne Horbal, prominent feminist and supporter of gay rights, as the US representative to the UN's Commission on the Status of Women.[23] It would take another fourteen years for a president to appoint an openly gay person to a federal department or agency; in 1993, Clinton appointed Roberta Achtenberg, an open lesbian, as Assistant Secretary at HUD's Office of Fair Housing and Equal Opportunity.[24] Although Carter had not appointed any open gay as a top White House aide, he had already appointed Costanza, who was an outspoken and fierce supporter of gay rights; although she was a closeted lesbian, her sexual preference was known to Carter and his aides. Carter had appointed four openly gay people – Abram, O'Leary, Rustin and Schropp – to presidential committees, while in 1978 he had invited Rustin to be an official delegate of the US delegation to Israel to attend Golda Meir's funeral. Carter did not personally meet with gay rights activists for official talks; it would be over fifteen years before an American president, Clinton, did so. As for an American president personally attending or addressing a gay organization or a gay-oriented event, it would take another eighteen years for this to happen; in 1998, Clinton spoke at the Human Rights Campaign's annual dinner.[25] Carter did not speak to the gay press; another seventeen years would pass before a President, again Clinton, did so. Asked by the author whether the demands were perhaps far-fetched and unrealistic for the climate of the time, Bush said:

> Definitely. . . . [but also] it was an indication of both an openness to have a dialogue, which would have never taken place at this level previously . . . I think it was very ambitious, but I understand doing a roadmap. But I think there was a long way to go on that road before they got there.*

Clay, asked the same question by the author, said,

> Well, yes, I will agree with you. The demands demonstrated how comfortable we were with him. We would never have considered making such demands to Reagan

22 Perry and Wilson, author interviews.

23 Weddington, author interview.

24 Donald Padgett, 'Before Buttigieg: Roberta Achtenberg, First LGBTQ+ Senate Confirmation', *Out*, 11 March 2021.

25 Chris Bull, 'A Gay-Friendlier White House: An Interview with Virginia Apuzzo', *The Advocate*, 20 January 1998.

> or Nixon, but Carter was approachable and we just kind of tested the ground to see how far we could go with him. These guys [who made the demands] were not stupid, they knew they were asking too much, and I believe they were just fishing and hoping to catch as much as possible.*

Even so, Carter went on to fulfil some of the new requests. In addition to his mother attending an MCC service, he appointed openly gay people like Apuzzo, Pou and Schropp to prominent and visible positions in his election campaign team (see Chapter 14). To the extent, which is not clear from the record, that the NGTF's list of demands represented conditions for its support of Carter's re-election bid, a degree of overconfidence about the future and forgetfulness about the past can certainly be diagnosed.

The NGTF was also awaiting a response (which it had demanded be signed by either Carter or Robert Strauss, the president of his election campaign) to its questions submitted to candidates. An early draft, in December, was leaked to activists, who found it to be 'disappointing'.[26] Eizenstat and Wexler wrote to Carter on 19 December, noting that

> the sensitivity of the press and general public to gay issues insure that the responses to this questionnaire will receive wider dissemination and analysis than in the typical case. For this reason, we believe it is important for you to personably approve the recommended responses or to modify them to reflect your true positions.

They suggested that the response should highlight the administration's accomplishments and avoid making many promises for the future.[27] Evidently, the political calculus was becoming increasingly complicated.

A challenge from the left

Meanwhile, Kennedy was actively seeking the gay vote in California and had personally campaigned along with his wife and son in gay areas of San Francisco.[28] In early January 1980, in a highly controversial move, the GSDC endorsed Kennedy. The endorsement came by the closest of margins, 28–27, and after a series of heated arguments between members of the Club and other activists. The endorsement came after Kennedy struck a deal with the Club that he would have at least two openly gay delegates, one full and one alternate, to the Democratic National Convention. Several members of the GSDC and other activists questioned the depth of Kennedy's commitment, pointing out that he had not co-sponsored a Senate gay rights bill, that

26 Lou Chibbaro Jr., 'Carter Statement Viewed as Retreat', *The Blade*, 20 March 1980.
27 Memorandum, Anne Wexler and Stu Eizenstat to President Carter, 19 December 1979. BASF, GR, JCPL.
28 Stanley, *Kennedy vs. Carter*, 106.

he had appointed a homophobe to his campaign staff, and that while chairman of the Senate Judiciary Committee he had not paid any attention to gay rights issues. Bastow, the Club's former President, who was confident that Kennedy would win, had warned that the GSDC would 'isolate' itself by not endorsing Kennedy and that a Carter endorsement would bring another four years 'of the same old shit'.[29] The NGTF and other activists were unhappy about the GSDC's endorsement, while Bastow, who had not had any dealings with Carter's administration over the previous three years, came under criticism from activists like Kameny for his comments about Carter. The NGTF remained largely divided about who to support, so they followed the organization's usual policy of not publicly endorsing any candidate for public office. Privately, some, like Valeska, believed that Carter had done more than enough and deserved their support and another four years, while others, like Brydon, although acknowledging Carter's accomplishments, believed that Kennedy would deliver even more.[30]

Carter's aides continued discussing how to respond to the NGTF's candidate questions. It would take them almost three months to respond, something that did not go down well with the NGTF,[31] especially since most of the candidates (John Anderson, Howard Baker, Brown, George H.W. Bush and Kennedy) had replied by mid-January 1980, while the others (Ronald Reagan, Robert Dole, Phillip M. Crane and John Connally) never responded.[32] Carter's delay could perhaps be explained by the fact that since he had received the questions, he had had to face the biggest crises of his presidency: the Iran hostage-taking, The Shah, the invasion of Afghanistan and the withdrawal of the SALT II treaty. The response was written on 3 March, by Eizenstat, Weddington and Wexler, approved by Carter, and signed by Strauss as the NGTF had requested.[33] It pledged to continue the administration's anti-discrimination policy, avoided making any promises for the future and highlighted some of the administration's accomplishments.[34] Surprisingly, the letter did not list all of these, with the most glaring omissions being the SDRP and Carter's appointments of openly gay people to presidential commissions. Nevertheless, Larry Bush wrote in *The Sentinel* that this letter made Carter the 'first incumbent president to tell gay voters that he deserves their support because of his accomplishments for them'.[35]

On 6 March, an NGTF press release publicized the contents of Carter's letter and declared, 'No other President has shown the courage evidenced by this Administration on the gay rights issue. We commend the actions taken so far and look forward to continued cooperation and momentum'. It concluded, 'reservations [over the requested

29 Steve Mertz, 'Gertrude Stein Chooses Kennedy', *The Blade*, 10 January 1980.

30 Bastow, Bush, Clay and Vida, author interviews.

31 Lou Chibbaro Jr., 'Carter Statement Viewed as Retreat', *The Blade*, 20 March 1980.

32 Anderson, Brown and Kennedy had responded favourably to all the questions in the questionnaire. Baker and Bush had not answered any of the questions and had merely stated that they opposed discrimination against gay people. Connally, although he did not respond to the questionnaire, had previously publicly declared not only his support for equal rights for gay people, but also that they should not serve in sensitive government jobs ('Candidates Take Stand on Gay Rights', *Gaze*, April 1980).

33 Memorandum, Stu Eizenstat, Anne Wexler and Sarah Weddington for President Carter, undated. BASF, GR, JCPL.

34 Letter, Robert Strauss to Charles Brydon and Lucia Valeska, 3 March 1980. RMSF, GH1, JCPL.

35 Larry Bush, 'White House Claims Solid Record on Gay Issues', *The Sentinel*, 16 May 1980.

Executive Order, H.R.2074 and the gay rights plank] aside, the Carter Administration can point to a solid track record'.[36]

Subsequently, the administration made three highly significant moves for gay rights. First, it requested from gay rights organizations a list of people they wanted to nominate as candidates for delegates to the Democratic Party's National Convention. It was the first time that a president had taken such an initiative. Secondly, on Wexler's advice, Carter approved the appointment of Apuzzo, at the time Director of the Fund for Human Dignity, to his Party's Platform Committee. Apuzzo's appointment made her the first openly gay person to be picked by a president for this committee. Finally, Carter approved the nominations as delegates of dozens of open lesbians and gay men who were put forward by the activists. It was the first time that a president had approved so many openly gay people as candidates to be delegates.[37]

Nevertheless, on 18 March, the day of the primary in Illinois, the local NGTF office issued a press release purporting to outline the positions of each of the candidates on gay issues. It said Carter had

> promised that the federal government would reflect his commitment to end discrimination on the basis of sexual orientation. . . . But Armed Forces regulations have become more anti-gay since 1976. Lesbians and gay men are still harassed by immigration authorities and fired by federal agencies such as the FBI and CIA. In 1980, Carter has declined to support a gay rights plank in the Democratic platform, or to sign an executive order banning federal discrimination on the basis of sexual orientation. No-one close to Carter has campaigned for gay votes this year. The Carter campaign has made no significant effort to involve gay people.[38]

The release offered an inaccurate and ill-informed picture of Carter and was entirely different in tone from the NGTF release of just twelve days earlier. The greatest distortions concerned the military and immigration. The authors seemed to be unaware of Carter's SDRP, reform of immigration procedures, or the CSRA, and it misrepresented Carter's 1976 position on federal employment in the security sector. Furthermore, Carter had not declined to support the gay rights plank and the administration had already appointed a number of openly gay people to its election campaign team, the best known being Apuzzo. In reference to the other candidates, the release showed a clear preference for Kennedy, saying he was the only candidate who had promised to issue the requested executive order, while he had also involved many gay people in his campaign.[39] The Illinois release brought the anger of the NGTF head office in New York which distanced itself from it.[40]

36 'Carter Appeals for Gay Support', News from NGTF, 6 March 1980. RMSF, GTFN1, JCPL.

37 Apuzzo and Weddington, author interviews; Andrew Humm and Betty Santoro, 'If We Gay Men and Lesbians Stand Up', *NYT Magazine*, 1 November 1980.

38 Illinois NGTF, 'The Candidates on Gay Rights', 18 March 1980. NGTFR, B.141, F.14, CU.

39 Ibid.

40 Bush and Clay, author interviews.

Carter started the primaries well, although Kennedy managed to win important victories in four Northern states.[41] On 20 March, Lou Chibbaro Jr reported in *The Blade* that it appeared to a section of the gay community that Carter was not courting the gay vote with the same zeal he had showed in 1976. The main source of this information was Bastow, who told Chibbaro that he had noticed a 'cooling' in Carter's campaign; he cited as evidence the fact that Carter's campaign workers had declined to participate in candidate forums sponsored by the GSDC as well as other gay groups in Florida and Illinois. Other evidence cited was Carter's belated response to the NGTF's questionnaire and his failure to commit to supporting H.R.2074. Furthermore, Chibbaro had been told by gay people from the states that had held the previous four primaries that Carter staffers had conveyed strong 'hints' to them that he would shortly come out in support of the Congressional gay rights bill and the plank in the Democratic Party platform, but that this eagerness faded away when Carter took the lead over Kennedy with a landslide win in the Iowa caucuses.[42] However, Chibbaro failed to mention that the GSDC, as well as the gay groups in Florida and Illinois, had publicly endorsed Kennedy and severely attacked Carter during the primaries, which explains the reluctance of Carter aides to participate in events organized by these clubs.[43] Bastow admitted as much to the author, but added,

> On the other hand, in politics, the wisdom in Washington has always been, 'You have no permanent friends or permanent enemies'. If Carter's people had been sharper, they would have . . . don't give up on anybody. But you're right. We wanted to hunt with the hounds and run with the hares.[*]

Meanwhile, the GSDC intensified its efforts in support of Kennedy and took out full-page ads in *The Blade*.[44] One of these was particularly critical of Carter, alleging that his 'weak and indecisive leadership has contributed measurably to our country's growing problems' and highlighting the fact that Kennedy had pledged to issue the requested executive order. The ad asked the gay community:

> Do we, we lesbians and gay men, uphold Carter who has allowed the military to pursue its irrational attempt to exclude all of us from the armed services?
>
> Are we to approve a man who permitted certain federal agencies to fire some of us solely because of our sexual orientation?
>
> Are we to sanction an administration which only last December accepted its Justice Department's legal interpretation that resumed efforts to bar all foreign gay people at U.S. borders . . . Kennedy decried the Carter Administration's Immigration ban on homosexual foreigners.[45]

41 Dumbrell, *The Carter Presidency*, 7.
42 Lou Chibbaro Jr., 'Carter Statement Viewed as Retreat', *The Blade*, 20 March 1980.
43 Bastow, author interview.
44 GSDC Adverts in *The Blade*: 'On May 6, Gay Clout Is on the Line. Vote for Edward Kennedy for President', 1 May 1980, and 'American Gays at the Crossroads: Kennedy vs. Carter', 3 April 1980.
45 GSDC Advert, 'American Gays at the Crossroads: Kennedy vs. Carter', 3 April 1980.

The ad was highly misleading and inaccurate. Carter had already passed the CSRA, and all the non-security federal agencies had reversed their anti-gay policies during his presidency, while the remaining 5 per cent could not have been protected by an executive order. It was impossible for Carter to secure legislation ending discrimination in the military, but his actions had led to significant gains for gay people in the military. Another big distortion of the truth was the suggestion that Carter was responsible for the ban on gay aliens. Absent from the ad were not only Carter's accomplishments in the area of gay rights but also the fact that members of the GSDC had met on several occasions with Carter aides such as Costanza, Haft, Thomas and Wales, in the White House or in the Club's offices, while Haft had even been a keynote speaker at one of the Club's events (see Chapter 11).

In the end, the gay community remained divided between Carter and Kennedy, although the majority supported the latter. Carter received the support of the majority of the local gay community in Georgia, Mississippi, Oregon, Ohio and Wyoming, while Kennedy prevailed in the states of California, the District of Columbia, Florida and New York.[46] Carter's loss to Kennedy in New York, by 59–41 per cent,[47] was attributed by Herb Rickman, past executive director of the New York State Democratic Committee, to gay support for Kennedy.[48] Gay rights activists also attributed Carter's 37–63 per cent loss to Kennedy in the District of Columbia to the gay vote, despite the fact that Carter had received overwhelming support from the local Black gay community.[49]

Prior to California primary, set for 3 June, Wayne Friday, a prominent gay rights activist and journalist, endorsed Kennedy in his regular column in the *Bay Area Reporter*.[50] Two of San Francisco's gay Democratic clubs, the Harvey Milk and the Alice B. Toklas, also endorsed Kennedy, attacking Carter's policies on women, gay rights and the economy.[51] The White House perceived the lesbian community in San Francisco to be 'more politically astute and more supportive' towards Carter than the 'very anti-Carter' gay men's community.[52] During a rally in San Francisco, Kennedy called Carter a 'clone' of Reagan, while his daughter and nephew campaigned in San Francisco's gay bars.[53]

Subsequently, Apuzzo travelled to California on her own initiative to meet with the local gay community and urge it to support Carter. The community was divided and although the majority supported Kennedy, Carter maintained significant support and the endorsement of prominent local activists like Sheldon Andelson who had been relentlessly campaigning for him. Apuzzo pleaded with the Municipal Elections Committee of Los Angeles (MECLA), the first gay and lesbian American Political Action Committee as well as the biggest and most powerful fundraiser in the city, to

46 Apuzzo, Bastow, Clay, Gerald, Jones-Hennin, McReynolds, Perry and Warburton, author interviews.

47 Larry M. Bartels, *Presidential Primaries and the Dynamics of Public Choice* (Princeton, NJ: Princeton University Press, 1988), 222.

48 'Democrats Need Gay Vote to Win Election', *The Sentinel*, the date is not visible. RMSF, G/L1, JCPL.

49 'Gays Tip Capital against Carter', *BAR*, 5 June 1980; Jones-Hennin, author interview.

50 Wayne Friday, 'Kennedy for President', *BAR*, 22 May 1980.

51 Jonathan Ball, 'Making Sexual Citizens: LGBT Politics, Health Care, and the State in the 1970s', in Bell, *Beyond the Politics of the Closet*, 77.

52 Note, Allison Thomas to Tom Belford, 5 September 1980. TBSF, Gays, JCPL.

53 'Kennedy Rips Carter at S.F. Rally', *Organized Labor*, 9 June 1980.

support Carter. She argued that Carter had a much better chance of defeating Reagan, who she claimed would be a disaster for gay rights, as Kennedy was too liberal to retain the support of moderate Democrats. However, MECLA's leaders, David Mixner and Dianne Abbitt, maintained their support for Kennedy, believing that he could beat both Carter and Reagan.[54] Mondale also made an attempt to win some support in the state; he visited San Francisco where he had breakfast with local political leaders, including the openly gay Larry Eppinette, Del Dawson and Lee Allen.[55]

Meanwhile, *The Sentinel* and *The Advocate* published Bush's articles on the administration's achievements, 'a record that holds a number of surprises, lending credence to White House claims that substantive gains have been made with little fanfare'.[56] The articles helped to change the minds of many members of the gay community about Carter.[57] Brydon, who strongly supported Kennedy, was interviewed by Bush for his *Advocate* article, and graded Carter's efforts on gay rights as 'C-'.[58] Bush later characterized the grading as a 'calculated insult'[59] which aimed to propel the gay community towards Kennedy. Nevertheless, in the same interview Brydon also provided apparently an upward revision of this grade, 'I think the administration's heart is in the right place, but I think they are frightened to death of the issue'.[60]

But although Kennedy went on to win in California, the tide was clearly turning towards Carter. Moderates and conservatives among Democrats preferred Carter and considered Kennedy too far to the left; the gay demographic would be unusual in skewing slightly in favour of Kennedy. Carter went on to win eleven straight primaries.[61] Carter eventually easily prevailed and retained the Democratic nomination, receiving 50 per cent of all the votes and Kennedy just 38 per cent.[62]

The gay rights plank

As the Convention approached, the agenda of gay rights began to centre on the question of a plank in the party platform. As early as October 1979, activists had begun pressing Carter to include it. They believed that in the event of a Democratic victory it would significantly increase the chances of favourable legislation being passed by Congress.[63] Although Carter personally, as well as his administration, 'fully supported' the inclusion of the plank,[64] the party and its Platform Committee were bitterly divided about it, with many, especially in the South, strongly opposed. Carter

54 Apuzzo, author interview.
55 Wayne Friday, 'Politics & Poker . . .', *BAR*, 22 May 1980.
56 Larry Bush, 'The Carter Administration. More Done Than Said?', *The Advocate*, 12 June 1980; Larry Bush, 'White House Claims Solid Record on Gay Issues', *The Sentinel*, 16 May 1980, quotation from the latter.
57 Bush, DeBaugh, Kent and McReynolds, author interviews.
58 Larry Bush, 'The Carter Administration. More Done Than Said?', *The Advocate*, 12 June 1980.
59 Clendinen and Nagourney, *Out*, 456.
60 Larry Bush, 'The Carter Administration. More Done Than Said?', *The Advocate*, 12 June 1980.
61 Dumbrell, *The Carter Presidency*, 8.
62 Eugene Robinson, 'The Democrats in New York', *WP*, 13 August 1980.
63 Dan Daniel, 'National Convention Project Launched', *GCN*, 10 November 1979.
64 Apuzzo, Bush, Eizenstat, Maddox and Weddington, author interviews.

received numerous phone calls and letters from conservative Democrats asking him to kill the plank otherwise they would not vote for him.[65] Eizenstat said, 'We had both southern Democrats and conservative Democrats who were concerned that this would hurt their races for front office and hurt Carter's chance of getting elected'.*

With the Kennedy challenge disposed of, politically it would have been beneficial for Carter to reject the plank. Even the liberals and feminists had some tactical doubts about it, although most of them supported it, but they were in any case a smaller component of the democratic coalition than moderates and conservatives.[66] Furthermore, Carter's largest support in 1976 had come in the South, especially, and crucially, among conservative religious people, including evangelicals. The evangelicals alone, as Falwell proudly declared in January 1980, were a force to be reckoned with as they constituted 40 per cent of the electorate, a far bigger electoral bloc than the gay community;[67] evangelicals numbered about eighty million,[68] in comparison to the estimated 15–20 million gay people.[69] The South was absolutely vital to the elections. Despite his awareness of these by now quite visible threats, Carter decided to do what he believed was morally right: support the plank. However, it was agreed that this should be done in a way that would (it was hoped) minimize the losses. This led to a concern with language – the words 'gay' and 'lesbian' – which as before would create political entanglements.[70]

Bastow and Pou had written a draft gay rights plank for the party's platform. This called for all anti-gay laws to be repealed, for a law protecting the rights of gay people, and for an executive order banning all anti-gay discrimination in federal sectors that were not covered by Carter's CSRA. Bastow, Pou and other activists had spent the first months of 1980 discussing the plank with various Democratic platform drafting subcommittees and Carter's administration. When the activists were due to meet with the Platform Committee in Washington, D.C., they invited Chanin, who at the meeting expressed the administration's support for the plank.[71] However, the administration was not happy with the language, which explicitly referred to gay men and lesbians, as they believed it would be harmful to party unity. Thus, Wexler, Thomas and David Rubenstein, Eizenstat's Deputy Assistant, began working with gay delegates of the Platform Committee, along with the NGTF and the NCP, trying to find language that would be acceptable to both the administration and the activists.[72]

While still locked in negotiations with activists about the language, Thomas took the initiative and asked the National Committee for Sexual Civil Liberties[73] for their

65 Eizenstat, Maddox and Weddington, author interviews; also see letters in various GR folders in JCPL.

66 Dukakis and Weddington, author interviews.

67 George Vecsey, 'Militant Television Preachers Try to Weld Fundamentalist Christians' Political Power', *NYT*, 21 January 1980.

68 George Vecsey, 'Carter Sways Some Evangelicals in 2-Day Blitz to Regain Support', *NYT*, 29 January 1980.

69 Harvey Milk's speech at Gay Freedom Day, 25 June 1978. MCSF, [GR-HMSL], JCPL.

70 Eizenstat and Weddington, author interviews.

71 Apuzzo and Bastow, author interviews.

72 Apuzzo, author interview; Memorandum, Allison Thomas for Anne Wexler, 28 May 1980. CHSF, GR, JCPL.

73 A high-level think-tank comprising jurists, doctors, academics, scholars and various other professionals that aimed to achieve legal reform and end all discrimination against gay people.

opinion regarding the wording.[74] Two days later, Carter appointed Jack Watson to replace Hamilton Jordan as his Chief of Staff.[75] Watson's appointment delighted gay rights activists because of his support for gay rights.[76] The same day, Apuzzo, who had been elected national co-chair of the Democratic Party's Lesbian and Gay Caucus, the two other openly gay members of the Platform Committee, Sheldon Andelson, a Carter delegate, Bill Kraus, a Kennedy delegate, along with Bastow and Pou met in the White House with Thomas, Chanin, Rubenstein and Mary Frank (research director for the Carter campaign) to discuss the plank. Carter's aides expressed the administration's willingness to include a gay rights plank but disagreed with the language in the proposed draft, insisting that the words 'lesbian' and 'gay' should not be included. They also warned that there could be 'trouble' if the lobbyists pushed too hard on the Carter-backed language.[77] Carter's proposal read: 'We must affirm the dignity of all people and the right of each individual to have equal access to and participation in the institutions and services of our society, including actions to protect all groups from discrimination based on race, color, religion, national origin, sex or sexual orientation'.[78]

Bastow told the author, 'I've got to give the Carter administration credit for going as far as they did'.[79] Although Andelson, Apuzzo and Pou were happy with Carter's proposed wording, Kraus was not satisfied as he believed that explicit language regarding gay men and lesbians was needed. Thus, the activists asked for a few hours to discuss Carter's proposed plank with their colleagues. The same evening, the six openly gay members of the 158-member Platform Committee of the Democratic Party who had first brought the issue forward – Andelson, Apuzzo, Gary Grefenberg, Kraus, Tim Mayhew and Janna Zumbrum – met with Bastow, Jack Campbell, Endean, Pou and Valeska to discuss Carter's proposed plank. Kraus strongly insisted on explicit wording and proposed forcing the matter to a vote on the convention floor; even if they lost, he argued, the national TV exposure would make it worth doing. On the other side, Andelson and Apuzzo argued that they had already won a big victory for gay rights with the plank and that it would be dangerous and foolish to jeopardize it. They reminded the activists that Carter forces were in control of the convention and might attempt to vote the plank down completely if they did not agree with the wording.[80] Endean strongly agreed and advised Bastow, as the latter recalled to the author, that he 'should be advocating strongly for the Carter plank because . . . the important thing wasn't just what it said, but . . . was to get in the Democratic platform that we were part of the Democratic coalition'. In retrospect, Bastow said, 'Steve [Endean] was absolutely right'. However, at the time he took no position as he believed it was up to the six delegates to decide.* Endean and other activists 'passionately' insisted that 'no one remembers

74 Letter, Anthony Silvestre to Allison Thomas, 11 June 1980. RMSF, G/L1, JCPL.

75 Steven R. Weisman, 'President Appoints Jack Watson to Replace Jordan as Staff Chief', *NYT*, 12 June 1980.

76 Bush, Clay, Kent and McReynolds, author interviews.

77 Apuzzo and Bastow, author interviews; Steve Martz and Lou Chibbaro, Jr., 'Gay Rights Included in Dem. Platform', *The Blade*, 26 June 1980.

78 Michael Glover, 'Carter Supports Gay Plank for Democratic Platform', *GCN*, 21 June 1980.

79 Bastow, author interview.

80 Apuzzo and Bastow, author interviews; Endean, *Bringing Lesbian and Gay Rights into the Mainstream*, 62–4.

the exact language of platform planks anyway', and that 'the wording was frankly irrelevant' since the important thing was the 'vital inclusion of nondiscrimination based on "sexual orientation". Accept Carter's deal, proclaim victory, and come out of the 1980 Democratic National Convention with a historic inclusion of gay and lesbian civil rights plank'.[81] When Kraus resisted, Apuzzo told him to 'get real', which led him to break down in tears, but he eventually backed down and everyone agreed to accept the proposed plank.[82] The following day, 12 June, the plank, wording unaltered, was included among Carter's proposals submitted to the Democratic Party's Platform Committee. The gay rights activists involved with the plank welcomed the decision as a 'clear victory' for the gay community, although they accepted that the language was less bold than they wanted.[83] Despite the fact that Carter's administration and his delegates supported the plank, a number of conservative members of his Party strongly opposed it and Carter was criticized for accepting it.[84]

On 19 June, a week after he had submitted it to his Party Committee, Carter, through Eizenstat who attended, publicly endorsed the passage of the gay rights plank at the opening session of the full Platform Committee in Washington, D.C. Eizenstat emphasized Carter's endorsement of the plank and urged the Committee to adopt it in order to 'ensure that no American is treated unfairly'. Bastow said at the time of Carter's statement, 'The President's statement represents the first time [that] an incumbent President has spoken out for the rights of gay Americans. This time they're supporting us. I think the process is moving'.[85] The plank was also supported by Kennedy.[86] The news that Carter had supported the gay rights plank angered many Democrats, especially in the South.[87] Pou said that Carter was 'lambasted in the South for his gay rights views'.[88]

On 24 June, despite strong opposition from several prominent members of the party, senior Carter aides including Eizenstat, Maddox, Weddington and Wexler convinced the Platform Committee to accept the gay rights plank. All of Carter's delegates were told by his aides to support the plank and the vast majority of them did. This meant the plank would be included in the platform without requiring a vote at the convention.[89] Also crucial was Maddox's intervention as he had managed to convince a number of conservative religious delegates to support it.[90] Martin Franks, Carter campaign's Research Director, told reporters afterwards that 'we went as far we could' in terms of the language used in the plank and argued that stronger language would have caused problems for all Democratic candidates across the country.[91]

81 Endean, *Bringing Lesbian and Gay Rights into the Mainstream*, 63.
82 Bastow, author interview.
83 Apuzzo and Bastow, author interviews; Steve Martz and Lou Chibbaro, Jr., 'Gay Rights Included in Dem. Platform', *The Blade*, 26 June 1980.
84 Eizenstat and Weddington, author interviews.
85 Larry Bush, 'Carter Calls on Democrats to Adopt Gay Rights Plank', *The Sentinel*, 20 June 1980.
86 'Notes from the Co-Execs', *It's Time*, July–August 1980. RMSF, G/L2, JCPL.
87 Eizenstat and Weddington, author interviews.
88 Don Leavitt, 'Latest Carter Move Termed "A Step Forward"', *The Washington Blade*, 10 October 1980.
89 Apuzzo, Eizenstat, Fiscal, Maddox and Weddington author interviews; Steve Martz and Lou Chibbaro, Jr., 'Gay Rights Included in Dem. Platform', *The Blade*, 26 June 1980.
90 Maddox and Weddington, author interviews.
91 Eric Planin, 'Party Adopts Gay-Rights Plank', *WS*, the date is not visible. RLMSF, GI, JCPL.

Despite the inexplicit language, the plank still condemned discrimination due to sexual orientation, and it was still a very important win for gay rights. The plank received widespread public attention and was hailed as a major historical achievement by the gay community and the gay press.[92] At a press conference by the NCP, a delighted Bastow stated, 'For the first time in American history, a major political party has endorsed the civil rights of gay people'.[93] A few months later, the NGTF and Kameny publicly acknowledged Carter's crucial contribution in convincing his party to adopt the plank.[94]

Carter was denounced by conservative Christians, especially evangelicals, and a large number of Democrats for supporting the plank, something that led to a split within the party.[95] Patrick Buchanan, who had served as special consultant to Presidents Nixon and Ford, and would go on to do the same with Reagan, saw this as confirmation that Carter was 'a lackey' of the gay rights lobby,[96] and sought to 'provide special protected status in law for individuals who profess and practice a life style that Carter's church teaches is aberrant, sinful and immoral'.[97] Bush, who closely covered these developments for the gay press, said that after the plank was announced, the White House press corps thought 'that that was suicidal' for Carter.*

A less visible but still important sequel was the amendment of the party's Charter to include non-discrimination clauses that referred to sexual orientation. At a meeting of the party's Rules Committee on 9 July, this amendment was proposed by two openly gay Kennedy delegates, Jo Daly and Stephen Weltman. The proposed amendment caused heated arguments in the Committee, in which, for example, Joseph Fauliso compared gay people to arsonists and rapists. But the majority of Carter delegates on the Committee supported, and in the case of Apuzzo and Diane Feinstein strongly promoted, the Kennedy delegates' amendment. Weddington and Wexler conveyed to the Committee that Carter strongly supported it and lobbied some of the Committee's members, which swung several undecided or opposed members, and the amendment was adopted.[98] Although it was an internal matter, the amendment to the Charter was important as it, unlike the platform, was a permanent document. The NCP leaders said they were 'extremely pleased' with the adoption of this amendment, which they said added 'further legitimacy to the participation of lesbians and gays' within the Democratic Party. Pou stated that its passing was 'a signal from Jimmy Carter that he and his re-election campaign take the gay vote very seriously'.[99] Shortly before the 1980 presidential election, Kameny included the amendment to the Party Charter as one of

92 Apuzzo and Bastow, author interviews; Andrew Humm and Betty Santoro, 'If We Gay Men and Lesbians Stand Up', *NYT Magazine*, 1 November 1980; Steve Martz and Lou Chibbaro, Jr., 'Gay Rights Included in Dem. Platform', *The Blade*, 26 June 1980.

93 Steve Martz and Lou Chibbaro, Jr., 'Gay Rights Included in Dem. Platform', *The Blade*, 26 June 1980.

94 NGTF, 'What Has Jimmy Carter Ever Done for Gays?', 1980 and AHMCC, 'While Others Talk … President Carter Acts', undated, both in NGTFR, B.6, F.3, CU.

95 Bourne, Eizenstat and Weddington, author interviews.

96 Patrick J. Buchanan, 'Carter's Pact with Gay Liberation', *Christian News*, 21 July 1980.

97 Patrick J. Buchanan, 'Is Mr. Carter a Born-Again Pagan, Too?', *The Greensboro Record*, 4 July 1980.

98 Apuzzo and Weddington, author interviews; Gay Vote 1980 Press Release, 11 July 1980. NGTFR, B.6, F.2, CU.

99 Gay Vote 1980 Press Release, 11 July 1980. NGTFR, B.6, F.2, CU.

Carter's accomplishments in a pamphlet and ads that he placed in the gay press seeking the gay community's vote for Carter.[100]

At the Convention

The 1980 Democratic National Convention met at Madison Square Garden in New York City from 11 August to 14 August. Unlike the 1976 convention, this one proved to be an ill-tempered affair, with flare-ups between Carter and Kennedy. The gay community had a visible presence as it boasted seventy-seven openly gay delegates (fifty-four for Kennedy and twenty-three for Carter), including twenty-two lesbians, compared to only three, and by the end of the proceedings, four declared gays in 1976.[101] Some of Carter's former associates had now sided with Kennedy; Abzug was heading Kennedy's forces on the Platform Committee, Costanza had publicly endorsed him, while O'Leary was a Kennedy delegate.[102]

The increased number of openly gay delegates was a vivid demonstration of the progress gay people had made over the past four years. Hundreds more came to support the gay rights plank,[103] further evidence of how the national discourse on gay rights had been changed by Carter's actions. However, the progress that had been made over the previous four years had expanded expectations on the part of activists who kept on asking for more. At the time of the Convention, thousands of activists demonstrated outside the hall, warning Carter by means of a large banner: 'No More Broken Promises'.[104] This was despite the fact that he had not broken any promises and had in fact delivered more than he had promised.

With the gay rights plank secured, gay rights activists focused on their other major goal: to make their presence felt, to raise their visibility and become a recognizable movement nationwide, as well as to bring their issues to the attention of the American people. In particular, they wanted to prove that they were accepted as a legitimate and respected political force by at least one of the two major political parties. Since the Lesbian and Gay Caucus was the largest ever to attend a national political gathering, this should not have been a problem. However, despite their numbers, the activists failed initially to make the desired breakthrough into public consciousness as they were completely ignored by the mainstream press. Bastow admitted, 'So far, we're not having much of an impact. There are a lot of groups here competing for press attention. You've got to figure some kind of strong angle to get it'.[105]

The angle chosen was to nominate an openly gay man for Vice President because candidates got fifteen minutes for a speech and thus national TV exposure. The candidate

[100] AHMCC ads in *The Washington Blade*, 'While Others Talk . . . President Carter Acts', 25 September 1980 and 24 October 1980.

[101] Lisa M. Keen, 'A Look at the Personnel and Political Diversity', *The Blade*, 21 August 1980; Eugene Robinson, 'The Democrats in New York', *WP*, 13 August 1980.

[102] Mattingly, *A Feminist*, 207–8; O'Leary, 'From Agitator to Insider', 94; Spruill, *Divided We Stand*, 284.

[103] Eugene Robinson, 'The Democrats in New York', *WP*, 13 August 1980.

[104] John Block, 'Protestors Giving Delegates Plenty to Think About', *AP*, 10 August 1980.

[105] Eugene Robinson, 'The Democrats in New York', *WP*, 13 August 1980.

was Melvin Boozer who was the nation's first openly gay Black person to run for the office of Vice President.[106] Boozer gave a brave speech from the podium which was televised in primetime and asked the party to support gay rights, which he compared with the struggle of Black Americans for civil rights.[107] Inevitably, the nomination was unsuccessful and Mondale was selected to run as Carter's Vice President. However, what disappointed the activists was that Boozer's nomination received little media coverage beyond the broadcast of Boozer's speech, apart from rather superficial mentions from D.C. newspapers such as the *Washington Post* and the *Washington Star*.[108]

An event of considerable importance inside the gay community took place on 13 August, when Wexler, accompanied by Chanin and Thomas, gave a presentation to the Lesbian and Gay Caucus. Wexler talked about the administration's accomplishments on gay rights and conveyed Carter's personal message and commitment to them that if re-elected, not only would he continue being committed to their cause but that he would achieve even more in a second term. Those present were 'appreciative' (in Apuzzo's recollection) of Wexler and acknowledged that Carter had indeed delivered on his promises but expressed their frustration about him not issuing the executive order eliminating remaining federal employment discrimination. Wexler explained that the administration had explored this option and had concluded that it would not have made a real difference as it would have no purchase on the military and agencies that were not covered by the CSRA. She also reminded them that such an order would cause controversy and could be very easily overruled by the next president or Congress, citing how quickly the Congress had moved to stop some of the administration's efforts on gay rights, such as on housing and gay veterans' benefits. Wexler insisted that the strategy would not only fail to benefit the gay employees but that the controversy and backlash that it would cause could hinder other gay rights efforts.[109] Wexler admitted that 'we [Carter's administration] are not perfect', and called for a 'continuing dialogue', reminding them that the 'White House is open to the Gay community at all times' and about 'what's at stake in [*sic*] Ronald Reagan'.[110]

At the end of her presentation, Wexler answered all the activists' questions, with the most contentious issue being the executive order. Some were not convinced by Wexler's claims about its ineffectiveness or insisted that Carter should issue it anyway. Wexler expressed Carter's willingness to work with the activists and try to find a solution to all their issues, but avoided committing Carter to successfully fulfilling all of the requests, and clearly stressed that it would be extremely difficult to end the military's discrimination against gay people. The majority of the activists were delighted with Wexler's comments. Particularly pleasing for the activists was the fact that Wexler had not just given a presentation but had very patiently answered all their questions, often explaining in great detail what could be done in order to address the issues. Given that Kennedy's promise to sign the executive order was the biggest difference between

106 Don Leavitt, 'The Nation's First Openly Gay VP Candidate', *The Blade*, 21 August 1980.
107 Rutledge, *The Gay Decades*, 156.
108 Don Leavitt, 'The Nation's First Openly Gay VP Candidate', *The Blade*, 21 August 1980.
109 Apuzzo and Warburton, author interviews; Don Leavitt and Lisa M. Keen, 'VP Candidate Route to Gay Visibility', *The Blade*, 21 August 1980.
110 Don Leavitt and Lisa M. Keen, 'VP Candidate Route to Gay Visibility', *The Blade*, 21 August 1980.

the two sides, some activists remained dissatisfied. Notwithstanding this, Wexler's presence and her presentation marked the first time that a senior presidential aide had addressed a gay and lesbian caucus.[111]

Six days later, Brydon and Valeska sent a letter to Wexler and thanked her for the presentation and commented that her presence and remarks there represented 'a willingness on the part of the Carter Administration to continue a vital dialogue with the national gay community'. They noted that some of the issues discussed, without mentioning them but clearly meaning the executive order and the military, 'seem to represent enormously frustrating and seemingly impenetrable obstacles, from our standpoint as well as from yours', but they expressed the 'hope that by continuing to work together we will find . . . creative solutions'.[112]

Carter easily secured the nomination with 2,129 votes to 1,150.[113] After his win, Kennedy offered congratulations and declared that he would 'support and work for the re-election of President Carter', urging 'all Democrats to join in that effort'.[114] Nevertheless, despite Kennedy's public statements, it was evident that the party was not united behind Carter. Journalists and political commentators questioned how enthusiastic Kennedy's backers would be about transferring their allegiance to Carter when the Senator himself had appeared rather reluctant to do so after his defeat.[115] Kennedy's gay supporters were reluctant to switch to Carter, with some of them indicating their preference for independent candidate John Anderson.[116]

Following the Convention, Carter found himself not only with a divided party but also without the support of most of his co-religionists the evangelicals, who were aghast at the gay rights plank and saw it as proof of Carter's endorsement of homosexuality. Maddox was condemned for campaigning for the plank, and he and Carter received numerous protest letters.[117] For example, Kenneth Bowden, a Baptist pastor, wrote to Maddox that he was 'appalled at the fact that you, a Southern Baptist Minister, would condone the dreadful sin of sodomy by approving and encouraging others to approve the Gay rights plank', and that he was going to 'encourage as many of the evangelicals' he came in contact with to vote for Reagan because he wanted 'no part of such a whitewash as you put on homosexuality'.[118] In 1981, Gary Jarmin, the national director of Christians for Reagan, said:

> We were working on school prayer, but then we found that almost everybody was unaware of Jimmy Carter's support for the gay rights plank. This is an issue which symbolized a drastic departure from Christian morality. Christians debate among themselves over school prayer, but when it comes to homosexuality, it is

[111] Apuzzo and Warburton, author interviews; Letter, C.F. Brydon and Lucia L. Valeska to Anne Wexler, 19 August 1980. NGTFR, B.6, F.2, CU.

[112] Letter, C.F. Brydon and Lucia L. Valeska to Anne Wexler, 19 August 1980. NGTFR, B.6, F.2, CU.

[113] Stanley, *Kennedy vs. Carter*, 168.

[114] Robert G. Kaiser and Martin Schram, 'A Formal Peace over Platform', *WP*, 14 August 1980.

[115] Hedrick Smith, 'Some Doubt Kennedy Enthusiasm after Podium Finale with Carter', *NYT*, 16 August 1980.

[116] Eugene Robinson, 'The Democrats in New York', *WP*, 13 August 1980.

[117] Maddox, author interview.

[118] Letter, Kenneth Bowden to Robert Maddox, 21 August 1980. RLMSF, GI, JCPL.

> so clearly wrong that to find a born-again President supporting gay rights is a real eye-opener. That's when we really got the 'ohs' and 'ahs' and gasps.[119]

What had particularly upset the evangelicals was that it was they who had helped Carter to come to office, being not fully aware of his social liberal views. Colonel Donner, chief strategist of Christian Voice, said, 'It was a tremendous let-down, if not a betrayal, to have Carter stumping for the ERA, for not stopping federally paid abortions, for advocating homosexual rights. Christians gave Jimmy Carter his razor-thin margin of victory in 1976. We plan to reverse that in 1980'.[120]

☙

As he had done four years earlier Carter sought the gay vote and appointed a number of open gay people to his campaign team during the primaries. Furthermore, Apuzzo's appointment to the Platform Committee made her the first openly gay person ever named to the committee of one of the two major parties. At one stroke, the highest authority in the nation signalled that gay people were to be treated as legitimate players on the political scene. Inevitably, the convention had the opposite effect on conservative Christians, who saw the gay rights plank as further proof of the moral decay of the nation under Carter.

Although Carter had done more for gay rights than any previous president, much of the gay community turned its back on him and supported Kennedy. This chapter has explored some of the reasons why. Meanwhile, despite being painfully aware of the damage his gay rights policies had done to his relationship with the evangelicals and other conservatives, Carter took a stand for his principles and was not afraid to clash with them. For the gay community, the plank and the non-discrimination amendment of the Charter brought symbolic as well as some practical benefits, with a permanent change to the party's internal rules and the prospect (not realized, as it happened) of a presidency expressly committed and with a mandate for progressive change in gay rights. Furthermore, 77 openly gay delegates attended the 1980 Democratic Convention compared to four at the 1976 Convention, another sign of the massive progress that had been made in less than four years. O'Leary wrote in 1999 about the convention's impact,

> The 1980 convention was an enormous success. We were in the platform for the first time and permanently included in the Charter of the Party. We had gotten national visibility and increased our respect from within the party. All in all, the gains reflected the ones we had made in the larger culture. We were definitely making progress.[121]

That progress was about to come to a screeching halt.

[119] Larry Bush and Richard Goldstein, 'A Chill Wind for Gay Rights', 9 July 1981, in Chris Bull (ed.), *Witness to Revolution: The Advocate Reports on Gay and Lesbian Politics, 1967–1999* (Los Angeles and New York: Alyson Books, 1999), 130–1.

[120] Allan J. Mayer et al., 'A Tide of Born-Again Politics', *Newsweek*, 15 September 1980.

[121] O'Leary, 'From Agitator to Insider', 95.

14

The end of the beginning

Gay rights and the 1980 presidential election

Carter had survived the challenge, an unusually strong one against a sitting president, of Edward Kennedy, to which internecine political rivalries among gay rights activists, a weak gay media apparatus, rapidly expanding expectations, and hesitant and inadequate communication of its achievements by the administration itself had all contributed. Warnings about the potential undermining of Carter in the face of the oncoming general election challenge had not been entirely heeded; indeed some activists were sufficiently dissatisfied with Carter that they suggested Reagan would be no worse for their cause than he had been. As the preceding chapter argued, the very status of Carter as a pioneer in this field produced both hesitancy and rising expectations. But the possibility that this promising beginning could come to an abrupt end was not sufficiently appreciated.

Gay rights and other problems

By 1980, Carter faced a range of issues, including recession, rampant inflation and high unemployment, while he had also to deal with a renewed oil crisis, the Soviet invasion of Afghanistan, the Iranian revolution and the embassy hostage crisis. Although he had inherited a difficult economic and political situation, Carter was blamed for many of the difficulties the American people continued to endure.[1] The difficult political and economic conjuncture of the late 1970s was not, in fact, unique to the United States, and helped to create what some analysts have understood as a 'paradigm shift' in politics and economic management, initially in the US and Britain, and later in other Western industrial countries.[2]

Carter had fulfilled, by one calculation, 80 per cent of the promises he had made during his 1976 election campaign, but critics considered these achievements to

1 Dukakis, author interview.

2 Peter A. Hall, 'Policy Paradigms, Social Learning, and the State: The Case of Economic Policymaking in Britain', *Comparative Politics* 25, no. 3 (1993): 275–96.

be of less importance than the promises he had failed to deliver.[3] Heading into the 1980 presidential election, Carter was in serious trouble. His public approval rating slumped to a historic low of 22 per cent.[4] Even though the realignment of the Southern white conservative vote was a long-term process that both preceded and continued after Carter's presidency,[5] his policies and decisions had contributed to it, dividing his own party and alienating conservative religious groups, especially evangelicals, who had played an important role in his 1976 victory.[6] At the same time, Carter had also managed to alienate the political left and progressive evangelicals who believed he was not progressive enough.[7]

The high expectations evangelicals and other religious conservatives initially harboured about Carter had turned to severe disappointment. Carter had supported gay rights and the ERA, had not opposed abortion to the extent they wanted, had not spoken out for prayer in schools and had appointed gay people to his administration and to public, visible posts while appointing no evangelicals.[8] For some conservative Christians, Carter came to be seen as not just indifferent to their cause but its enemy. With gay people increasingly visible and discourse on homosexuality becoming mainstream, their bitterness led some zealots to denounce Carter as the anti-Christ,[9] and many others to question whether Carter was indeed a Christian.[10] Mel White, biographer of James Dobson, Billy Graham, Jerry Falwell and Pat Robertson, told the author that 'all these fundamentalist Christian leaders saw Carter as a traitor to the Christian cause for his progressive stance on so many issues, including homosexuality'.* Indicative of how Carter was perceived at the time by a large number of conservative Christians was the statement of former Congressman John Conlan: 'Carter's had gay liberation people in the White House, sent Midge Costanza down to Florida to fight Anita Bryant on the anti-gay ordinance, has done nothing to advance the pro-life cause, fought the tuition tax bill and had his Internal Revenue Service commissioner harassing Christian schools'.[11] The new-found political zeal and prominence of religious conservatism, which seemed to resolve the tension between political withdrawal and engagement that had been prominent since fundamentalism emerged in the early twentieth century, with the latter view retreating after the public relations disaster of the Scopes Trial of 1925,[12] meshed seamlessly with the growing professionalism and technological innovation of the 'New Right', especially its early adoption of the techniques of computerized direct mailing. By this means, whatever the logical compatibility between conservative religion and the social change unleashed

3 Michael G. Krukones, 'The Campaign Promises of Jimmy Carter: Accomplishments and Failures', *Presidential Studies Quarterly* 15, no. 1 (1985): 136–44.
4 Stanley, *Kennedy vs. Carter*, 237n22.
5 J. Morgan Kousser, 'The Immutability of Categories and the Reshaping of Southern Politics', *Annual Review of Political Science* 13 (2010): 365–83.
6 Doukakis, Eizenstat and Maddox, author interviews.
7 Swartz, *Moral Minority*, 220–4; Weddington, author interview.
8 Bourne, *Carter*, 467.
9 Robert Maddox Exit Interview, 12 August 1980, WH Staff Exit Interviews, JCPL.
10 Maddox, *Preacher*, 137, 160–6.
11 'Reagan Backed', *The Desert Sun*, 3 December 1979.
12 Frank Lambert, *Religion in American Politics: A Short History* (Princeton, NJ and Oxford: Princeton University Press, 2010), 126–7.

by market deregulation, an effective coalition was created, and it found an effective figurehead in Reagan.

The novelty of Reagan's New Right candidacy, thanks to the divisions it opened up in the Republican Party, created another problem for Carter, with particular relevance to his gay rights appeal, when liberal John Anderson, an Illinois Republican Congressman, dropped out of the Republican primaries and announced an independent campaign for the presidency. Anderson had reached out to the gay community and publicly courted the gay vote. He had come out strongly in favour of gay rights and had recently co-sponsored House bill H.R.2074; in 1979 he had strongly opposed Laxalt's Family Protection Act, and in 1977 he had done the same with a bill that would have prohibited federally funded legal service for gay rights litigation.[13]

Carter and the 'national nightmare' of the religious right

Unlike the gay rights activists, evangelicals perceived no ambiguity in Carter's embrace of gay rights – he was seen as their avatar. Plainly, Carter's own religious background added force to the perceived threat; the charge of apostasy could be added to it, even though Carter's church had itself shifted position considerably. Carter told Professor Randall Balmer that 'when he learned that conservatives had taken over his own denomination, the Southern Baptist Convention, in June 1979 he knew he was in trouble'. Balmer argued that 'by then, arguably, it was already too late to reverse the damage, although he brought in Maddox to try to staunch the bleeding'.[14] Since his appointment as Religious Liaison, Maddox had been 'pushing all along' to convince Carter to meet with some prominent evangelical leaders. However, Carter was unwilling to do it, thinking that 'it could get out of hand'. Nevertheless, in January 1980, Carter reluctantly accepted Maddox's request in an attempt to regain some of his evaporating evangelical support. Maddox invited fourteen prominent evangelical preachers, including Falwell,[15] for breakfast in the White House with Carter. The breakfast took place on 22 January and Carter answered questions about issues such as arms, prayer in public schools, the ERA and abortion.[16] Falwell's question was, 'Is it fair to say that your definition of a family would not include the marriage of homosexual men or lesbians?' Carter nodded without saying anything.[17] Morris Sheats, founder of the Trinity Church and one of the participants, told the author that 'very few pastors were pleased' with Carter's response to their questions.*

13 'Anderson Takes Pro-Gay Stand', *Gaze*, May 1980; 'Candidates Take Stand on Gay Rights', *Gaze*, April 1980.

14 Balmer, author interview.

15 The others were Jimmy Allen, Jim Bakker, Robert Dugan, Brandt Gustavson, Rex Humbard, Howard Jones, James Kennedy, Tim LaHaye, Oral Roberts, Demos Shakarian, Dr Morris Sheats, Ronald Sider and Charles Stanley.

16 Maddox, author interview.

17 Dudley Clendinen, 'White House Says Minister Misquoted Carter Remarks', *NYT*, 8 August 1980; Maddox and Sheats, author interviews.

During the Republican primaries it quickly became obvious that Reagan would be his party's choice as candidate. Throughout his campaign, Reagan followed a stridently and openly anti-gay line. He refused to engage with gay rights activists at all on the basis that he was opposed to their cause on moral and religious grounds and continued to be in tune with the highly politicized religious right. For example, on 6 March, in an interview with the *Los Angeles Times*, Reagan stated that the gay community was trying to achieve 'a recognition and acceptance of an alternative lifestyle which I do not believe society can condone, nor can I'. Asked why, Reagan responded, 'Well, you could find it in the Bible. It says that the eyes of the Lord, it is an abomination'.[18] While, in the same interview, he said there should be no discrimination against gay people, in the context of his other remarks, the gesture was obviously a hollow one. Reagan was able to communicate with the religious right in their language, claiming, among other things, that he was an evangelical Christian.[19] He began meeting with evangelical fundamentalists who had declared war on homosexuality and gay rights like Jim Bakker, Falwell and Robertson, and he appointed Senator Laxalt as national co-chairman of his presidential campaign and Connie Marshner as Chair of his Family Policy Advisory Board, which aimed to establish links with pro-family and conservative organizations.[20]

Meanwhile, Bastow and some gay Republicans attempted to get the Republican Party to include a gay rights plank in its platform. They were of course rebuffed. In fact, the Republican platform, which also repudiated the ERA commitment that had been in place for forty years, contained a number of anti-gay resolutions. On the other hand, some proof of the progress that had been made during the previous four years in at least increasing tolerance of homosexuality could be seen in the fact that for the first time in the party's history, there were two openly gay delegates at the Republican convention.[21]

Despite Reagan's overtures to conservatives and his public opposition to homosexuality, some in the gay community perceived him as not much different from Carter with regard to gay rights. They believed that the openings that Carter had provided and the precedents he had set would continue with Reagan as president. *Gay News* even suggested that he would offer more for gay rights than Carter had. Its article cited Reagan's opposition to the Briggs Initiative and his not vetoing a sodomy repeal bill while Governor of California, and made the astonishing, and inaccurate, claim that Reagan could take credit for as many accomplishments with regard to gay rights as Carter.[22] On another occasion, the newspaper even claimed that Carter's record on gay rights 'sounds hollow'.[23] These naïve and inaccurate articles did not mention any of Carter's accomplishments, or note that Reagan, although he had not vetoed the

18 Clendinen and Nagourney, *Out*, 421.

19 Randall Balmer, *God in the White House: How Faith Shaped the Presidency from John F. Kennedy to George W. Bush* (New York: HarperCollins, 2008), 117–19.

20 Donald T. Critchlow, *Phyllis Schlafly and Grassroots Conservatism: A Woman's Crusade* (Princeton, NJ: Princeton University Press, 2005), 265, 275; Flippen, *Jimmy Carter*, 299.

21 'Gay Delegates Unhappy with Reagan Platform', *Gaze*, August 1980; Don Leavitt, 'A Dimmed Ray of Hope', *The Blade*, 24 July 1980.

22 'Reagan for President?', *GN*, 21 March–3 April 1980.

23 'Carter Solicits Gay Support, but his Record Sounds Hollow', *GN*, 3 April 1980.

sodomy repeal, had opposed it.[24] Ill-informed articles like this played a part in shaping an erroneous view in parts of the gay community about Carter's accomplishments on gay rights.

Falwell's campaign to get Carter out of the White House reached a new low in March. During a rally in Anchorage, Alaska, Falwell recounted an exchange that he said had taken place during the January breakfast meeting. Falwell told the audience that he had asked Carter, 'Why do you have known practicing homosexuals on your staff?' Carter supposedly answered, 'Well, I'm President of all the people', whereupon, Falwell claimed, he riposted: 'Why don't you have some murderers and burglars on your staff?' When the White House denied the alleged exchange, Falwell said this was Carter's attempt 'to discredit evangelical ministers who disagree with him on many social and political issues', and produced what he said was a transcript of a tape recording from the meeting. On 7 August, Maddox made the actual transcript of the breakfast meeting available to the media. It revealed that Falwell's only question to Carter was about his definition of families. Falwell's recorder has not caught any response from Carter but had picked up Falwell subsequently saying, 'Thank you – thank you very much', which practically confirmed that Carter had just nodded without saying anything.[25] Falwell had evidently lied and supported the lie with a concocted transcript. He eventually conceded that his version of Carter's remark was 'obviously' a 'reckless statement'. Asked if he planned to apologize to Carter, he said, 'I am doing it right now'.[26] He then gave a rambling and confused explanation of his action, saying 'I gave what I believed to be a parable of a president's position on gay rights', apparently suggesting that he was speaking metaphorically rather than literally, insisting that this was 'an absolute accurate statement of the President's record and position on gay rights'.[27]

The most surprising aspect of the affair was that Falwell was the source of the recorded evidence of his lie. He had received permission to tape the breakfast meeting, with the understanding that it was off the record, and had even sent Maddox a courtesy copy of the transcript afterwards – the one that Maddox eventually released to the press.[28] After this episode, Carter gave up altogether the attempt to win back his former allies and began a lifelong feud with Falwell. When he was invited by some conservative leaders to speak at the anti-ERA, anti-gay and anti-abortion Washington for Jesus march of 29 April, he turned down the request, as he did all others that followed from conservative leaders. He instructed Maddox, 'if they call again, the answer is no!'[29]

In order to ensure that all his followers got his message about who Carter was, Falwell used extensive mailing to communicate with them. A fund-raising letter said that though Carter called himself a Christian, he did not act like one.[30] A shock tactic employed by Falwell at his rallies was a ninety-minute video which beamed out repeated

24 Letter, C.F. Brydon and Lucia Valeska to *The Blade*'s Editor, 19 September 1980. NGTFR, B.6, F.3, CU.

25 Dudley Clendinen, 'White House Says Minister Misquoted Carter Remarks', *NYT*, 8 August 1980.

26 'Campaign Report: Fundamentalist Preacher Makes Apology to Carter', *NYT*, 13 October 1980.

27 Clendinen and Nagourney, *Out*, 421.

28 Dudley Clendinen, 'White House Says Minister Misquoted Carter Remarks', *NYT*, 8 August 1980.

29 Flippen, *Jimmy Carter*, 9–10.

30 Letters to Robert Maddox by Jerry Falwell, 1 November 1980, and by Ruth Bell Graham, 2 November 1980, both in RLMSF, Correspondence File, B.102, JCPL.

images of nuclear explosions, men kissing each other, discarded foetuses in hospital sluice pans, the face of Charles Manson and sex movie houses in New York's Times Square. The video was titled, 'America, You Are Too Young to Die!'[31] Maddox said, 'They just wanted to make it perfectly clear that they felt any kind of homosexuality was of the devil and anything Jimmy Carter did to foster them was satanic'.[32] Reagan continued to court religious and cultural conservatives. In July, he publicly gave his support to the Family Protection Act.[33] His choice of George Bush, his main rival for the nomination, as running mate was as usual an attempt to cover the bases, though in regard to gay rights the spread was not wide. Bush had also come out against gay rights during the Republican primaries stating, 'I don't think homosexuality is normal behaviour and I oppose codification of gay rights'.[34] However, after his defeat to Reagan, Bush had taken a slightly less hostile line, stating that while he was opposed to gay rights, he did not think that gay people should be harassed,[35] while in August he said, 'Maybe I could accept homosexuals in White House staff positions if there were positions for which they were uniquely qualified'.[36]

Carter's public endorsement of the gay rights plank consolidated the evangelicals' alignment with Reagan. Falwell relentlessly attacked Carter, claiming he 'had given undue recognition to homosexuals, to a perverted lifestyle, giving them unreasonable privileges [and adding] It is something the President does not have to do, popularizing the existence of this "minority"'.[37] The Moral Majority gave its backing to a group named Christians for Reagan, which solicited funds by direct mail, charging that Carter 'supported the lesbian-backed, anti-family ERA and the goals of the Gay Militants – even opening the White House doors to them!'[38]

Religious right leaders marked the final months of the campaign by staging rallies, workshops and seminars all around the country. They aimed to coach church ministers in the best methods of motivating their congregations to convert their beliefs and values into votes. Central to this effort was Ed McAteer's Religious Roundtable, which, in Dallas on 21 August, organized a conference of conservative Christians. Carter and Anderson declined an invitation to attend, but Reagan accepted it. When Reagan spoke, he made no mention of gay rights, abortion or the ERA,[39] but he told the crowd, 'I know this is a nonpartisan gathering, and so I know that you can't endorse me, but I only brought that up because I want you to know that I endorse you and what you are doing'.[40] By this time, it was not necessary for Reagan to state his commitments. Richard Cohen of the *Washington Post* commented about Carter's non-attendance, 'Whatever his reason, he has been a lot better than Reagan at understanding that

31 Flippen, *Jimmy Carter*, 291.

32 Larry Bush, 'Exit Interviews with the Carter Administration', *The Sentinel*, 20 February 1981.

33 Margot Hornblower, '"Pro-family" Push: Political Minefield', *WP*, 25 July 1980.

34 Shilts, *Conduct Unbecoming*, 368.

35 Andrew Humm and Betty Santoro, 'If We Gay Men and Lesbians Stand Up', *NYT Magazine*, 1 November 1980.

36 'Gays in a Reagan Administration?', *GN*, 22 August–4 September, 1980.

37 Shilts, *Conduct Unbecoming*, 368–9.

38 Michael Putzel, 'Pro-Reagan Groups Getting Tough on Carter', *AP*, 12 October 1980.

39 Kathy Sawyer, 'Reagan Sticks to Stand on Taiwan Ties', *WP*, 23 August 1980; Michael Sean Winters, *God's Right Hand: How Jerry Falwell Made God a Republican and Baptized the American Right* (New York: HarperOne, 2012), 139–43.

40 Winters, *God's Right Hand*, 143.

there is a distinction between his personal beliefs and policy – that his literal truth may not be everyone's'.[41] That is, of course, a reference to what has been called in this book Carter's 'wall of separation'. Carter sought at considerable electoral risk and with dignity (illustrated by his response via Maddox to Bob Jones III; see Chapter 6) to reconcile his religious and his political commitments. Reagan, far more comfortable and practised in the arts of political dissimulation, faced no similar hazard, whatever his 'literal truth' might have been.

As the elections neared, the religious right and groups like Christians for Reagan, Christian Voice and of course the Moral Majority greatly intensified their anti-Carter efforts, spending millions of dollars on advertisements. For a number of Reagan voters, Carter's open-door policy to gay rights activists was like a 'national nightmare', as Larry Bush wrote in 1981.[42] Carter's record on gay rights, up to and including his acceptance of the gay rights plank, was in effect weaponized.[43] According to Maddox, the anti-Carter groups portrayed Carter as 'a flaming liberal straight from the pits of hell'.[44] Reagan's campaign team both benefited from such ads and maintained some distance from them, as they were funded by the groups just mentioned. Two TV spots depicted Carter as being soft on 'perverts' and associated with 'militant' gay people, with homosexuality being depicted as one of the social ills that had been allowed to flourish under his presidency. They were widely run mainly in the Southern states during the last weeks of the campaign, although some clips appeared on national network news programmes. A number of stations deemed them offensive and declined to run them. Gary Jarmin, national director of Christians for Reagan and responsible for the ads, stated that they aimed to inform the public about Carter's 'support of homosexual rights', as he believed that 'there is no issue which will cause evangelicals to defect from Carter more than this one'.[45] The ads came in the form of two thirty-second spots, one portraying gay people as ridiculous and repulsive and the other playing up the perceived normality of a Reagan-style American family. The former showed scenes from San Francisco's Gay Freedom Day Parade where drag queens and men in colourful costumes were kissing each other, while a voiceover declared:

> Militant homosexuals parade in San Francisco, flaunting their life style. Flexing their political muscle, they elect a mayor . . . now the march has reached Washington. And President Carter's platform carries his pledge to cater to homosexual demands . . . Carter advocates acceptance of homosexuality. Ronald Reagan stands for the traditional American family.[46]

In the second ad, a woman in a woollen cardigan sat on a lawn chair next to a wood frame house. Looking into the camera, she declared,

41 Richard Cohen 'New Time Religion: Forgetting Civil Rights', *WP*, 2 September 1980.
42 Larry Bush, 'Exit Interviews with the Carter Administration', *The Sentinel*, 20 February 1981.
43 Shilts, *Conduct Unbecoming*, 369.
44 Maddox, *Preacher*, 166.
45 Lou Chibbaro, Jr., 'Anti-Gay Ads Rejected by TV Stations', *The Washington Blade*, 7 November 1980; Thomas Morgan, 'Pro-Reagan TV Spots Depict President as a Gay Rights Advocate', *WP*, 31 October 1980.
46 Ibid.

> As a Christian mother, I want my children to be able to pray in school. I don't want them being taught that abortion and homosexuality are perfectly all right. I was very sorry to learn that President Carter disagrees with me on all of these issues. Because of this, I'm duty bound as a Christian and a mother to vote for Ronald Reagan, a man that will protect my family's values.[47]

Gay rights activists expressed outrage at the portrayal of gay people in the ads. Kameny said, 'it's the same effort of the militant evangelicals to impose their beliefs on everybody. If they succeed, it will mark the death of this nation'. DeBaugh characterized them as 'dangerous' and said that they would undoubtedly contribute to 'irrational hate and bigotry' against gay people.[48] Carter characterized the advertisements as 'very vicious' and accused Reagan of responsibility for them,[49] while for the first time he publicly criticized the Moral Majority and 'others like them', claiming that they had introduced a 'narrow definition of what a Christian is and also what an acceptable politician is, and I don't want to see that happen'.[50]

The gay community on Carter: From 'purism' to 'all could be lost'

In the 1980 presidential campaign Carter actively sought the gay vote and followed the same pattern that he had in 1976: he made a direct appeal to the gay community to support him, he advertised in the gay press, some of his aides, like Chanin, Malson, Thomas, Weddington and Wexler worked on a daily basis with gay rights activists and campaigned all over the country by visiting local gay communities and appearing in several events and fundraisers organized by the gay community, his mother Lillian and his son Chip campaigned in the gay community, and he appointed openly gay people to his campaign team.

After Carter secured the Democratic nomination, several prominent gay rights activists and members of the gay community voluntarily mobilized to support him, and several Gays for Carter groups were formed across the country. But as the campaign got underway, many organizations in the gay community remained unenthusiastic about Carter. It perhaps took some time for the adversarial mindset generated by the nomination battle to be reset for the struggle against Reagan. Indeed a trajectory of growing consolidation and visibility of gay support for Carter as the election neared can be observed. It can be found, we will see, even in the trajectory of individual activists, such as Lucia Valeska of the NGTF.

47 Ibid.
48 Ibid.
49 Steven R. Weisman, 'Appeals Backing G.O.P. Said to Portray Views as Contrary to Bible', *NYT*, 1 November 1980.
50 Steven R. Weisman, 'Carter and Reagan Comments Tangle Campaigns in a Controversy Surrounding Evangelicals', *NYT*, 10 October 1980.

Some maintained consistent strong support for Carter. Kameny, who had dealt extensively with the administration and was aware of its efforts and accomplishments on gay rights, was particularly disgruntled at the gay community's failure to recognize these gains. He voluntarily joined Carter's election campaign, even refusing to accept money for his expenses, and relentlessly campaigned, sometimes alongside Thomas and Weddington, among the gay community in Washington, D.C.[51] In California, Troy Perry publicly endorsed Carter and the MCC all over the country mobilized in his support.[52] Several other prominent gay rights activists voluntarily joined Carter's campaign and campaigned for him, including Sheldon Andelson, Louie Clay, Jeanne Córdova, Steve Endean, Donald Knutson, Phyllis Lyon, Del Martin and Clayton Wells. Even Jo Daly and Bill Kraus, who had been Kennedy supporters, joined the campaign.[53] Kraus pointed out that Carter had 'more of a (Gay rights) record than any of the other candidates'.[54] Hundreds of openly gay people were appointed by Carter's election team to various paid positions within the campaign and across the whole country, with a focus on states and cities with large gay communities, while several hundred joined as volunteers.[55] Two of those appointed were Mary Spottswood Pou as campaign deputy press secretary in Northern California[56] and Jill Schropp as the campaign's Press Secretary in the state of Washington.[57]

Chip Carter campaigned again in California, visiting gay establishments and attending fundraisers organized by local gay rights activists; in a tour around the gay community in San Francisco, Chip was accompanied by Kraus. However, this time Chip was not as well received as he had been in 1976 due to the disappointment of portions of the community who believed that his father should have done even more for gay rights. Chip was even disinvited from a gay fundraiser in San Francisco due to protests from the local Jewish community at what they perceived as his father's pro-Palestinian and anti-Israeli stance.[58] Malson also campaigned in the gay community in California and appeared at numerous events organized by local gay rights activists; for example, on 8 October, in a fundraiser in San Diego, organized by Brad Truax, a local physician and prominent activist.[59] In Washington, D.C., Chanin, Malson, Thomas, Weddington and Wexler, often accompanied by local gay rights activists such as Endean and Kameny, campaigned in the local gay community. Weddington, often accompanied by Apuzzo or Valeska, also campaigned in the gay community in New York City and Texas.[60] Lillian Carter attended a fundraising event in Atlanta organized by the local Gays for Carter group, which was led by Ray Kluka and Gary Piccola, and she also visited the Atlanta Gay Centre.[61]

51 Kent and Weddington, author interviews.
52 DeBaugh, Perry and Wilson, author interviews.
53 Britt, Clay and Perry, author interviews.
54 Don Leavitt, 'Latest Carter Move Termed "A Step Forward"', *The Washington Blade*, 10 October 1980.
55 Apuzzo and Weddington, author interviews.
56 Don Leavitt, 'Latest Carter Move Termed "A Step Forward"', *The Washington Blade*, 10 October 1980.
57 White House News on Women, II, VIII, December 1980.
58 Fiscal, author interview.
59 Gay talking points, 8 October 1980. RMSF, G/L2, JCPL; Malson, author interview.
60 Apuzzo and Weddington, author interviews.
61 Clay, author interview.

In addition to being appointed to the Democratic Party's Platform Committee, Apuzzo was asked by Carter, again on Wexler's advice, to campaign for him in the gay community across the country and to run his New York City campaign. The administration felt let down by the community because of the lack of acknowledgement of its efforts and accomplishments; Apuzzo's mission was to rectify this lack of credit. Aware of the mismatch between accomplishment and acknowledgement, Apuzzo accepted the task but refused to accept any money for it. Thus, Apuzzo began campaigning for Carter, raising money with the help of the gay community; the NGTF, which supported her logistically, called her campaign 'The Apuzzo Road Show'. Further to her campaign efforts in New York City, Apuzzo toured key states with large lesbian/gay populations such as Texas, Ohio, Pennsylvania and California. Chip Carter and Wexler appeared alongside her at several events in gay communities across the country.[62]

On 25 July, *Out Front* magazine published an interview with Valeska in which she recognized that gay people would 'do better' under Carter than Reagan, who she expected would affect them 'detrimentally', and also acknowledged that 'Regardless of who is in office, our basic problem is going to come from the right wing in the next few years'. Along with this somewhat weak display of enthusiasm, Valeska reiterated the inaccurate trope that Carter

> could have done much more for us than he has done. It is unfortunate he hasn't lived up to some of his promises. In the past four years, we have made some progress with the current administration and that is not to be taken lightly. A lot of that is not a result of Carter personally on this issue. He stays as far away from gay rights issues as he can. But we have established some good relations with some people close to the top of the administration. There is certainly room for progress.[63]

A first for gay rights occurred when the Socialist Party of the United States of America chose David McReynolds, an openly gay man and prominent anti-war activist, to run for president, whereby it became the first American political party to nominate an openly gay person for the highest office in the land. McReynolds's nomination had nothing to do with gay rights or gay rights activists. His nomination did not receive any support from the gay community and the gay press and was in fact completely ignored by both. It also received hardly any coverage from the mainstream media: 'You won't find anything in the newspapers', McReynolds told the author. Apart from the fact that the Socialist Party was very small and generally ignored by the media, the majority of gay rights activists and the gay press were reluctant to publicly support someone seen as Communist, even if he was gay.*

Rather more visibly, John Anderson was actively courting the gay vote. He appointed a number of openly gay people to his campaign team. He wrote in *The Sentinel* that if elected he would issue an executive order banning discrimination based on sexual orientation in all federal sectors. He advertised in gay publications such as

62 Apuzzo, author interview.
63 Phil Nash, 'Gays in Politics: Lucia Valeska', *Out Front*, 25 July 1980.

Gaze, and his aides campaigned in gay communities across the country. As a result of this, Anderson became very popular in the gay community, among both Republicans and Democrats. Gay rights activists in various cities, such as San Francisco and New York, formed groups to support him, while a number of gay organizations, such as San Francisco's Stonewall Democratic Club and the Tennessee Gay Coalition for Human Rights, endorsed him.[64] In September, Bob Wechter, who was openly gay and was serving in Anderson's campaign as its liaison to the gay community, resigned from his post and joined Carter's campaign team. Wechter said that despite Anderson's firm support for gay rights, the people in charge of his campaign had no interest in reaching out to the gay community. Carter's team assigned Wechter to spearhead, along with Apuzzo, his campaign in the gay community.[65]

On 11 September, *The Blade* published a lengthy commentary by Bastow with the title 'Making the Right Choice in November', arguing that the interests of gay people 'clearly point toward the re-election' of Carter. Bastow claimed that Reagan's election 'would be a serious setback to achievement of the goal that many of us have been working for during the last decade – the acceptance of Lesbians and Gay men as a legitimate element of diversity in American society'. He argued that Anderson had no chance of winning, so any vote for him would be a waste and would benefit Reagan. He wrote about Carter, 'Most of us are painfully aware of President Carter's inadequacies. But we tend to forget that he also has a record of genuine accomplishment on behalf of civil rights of Gay people'.[66]

Also on 11 September, the GSDC met in Washington D.C. to discuss whether to endorse Carter. Many of the city's gay leaders, such as Kameny, Kuntzler, Pou and even Peter Edelman, who had been one of Kennedy's top aides, strongly urged the hundred or so members of the Club to publicly endorse Carter. They claimed that a vote for Anderson would be a vote for Reagan, whose election would be disastrous for the gay community. Bastow also asked for the endorsement, reminding the Club's members of Carter's contribution to the 'historic first' gay rights plank. Their request led to a heated debate. The opposition to the endorsement was led by Frank Zampatori and Melvin Boozer who asked for 'another month' to see whether Carter would take any 'significant' and 'visible' action for gay rights. Zampatori asserted that only the much-sought executive order would be enough for Carter to secure the Club's endorsement. Boozer said he would not give in to 'blackmail' by Carter supporters who were trying to frighten the gay community into supporting Carter by invoking the 'horrors' of a Reagan administration. In the end, the Club refused to endorse Carter.[67]

Subsequently, Steve Brown, the GSDC's President, sent an open letter to over a hundred gay groups all over the country urging them to withhold endorsing any presidential candidate until mid-October. The letter was very critical of Carter, incorrectly claiming he had 'either ignored or assigned a low priority' to gay rights

64 'S.F. Democrats Endorse Anderson – D.C.'s Remain Uncommitted', *Gaze*, October 1980; for the Anderson's ads see for example, *Gaze*, August 1980: 6–7 and September 1980: 12; McReynolds, author interview.

65 'Anderson's Gay Liaison Joins Carter Camp', *Out Front*, 31 October 1980.

66 Tom Bastow, 'Making the Right Choice in November', *The Blade*, 11 September 1980.

67 Lou Chibbaro, Jr., 'Stein Club Declines Carter Endorsement', *The Blade*, 25 September 1980.

issues for the previous three-and-a-half years and had only now begun courting gay voters. The statement acknowledged that the gay community had 'finally been recognized as possessing nationwide impact and significance' and asked gay voters to use this 'leverage' with Carter to lobby the White House via mail and phone calls telling his aides that they would not vote for him without receiving 'some positive, firm, and public commitment' that he would sign the requested executive order.[68]

The GSDC was severely criticized by gay leaders for its failure to endorse Carter and its general attitude towards him. A number of prominent activists, including Andelson, Brydon, Endean, Kameny, Valeska, Voeller and even O'Leary, publicly expressed their disappointment and condemned the Club's letter and actions.[69] Brydon and Valeska wrote to *The Washington Blade*'s editor arguing that 'by abandoning Jimmy Carter, you abandon gay people to those who will take our hard-won gains'. They argued that although Carter had not 'fulfilled all our ideals', he had nevertheless been 'the first President with the courage to do something about the concerns of gay people. Every action by the Carter administration on behalf of our interests has set a precedent' and urged the gay community to 'unite and support [him] vigorously'.[70]

One of the strongest critiques of the GSDC came from Kameny. On 10 October, he wrote a lengthy article in *The Washington Blade* in support of Carter, attacking the GSDC, calling its decision 'unfortunate and unrealistic', and other members of the gay community who had not appreciated Carter's efforts. He highlighted some of Carter's accomplishments and made the point that a vote for Anderson would be wasted and that a Reagan win would be an 'unmitigated disaster' for the gay community. Kameny's analysis is worth quoting at length:

> There has developed in the Gay community a strange mythology to the effect that Carter has done nothing for us. This flies squarely in the face of the facts, which demonstrate beyond controversion that Carter had not only done more for the gay community than any other president, but he had done more for us *than all other presidents put together.*
>
> As one who spent 15 years writing to president after president, from Kennedy to Ford, to ask for a meeting with our president or White House staff, without ever getting so much as the decency of a reply or even the common courtesy of an acknowledgement, and who picketed in front of the White House gates for such a meeting, it was particularly gratifying, in 1977, to come through those gates to meet with presidential staff inside the White House, to see numerous such meetings with Gay community leaders follow that notable first meeting, and to see the kind of *responsive* access which we have had in the years since; to what

68 Steve Brown, 'An Open Letter to Lesbian and Gay Male Voters', 17 September 1980. RMSF, G/L2, JCPL.

69 Franklin E. Kameny, 'Gay Survival and Practical Politics: Support for Carter', *The Washington Blade*, 10 October 1980; Letter, C.F. Brydon and Lucia Valeska to *The Blade*'s Editor, 19 September 1980. NGTFR, B.6, F.3, CU; Bastow, Bush and McReynolds, author interviews.

70 Letter, C.F. Brydon and Lucia Valeska to *The Blade*'s Editor, 19 September 1980. NGTFR, B.6, F.3, CU.

> became for the first time, *our*, White House, as it had been before then for all other Americans except us.
>
> This negativism toward Carter seems to arise from a kind of 'purism' of the type which we tend to associate, these days, with the New Right fanatics and zealots, but which is unseemly for a Gay community which is learning to take pride in its political sophistication. In order to gain support, under this purism, a candidate must have done *everything* we want, must have done it in precisely the way and in the style that we wanted it done, and must have done it yesterday (if not the day before). Such a demand for perfection as a pre-condition for support is puerile. That kind of perfection is never in the cards, politically.
>
> The Federal government has been one of our chief adversaries for some 200 years. . . . To expect *all* of that to have been reversed in the three or four short Carter years from 1977 through 1980, as the purists do, is irrational. To argue that because there still remain some things to be done at the presidential level, that because Carter has not yet done them, and that because some of the things he has done were done more quietly and less flamboyantly (but no less effectively), or otherwise differently than some of us might have liked, Carter should be faulted and therefore we should not support him, is yet again irrational. Utopianism and perfectionism do not get one very far in real-life politics . . . [I]f we do not give Carter a chance to at least double his already-impressive record of accomplishment for us, by a second term, we will have only 'might have beens', as our lives recede back into the bleakness and desolation of past years. . . . *Carter is worthy of Gay support: he has earned it; and he should have it.* Our future as Gay people and as American citizens depends upon it.[71]

Kameny remained a passionate supporter of Carter's record on gay rights until his death, believing that he had been unjustly treated by history and by some within the gay community with regard to his efforts and accomplishments on gay rights.[72] As confirmation, the edition of *The Washington Blade* that contained Kameny's article also contained an article by John Gilbert in which he strongly argued in favour of Reagan, claiming that he was not anti-gay and that his attitude towards gay people was 'live-and-let-live'.[73]

In late September, Kameny and Pou, determined to help Carter, joined by Jeannie Craciun and other members of the GSDC who supported Carter, founded the Allan Hoffard Memorial Campaign Committee (AHMCC), named for one of the founders of the GSDC, a closeted gay and a close associate of Kameny. The sole purpose of the Committee was to mobilize the gay community to vote for Carter and it would disband after the election.[74] The AHMCC embarked on a national campaign that included ads in gay publications, leaflets, mails and public speeches, aiming to inform

71 Franklin E. Kameny, 'Gay Survival and Practical Politics: Support for Carter', *The Washington Blade*, 10 October 1980.

72 Kent and McReynolds, author interviews.

73 John Gilbert, 'Claiming a Share in America's Destiny', *The Blade*, 10 October 1980.

74 Lou Chibbaro, Jr., 'Carter Committee Formed', *The Blade*, 25 September 1980.

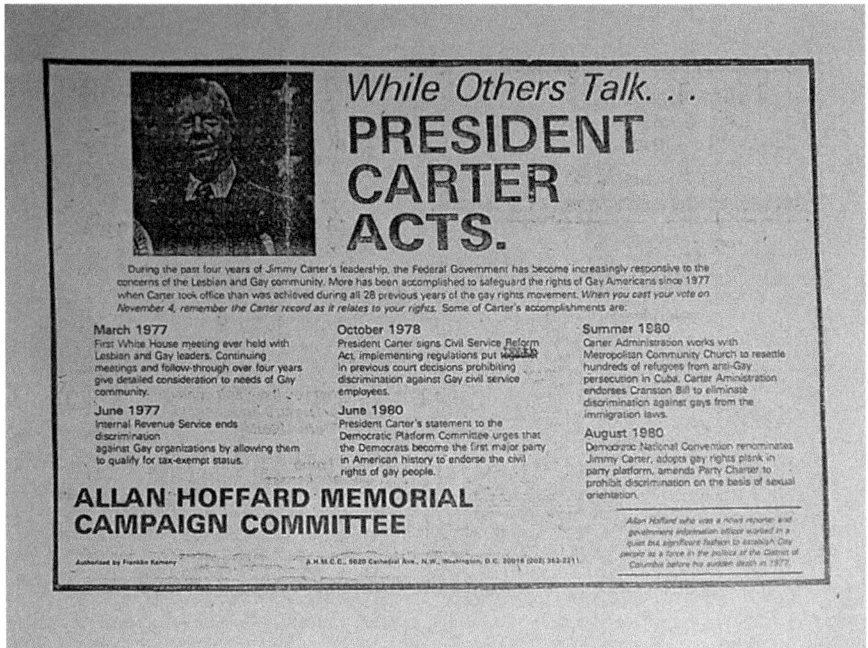

Figure 8 One of the Allan Hoffard Memorial Campaign Committee ads. NGTFR, B.6, F.3, CU.

the community of the administration's accomplishments and to convince it to vote for Carter (Figure 8).[75]

Faced with the onslaught of the religious right, many prominent gay rights activists and organizations were involved in ensuring that gay Americans got out and used their vote for Carter. State and national gay organizations, like the Dade County Coalition for the Humanistic Rights of Gays, Integrity, the Lambda Independent Democratic Club, the Mississippi Gay Alliance, the NCBG, and two out of three major gay organizations in Texas publicly endorsed Carter, and some of their members campaigned for him.[76] Bob Basker had remained a passionate Carter supporter; once again, he voluntarily participated in his election campaign and organized several fundraisers in the gay community.[77] Vogel and Andelson warned gay voters that Anderson had no chance of winning and that it would be a disaster for gay people if Reagan won the election.[78] Nevertheless, a number of gay Democratic clubs, such as the Stonewall of San Francisco,

[75] AHMCC ads in *The Washington Blade*, 'While Others Talk . . . President Carter Acts' and 'On November 4 We Will Choose Between Two Futures'. 25 September 1980, 10 October 1980 and 24 October 1980; Bush and Kent, author interviews.

[76] Clay, DeBaugh, Jones-Hennin and Sandifer, author interviews; Letter, Peter Vogel to Joel McClaery, 24 February 1980. NGTFR, B.6, F.3, CU.

[77] Kent, author interview.

[78] Lou Chibbaro, Jr., 'Carter's Efforts Not Enough Activists Warn', *The Blade*, 10 July 1980.

endorsed Anderson.[79] On the other hand, although McReynolds was openly gay, he was not endorsed by any gay organization.[80]

The NGTF had never previously endorsed a candidate for public office. On 14 September, its Board of Directors voted unanimously to endorse Carter.[81] In its resolution on endorsement, the NGTF wrote that Carter had opened the White House's doors to the gay and lesbian community in 'an unprecedented fashion, resulting in more substantive advances for gay rights than under any previous administration'. Valeska and Brydon wrote in *It's Time* that although the NGTF usually did not endorse candidates for public office, they strongly urged the gay community to vote for Carter.[82] On 2 October, the NGTF took an even stronger stand for Carter, urging the gay community to vote for him. The statement, written by Brydon and Valeska, read:

> This administration has a solid record of achievement. From funding of gay health services, to the change in tax policy that enabled otherwise qualified gay foundations to receive 501 (c) 3 tax deductible status, to being the first administration in history to formally support a piece of gay rights legislation in Congress – the Cranston immigration bill –, to its sensitive decision on enforcement of the immigration law and assistance and support of the resettlement of gay Cuban refugees and other actions, the record is positive. This does not mean that President Carter has achieved all that we would want in the area of civil rights for the gay community. There remains an agenda for Presidential action that includes an Executive Order to establish across the board the principle of nondiscrimination on the basis of sexual orientation, administration leadership for passage of the federal gay rights bill and the Cranston immigration reform bill, and the appointment of qualified lesbians and gay men to executive and judicial positions. We feel that Mr. Carter has shown considerable sensitivity and is the candidate who would be best able to continue this progress.[83]

On 4 October, Valeska gave a speech at NOW's annual conference in San Antonio and repeated the same address to the Dorian Group in Seattle fifteen days later. She concluded her speeches with a plea for coalition efforts to re-elect Carter, citing the progress that had been made under him and warning that 'all could be lost' if Reagan won the election. Despite Valeska's plea, the conference did not endorse Carter or any other presidential candidate.[84] The same month, Carter released issue papers with his main achievements in each area, as well as his position on each issue (see Chapter 11). Although he was under tremendous pressure from conservatives over his gay rights policies, one of these papers was on gay rights; apart from listing his achievements in

79 Wayne Friday, 'Stonewall Recommends Anderson', *BAR*, 11 September 1980.
80 McReynolds, author interview.
81 NGTF's resolution on endorsement, 15 September 1980. NGTFR, B.6, F.3, CU.
82 Charles Brydon and Lucia Valeska, 'Notes from the Co-Execs', *It's Time*, September 1980. NGTFR, B.6, F.3, CU.
83 'National Gay Task Force Directors Express Support for Carter', News from NGTF, 2 October 1980. NGTFR, B.6, F.3, CU.
84 Georgia E. Fuller, 'NOW Acts on Lesbian Concerns', *The Washington Blade*, 10 October 1980; Valeska, 'NOW Speech'.

the area so far, it contained the clear and strong statement he had made in support of gay rights on NBC the previous January (see Chapter 11).[85] Meanwhile, since she had begun campaigning for Carter, Apuzzo had asked local gay organizations all over the country to track gay voters precinct by precinct. The results showed that support for Carter had significantly increased compared to the 1976 elections.[86]

As the election approached, the NGTF took another unprecedented step and placed its own ads in support of Carter in its publications and leaflets.[87] Its language in support of Carter became stronger. In a pamphlet, the NGTF summarized Carter's record and urged gay people to vote for him. Its headline was 'What has Jimmy Carter Ever Done for Gays?' The organization answered the question thus: 'More than any other president in American history, that's what'. It then went on to commend his accomplishments on gay rights, his stand against the religious right which was 'crusading' against gay people, and his support for 'the first gay rights plank in history'. It concluded by warning that a Reagan win would 'roll back every step we've taken'.[88] On 31 October, just four days before the election, *Out Front* magazine endorsed Carter. Its editorial stated that Carter's record on gay rights 'has not been unimpressive. His administration responded well to our initiatives to achieve equality – more than all other administrations combined. . . . We commend Carter and his Cabinet for making bold attempts at solving problems that previous Administrations failed to address – some which previous Administrations even created'.[89]

As election day neared, most gay voters seemed to conclude that Carter was their best option. All the gay rights activists interviewed for this book, apart from McReynolds who obviously voted for himself, voted for Carter, as did most of the gay people they knew. Many gay voters did so in acknowledgement of Carter's contribution to gay rights, while others acted mainly to stop Reagan. However, a substantial portion of the gay community voted for Anderson or Reagan.[90]

Carter loses: 'Shut out'

Despite the fact that a Gallup poll had predicted that the election would be close, on 4 November Reagan won a landslide victory, with 51 per cent of the vote to Carter's 42 per cent, Anderson taking about 7 per cent.[91] The South contributed to Carter's defeat; of the fifteen Southern states, Carter won only two, in contrast to the thirteen he had won in 1976.[92] White, married, middle-class women tended to vote for Reagan because they felt he was stronger on 'family values', while white single women, and

85 Don Leavitt, 'Latest Carter Move Termed "A Step Forward"', *The Washington Blade*, 10 October 1980.
86 Larry Bush, 'TV Network Finally Discovers Gay People', *The Advocate*, 20 November 1990.
87 Letter, Elaine Noble to Charles Brydon, 5 November 1980. NGTFR, B.6, F.3, CU.
88 NGTF, 'What Has Jimmy Carter Ever Done for Gays?', 1980. NGTFR, B.6, F.3, CU.
89 'Endorsements: Vote Carter for President', *Out Front*, 31 October 1980.
90 Apuzzo, Bastow, Bunch, Bush, Clay, Kent, McReynolds and Perry, author interviews.
91 Critchlow, *Schlafly*, 265.
92 Eizenstat, author interview.

ERA supporters generally, tended to vote for Carter;[93] 63 per cent of the pro-ERA women voted for Carter and 69 per cent of the anti-ERA women for Reagan.[94] As for evangelicals, 56 per cent voted for Reagan and only 34 per cent for Carter, contributing greatly to Reagan's wins in the South. A poll showed that 61 per cent of the 'born-again white Christians' had voted for Reagan.[95] Pollster Louis Field determined that, without evangelical support in the 1980 presidential election, Reagan would have lost to Carter by 1 per cent of the popular vote.[96] Jarmin claimed that his ads portraying Carter as a gay rights advocate played a significant role in swinging targeted voters, including Southern Christians: 'I think it was the Christian votes that put Reagan over the top in most of the Southern states. We won with a particularly close margin in Alabama, Arkansas and the Carolinas'.[97] The religious right quickly attempted to take credit for its contribution to Reagan's win; Robertson's first broadcast after the election claimed proudly that conservative Christian voters had been the decisive factor. He went on to itemize problems he had had with a number of White House staffers under Carter, and referred to Costanza as having been 'repugnant to Christians' for having advocated gay rights.[98]

Gay rights activists were downcast. Endean wrote 'our hearts sank',[99] while Bastow said, 'It's a disaster. An obvious setback. People that advance the idea that we're a legitimate minority were beaten'. Kameny stated, 'There is a lot of anxiety in the community verging on panic'.[100] Retrospective judgements were yet more categorical: O'Leary wrote in 1999, 'Unfortunately, Carter lost the election and we were faced with Ronald Reagan and what would evolve into twelve long years under Republican White House leadership',[101] while Nancy Wilson recalled to the author the sense not only of loss but also of uncertainty at the time, saying, 'That was a *terrible* election to lose, and we knew it when we lost it, and I don't know that we knew how much we lost and how much it would impact us'.* Bunch argued that Carter's innate 'decency' played a role in his defeat; 'the politics of decency is at such a contradiction to this kind of right wing ruthlessness and I think Carter was very much a victim of that. And every time he tried to stand up for principles he was made to seem weak'.*

On 19 January 1981, the day before Carter's last day in the White House, Brydon and Valeska sent him a mailgram which read:

> On behalf of our members and staff, the National Gay Task Force would like to express its gratitude and heartfelt thanks for your successful commitment to open the government to all citizens, for your concern for human rights and justice and

93 Zillah Eisenstein, 'Antifeminism in the Politics and Election of 1980', *Feminist Studies* 7, no. 2 (1981): 187–205.

94 Critchlow, *Schlafly*, 265.

95 Winters, *God's Right Hand*, 158.

96 Randall Balmer, *Thy Kingdom Come: How the Religious Right Distorts the Faith and Threatens America: An Evangelical Lament* (New York: Basic Books, 2006), xvii.

97 Quoted in Lou Chibbaro, Jr., 'Anti-Gay Ads Rejected by TV Stations', *The Washington Blade*, 7 November 1980.

98 Flippen, *Jimmy Carter*, 312.

99 Endean, *Bringing Lesbian and Gay Rights into the Mainstream*, 90.

100 'Thoughts on Things to Come', *The Washington Blade*, 7 November 1980.

101 O'Leary, 'From Agitator to Insider', 95.

> for the positive steps taken by your administration to advance the civil rights and human dignity of all gay people.
>
> We particularly have appreciated your administration's openness in discussing gay issues, its opposition to employment discrimination in the federal government because of private non-job related behaviour and the permission to enter the United States granted to gay Cuban refugees.
>
> Thank you for being a decent, caring and compassionate President. May the months and years ahead offer you personal fulfilment and satisfaction as you reflect on your achievements in the past four years . . . our hearts are with you.[102]

Immediately after the election, the NGTF had sent a message to Reagan congratulating him for his 'overwhelming victory' and expressing the hope that he would 'understand' and 'listen' to their 'reasoned voice'.[103] However, the hope was soon dashed, if it had ever really existed, as Reagan not only failed to respond to the message but abruptly ended the access the gay community had enjoyed under Carter to the White House, the administration and the federal government more generally. A December 1981 letter from the NGTF to its members gave a clear picture of the situation which gay rights activists would face throughout the 1980s. It said, 'We have been shunned by the White House . . . our contacts at the numerous agencies of the federal government have been cut off or severely restricted'.[104] Wilson told the author, 'I think none of us were quite prepared for how shut out we would be in a Reagan administration'.* It was the religious right that now enjoyed access and a new wave of social conservatism rose under Reagan. While evangelicals would in the end experience some disappointment with Reagan's actions and achievements in their field of interest (most obviously in abortion law),[105] his accommodating rhetoric prevented anything resembling the break they had made with Carter (or, as they saw it, his with them). Not until two and a half years into Reagan's presidency would representatives of the gay community visit his White House for the first time. The meeting was held on 21 June 1983, and it discussed not gay rights in general or the community's broader agenda, but the AIDS pandemic.[106] Gay rights activists must have seen the change coming quite early in Reagan's administration: within four months of his inauguration, the White House cancelled its subscription to *The Advocate*,[107] and presumably the other gay publications that Carter had taken.

☙

102 Mailgram, Charles Brydon and Lucia Valeska to President Carter, 19 January 1980. NGTFR, B.6, F.3, CU.

103 'A Note of Congratulations', *The Washington Blade*, 7 November 1980.

104 'Dear Friend', NGTF announcement, December 1981. NGTFR, B.3, F.11, CU.

105 After twelve years of Republican control of Supreme Court nominations, under Reagan and George H. W. Bush, the Court in 1992 handed down its decision in *Planned Parenthood v. Casey*, which modified *Roe v. Wade* but nevertheless maintained the nationwide right to abortion access which it had established, falling short of the religious right's most important goal.

106 Rutledge, *The Gay Decades*, 208–9.

107 'For the Record: Maybe Nancy Dislikes the Pink Section', *The Advocate*, 14 May 1981.

The election was characterized by the GRNL as 'a milestone' for the gay community.[108] In its usual sense of a significant marker of forward progress, this metaphor can be questioned, as the election result triggered not just a setback, but a prolonged reversal for the cause of gay rights. Even so, the conduct of the election did represent significant forward progress for the gay community. Carter sought the gay vote even more vigorously than he had done in 1976. He made a direct appeal to the gay community to vote for him; he sent members of his family and his administration to campaign in the gay community and at gay events; he advertised in the gay press; he appointed open gay people to his campaign team; and he became the first president to publish an issue paper on gay rights.

The election is often discussed with regard to the unprecedented mobilization and contribution of the religious right; however, the gay community also mobilized as never before. Although the community had got together to support Carter in 1976, the extent of the 1980 exercise was unprecedented, despite the fact that the changed setting created in part by Carter's own achievements, and the resulting expansion of expectations, created gaps in this support. As this chapter has documented, such dissenting views or lukewarm approval tended to diminish as the election grew closer, and intimations of a future without President Carter grew more vivid. In addition to the formation of the Gays for Carter groups and the campaigning of several prominent gay leaders in support of Carter, prominent gay rights activist Kameny formed the AHMCC to aid Carter's campaign, while for the first time the NGTF endorsed a candidate and took out ads to support Carter.

There were two other noteworthy firsts with regard to gay rights; for the first time, there were openly gay delegates, if only two, at the Republican convention, while an openly gay man, McReynolds, set a precedent as a presidential candidate. Although Carter was not directly involved in either of these developments, they provide further evidence of the changes that had occurred during his presidency. That gay people felt emboldened to declare their identities to the nation and to seek office at the highest levels clearly owed much to the atmosphere of acceptance and respect engendered by the Carter administration. Chanin was expressing an evident truth when he told the gay community that Carter had 'begun to change the attitudes of people'.[109]

[108] 'Does Support for Gay Civil Rights Spell Political Suicide?', GRNL, n.d. RMSF, G/L1, JCPL.

[109] Bill Peterson, 'Brown's Support for Gays Brings Cheers', *WP*, 28 November 1979.

15

Conclusion

Carter's gay rights legacy

As well as summarizing the key achievements of the Carter presidency in the field of gay rights, this chapter examines difficult questions of causation and responsibility, though it cannot hope to resolve them. It relates the Carter years to broader changes in political culture, some of which extended beyond the United States, and emphasizes that the sequel of these years was a long hiatus, which casts an even more vivid light on their pioneering character. The last words of this book are, however, left to the activists, politicians, officeholders and others who generously gave their time to talk about Carter's gay rights achievements with the author and who are far better placed than he to express the true meaning of Carter's gay rights legacy.

Gay rights gains, revisited

- As the Democratic nominee in 1976, Carter stated at a news conference, 'I don't think that the government at the local, state or federal level should single out homosexuals for special abuse or special harassment, or special prosecution under existing laws'; his campaign team issued a press release entitled 'Jimmy Carter Speaks Out on Gay Rights', and his campaign placed advertisements in the gay press. He was the first nominee to make such statements.
- Openly gay people were appointed to Carter's campaign organization, an Advisory Committee on Gay People was formed inside the organization, and a gay rights caucus was accepted at the 1980 Democratic National Convention.
- Carter's White House staff contained numerous staffers with a history of gay rights advocacy, and readily addressed its concerns in public forums, with Carter's approval; Midge Costanza of the Office for Public Liaison was a prominent example, but one of many. Some appointees were publicly or among colleagues known to be gay, about which Carter had no qualms.
- Openly gay people were invited to Carter's inauguration, and were appointed to various advisory committees and commissions, for the first time.
- After a preliminary meeting in February marking the first talks in the White House for gay rights activists, in March 1977 a delegation of fourteen activists

attended for what the NGTF called 'the biggest opportunity in our movement's history', presenting a wide-ranging agenda of concerns, most of which were acted upon. Subsequently, twenty-one meetings between Carter's aides and gay rights activists took place in the White House, while his administration facilitated over thirty meetings between gay rights activists and federal departments and agencies.

- Over time, the White House also began to appreciate the internal complexity of the gay community, by, for instance, inviting representatives of racial minorities within that community, and gay religious leaders, for talks about their interests; thus even its embrace of the community as a whole, already a dramatic advance, was further improved upon in a more differentiated engagement with it.
- Carter's Civil Service Reform Act, a major legislative initiative, established for the first time the job security of gay people in 95 per cent of federal government employment. After White House intervention the Civil Service Commission began hearing harassment cases against gays, and gay people were no longer barred from access to government volunteer programmes such as the Peace Corps.
- The IRS granted tax-exempt status to gay rights community organizations, having previously made it a condition that they accept that homosexuality is a disease; this made more of their funds, largely obtained through donations, available for beneficial use, and of course marked an important moment of recognition. In addition, it unlocked numerous sources of direct federal funding for gay organizations and the community.
- The FCC revised its regulations for its 'ascertainment' procedure and its 'fairness doctrine' to ensure consultation with the gay community and representation of its viewpoint in broadcast media.
- While amendment of immigration law to remove a provision explicitly excluding people with 'sexual deviancy' from entry to the United States proved impossible, the administration brought about a radical change in its implementation which in effect established a 'don't ask, don't tell' policy at the border. The administration also worked proactively with the MCC to ease the plight of gay people among the Mariel boatlift from Cuba and waived immigration restrictions on a humanitarian basis.
- Carter's post-Vietnam Special Discharge Review Program was extended to cover the cases of gay veterans who had received 'less-than-honourable' discharges on the exclusive account of their homosexuality; many were upgraded, making them eligible to receive various veterans' benefits. While policy going forward reaffirmed the 'incompatibility' of homosexuality with military service, the policy of less-than-honourable discharge was abolished. Carter's judicial appointees contributed significantly in the longer term to dismantling the assumed 'rational basis' for the discharges. The administration intervened to enable gay representatives to participate in ceremonial commemoration of those in their community who had died in military service.
- Gay inmates of federal prisons won the right to access non-pornographic publications serving gay people, and to receive support and ministry from the MCC; the word 'homosexual' was removed when reporting a sexual crime in

prison, and sensitivity training, in which gay people participated, was introduced for prison guards.

- The administration's plans to memorialize the Holocaust were expanded to incorporate the victimization of gay people.
- Through Carter's Office for Families, the government promoted gay youth group peer counselling for state agencies dealing with young gay runaways, while the Office's model adoption code placed no restrictions on same-sex couples' adoptions and urged that 'non-traditional' family environments should be considered equally and on merit.
- Well after Carter's presidency, his judicial appointees contributed to major rulings abolishing discriminatory anti-sodomy statutes and establishing the legality of same-sex marriage.

As already noted, many of the above examples of progress for gay people, and the many others charted in preceding chapters, combine practical aspects, such as access to employment or to financial assistance, with symbolic ones. But about the symbolic aspect of Carter's policies on gay rights issues there is more to be said. It is easy to think of the visibility gained by the gay community, and by gay people, during this period as simply a raising of their profile and their political influence, but it is important to remember that it has an almost literal meaning, against a long background not only of derogation but of exclusion from any means of rectifying it politically. Carter's made unprecedented contributions to gay rights which, though not widely recognized, were hugely important in the march towards dignity and acceptance for gay Americans, and hence their ability to live an open way of life.

Carter had very little political scope to introduce new laws with respect to gay rights due to Congress's strong opposition to them. However, where and when he had scope to implement the existing laws in a more liberal way, he did so. Whenever possible he used the White House's influence and power to enable significant positive changes. The resulting practical and symbolic gains did not immediately reduce the expression of hostility to gay people, indeed they may well have increased it since there was now a much more visible 'threat' from the perspective of those who saw gay people in a threatening light. But even this should be seen as a form of progress, as the gay community itself was now an audible and officially recognized interlocutor in these debates.

Gay people in the process also became more visible *to themselves*. In the mid-1970s, few gay people were active in the cause of gay rights. The NGTF, the largest gay organization, was formed in October 1973 and was taking its first, mostly unsuccessful, steps, as it was unable to establish any communication with the government or federal agencies. Many gay people could not see any reason to become active in the struggle as there was no end product, and many gay organizations were more like social clubs than special interest groups. All this changed during Carter's presidency. The growing visibility and legitimation of the movement, along with the fast-changing public discourse on homosexuality, prompted many gay people to organize seriously. The March 1977 Meeting in particular was a catalyst for the enlargement and strengthening of the NGTF and other organizations. The NGTF consisted in 1976 of 2,500 members while in 1979, just three years later, it had quadrupled in size.[1] Activists realized that they could get results by organizing and lobbying. Early successes following the meeting were hugely important and persuaded many gays to join the struggle for their rights, convinced that at last they could be heard and could influence policy. The same applies to the NCBG whose membership of a few dozen increased overnight to several hundred and soon after to several thousand after the organization's meeting in the White House.[2]

A telling indicator of the symbolic effects of policy changes, meetings in and with government, and the visibility created by the president's own statements about the need to end discrimination against gay people is the contention by all the gay rights activists interviewed for this book that during Carter's presidency, for the first time, gay people were coming out willingly and on their own terms. David Mack Henderson, a gay rights activist and founder of Fairness Fort Worth, said that 'Carter changed the perception of how we were seen and therefore how we were treated. Carter removed what was seen as the stigma [of being gay]'. A lot of gay people he knew 'came out during Carter's time' as 'they were not embarrassed to admit they were [gay] anymore. This, for me, was his major achievement: getting rid of the stigma'.* Bush said:

> I wrote a piece in the *Advocate*, a few years after that, that said that while much of what we do with politics is important and makes a difference to people's lives, the most important thing is people coming out, because as you come out, more people become aware of *who* we really are, instead of who people *say* we are. And I still think that that's the most critical turning point. . . . So, as much as what Carter did, . . . he made it more likely that people would come out on their own terms, instead of being forced out by a government action.*

Carter and changing political culture: Demiurge or victim?

It has been a theme of this book that the Carter administration's response to and embrace of the concerns of the gay community was both an extension of political cultural changes that had been underway since the 1950s and also a major cause of the growing cultural backlash that soon became known as the religious right. The answer to the question posed in the subtitle above is, therefore, 'both'.

Carter and his administration's efforts, often not only responsive but also sometimes proactive, have just been recapitulated. Previous chapters have also considered episodes in which these efforts generated new pressures to which the administration had to respond. The issue of lesbian participation on the conference to recognize the UN International Women's Year might not have loomed large when the conference was conceived by the Ford administration, but the new environment

1 Letter, Jean O'Leary to members of the Congress, 8 January 1979. NGTFR, B.139, F.1, CU; Bruce Voeller, 'NGTF: Our Past and Future', *It's Time*, 1976 Special bonus issue, n.d. SWSF, [NGTF-CR], JCPL.

2 Gerald and Jones-Hennin, author interviews.

created by Carter made this important lesbian dimension highly visible. New opportunities for participation by previously excluded people in turn evoked a growing response from organizations and sections of the public who were hostile to them and wished them to remain excluded and invisible. And this dialectic in turn created tactical dilemmas and debates among liberal and progressive advocates as to which issues to prioritize, what language to use and how best to oppose the growing reactionary forces.

Beyond the IWY Conference, the Carter administration faced the challenge of positioning itself in relation to the growing backlash. While Carter himself consistently maintained a balance between personal religious disapproval of homosexuality and his political commitment to human rights and non-discrimination, which was described above as his 'wall of separation' between religion and politics, many others could not accept this balance and found one or the other side of it to be insupportable. Carter's finessing of the issue showed consistency of principle, but was not always persuasive, as when he avoided until a very late stage making a public comment on California's discriminatory Proposition 6 while allowing very visible advocacy and participation in the campaign by Midge Costanza. The difficulties came to a head in the delayed, and renamed, White House Conference on Families, which in effect bookended the administration's gay rights efforts just as the Women's Conference had, but in a much alert and attentive external cultural environment. By this time, the religious right was more than hinting at its mobilizational potential and deployed it effectively in the process of electing delegates to the Conference, until modifications were made to prevent this. Simultaneously, the expectations of gay rights activists had expanded rapidly: it was not only in the economy that Carter faced a problem of inflation. These forces converged on Carter in 1980, first in the nomination battle with Kennedy, which Carter won thanks to moderates and conservatives in his party, *despite* Kennedy's greater appeal to gay Democrats, and then in the general election where a growing sense of tactical realism belatedly consolidated the gay community's support for him.

Fear of Reagan was by no means a misplaced component of this sense of realism. Despite the absence of a record of religious motivations in Reagan's political conservatism (in fact, probably because of it), and despite his background as a twice-married film actor who had inhabited the relatively permissive Hollywood milieu for some time and with some success, he was better able than Carter to associate himself with the rising political power of the religious right. While, in a further irony, the causes of evangelicals did not in general receive high priority from the Reagan administration, in the matter of gay rights Reagan had no difficulty obliging them. A long hiatus in the progress of gay rights ensued. It would be rendered much more harmful by the AIDS epidemic that was about to strike, and to which the administration responded very weakly, on plainly discriminatory grounds.

There was indeed, beginning around 1980, a substantial inflection in the politics of leading democratic countries, with the accession, first in Britain and the United States, of governments committed to a neoliberal policy of market deregulation and anti-statism. In several instances, this policy paradigm was combined with conservative positions on social policy and social change – an unstable combination in view of the tendency of unfettered markets to bring about considerable social disruption, but nevertheless a politically effective one at the time,[3] and sometimes since. Carter's presidency can be seen as a casualty of this widespread change of public mood. He was also, however, a victim of his own success in respect of the gay rights movement: its beneficiaries began (until very late in the day) to take their future prospects for granted, while its opponents began a long upswing in political influence in the United States. In this sense Carter combines the status of cause and effect, demiurge and victim. The duration of the resulting setback testifies to his significance.

Gay rights after Carter

As a result of the AIDS catastrophe, gay organizations were distracted throughout the 1980s and 1990s from their quest for greater civil rights, focusing instead on the urgent need for research into the disease, and on the even more urgent need for the sick to receive care.[4] But the gay community itself, and its organizations, despite the ravages of the AIDS crisis, never returned to its previous condition of obscurity: its visibility was a permanent achievement.

It is beyond doubt that a second-term Carter presidency would have responded much more effectively to the crisis than his successor did. O'Leary argued in 2004, 'If Carter had been there when the AIDS crisis came up, it would have been a whole different story. It would have been treated like a legitimate disease'.[5] Apuzzo told the author, 'I never doubted that had President Carter prevailed in the 1980 election, the course of the AIDS epidemic would have been significantly different'.* Further evidence for this hypothesis of alternative history came in the late 1980s, when Carter organized a series of meetings on AIDS at the Carter Presidential Center, with the participation of religious groups. Among the participants were Christian fundamentalists – at a time when several of their co-religionists were saying that 'AIDS was God's gift to gay men' – and religious gay leaders, such as Troy Perry. Carter's aim was to raise awareness among the churches about the true causes of AIDS and increase their understanding about the disease, as well as to find some common ground in the fight against the pandemic. Lastly, but very importantly, he wanted to put an end to the hate language used by some religious leaders against gay people. It was the first-ever meeting of this kind, and Carter was widely praised by the gay community for the initiative.[6]

Another post-presidential contribution of Carter's came in 1992, when he agreed to be the honorary co-chair at the annual dinner of the Human Rights Campaign in Atlanta. The organization had been founded in 1980 by Steve Endean and over the years grew to become the largest advocacy and lobbying organization for gay rights. The organization's dinner in Atlanta drew 1,200 people, and Carter expressed his

[3] Andrew Gamble, *The Free Economy and the Strong State: The Politics of Thatcherism*, 2nd edn (New York: New York University Press, 1994).

[4] Apuzzo, Bush and Perry, author interviews.

[5] Karen Ocamb, 'O'Leary's Toughest Fight', *The Advocate*, 2 March 2004.

[6] Perry, author interview.

support for gay rights, at the same time becoming the first former president to attend a gay event.[7]

That it took almost thirty years after Carter left office for gay Americans to make further significant gains testifies to the difficulties he had faced. The long hiatus of the Reagan years shows that Carter was far ahead of his time. It also indicates the contingent effect of his personal interest in the issue. Ford, Carter's predecessor as president, and Reagan, after him, governed in different political environments, but in the area of gay rights Carter's environment presented challenges that were partly the result of his own important initiatives and responses. Ford had been caught off guard when he was asked about 'civil rights for gay people', replying 'civil rights for whom?', before calling it 'a very new and serious problem' to which 'it would be dishonest to give a pat answer' (see Chapter 1).[8] He was in office just at the end of the period in which such a polite and arguably decent, but also evasive, response to the question could be effective. Reagan, on the other hand, sought and gained the presidency at a time when calling homosexuality a biblical 'abomination' was a profitable political gesture. Carter not only straddled this epochal difference but greatly contributed to its existence.

Further substantial progress for gay rights did not arrive until Obama's election in 2008. However, even then, it was still possible for people to be fired because of their sexuality. Carter's CSRA had protected gay people in 95 per cent of federal employment, basically everywhere but the security services and the military. That 5 per cent remained outstanding and the situation would remain exactly as Carter left it for nearly thirty years. It was the same for military service. That Carter upgraded several dishonourable discharges to honourable was the best thing that any president did for gay soldiers until Obama permanently removed discrimination in terms of sexual preference from the military. Without downgrading Obama's achievements, it was easier for him to support gay rights than it was for Carter during the second part of the 1970s. By 2008, the public attitude towards gay people had changed markedly. However, this change started with Carter's presidency and was the result of his policies and decisions. If some of Carter's achievements appear unimportant today, when same-sex marriages are legal throughout the United States, it is important to remember that he acted at a time when homosexuality was considered by many Americans to be abhorrent, a disease and a dire threat to children (though this last element is by no means absent in the present climate of political debate, around the question of transgender). In judging Carter's achievements in this field, it is essential to set his actions against the environment and attitudes of his time, not the way things are today.

Last words

Although Carter's role in advancing gay rights has been underestimated and little publicized, it has not gone entirely unnoticed. Prominent gay rights activists from the

7 Endean, *Bringing Lesbian and Gay Rights into the Mainstream*, 100.

8 'Ford Has "No Pat Answer", *The Advocate*, 7 April 1976'.

era who were actively involved in the struggle for gay rights and had direct dealings with Carter's administration have praised President Carter's efforts. For example, Elaine Noble stated that she was 'quite amazed' and 'surprised the Carter administration made as many commitments as it did, to open doors for us', comparing the situation favourably to that during the Kennedy administration, when all of their requests for a meeting had been ignored; she said, 'a lot of us have picketed on the outside. Now we see ourselves inside the fence'.[9] In 1980, the two biggest gay newspapers, *The Advocate* and *The Sentinel*, praised Carter's achievements in the area of gay rights, while observing that these had not been adequately appreciated by the gay community.[10] Frank Kameny and Jeannie Craciun wrote in 1980 that Carter had 'achieved a number of genuine advances for the civil rights of lesbians and gay men'.[11] Apuzzo highlighted the 'growing understanding' that Carter and his administration had regarding gay rights and added,

> My feeling is he went further than he thought he could go. I think he really moved on the issue significantly and that was wonderful, and I come back to my point, that elections matter, just ask yourself would it have been a different story if Reagan hadn't been the president during AIDS and Carter had been the president during AIDS, it would have been a completely different response on the part of the government. I believe it in my soul, I believe it in my soul. This man could not have looked with such benign neglect at what was going on. One of the great sadnesses in my life is that we couldn't get him elected because what happened later so needed a man with his integrity and compassion.*

Bunch said about Carter,

> I think that he did more than we realised at the time. I think that . . . you know, we were the impatient activists. We wanted 100 per cent from him, from Bella Abzug, from everyone, and he wasn't 100 per cent. In retrospect, I think he did a great deal. And you're even telling me more that I didn't know. I think he *did* do a lot that we didn't see, because we wanted more. But what we *did* get was very important, and you see how important it is when you see Reagan trying to push back against it all. I think we underestimated how much Carter did at the time. And as I said before, his support [for gay rights] *after* being president has been even more important.*

And Bush said:

> I think that the Carter administration marked a turning point, both for government and for the LGBT community. The turning point was that there began to be an

9 Austin Scott, 'Carter Aide Meets with Gay Activists', *WP*, 27 March 1977; Lou Romano 'Gays Meet with Carter Aides', *The Blade*, April 1977.

10 Larry Bush, 'The Carter Administration. More Done Than Said?', *The Advocate*, 12 June 1980; Larry Bush, 'White House Claims Solid Record on Gay Issues', *The Sentinel*, 16 May 1980.

11 'On November 4 We Will Choose Between Two Futures', Allan Hoffard Memorial Campaign Committee, undated. NGTFR, B.6, F.3, CU.

> understanding that we needed to have a dialogue, and that we needed to correct some of the injustices that had existed. . . . You could not argue about the gay Cuban refugees as being anything other than significant.*

Clay believed that Carter 'legitimized' the gay community and changed public discourse about gay rights, while he also 'humanized' gay people. He reflected in 2014,

> I think Mr Carter himself would probably . . . reflect that no, he wasn't as bold as he might have been, but I think that's more from the point of view of what came later. He certainly has been a major advocate for example in his retirement for marriage equality. . . . I think the reforms [regarding gay rights] were highly significant. They set a model for the country and I think they opened the country's experience.*

Hayden said, 'Carter's administration created an era in which the movement for LGBT rights began to impact the political and policy processes. It took three or four decades before the seeds really began to grow in the present. It is important to recall the hard times'.* Montgomery argued that 'there can be no doubt that all these efforts by President Carter were of the utmost importance for us and that really made a difference to the improvement of our lives'.* McReynolds considered Carter to be 'the best ex-president' in terms of contributing to gay rights and that his actions during his presidency were 'very courageous' as 'gay rights then were not what they are today'.* Schockman said,

> I think Carter was the silent force [of his administration's efforts on gay rights] until times when he did speak out, but it was very appropriate when he spoke out, it wasn't off the wall, he was very methodical. And again, times were so different then, very different. [Carter and Rosalynn] were both visionaries before their time and activists after their time and one of the greatest living presidents, I think, that we have ever seen.*

Doubleday said, 'Carter is a very honourable man. I would say that he might be the most honourable president in my lifetime. I've always had great admiration for him. I pray for him daily'.* DeBaugh said,

> I think Carter was excellent in terms of his support for LGBTQ people and gay rights in general, and he directed his staff to assist us in whatever ways they could. You know, you've got to also understand that the President of the United States has lots and lots of issues on their plate, and so we weren't necessarily a number one priority. But we *were* a priority, and they did support us as much as they could.*

Wilson said about Carter, 'first of all, he was the first person to *really* recognise LGBT rights as a legitimate area of concern for the White House. And just the fact that he would begin to open the doors and begin to look at non-discrimination – it was, I think, in some ways, the most powerful thing that he did'.* Hallman said,

> Carter's contribution in advancing gay rights is for me unquestionable and I am actually surprised that it is not very hyped. He was the one who set the wheels in motion in the 1970s in a very difficult period for us. I think he was a very brave president who did the right thing and what his conscience told him to do, but as it often happens it was not appreciated at the time.*

Jones-Hennin agreed that Carter did much more for gay rights than he gets credit for and added in a more personal vein,

> I *love* Jimmy Carter. I absolutely *adore* him. In my mind, he was one of our best presidents. And I think he especially highlighted . . . post-presidency, after he left the White House, I think it highlighted what a good guy he is. In fact, I think he didn't get re-elected, in part, because he was too nice. He was too pure. He was incapable of being nasty.*

Afterword

Lillian Faderman[1]

In 1962, the year Jimmy Carter won his first political bid and became a Georgia state senator, most of America still thought of homosexuals as loonies, lawbreakers, subversives, and sinners. In the *Diagnostic and Statistical Manual of Mental Disorders*, which was the virtual 'bible' of the American Psychiatric Association, homosexuality was presented as a sickness. It required intervention, sometimes even treatment such as aversion therapy, electroshock, or lobotomy.

In every state of the union except Illinois (which had voted to repeal its sodomy law the year before Carter's first election) homosexuals were presumptive criminals. Many states defined sodomy not just as anal sex but as any sex act other than heterosexual intercourse, which meant that lesbians too were subject to sodomy laws. In Illinois, before the state's sodomy law was repealed, convicted homosexuals could be held as psychiatric prisoners until they 'recovered'; and if they 'recovered' they could be criminally tried for having committed sodomy. In all the forty-nine states that continued to have sodomy laws throughout the 1960s, sodomy was a felony; it was punishable in some states by up to twenty years in prison.

To the federal government, homosexuals were also security risks: that was because homosexuality was illegal and reprehensible, and so, the argument went, homosexuals could easily be blackmailed into giving away state secrets. Homosexuals were thus witch-hunted out of federal jobs. Indeed, by almost universal consensus, homosexuality was so awful that known homosexuals could be fired from any job, whether in the public sector or the private sector – lest they spread their moral contagion to other workers.

No religious denomination in America officially welcomed unrepentant homosexuals. Notwithstanding the handful of individual churches, such as the Glide Memorial Methodist Church in San Francisco which opened its doors to gay people in 1963, homosexuals were all sinners. To Southern Baptists, Jimmy Carter's religious affiliation, homosexuality was a manifestation of a depraved nature.

In the years following the 1969 Stonewall Riots, gay and lesbian organizations grew in number and savvy, and they were learning to fight back effectively. By the time

1 Lillian Faderman is a professor of history, specializing in lesbian and LGBT history. She is the author, among others, of *Woman: The American History of an Idea* (2022), *Harvey Milk: His Lives and Death* (2018), *The Gay Revolution: The Story of the Struggle* (2015), *Gay L. A.: A History of Sexual Outlaws, Power Politics, and Lipstick Lesbians*(2006), *To Believe in Women: What Lesbians Have Done For America – A History* (1999), *Odd Girls and Twilight Lovers: A History of Lesbian Life in Twentieth-Century America* (1991).

Carter was elected president in 1976, they had already had some notable successes. The American Psychiatric Association had declassified homosexuality from its list of mental disorders in 1973. That same year a federal judge, Charles Fahy, had declared in the case of *Benning Wentworth v. Melvin Laird, Secretary of Defense* that the Department of Defense had conducted an 'unreasonable encroachment' into Wentworth's private life by its investigation, and unless there was a *nexus* between his homosexuality and his ability to safeguard state secrets, his security clearance must be restored. By 1975, ten states had joined Illinois in repealing their sodomy laws, and the year Carter was elected, five more states repealed their sodomy laws.

But despite such advances, most Americans still considered gays and lesbians pariahs. For instance, in 1977, the year Carter took office, Gallup pollsters asked Americans about their opinions concerning homosexuals and employment: 73 per cent said homosexuals should not be hired to teach children; 64 per cent said they should not be hired in the clergy; 56 per cent said they should not be hired as doctors. The hateful stereotypes of gays and lesbians as child molesters, sinners, unstable, and untrustworthy persisted and helped to justify their treatment as second-class citizens.

It was highly unlikely in this climate that a born-again evangelical, a church deacon since he was eighteen years old, an avid member of the Southern Baptist Church – a church that defended 'biblical morality' and resisted any move that would help legitimize those who indulged in same-sex relations – might become the first US president to make serious efforts to give gays and lesbians the rights of first-class citizenship. Yet as Harris Dousemetzis has persuasively argued in this book, that is precisely what Jimmy Carter did during his term in office.

Carter could not escape from the Southern Baptist shibboleth that deemed homosexuality sinful, but his commitment to fairness and equality and to the principle of the separation of church and state made him intent on advancing the civil rights of gay and lesbian Americans. Nevertheless, to protect himself against the disfavour of his fellow evangelicals, who comprised more than one-third of the electorate and had helped sweep him into the presidency, Carter often felt that when it came to supporting gay concerns, he had to work in the dark, to finesse, to assure his constituency on the religious right that he was certainly not encouraging homosexuality as a 'viable alternate lifestyle'; he simply believed that no American citizens should be deprived of their civil rights.

His care to thread the needle did him little good, of course. Most gays and lesbians were ignorant of what he was doing on behalf of their community. And the religious right was all too cognizant. Carter was constantly bombarded by letters and petitions from conservative Christians who were outraged that he was allowing homosexuals to work in federal agencies and enjoy the civil rights that should be reserved for Americans with better morals. In the end, as Dousemetzis shows, Carter lost his re-election bid because these former supporters defected to Ronald Reagan as the more reliably Christian conservative candidate.

But in his four years in office, despite the outrage coming from the right, Carter accomplished a remarkable lot for gay and lesbian people. He was the first president to help them to dignity and to a sense of being first-class citizens by permitting their leaders to come into the White House and deliver gay and lesbian grievances and requests. He upgraded the dishonourable discharges that gay veterans had received. He made sure that gay organizations would be eligible for federal funding and for IRS tax exemptions. He approved funding for gay health services. He opened the Job Corps and White House Fellowship Program to young gays and lesbians. He authorized a resettlement program for gay refugees from Cuba. He endured the ire of religious conservatives, right-wing politicians, and even the Army by intervening to get permission for the Gay Activists Alliance to lay a wreath at the Tomb of the Unknown Soldier. With his encouragement, the 1980 Democrat platform included the first plank in US history to promote equality regardless of sexual orientation. He appointed liberal federal judges who would go on to hear cases on sodomy laws, gays in the military, and same-sex marriage – and would invariably find in favour of gays.

Carter lost his re-election bid at least partly because he helped gays and lesbians in their struggles to become first-class citizens. His defeat by Ronald Reagan in 1980 was a disaster for the gay community in ways that could not have been predicted at the time. During Carter's presidency, gay health clinics had received generous federal funding. They were able to hire expert personnel, expand their facilities, and conduct research on sexually transmitted diseases. Reagan took office in 1981. It was the same year that the first cases of AIDS were diagnosed in the United States. Soon after the start of the Reagan presidency, the funding for gay clinics was drastically reduced. It was the worst time possible to starve *precisely* those medical facilities that could have had a direct influence on staunching the rapid spread of the disease throughout the gay male community.

The Reagan administration chose to ignore AIDS throughout Reagan's first term. At a 1982 press conference, his press secretary, Larry Speakes, was asked what Reagan's response was to the Centers for Disease Control announcement that hundreds of men had already died from AIDS. 'What's AIDS?' Speakes asked. On being told 'it's known as the gay plague', Speakes's response was to laugh and then quip, 'I don't have it. Do you?' Speakes's boss took the disease no more seriously than he did. At a 1984 press conference, when 300,000 people had already been diagnosed with HIV, Speakes was again asked about the president's response. 'I haven't heard him express concern', he answered, still with jocularity.

It was not until September 1985, after thousands had died and it was already clear that a diagnosis of HIV was tantamount to a death sentence, that Reagan finally uttered the word 'AIDS' in public. The budget he requested for AIDS research funding was so low that Congress saw fit to increase it by $70,000,000. Throughout all of Reagan's first term as president of the United States, as myriads were dying, he was mum. It was truly a tragedy for the gay community that Jimmy Carter, with his quiet commitment to gay causes, was no longer in the White House.

Abbreviations

Used in the Text and Footnotes

ACLU	American Civil Liberties Union
BOP	Bureau of Prisons
CCR	Commission on Civil Rights
CHTF	Cuban-Haitian Task Force
CRTF	Cuban Refugee Task Force
CSC	Civil Service Commission
DoJ	Department of Justice
DHR	Department of Human Resources
ERA	Equal Rights Amendment
FCC	Federal Communications Commission
GAA	Gay Activists Alliance
GSDC	Gertrude Stein Democratic Club
HEW	Department of Health, Education and Welfare
HUD	Housing and Urban Development
INS	Immigration and Naturalization Service
IRS	Internal Revenue Service
IWY	International Women's Year
MCC	Metropolitan Community Church
NACW	National Advisory Committee for Women
NGTF	National Gay Task Force
NOW	National Organization for Women
NWC	National Women's Conference
OPL	Office of Public Liaison (White House)
PACW	President's Advisory Committee for Women
PHS	Public Health Service
SDC	Stonewall Democratic Club
USAID	US Agency for International Development
WHCF	White House Conference on Families

Publications, Used in Footnotes Only

AGN	*Arizona Gay News*
AP	*The Associated Press*
GCN	*Gay Community News*
GN	*Gay News*
NYP	*New York Post*
NYT	*New York Times*

LT	*The Lesbian Tide*
USCSCHR	United States Congress, Senate Committee on Human Resources, Subcommittee on Child and Human Development
WH	White House
WHCF1978	White House Conference on Families, Joint Hearings before the Subcommittee on Child and Human Development of the Committee on Human Resources, 2 and 3 February, 1978
WSJ	*Wall Street Journal*
WP	*Washington Post*
WS	*Washington Star*

Archives, Used in Footnotes Only

ATSF	Allison Thomas' Subject Files
AWSF	Anne Wexler's Subject Files
B.	Box (followed by number)
BASF	Bill Albers' Subject Files
CF	[CF, O/A 728]
CHR	[Commission on Human Rights] 3/77 [O/A 4496]
CPP	Carter Presidential Papers-WHCF
CR	Civil Rights 10/76-2/78 [O/A 4609]
CLC	[Christian Life Commission], 2/16/77-9/23/77 [CF, O/A 84]
CHSF	Michael Channin's Subject Files
CHTF	Cuban-Haitian Task Force
CU	Cornell University
DTSF	Dennis Tapsak's Subject Files
F.	Folder (followed by number)
FCC1	[Federal Communications Commission] 3/77 [O/A 4496]
FCC2	Federal Communications Commission, 2/78 [O/A 4499]
F+P	Flyers & Publications, 12/76-3/77 [O/A 4499]
FG	Federal Government
FG300	FG 300 1/20/77-1/20/81
GHD	Gays and Honorable Discharge, 7/75-2/78 [O/A 4499]
GI	Gay Issues
GH1	[Gay]-Homosexuals, [7/20/79-5/31/79]
GH2	[Gay] Homosexuals [2]
GH3	[Gay] Homosexuals [3]
G/L1	Gay/Lesbians, [2/8/79-6/30/80]
G/L2	Gay/Lesbians, [7/1/80-n.d.]
GR	Gay Rights
GR:	C [Gay Rights: Correspondence] 5/76-7/78 [O/A 5771]
GR:	P [Gay Rights: Publications] 3/75-1/78 [O/A 5771]
GRJCV [Gay Rights:	Jimmy Carter's Views on] 10/76 [O/A 5772]
GTFN1	Gay Task Force, National, [10/79-3/24/80]
GTFN2	Gay Task Force, National, [4/1/80-n.d.]
GR&FG	Gay Rights and Federal Government
GRPH	Gay Rights & Public Health 8/76-1/78 [0/A 5772]

GV	Gay Views
HC	Homophobic Correspondence
HMSL	Harvey Milk Speech & Letter
IWY	International Women's Year, 3/77-3/78 [CF, O/A 424]
JCPL	Jimmy Carter Presidential Library
JWSF	Jane Wales' Subject Files
LBP	Larry Bush papers
LBSF	Landon Butler's Subject Files
MECOCL	Memos, Correspondence, Clippings 5/76-8/78 [O/A 5771]
MCI	Midge Costanza Institute
MCSF	Midge Costanza's Subject Files
MMSF	Margaret McKenna's Subject Files
NGTFJW	National Gay Task Force 4/77-5/77 [O/A 4461]
NGTFR	National Gay Task Force Records
[NGTF] SG	[NGTF meeting with] Surgeon-General, 3/78 [O/A 4499]
NLGA	National Gay & Lesbian Archives
NSSF	Noel Sterret's Subject Files
OPLF	Office of Public Liaison Files
OSS	Office of the Staff Secretary
OWHPS	Office of the White House Press Secretary
PCC1	Prisons [Carlson Case] 7/77-3/78 [O/A 4499] [1]
PCC2	Prisons [Carlson Case] 3/78 [O/A 4499] [2]
PCC3	Prisons [Carlson Case] 3/78 [O/A 4499] [3]
RCHTF	Records of the Cuban-Haitian Task Force
RLMSF	Robert Lee Maddox Subject Files
RMSF	Robert Malson Subject Files
RWHPO	Records of the White House Press Office
SDCR	Stonewall Democratic Club Records
SESF	Stuart Eizenstat's Subject Files
SFE	Subject File-Executive
SFG	Subject File-General
SWOF	Sarah Weddington's Office Files
SWSF	Seymour Wishman's Subject Files
TBSF	Tom Belford's Subject Files
TCFODF	Tim Craft's Field Operation Director's Files
USC	University of Southern California
WHCOF	White House Central Office Files

Sources

Primary Sources

Archives

Larry Bush papers, 1977–1984. Division of Rare and Manuscript Collections, Cornell University.

Foster Gunnison, Jr. papers. University of Connecticut.

Jimmy Carter Presidential Library. Atlanta, Georgia.

James Guy Tucker, Jr. Papers. University of Arkansas.

Midge Costanza Papers. Midge Costanza Institute, San Diego, California.

National Commission on the Observance of International Women's Year. Digital Collections, University of Houston.

National LGBTQ Task Force records, 1973–2017. Division of Rare and Manuscript Collections, Cornell University.

Merrill-Palmer Institute: Dr. Francis H. Palmer Records. Walter P. Reuther Library, Wayne State University.

Stonewall Democratic Club records, 1975–1995. ONE National Gay & Lesbian Archives, USC Libraries, University of Southern California.

Court Cases

Baker v. Wade, 563 F. Supp 1121 (N.D. Tex. 1982), 769 F. 2nd 289 (5th Cir. 1985).

Bowers v. Hardwick, 478 U.S. 186 (1986).

In re Brodie, 394 F. Supp. 1208 (D. Or. 1975).

Dahl v. Secretary of U.S. Navy, 830 F. Supp. 1319 (E.D. Cal. 1993).

Glenn v. Brumby, 724 F. Supp. 2d 1284 (N.D. Ga. 2010), aff'd, 663 F. 3d 1312 (11th Cir. 2011).

High Tech Gays v. Defense Industrial Security Clearance Office, 895 F. 2d 563 (9th Cir. 1990).

Hollingsworth v. Perry, 570 U.S. 693 (2013).

Lawrence v. Texas, 539 U.S. 558 (2003).

Matlovich v. Secretary of the Air Force, 591 F. 2d 852 (D.C. Cir. 1978).

Meinhold v. U.S. Department of Defense, 808 F. Supp. 1455, 1457 (C.D. Cal. 1993), 123 F. 3d 1275, 131 F. 3d 842 (9th Cir. 1997).

Miriam Ben-Shalom v. Secretary of the Army, 807 F. 2d 982 (Fed. Cir. 1986).

Obergefell v. Hodges, 576 U.S. 644 (2015).

Pruitt v. Cheney, 943 F.2d 989 (9th Cir. 1991).

Rene v. MGM Grand Hotel, 243 F.3d 1206 (9th Cir. 2001).

Romer v. Evans, 517 U.S. 620 (1996).

Selland v. Aspin, 832 F. Supp. 12 (D.D.C. 1993).

Shahar v. Bowers, 836 F. Supp. 859 (N.D. Ga. 1993), 70 F. 3d 1218 (11th Cir. 1995), 114 F. 3d 1097 (11th Cir. 1997).
Society for Individual Rights, Inc. v. Hampton, 63 F.R.D. 399 (N.D. Cal. 1973).
United States v. Windsor, 570 U.S. 744 (2013).
Watkins v. U.S. Army, 875 F. 2d 699 (9th Cir. 1989).

Government Publications

National Commission on the Observance of International Women's Year. *The Spirit of Houston*. Washington, DC: National Commission on the Observance of International Women's Year, 1978.
National Institute for Advanced Studies. *Summary of National Hearings of the White House Conference on Families*. Washington, DC: White House Conference on Families and the Department of Health, Education, and Welfare, 1980.
Public Papers of the Presidents, Jimmy Carter, 1977–1980. Washington, DC.: U.S. Government Printing Office, 1980.
United States Congress. *White House Conference on Families, 1978 Joint Hearings before the Subcommittee on Child and Human Development of the Committee on Human Resources . . . February 2 and 3, 1978*. Washington, DC: U.S. Government Printing Office, 1978.
U.S. Merit Systems Protection Board, 'Sexual Orientation and the Federal Workplace: Policy and Perception'.
White House Conference on Families, *Listening to America's Families, Action for the 80's*, Washington, DC: The White House Conference on Families, 1980.

Interviews

All interviews were conducted and recorded personally by the author.

David Addlestone, 13 July 2021.
Virginia Apuzzo, 9 March 2014 and 3 March 2021.
Bob Arthur, 28 June 2021, 2 May 2022 and 27 February 2023.
Tom Bastow, 25 January 2021.
Harry Britt, 11 February 2018.
Charlotte Bunch, 17 June 2014 and 9 February 2021.
Larry Bush, 14 October 2020 and 22 November 2021.
Tony Campolo, 30 April 2014.
Louie Crew Clay, 3 March 2014 and 4 December 2018.
Adam DeBaugh, 10 September 2020 and 19 January 2021.
William Doubleday, 1 September 2020.
Paula Fiscal, 26 June 2020.
Gill Gerald, 12 September 2020.
Donald Hallman, 28 March 2014.
Tom Hayden, 4 March 2014.
David Mack Henderson, 26 March 2014
Nancy Higgins, 17 June 2016 and 17 December 2018.
Craig Howell, 21 March 2016 and 21 January 2021.
ABilly Jones-Hennin, 1 September 2020.
Eric Marcus, 18 February 2015 and 24 October 2020.

David McReynolds, 27 March 2017 and 7 May 2017.
Rick Melchionno, 7 August 2020 and 20 February 2023.
Denny Meyer, 19 June 2016.
Jeffrey Montgomery, 11 March 2014.
Walter Naegle, 20 September 2020.
Dana Naparsteck, 28 August, 2020.
Norman E. Kent, 16 October 2020.
Jan Peterson, 13 April 2021.
Troy Perry, 22 January 2021, 16 March 2021 and 20 April 2021.
Eddie Sandifer, 6 March 2014.
Eric Schockman, 27 November 2020.
Carol Ruth Silver, 1 September 2020.
Lenny Swerdlow, 1 June 2021.
Robin Tyler, 18 July 2020.
Ginny Vida, 21 January 2021.
Bob Warburton, 13 March 2021.
Nancy Wilson, 29 June 2020.
Mel White, 7 March 2014.

Carter Administration Staff

Peter Bourne, 13 March 2014 and 4 February 2021.
Bert Carp, 18 May 2021.
Evan Dobelle, 5 July 2020.
Stuart Eizenstat, 19 January 2021 and 23 April 2021.
James Fallows, 24 February 2017.
Marilyn Haft, 12 April 2014, 2 February 2021 and 23 February 2021.
Margaret McKenna, 3 July 2020.
Robert Maddox, 26 January 2023.
Robert Malson, 24 October 2020.
Jane Wales, 19 May 2021.
Sarah Weddington, 30 May 2015 and 12 January 2018.

Academics, Journalists, Ministers

Randall Balmer, 18 June 2014.
Michael Dukakis, 27 April 2014.
Lisa Keen, 4 March 2017.
D. Michael Lindsay, 4 March 2014.
Doreen Mattingly, 11 February 2017 and 12 February 2021.
Mark J. Rozell, 12 March 2014.
Byron E. Shafer, 31 March 2014.
Morris Sheats, 6 April 2014.

Memoirs

Abzug, B., Kelber, M. *Gender Gap: Bella Abzug's Guide to Political Power for American Women*, Boston: Houghton Mifflin, 1984.

Califano Jr., J.A. *Governing America: An Insiders Report from the White House mi the Cabinet*, New York: Simon and Schuster, 1981.
Carter, J. *Keeping Faith: Memoirs of a President*, Fayetteville: The University of Arkansas Press, 1995.
Carter, J. *White House Diary*, New York: Farrar, Straus and Giroux, 2010.
Córdova, J. *When We Were Outlaws*, Midway: Spinsters Ink, 2011.
Friedan, B. *Life So Far: A Memoir*, New York: Simon & Schuster, 2001.
Ginsburg, R.B., Hartnett, M., Williams W.W. *My Own Words*, New York: Simon & Schuster, 2018.
Henry, A., Curry, C.C. *Aaron Henry: The Fire Ever Burning*, Jackson: University Press of Mississippi, 2000.
Maddox, R.L. *Preacher at the White House*, Nashville: Broadman Press, 1984.
Perry, T.D., Swicegood, T.L.P. *Don't Be Afraid Anymore: The Story of Reverend Troy Perry and the Metropolitan Community Churches*, New York: St Martin's Press, 1992.
Powell, J. *The Other Side of the Story*, New York: Morrow, 1984.
Weithorn, S.W. *Love, Death, and Taxes: My Life in Politics, Social Activism, and the Law*, Bloomington: Archway Publishing, 2013.

Newspapers and Periodicals

The Advocate
Arizona Gay News
Bay Area Reporter
The Blade (later *The Washington Blade*)
Capitol Hill
Chicago Gay Life
Christianity and Crisis
Christianity Today
Eagle Forum
Esquire
Gay Community News
Gay Era
Gaze
Harper's
It's Time: The Newsletter of the National Gay Task Force
The Lesbian Tide
Los Angeles Times
Miami Herald
Miami News
The Nation
National Inquirer
Newsweek
New York Post
Off Our Backs
Out Front
Playboy
San Francisco Chronicle
The Sentinel
Time

The Wall Street Journal
Washington Post
Washington Star

Personal Collections

Eric Marcus's Personal Collection of interviews with gay rights activists.

Secondary Sources

Abernathy, M.G. 'The Carter Administration and Domestic Civil Rights'. In *The Carter Years: The President and Policy Making*, edited by M.G., Abernathy, D.M. Hill, P. Williams, 106–22. London: Frances Pinter, 1984.
Armstrong, E.A. *Forging Gay Identities: Organizing Sexuality in San Francisco, 1950–1994*, Chicago: University of Chicago Press, 2002.
Azicri, M. 'Twenty-six Years of Cuban Revolutionary Politics: An Appraisal'. *Contemporary Marxism*, no. 14, Dialectics of Democracy in Latin America (1986): 65–96.
Baim, T. *Gay Press, Gay Power: The Growth of LGBT Community Newspapers in America*. Chicago: Prairie Avenue Productions and Windy City Media Group, 2012.
Ball, C.A. *The First Amendment and the LGBT Equality: A Contentious History*, Cambridge, MA: Harvard University Press, 2017.
Balmer, R. 'Fundamentalism, the First Amendment, and the Rise of the Religious Right'. *William and Mary Bill of Rights Journal*, 18, 4 (2010): 889–900.
Balmer, R. *God in the White House: A History. How Faith Shaped the Presidency from John F Kennedy to George W. Bush*, New York: Harper One, 2008.
Balmer, R. *Thy Kingdom Come: How the Religious Right Distorts the Faith and Threatens America: An Evangelical Lament*, New York: Basic Books, 2006.
Balmer, R. *Redeemer: The Life of Jimmy Carter*, New York: Basic Books, 2014.
Bamforth, N. *Sexuality, Morals and Justice: A Theory of Lesbian and Gay Rights Law*, London and Washington: Cassell, 1997.
Bartels, L.M. *Presidential Primaries and the Dynamics of Public Choice*, Princeton: Princeton University Press, 1988.
Bell, C.A. *The Rights to be Parents: LGBT Families and the Transformation of Parenthood*, New York and London: New York University Press, 2012.
Bell, J. 'Making Sexual Citizens: LGBT Politics, Health Care, and the State in the 1970s'. In *Beyond the Politics of the Closet: Gay Rights and the American State since the 1970s*, edited by J. Bell, 58–80. Philadelphia: University of Pennsylvania Press, 2020.
Benford, Robert D. and David A. Snow, 'Framing Processes and Social Movements: An Overview and Assessment'. *Annual Review of Sociology*, 26 (2000): 611–39.
Berkowitz, E.D. *Something Happened: A Political and Cultural Overview of the Seventies*, New York: Columbia University Press, 2007.
Bockris, V. *The Life and Death of Andy Warhol*, New York: Bantam Books, 1989.
Bourne, P.G. *Jimmy Carter: A Comprehensive Biography from Plains to Postpresidency*, New York: Scribner, 1997.
Branch, T. 'Closets of Power'. In *Homosexuality and Government, Politics and Prisons*, edited by W.R. Dynes and S. Donaldson, 1–16. New York and London: Garland, 1992.

Burrows, T.J. 'Family Values: From the White House Conference on Families to the Family Protection Act'. In *Creating Change: Sexuality, Public Policy, and Civil Rights*, edited by J. D'Emilio, W.B. Turner and U. Vaid, 336–60. New York: St. Martin's Press, 2000.

Bush, L., Goldstein, R. (1999), 'A Chill Wind for Gay Rights'. In *Witness to Revolution: The Advocate Reports on Gay and Lesbian Politics, 1967–1999*, edited by C. Bull, 130–6. Los Angeles and New York: Alyson Books, 1999.

Canaday, M. *The Straight State: Sexuality and Citizenship in the Twentieth-Century America*, Princeton: Princeton University Press, 2009.

Capo Jr., J. 'Queering Mariel: Mediating Cold War Foreign Policy and U.S. Citizenship among Cuba's Homosexual Exile Community, 1978–1994'. *Journal of American Ethnic History*, 29, 4 (2010): 78–106.

Capsuto, S. *Alternate Channels: The Uncensored Story of Gay and Lesbian Images on Radio and Television*, New York: Ballantine Books, 2000.

Carpenter, D. *Flagrant Conduct – The Story of Lawrence v. Texas*, New York: W.W. Norton & Company, 2013.

Carroll, S.J. 'Women Appointed to the Carter Administration: More or Less Qualified?'. *Polity*, 18, 4 (1986): 696–706.

Clendinen, D., Nagourney, A. *Out for Good: The Struggle to Build a Gay Rights Movement in America*, New York: Simon & Schuster, 1999.

Clark, M.L. 'Carter's Groundbreaking Appointment of Women to the Federal Bench: His Other 'Human Rights' Record'. *American University Journal of Gender, Social Policy & the Law*, 11, 3 (2003): 1131–63.

CM.T. 'Notes on Church-State Affairs'. *Journal of Church and State*, 20 (1978): 1.

Critchlow, D.T. *Phyllis Schlafly and Grassroots Conservatism: A Woman's Crusade*. Princeton: Princeton University Press, 2005.

D'Emilio, J. 'Cycles of Change, Questions of Strategy: The Gay and Lesbian Movement after Fifty Years'. In *The Politics of Gay Rights*, edited by C.A. Rimmerman, K.D. Wald and C. Wilcox, 31–53. Chicago and London: The University of Chicago Press, 2000.

D'Emilio, J. *Lost Prophet: The Life and Times of Bayard Rustin*, New York: The Free Press, 2003.

D'Emilio, J., Turner, W.B., Vaid, U. (eds.). *Creating Change: Sexuality, Public Policy, and Civil Rights*, New York: St. Martin's Press, 2000.

Dumbrell, J. *The Carter Presidency: A Re-evaluation*, Manchester and New York: Manchester University Press, 1995.

Dowland, S. '"Family Values" and the Formation of a Christian Right Agenda'. *Church History*, 78, 3 (2009): 606–31.

Eisenstein, Z. 'Antifeminism in the Politics and Election of 1980'. *Feminist Studies*, 7, 2 (1981): 187–205.

Eizenstat, S.E. *President Carter: The White House Years*, New York: St. Martin's Press, 2018.

Endean, S. *Bringing Lesbian and Gay Rights into the Mainstream. Twenty Years of Progress*, New York and London: Routledge, 2006.

Eskridge, W.N., *Dishonorable Passions*, New York: Viking, 2008.

Eskridge, Jr., W.N. Gaylaw: Challenging the Apartheid of the Closet, Cambridge, MA: Harvard University Press, 1999.

Faderman, L. *The Gay Revolution: The Story of the Struggle*, New York: Simon & Schuster, 2015.

Faderman, L. *Harvey Milk: His Lives and Death*, New Haven and London: Yale University Press, 2019.

Fejes, F. *Gay Rights and Moral Panic: The Origins of America's Debate on Homosexuality*, New York: Palgrave MacMillan, 2008.
Felsenthal, C. *Phyllis Schlafly: The Sweetheart of the Silent Majority*, Chicago: Regnery Gateway, 1981.
Fink, G.M., Graham, H.D. (eds.). *The Carter Presidency: Policy Choices in the Post-New Deal Era*, Lawrence: University Press of Kansas, 1998.
Flippen, J.B. 'Carter, Catholics and the Politics of Family'. *American Catholic Studies*, 123, 3 (2012): 27–51.
Flippen, J.B. *Jimmy Carter, The Politics of Family, and the Rise of the Religious Right*, Athens: The University of Georgia Press, 2011.
Fowler, W.G. 'A Comparison of Initial Recommendation Procedures: Judicial Selection under Reagan and Carter'. *Yale Law & Policy Review*, 1, 2 (1983): 299–356.
Frank, G. '"The Civil Rights of Parents": Race and Conservative Politics in Anita Bryant's Campaign against Gay Rights in 1970s Florida'. *Journal of the History of Sexuality*, 22, 1 (2013): 126–60.
Freedman, R. 'The Religious Right and the Carter Administration'. *The Historical Journal*, 48, 1 (2005): 231–60.
Frieder, M.I. 'Lesbian Lawyer's Appeal Succeeds'. *American Bar Association Journal*, 82 (1996): 40.
Frost, Cynthia J., 'Shahar v. Bowers: That Girl Just Didn't Have Good Sense'. *Minnesota Journal of Law & Inequality*, 17, 1 (1999): 57–95.
Gabriner, V. 'International Women's Year: "Mommy, When I Grow Up, Can I Be a Lesbian?"'. *Atalanta*, 12 (1977): 11–12.
Gamble, A. *The Free Economy and the Strong State: The Politics of Thatcherism*, New York: New York University Press, 1994.
Gilgoff, D. *The Jesus Machine. How James Dobson, Focus on the Family, and Evangelical America are Winning the Culture War*, New York: St Martin's Press, 2007.
Glendon, M.A. *Rights Talk: The Impoverishment of Political Discourse*, New York: Free Press, 1991.
Goldman, S. 'Carter's Judicial Appointments: A Lasting Legacy'. *Judicature*, 64, 8 (1981): 344–55.
Graham, H.D. 'Civil Rights Policy in the Carter Presidency'. In *The Carter Presidency: Policy Choices in the Post-New Deal Era*, edited by G.M. Fink and H.D. Graham, 202–33. Lawrence: University Press of Kansas, 1998.
Hall, P.A. 'Policy Paradigms, Social Learning, and the State: The Case of Economic Policymaking in Britain'. *Comparative Politics*, 25, 3 (1993): 275–96.
Hartmann, S.M. 'Feminism, Public Policy, and the Carter Administration'. In *The Carter Presidency: Policy Choices in the Post New-era*, edited by G.M. Fink and H.D. Graham, 224–44. Lawrence: University Press of Kansas, 1998.
Hirsch, L.P. 'A Wheel Within a Wheel: Sexual Orientation and the Federal Workforce'. In *Creating Change: Sexuality, Public Policy, and Civil Rights*, edited by J. D'Emilio, W.B. Turner and U. Vaid, 131–46. New York: St. Martin's Press, 2000.
Howard, J. *Men Like That: A Southern Queer History*, Chicago: The University of Chicago Press, 2001.
Inglehart, R. *Culture Shift in Advanced Industrial Society*, Princeton: Princeton University Press, 1990.
Ingraham, P.W., Perry, J.L. 'The Three Faces of Civil Service Reform'. In *The Presidency and Domestic Policies of Jimmy Carter*, edited by H.D. Rosenbaum and A. Ugrinsky, 677–88. Westport and London: Greenwood Press, 1994.
Isbell, F. 'Carter's Civil Libertarians'. *The Civil Liberties Review*, 4 (1977): 55–8.

Kameny, F.E. 'Government v. Gays: Two Sad Stories with Two Happy Endings, Civil Service Employment and Security Clearances'. In *Creating Change: Sexuality, Public Policy, and Civil Rights*, edited by J. D'Emilio, W.B. Turner and U. Vaid, 88–207. New York: St. Martin's Press, 2000.

King, J.D., Riddlesperger Jr., J.W. 'Diversity and Presidential Cabinet Appointments'. *Social Science Quarterly*, 96, 1 (2015): 93–103.

Knott, J., Wildavsky, A. 'Jimmy Carter's Theory of Governing'. *The Wilson Quarterly*, 1, 2 (1977): 49–50.

Kousser, J.M. 'The Immutability of Categories and the Reshaping of Southern Politics'. *Annual Review of Political Science*, 13 (2010): 365–83.

Krukones, M.G. 'Campaign and President: Jimmy Carter's Campaign Promises and Presidential Performance'. In *The Presidency and Domestic Policies of Jimmy Carter*, edited by H.D. Rosenbaum and A. Ugrinsky, 131–42. Westport and London: Greenwood Press, 1994.

Krukones, M.G. 'The Campaign Promises of Jimmy Carter: Accomplishments and Failures'. *Presidential Studies Quarterly*, 15, 1 (1985): 136–44.

Lambert, F. *Religion in American Politics: A Short History*, Princeton and Oxford: Princeton University Press, 2010.

Lengle, J.I., Shafer, B.E. *Presidential Politics: Readings on Nominations and Election*, New York: St. Martin's Press, 1980.

Leonard, A.S. 'Chronicling a Movement: 20 Years of Lesbian/Gay Law Notes'. *New York Law School Journal of Human Rights*, 17 (2000): 415–564.

Leonard, A.S. 'From *Bowers v. Hardwick* to *Romer v. Evans*'. In *Creating Change: Sexuality, Public Policy, and Civil Rights*, edited by J. D'Emilio, W.B. Turner and U. Vaid, 57–80. New York: St. Martin's Press, 2000.

Leonard, A.S. *Sexuality and the Law: An Encyclopaedia of Major Legal Cases*, New York and London: Garland Publishing, 1993.

Leonard, A.S., Cain, P.A. *Sexuality Law*. Durham: Carolina Academic Press, 2005.

Lewis, G.B. 'Lifting the Ban on Gays in the Civil Service: Federal Policy toward Gay and Lesbian Employees since the Cold War'. *Public Administration Review*, 57, 5 (1997): 387–95.

Loescher, G., Scanlan, J.A. *Calculated Kindness: Refugees and America's Half-Open Door, 1945 to the Present*, New York: The Free Press, 1993.

Lynch, E.J. 'White House Family Feud'. *Policy Review*, 13 (1980): 109–27.

MacPherson, M. *Long Time Passing: Vietnam and the Haunted Generation*, Bloomington and Indianapolis: Indiana University Press, 2002.

Mansbridge, J.J. *Why We Lost the ERA*, Chicago: University of Chicago Press, 1986.

Marcus, E. *Making History: The Struggle for Gay and Lesbian Equal Rights: An Oral History*, New York: HarperPerennial, 1993.

Massing, M. 'The Invisible Cubans'. *Columbia Journalism Review*, 19, 3 (1980): 49–51.

Masud-Piloto, F. *From Welcomed Exiles to Illegal Immigrants: Cuban Migration to the U.S., 1959–95*, New York: Rowman & Littlefield Publishers, Inc., 1995.

Mattingly, D. *A Feminist in the White House: Midge Costanza, the Carter Years, and America's Culture Wars*, New York: Oxford University Press, 2016.

Mattingly, D.J., Boyd, A. 'Bringing Gay and Lesbian Activism to the White House: Midge Costanza and the National Gay Task Force Meeting'. *Journal of Lesbian Studies*, 17 (2013): 365–79.

Mattingly, D.J., Nare, J.L. '"A Rainbow of Women": Diversity and Unity at the 1977 U.S. International Women's Year Conference'. *Journal of Women's History*, 26, 2 (2014): 88–112.

Mattson, K. *What the Heck are You up to, Mr President? Jimmy Carter, America's 'Malaise', and the Speech that should have Changed the Country*, New York: Bloomsbury, 2009.

Miller, M. *Out of the Past: Gay and Lesbian History from 1869 to the Present*, New York: Vintage Books, 1995.

Minter, S. 'Sodomy and Public Morality Offenses under U.S. Immigration Law: Penalizing Lesbian and Gay Identity'. *Cornell International Law Journal*, 26, 3 (1993): 771–818.

Mixner, D. Stranger Among Friends, New York: Bantam Books, 1996.

Murdoch, J., Price, D. *Courting Justice: Gay Men and Lesbians V. The Supreme Court*, New York: Basic Books, 2001.

Murray-Brown, R. *For A Christian America: A History of the Religious Right*, Amherst: Prometheus Books, 2002.

National Defense Research Institute. *Sexual Orientation and U.S. Military Personnel Policy: Options and Assessment*, Santa Monica: RAND Corporation, 1993.

Neustadt, R.E. *Presidential Power and the Modern Presidents: The Politics of Leadership from Roosevelt to Reagan*, New York: Free Press, 1991.

Novak, M. *The Spirit of Democratic Capitalism*, Lanham: Madison Books, 1982.

O'Leary, J. 'From Agitator to Insider: Fighting for Inclusion in the Democratic Party'. In *Creating Change: Sexuality, Public Policy, and Civil Rights*, edited by J. D'Emilio, W.B. Turner and U. Vaid, 81–114. New York: St. Martin's Press, 2000.

Peña, S. *Oye Loca: From the Mariel Boatlift to Gay Cuban Miami*, Minneapolis and London: University of Minnesota Press, 2013.

Perlstein, R. *Nixonland: The Rise of a President and the Fracturing of America*, New York: Scribner, 2008.

Peterson, M.A. 'The Presidency and Organized Interests: White House Patterns of Interest Group Liaison'. *The American Political Science Review*, 86, 3 (1992): 612–25.

Phillips, K. *American Theocracy: The Perils, Oil and Borrowed Money in the 21st Century*, New York: Viking, 2006.

Polikoff, N.D. 'Lesbian and Gay Couples Raising Children: The Law in the United States'. In *Legal Recognition of Same-Sex Partnerships: A Study of National, European and International Law*, edited by R. Wintemute and M. Andenaes, 153–68. Oxford and Portland: Hart Publishing, 2001.

Potter, C.C. 'Paths to Political Citizenship: Gay Rights, Feminism, and the Carter Presidency'. *The Journal of Policy History*, 24, 1 (2012): 95–114.

Pruitt, D. *Nomad for God*, Victoria, Canada: Trafford Publishing, 2020.

Reichley, A.J. 'The Evangelical and Fundamentalist Revolt'. In *Piety and Politics: Evangelicals and Fundamentalists Confront the World*, edited by R.J. Neuhaus and M. Cromartie, 69–95. Washington: Ethics and Public Policy Center, 1987.

Ribuffo, L.P. 'Family Policy Past as Prologue: Jimmy Carter, the White House Conference on Families, and the Mobilization of the New Christian Right'. *Review of Policy Research*, 23, 2 (2006): 311–37.

Rice, G.T. *Twenty Years of Peace Corps*, Washington: Peace Corps, 1981.

Rich, B.R., Arguelles, L. 'Homosexuality, Homophobia, and Revolution: Notes toward an Understanding of the Cuban Lesbian and Gay Male Experience, Part II'. *Signs*, 11, 1 (1985): 120–36.

Rimmerman, C.A. 'Beyond Political Mainstreaming: Reflections on Lesbian and Gay Organisations and the Grassroots'. In *The Politics of Gay Rights*, edited by C.A. Rimmerman, K.D. Wald and C. Wilcox, 54–78. Chicago and London: The University of Chicago Press, 2000.

Rimmerman, C.A., Wald, K.D., Wilcox, C. (eds.). *The Politics of Gay Rights*, Chicago and London: The University of Chicago Press, 2000.

Rossi, A.S. *Feminists in Politics: A Panel Analysis of the First National Women's Conference*, New York: Academic Press, 1982.

Rozell, M.J. 'President Carter and the Press: Perspectives from White House Communications Advisers'. *Political Science Quarterly*, 105, 3 (1990): 419–34.

Rozell, M.J. *The Press and the Carter Presidency*, Boulder and London: Westview Press, 1989.

Rutledge, L.W. *The Gay Decades: From Stonewall to the Present: The People and Events That Shaped Gay Lives*, New York: Plume, 1992.

Sears, J.T. 'Bob Basker (1918–2001): Selling the Movement'. In *Before Stonewall: Activists for Gay and Lesbian Rights in Historical Context*, edited by V.L. Bullough, 193–202. New York: Harrington Park Press, 2002.

Self, R.O. *All in the Family: The Realignment of American Democracy Since the 1960s*, New York: Hill and Wang, 2012.

Schram, M. *Running for President 1976: The Carter Campaign*, New York: Stein and Day, 1977.

Shafer, B.E. *Quiet Revolution: The Struggle for the Democratic Party and the Shaping of Post-reform Politics*, New York: Russell Sage Foundation, 1983.

Shilts, R. *Conduct Unbecoming: Gays & Lesbians in the U.S. Military, Vietnam to the Persian Gulf*, New York: St. Martin's Press, 1993.

Shilts, R. *The Mayor of Castro Street: The Life and Times of Harvey Milk*, New York: St. Martin's Press, 1982.

Shoup, L.H. *The Carter Presidency, and Beyond: Power and Politics in the 1980s*, Palo Alto: Ramparts Press, 1980.

Skowronek, S. *The Politics Presidents Make: Leadership from John Adams to Bill Clinton*, Cambridge, MA: The Belknap Press of Harvard University Press, 1997.

Spitko, E.G. *Antigay Bias in Role-Model Occupations*, Philadelphia: University of Pennsylvania Press, 2016.

Spruill, M.J. *Divided We Stand: The Battle Over Women's Rights and Family Values That Polarized American Politics*, New York: Bloomsbury Publishing, 2017.

Stanley, T. *Kennedy vs. Carter: The 1980 Battle for the Democratic Party's Soul*, Lawrence: University of Kansas Press, 2010.

Steding, W. *Presidential Faith and Foreign Policy: Jimmy Carter the Disciple and Ronald Reagan the Alchemist*, New York: Palgrave MacMillan, 2014.

Stone, A.L. *Gay Rights at the Ballot Box*, Minneapolis: University of Minnesota Press, 2012.

Stroud, K. *How Jimmy Won: The Victory Campaign from Plains to the White House*, New York: Morrow and Co, 1977.

Swartz, *Moral Minority: The Evangelical Left in an Age of Conservatism*, Philadelphia: University of Pennsylvania Press, 2012.

Turner, W.B. 'Mirror Images: Lesbian/Gay Civil Rights in the Carter and Reagan Administration'. In *Creating Change: Sexuality, Public Policy, and Civil Rights*, edited by J. D'Emilio, W.B. Turner and U. Vaid, 3–28. New York: St. Martin's Press, 2000.

Valeska, L. 'NOW Speech, 4 October 1980'. In *Speaking for Our Lives: Historic Speeches and Rhetoric for Gay and Lesbian Rights*, edited by R.B. Ridinger, 350–7. New York: Routledge, 2004.

Wald, K.D., Calhoon-Brown, A. *Religion and Politics in the United States*, Lanham: Rowman & Littlefield, 2014.

Walz, J.S., Comer, J. 'State Responses to National Democratic Party Reform'. *Political Research Quarterly*, 52, 1 (1999): 189–208.

Wheeler, L. *Jimmy Who? An Examination of Presidential Candidate Jimmy Carter*, Woodbury: Barron's Educational Series, 1976.

Wilcox, C. *God's Warriors: The Christian Right in Twenty-First Century America*, Baltimore: John Hopkins University Press, 1992.

Wilcox, C. *Onward Christian Soldiers? The Religious Right in American Politics*, Boulder and London: Westview Press, 1996.

Williams, D.K. *The Election of the Evangelical: Jimmy Carter, Gerald Ford, and the Presidential Contest of 1976*, Lawrence: University Press of Kansas, 2020.

Williams, D.K. *God's Own Party: The Making of the Christian Right*, Oxford: Oxford University Press, 2010.

Williams, J. Unbending Gender: Why Family and Work Conflict and What To Do About It, Oxford and New York: Oxford University Press, 1999.

Winters, M.S. *God's Right Hand: How Jerry Falwell Made God a Republican and Baptized the American Right*, New York: HarperOne, 2012.

Young, N.J. 'Worse than Cancer and Worse than Snakes'. *The Journal of Policy History*, 26, 4 (2014): 479–508.

Zarnow, L.R. *Battling Bella: The Protest Politics of Bella Abzug*, Cambridge, MA: Harvard University Press, 2019.

Index